FRENCH
MADE SIMPLE

FRENCH
MADE SIMPLE

Revised Edition

BY

Eugene Jackson

AND

Antonio Rubio

REVISED BY

Julien LaFontant

AND

Pamela Haze

BOOKS

A Made Simple Book
Broadway Books
New York

Produced by The Stonesong Press, LLC

FRENCH MADE SIMPLE. Copyright © 1990, 2001, 2006 by Broadway Books, a division of Random House, Inc.

For information, address Broadway Books, a division of Random House, Inc.,

1745 Broadway, New York, NY 10019.

Printed in the United States of America.

Produced by The Stonesong Press, LLC

Managing Editors: Typesetting: Publications Development Company

BROADWAY BOOKS and its logo, a letter B bisected on the diagonal, are trademarks of Random House, Inc. MADE SIMPLE is a trademark of Broadway Books.

Visit our website at www.broadwaybooks.com

First Broadway Books trade paperback edition published 2006.

The Library of Congress Cataloging-in-Publication Data

Jackson, Eugene.

French made simple / Eugene Jackson and Antonio Rubio.—Rev. ed. / revised by Julien Lafontant and Pamela Haze.

p.   cm.—(Made simple)

"A Made simple book."

ISBN 0-7679-1859-2

1. French language—Textbooks for foreign speakers—English.   2. French language—Grammar.   I. Rubio, Antonio, 1888–   II. Lafontant, Julien J.   III. Haze, Pamela.   IV. Title.   V. Made simple (Broadway Books)

PC2129.E5J33 2006

448.2'421—dc22   2006040511

ISBN 0-7679-1859-2

10   9   8   7   6   5   4   3   2   1

CONTENTS

PREFACE

About This Book

To the user of this book:

You may have studied French years ago, but never felt that you had acquired a solid foundation of French grammar or a knowledge of the distinctive meanings of many French expressions. Or, having wanted to learn French for years, you are now taking the first step to that goal by picking up this book. Alternatively, you may already be a teacher of foreign languages, including French, and want to see if you can supplement your teaching materials, or recommend a good self-study guide for a student or friend.

Whatever your reason for approaching the study of French, I hope that *French Made Simple* will serve as a great companion as you travel through its pages and obtain a sound understanding and active ability to communicate in this language.

The content of this text may be compared to that of a first-year college course in French. The written guidelines and illustrated descriptions of how to pronounce the language appear early in the book. First, you will discover how much French vocabulary you already know, due to the similarities between French and English. Then, a continuing saga of an international New York businessman and his informative and encouraging French tutor develops with each chapter.

The sections Vocabulary, French Expressions, and Grammar Notes are presented after the opening dialogue in each chapter. These are followed by several exercises of different formats to help you drill and absorb the new material, and at the same time, incorporate content from preceding chapters. A paragraph on How to Use the Text will be found at the beginning of Chapter 3. After every four or five chapters, a thorough Review of their concepts is presented.

Suggestions are also given on how you can best be your own French teacher, as well as methods to boost and supplement your growing command of the language. You will have an Answer Key, a Bilingual Dictionary, and a Verb Chart to help you check and recall your work. In this new edition of *French Made Simple*, a number of drawings and photos will give you a glimpse of the culture, especially that of France, and will, I hope, whet your appetite for real-life use of your new language.

ACKNOWLEDGMENTS

As editor responsible for revision and update, I would like to thank Stonesong Press for affording me the opportunity of bringing to life this edition of *French Made Simple*.

I wish to acknowledge several people who advised me at different points during this project. I greatly appreciate the suggestions from Rick Kulp, Susan Tarcov, and Monique Tranchevent regarding computer editing and modern French usage. Thanks to my Spring 2005 French students at Collins High School for helping me reflect upon useful methodology in beginning to learn a foreign language. And, of course, I am grateful for the input and support of my immediate family members, all of whom studied French for many years, with or despite my encouragement!

Pamela Rose Haze

CHAPITRE 1 (UN)

ON VOUS PRÉSENTE LA LANGUE FRANÇAISE

GETTING ACQUAINTED WITH THE FRENCH LANGUAGE

FRENCH IS NO STRANGER

As a speaker of English, you may be surprised to learn that you already know hundreds of French words. There are, in fact, several thousand words that have the same, or nearly the same, spelling in French and English. These words also have the same meaning. However, pronunciation of the French words differs, often greatly, from that of their English equivalents.

There are other words borrowed directly from the French language that have no change in spelling and almost no change at all in pronunciation.

Following are just a few examples of words—called *cognates*—that have the same spelling and same meaning in French and English:

- Words spelled alike and having the same meaning but different pronunciation

accident	active	automobile	avenue	blouse
cousin	danger	explosion	fruit	humble
image	index	journal	long	nation
profit	route	sacrifice	train	voyage

- Words of the same meaning, slightly different in spelling and pronunciation

| riche | oncle | balle | objet | carte | héros | brun | bleu |
| *rich* | *uncle* | *ball* | *object* | *card* | *hero* | *brown* | *blue* |

| salade | hôpital | rivière | chasse | famille | parfum | mètre | papier |
| *salad* | *hospital* | *river* | *chase* | *family* | *perfume* | *meter* | *paper* |

difficile	**individu**	**qualité**	**liberté**	**docteur**	**acteur**	**téléscope**	**télévision**
difficult	*individual*	*quality*	*liberty*	*doctor*	*actor*	*telescope*	*television*

visiter	**excuser**	**arriver**	**entrer**	**désirer**	**signer**	**honorer**	**inviter**
to visit	*to excuse*	*to arrive*	*to enter*	*to desire*	*to sign*	*to honor*	*to invite*

• English words borrowed directly from the French with no changes in spelling (except accent marks) and which are pronounced in almost the same manner.

In addition, each of the following words possesses at least one meaning that is the same in both languages. These words contain some good clues to French pronunciation:

café	garage	ennui	fleur de lis
route	chauffeur	encore	ensemble
rôle	liqueur	chemise	consommé
rouge	à propos	purée	à la carte
château	bouquet	matinée	entrée
coquette	rendez-vous	coup d'état	sabotage
nouveau riche	laissez-faire	savoir-faire	du jour

Some French words are only slightly different in spelling but have quite different meanings from their English counterparts. Thus, **blesser** means *to injure, to wound,* not *to bless;* **user** means *to wear out, to ruin,* not *to use.* Such words are called *false cognates* (**faux amis,** *false friends*).

FRENCH AND ENGLISH PRONUNCIATIONS DIFFER GREATLY

The similarities between French and English vocabulary will be of great help to you in learning French. However, French and English pronunciations are very different. You must learn not only to pronounce the French words correctly but also to understand them when you hear them. As in English, there are many silent letters. The vowel sounds in particular have a variety of spellings. Even many consonants are articulated with less force in French than they are in English.

You will have little difficulty with the spelling if you practice writing as well as saying new words and exercises. The most important words appear many times in this book, and this will help you remember spelling, meaning, and pronunciation.

In Chapter 2, the pronunciation of French sounds and their spelling is explained in detail. The description of the sounds and the pronunciation aids should enable you to pronounce them quite well. If possible you should also ask a native French speaker to help you with your pronunciation, for it is important to hear the sounds spoken correctly and to have your own pronunciation checked.

Another way you may improve your pronunciation and understanding of the spoken word is by listening to French recordings and radio broadcasts. French commercials are particularly valuable for this purpose, because they contain so much repetition and emphatic expression.

Cassettes of interviews and readings can often be borrowed free or for a small fee from public or university libraries or the Alliance Française in your community. At first, a few minutes of listening each day will probably be enough. Then, as you progress in your study of French, you should increase the amount of time you spend listening to the spoken language.

FRENCH IS SPOKEN BY MANY PEOPLE

French is spoken not only by the 60 million people of France but also by many other people throughout the world. It is a major language in several European countries, principalities, and islands. In the countries of North Africa and Central and West Africa that were once under French or Belgian rule, many people still speak French; in fact, it is the official language of more than twenty African nations. In the Western Hemisphere, French is the language of the Canadian province of Quebec; it is also spoken by large numbers of people in the Eastern Provinces, and it is one of the official languages of Canada. It is spoken in Haiti, Martinique, and Guadeloupe in the Caribbean; in French Guyana in South America; on the Mauritius Islands in the Indian Ocean; and it is recognized by many inhabitants of former French colonies in Southeast Asia, such as Cambodia and Laos.

For many years French was the sole language of diplomacy and the preferred foreign language among educated persons in Europe. That is no longer so, but even today French is probably the second most useful language after English for tourists and business persons traveling in Europe.

Knowing French is not merely of practical or commercial value. It opens the door to a better understanding of France, its people, its rich and colorful past, its contributions to art and technology, and its unique lifestyle. Further, it helps you to explore the origins, development, and current way of life of French-speaking people around the world. Finally, studying and mastering French will give you, the English-speaking learner, new insights into your own native tongue.

Alors, bon courage! Allons-y! Good luck and let's go!

CHAPITRE 2 (DEUX)

PRONONCIATION DU FRANÇAIS
FRENCH PRONUNCIATION

In Part 1 of this chapter, you will learn the elements of French pronunciation. The French words used to model the French sounds are in most cases the words you saw in Chapter 1. As you learn the correct French pronunciation of these words, you are reinforcing or adding to your French vocabulary.

The description of each French sound is accompanied by a pronunciation key, in parentheses, which indicates the nearest English equivalent of that sound. This key will be used throughout the book to ease your way in the pronunciation of new words, phrases, and sentences.

In Part 2 and Part 3 of this chapter you will practice correct French pronunciation in words and expressions useful for the traveler and in short easy dialogues.

French Vowel Sounds

LISTED BELOW ARE FRENCH VOWEL SOUNDS WITH THEIR NEAREST ENGLISH EQUIVALENTS AND PRONUNCIATION KEYS.

1. a is like *a* in *cat.* Key Symbol (a).
balle (bal).

NOTE I. French **a** is sometimes like *a* in *father*; here the Key Symbol is (ah), as in **classe** (klahs).

2. **i** is like *ee* in *feet.* Key Symbol (ee).
   riche (reesh), **Paris** (pa-**ree**).

NOTE 2. Stress (emphasize) slightly the last syllable in French words of more than one syllable. The last syllable is indicated by heavy type in the pronunciation key.

3. **é** is like *a* in *hate.* Key Symbol (ay).
   café (ka-**fay**), **matinée** (ma-tee-**nay**).

4. **è** is like *e* in *there.* Key Symbol (eh).
   scène (sehn), **rivière** (ree-**vyehr**).

5. **o** is like *u* in *but.* Key Symbol (u).
   poste (pust), **poème** (pu-**ehm**).

NOTE 3. French **o** is sometimes like *o* in *note;* the Key Symbol is (oh), as in **hôpital** (oh-pee-**tal**).

6. **ou** is like *oo* in *boot.* Key Symbol (oo).
   route (root), **touriste** (too-**reest**).

Première Partie (pruh-**myehr** par-**tee**) (First Part)

French Sounds in Familiar Words

Pronounce each sound and the words that demonstrate it three times. Stress (emphasize) lightly the syllable in heavy type in the pronunciation key of each word.

NOTE and remember: The last syllable—and only the last syllable—of French words is stressed.

a(a) madame (ma-**dam**) French **a** is generally like *a* in *cat.* Key Symbol (a). See Diagram 1. Remember: occasionally French **a** is like *a* in *father.* Key Symbol (ah). Practice:

balle (bal)	**place** (plas)	**salade** (sa-**lad**)
table (tabl)	**garage** (ga-**razh**)	**classe** (klahs)

i(ee) difficile (dee-fee-**seel**) French **i** equals *ee* in *feet.* Key Symbol (ee). See Diagram 2. Practice:

riche (reesh)   **image** (ee-**mazh**)   **famille** (fa-**meey**)   **Paris** (pa-**ree**)

é(ay) café (ka-**fay**) French **é** is like **a** in **hate**. Key Symbol (ay). See Diagram 3. The mark over this letter [´] is called the acute accent. Practice:

matinée (ma-tee-**nay**)   **désirer** (day-zee-**ray**)   **qualité** (ka-lee-**tay**)   **papier** (pa-**pyay**)

NOTE: French **-er** at the end of a word often equals **é** (ay). The **-r** is silent. French **qu** always equals *k.*

è(eh) scène (sehn) French **è** is like *e* in *there.* Key Symbol (eh). See Diagram 4. The mark over this letter [`] is called the grave accent. Other spellings of this sound are **ê** and very often **ai**. The mark [^] is called the circumflex accent. Practice:

mètre (mehtr)   **crème** (krehm)   **fête** (feht)   **laissez-faire** (leh-say-**fehr**)

e(uh) chemise (shuh-**meez**) French **e** without any accent mark is pronounced like *e* in *father,* when it ends the first syllable of a word. Key Symbol (uh). Practice:

menace (muh-**nas**)   **cheval** (shuh-**val**)   **regard** (ruh-**gar**)   **venir** (vuh-**neer**)

At the end of a word, **e** without an accent mark is silent except in words of one syllable. Practice:

le (luh)   **je** (zhuh)   **me** (muh)   **ne** (nuh)   **ce** (suh)   **de** (duh)   **que** (kuh)

e without an accent mark may sometimes be pronounced like **é** (ay), sometimes like **è** (eh). Practice:

et (ay)   **assez** (a-**say**)   **pied** (pyay)   **dessert** (day-**sehr**)
est (eh)   **elle** (ehl)   **effet** (ay-**feh**)

o(u) **poste** (pust) French **o** is like *u* in *but*. Key Symbol (u). See Diagram 5. Practice:

objet (ub-**zheh**)   **effort** (ay-**fur**)   **original** (u-ree-zhee-**nal**)
poème (pu-**ehm**)

ô(oh) **rôle** (rohl) French **ô** is like *o* in *note*. Key Symbol (oh). Other spellings of this sound are **au** and **eau**; sometimes **o** without the circumflex is also pronounced (oh).

hôtel (oh-**tehl**)   **au revoir** (oh-ruh-   **rose** (rohz)   **chapeau** (sha-**poh**)
                         vwar)

NOTE: French **oi** equals *wa*.

ou(oo) **route** (root) French **ou** is like *oo* in *boot*. Key Symbol (oo). See Diagram 6. Practice:

rouge (roozh)   **routine** (roo-**teen**)   **touriste** (too-**reest**)   **coup d'état** (koo-day-**ta**)

u(ü) **bureau** (bü-**roh**) French **u** is like *ee* spoken with lips held firmly in a small circle as for whistling. Key Symbol (ü). See Diagram 6. Practice:

nature (na-**tür**)   **public** (pü-**bleek**)   **avenue** (av-**nü**)   **excuser** (ehks-kü-**zay**)

eu(eu) **liqueur** (lee-**keur**) French **eu** is like *u* in *urge*. It is the sound (eh) spoken with lips firmly rounded on a somewhat larger circle than for French **u**. Key Symbol (eu). Practice:

docteur (duk-**teur**)   **acteur** (ak-**teur**)   **professeur** (pru-feh-**seur**)
chauffeur (shoh-**feur**)

French Nasal Vowel Sounds

In syllables ending in **n** and **m**, the **n** and **m** are not pronounced. Instead the preceding vowel sound is nasalized as described below. There are four nasal vowel sounds in French. As you will note, each of these nasal vowel sounds has a number of spellings. In the pronunciation key ñ indicates that the preceding vowel sound is nasalized.

1. an(ahñ) piquant (pee-kahñ) Say the English syllable *ahn* as in *want* loudly.

Mouth wide open. Hold the tongue down with a flat stick so that it cannot rise for the **n**, and try to say *ahn*. An excellent French nasal **an**, key symbol (ahñ), results. Now practice the sound without using a stick. Be sure to keep your tongue down. Other spellings of the nasal sound **an** (ahñ) are **am, en, em**. Practice:

France (frahñs)   **danger** (dahñ-**zhay**)   **encore** (ahñ-**kur**)   **absent** (ap-**sahñ**)

ensemble (ahñ-**sahñbl**)   **rendez-vous** (rahñ-day-**voo**)   **enveloppe** (ahñ-vuh-**lup**)

2. on(awñ) consommé (kawñ-su-may) Say the English sound *awn* as in *dawn*. Hold the tongue down with a flat stick, so that it cannot rise for the **n** and try to say *awn*. An excellent French nasal **on**, key symbol (awñ), results. Practice the sound without using the stick:

oncle (awñkl)   **nation** (nah-**syawñ**)   **station** (stah-**syawñ**)   **question** (kehs-**tyawñ**)

Another spelling of the nasal **on** is **om** in some words. Practice:

tombe (tawñb)
fall down

bombe (bawñb)

3. in(añ) lingerie (lañ-zhuh-ree) Say *an* as in the English word *ban*. Hold your tongue down with a flat stick so that it cannot rise for the **n**, and try to say *an*. The French nasal **in**, key symbol (añ), results. Practice the sound without using a stick. Other spellings of the nasal **in** are **im, ain, aim, ein**. Practice:

index (añ-dehks)   **faim** (fañ) hunger   **importateur** (añ-pur-ta-**teur**)
américain (a-may-ree-**kañ**)   **plein** (plañ) full

4. un(euñ) brun (breuñ) Pronounce the nasal sound **in** (añ). For the nasal sound **in** (añ) the corners of the lips are drawn back as in a smile. Round the lips as in Diagram 5 and try to say **in** (añ). The result is a good French nasal **un**, key symbol (euñ). Another spelling of the nasal **un** (euñ) is **um** (euñ). Practice:

un (euñ)   **brun** (breuñ)   **humble** (euñbl)   **parfum** (par-**feuñ**)
one   brown   perfume
chacun (sha-**keuñ**)
each

Summary of French Vowel Sounds

Letters:	a	é	è	e	i	o	ou	u	eu	au (eau)	oi
Symbols:	a ah	ay	eh	ay eh uh	ee	u oh	oo	ü	eu	oh	wa

Summary of French Nasal Sounds

Letters:	an (am, en, em)	in (im, ain, aim, ein, oin)	on(om)	un(um)
Symbols:	ahñ	añ	awñ	euñ

French Consonants

Most French consonant sounds are like the corresponding English consonant sounds, although native English speakers tend to emit more air in pronouncing a number of consonants than do the French (examples: **b, g, k, p**).

In addition, the following need special attention:

c before **e** or **i** is like *s* in *see*. **difficile** (dee-fee-**seel**)

c before any other letter (except **h**) is like *k*: **café** (ka-**fay**)

ç with cedilla is always like *s*: **français** (frahñ-**seh**)

ch is like English *sh*, **riche** (reesh)

g before **e** or **i** is like *s* in *measure*: **rouge** (roozh)

g before any other letter is like *g* in *goat*: **garage** (ga-**razh**)

h is always silent: **hôtel** (oh-**tehl**)

j is like *s* in *measure*: **je** (zhuh)

ll is often like *y* in *yes*, **famille** (fa-**meey**); other times it remains *l* as in *fall*: **ville** (veel)

r is a like a brief gargling sound, made at the front of your throat: **Paris** (pa-**ree**)

qu is always like *k*: **bouquet** (boo-**keh**)

gn is like *ny* in *canyon*: **espagnol** (ehs-pa-**nyul**)

NOTE: Final consonants in French are usually silent: **bouquet** (boo-**keh**), **Paris** (pa-**ree**), **regard** (ruh-**gar**)

However, the final consonants (c, f, l, r) are usually pronounced:

sac (sak)   **chef** (shehf)   **hôtel** (oh-**tehl**)   **car** (kar)

Deuxième Partie (deu-**zyehm** par-**tee**) Second Part

The second and third parts of this chapter contain important words and expressions frequently used. If you follow carefully the instructions for pronunciation practice, you will acquire many of these without difficulty. Do not try to memorize all of them at this point; they will appear again in later chapters, and you will have the opportunity to learn them thoroughly.

Some Useful Words and Expressions for the Traveler

Practice the French aloud. Stress slightly the key syllables in heavy type:

1. **Pardon (**par-**dawñ)**
2. **S'il vous plaît (**seel voo **pleh)**
3. **Monsieur (**muh-**syeu); Madame (**ma-**dam); Mademoiselle (**mad-mwa-**zehl)**
4. **Où est l'hôtel . . . ? (**oo eh loh-**tehl)**
5. **Combien coûte le livre? (**kawñ-byañ koot luh **leevr)**
6. **Je voudrais . . . (**zhuh voo-**dreh)**
7. **Merci beaucoup (**mehr-see boh-**koo)**
8. **Il n'y a pas de quoi (**eel nee-ya pah duh **kwah)**
9. **C'est trop cher (**seh troh **shehr). Très cher (**treh **shehr)**
10. **bon marché (**bawñ mar-**shay). meilleur marché (**meh-yeur mar-**shay)**

1. (I beg your) pardon.
2. Please; if you please.
3. Mr., Sir; Mrs., Madam; Miss, young lady.
4. Where is the hotel . . . ?
5. How much does the book cost?
6. I would like . . .
7. Thank you very much.
8. You are welcome.
9. It's too expensive. Very expensive.
10. cheap. cheaper

Read each question aloud, and complete it with the words listed below.

NOTE: In this book, the pronunciation aid for the definite articles **le** and **la,** and their translation *the* will generally be omitted.

Combien coûte . . . ? (kawñ-byañ koot)

Examples: **Combien coûte le chapeau? Combien coûte la chemise?** etc.
1. **le chapeau (**sha-**poh)** hat
2. **la chemise (**shuh-**meez)** shirt
3. **la blouse (**blooz)** smock
4. **le corsage (**kur-**sazh)** blouse
5. **la robe (**rub)** dress
6. **la montre (**mawñtr)** watch
7. **le parapluie (**pa-ra-**plüee)** umbrella
8. **le parfum (**par-**feuñ)** perfume

9. **la cravate** (kra-**vat**) necktie
10. **l'automobile** (lu-tu-mu-**beel**) automobile

Pardon, monsieur. Où est . . ., s'il vous plaît? (par-dawñ, muh-**syeu**. oo eh . . ., seel voo **pleh?**)

1. **la rue Drouot** (rü droo-**oh**) Drouot Street
2. **l'avenue de la République** (lav-nü duh la ray-pü-**bleek**) Republic Avenue
3. **la place de la Concorde** (plas duh la kawñ-**kurd**) Concord Place
4. **la gare du Nord** (gar dü **nur)** North Station
5. **l'Hôtel Albert** (loh-tehl al-**behr)** Albert Hotel
6. **le boulevard Saint-Michel** (bool-var sañ mee-**shehl)** Saint Michel Boulevard
7. **le bureau de poste** (bü-roh duh **pust)** post office.
8. **la salle d'attente** (sal da-**tahñt)** waiting room
9. **la toilette** (twah-**leht)** washroom

Je voudrais . . . (zhuh voo-dreh . . .)

1. **une chambre avec bain** (ün shahñbr avehk **bañ)** a room with bath
2. **de l'eau chaude** (duh loh **shohd)** some hot water
3. **des serviettes de bain** (day sehr-vyeht duh **bañ)** some bath towels
4. **la carte** (**kart)** menu
5. **l'addition** (la dee-**syawñ)** bill
6. **la revue** (ruh-**vü)** magazine
7. **le journal** (zhoor-**nal)** newspaper
8. **du savon** (dü sa-**vawñ)** some soap
9. **téléphoner** (tay-lay-fu-**nay)** to telephone
10. **changer de l'argent** (shahñ-zhay duh lar-**zhahñ)** to change money

Practice aloud, as often as possible, the numbers 1 to 21:

1. **un** (euñ), **une** (ün)	12. **douze** (dooz)
2. **deux** (deu)	13. **treize** (trehz)
3. **trois** (trwah)	14. **quatorze** (ka-**turz)**
4. **quatre** (katr)	15. **quinze** (kañz)
5. **cinq** (sañk)	16. **seize** (sehz)
6. **six** (sees)	17. **dix-sept** (dee-**seht)**
7. **sept** (seht)	18. **dix-huit** (deez-**üeet)**
8. **huit** (üeet)	19. **dix-neuf** (deez-**neuf)**
9. **neuf** (neuf)	20. **vingt** (vañ)
10. **dix** (dees)	21. **vingt et un** (vañ tay **euñ)**
11. **onze** (awñz)	

Troisième Partie (trwah-**zyehm** par-**tee**) Third Part

Liaison (lee-eh-**zawñ**) Linking

The final consonant of a French word is generally silent. However, when the next word begins with a vowel or silent **h**, the final consonant is usually pronounced and linked to the next word unless there is a natural pause. This is called **liaison** in French.

Final **s** and **x**, when linked, are pronounced like *z*; final **f** like *v* in **neuf ans** (neu vahñ) and **neuf heures** (neu veur); and final **d** like *t*.

Comment allez-vous?	beaux-arts	trois ans	neuf ans	le grand homme
(ku-mahñ ta-lay-**voo**)	(boh **zar**)	(trwah **zahñ**)	(neu **vañ**)	(grahñ **tum**)
How are you?	fine arts	three years	nine years	the great man

Élision (ay-lee-**zyawñ**) Elision

The letters **e** and **a** in the words **le, la, ce, je, me, te, se, de, ne, que** are dropped before words beginning with a vowel or a silent **h** and are replaced by an apostrophe. This process is called **élision**. Thus:

le + oncle becomes **l'oncle** (lawñkl) uncle
le + hôtel becomes **l'hôtel** (loh-**tehl**) hotel
la + école becomes **l'école** (lay-**kul**) school
je + ai becomes **j'ai** (zhay) I have
que + est-ce que c'est? becomes **qu'est-ce que c'est?** (kehs kuh **seh**) What is that?

The Stress in French Words and Sentences

1. **In French all the syllables of a word are spoken with equal force except the last.**

The last syllable of the word is stressed (emphasized) slightly.

général (zhay-nay-**ral) répéter** (ray-pay-**tay) madame** (ma-**dam) chauffeur** (shoh-**feur**)

2. **In short sentences all the syllables are spoken with equal force except the last.**

Only the last syllable of the sentence is stressed.

La leçon est difficile (la luh-sawñ eh dee-fee-**seel**) The lesson is difficult.

3. **In longer sentences, the last syllable of clauses and of other word groups is also stressed.**

Combien coûte le livre pour la classe de Français
(Kawñ-byan koot luh leevr poor la klahs duh frahñ-**say**)

Dialogue 1 (dya-**lug**)

Directions for Study.

1. Read the French text silently, sentence by sentence, using the English translation to get the meaning. Note that in French, long dashes are used to introduce alternating speakers, instead of quotation marks.
2. Read the whole French text aloud three or more times, using the pronunciation keys as aids. Stress lightly the syllables in boldface type.

Comment allez-vous (ku-mahñ ta-lay-**voo**)? How are you?

1. —**Bonjour, monsieur Picard. Comment allez-vous?** (Bawñ-zhoor, muh-syeu pee-**kar.** Ku-mahñ ta-lay-**voo?**)
2. —**Très bien, merci. Et vous?** (Treh byañ, mehr-**see.** Ay **voo?**)
3. —**Très bien, merci.** (Treh **byañ,** mehr-**see**)
4. —**Au revoir, monsieur Picard.** (Oh ruh-**vwar,** muh-syeu pee-**kar**)
5. —**Au revoir, Philippe.** (Oh ruh-**vwar,** fee-**leep**)

1. Good day, Mr. Picard. How are you?
2. Very well, thank you. And you?
3. Very well, thank you.
4. Goodbye, Mr. Picard.
5. Goodbye, Philippe.

Dialogue 2

Parlez-vous français? (par-lay-voo frahñ-**seh**) Do you speak French?

1. —**Parlez-vous français, Marie?** (Parlay-voo frahñ-**seh,** ma-**ree?**)
2. —**Oui, monsieur, je parle français!** (Wee muh-**syeu,** zhuh parl frahñ -**seh**)
3. —**Est-ce que Charles parle français?** (Ehs-kuh sharl parl frahñ-**seh?**)
4. —**Oui, madame, il parle bien le français!** (Wee, ma-**dam,** eel parl byañ luh frahñ-**seh**)
5. —**Est-ce que Louise parle français?** (Ehs-kuh loo-eez parl frahñ-**seh?**)
6. —**Non, madame, elle parle anglais.** (Nawñ, ma-**dam,** ehl parl ahñ-**gleh**)

1. Do you speak French, Marie?
2. Yes, sir, I speak French.
3. Does Charles speak French?
4. Yes, madam, he speaks French well.
5. Does Louise speak French?
6. No, madam, she speaks English.

NOTE: The definite article **le** is not used before the name of a language when the name of the language immediately follows the verb **parler** or the preposition **en.**

Est-ce que Louise parle français? but **Il parle bien le français.**

Dites-le en français.

Dialogue 3

Les jours de la semaine (lay zhoor duh la suh-**mehn**) The days of the week

1. —**Écoutez, Thomas! Combien de jours y a-t-il dans une semaine?** (Ay-koo-tay tu-**mah!** Kawñ-byañ duh zhoor ya-teel dahñ zün suh-**mehn?**)

2. —**Il y a sept jours dans une semaine.** (Eel ya seht zhoor dahñ zün suh-**mehn**)

3. —**Bien. Donnez-moi les noms des sept jours de la semaine, s'il vous plaît. (Byañ.** Du-nay-mwa lay nawñ day seht zhoor duh la suh-**mehn**, seel voo **pleh**)

4. —**Lundi, mardi, mercredi, jeudi, vendredi, samedi, dimanche.** (leuñ-**dee**, mar-**dee**, mehr-kruh-**dee**, zheu-**dee**, vahñ-druh-**dee**, sam-**dee**, dee-**mahñsh**)

5. —**Très bien. Écoutez, Georges! Quel jour de la semaine sommes-nous?** (Treh **byañ.** Ay-koo-tay **zhurzh!** Kehl zhoor duh la suh-mehn sum-**noo?**)

6. —**Aujourd'hui c'est lundi.** (Oh-zhoor-düee seh leuñ-**dee**)

7. —**Très bien, Georges.** (Treh byañ **zhurzh**)

---

1. Listen, Thomas! How many days are there in a week?

2. There are seven days in a week.

3. Good. Give me the names of the seven days of the week, please.

4. Monday, Tuesday, Wednesday, Thursday, Friday, Saturday, Sunday. NOTE: The French begin with Monday when they recite the days of the week.

5. Very good. Listen, George! What day of the week is it today? (*Literally:* What day of the week are we [on]?)

6. Today is Monday.

7. Very good, George.

NOTE: The normal convention in printed French is to omit accent marks over letters if the letters are capitalized. However, for pedagogical reasons, we are following the style of many beginning French texts, and including the accents, for the student's benefit.

Example: **Écoutez, Thomas!**

CHAPITRE 3 (TROIS)

QUI EST MONSIEUR BROWN?
WHO IS MR. BROWN?

You now have a good working knowledge of French pronunciation and are ready for a more in-depth study of the language. Practice the pronunciation aids after each conversational text and follow all directions for reading aloud and speaking. Remember: the only way you can learn to speak a language is by speaking it.

This chapter will introduce you to Mr. Brown, a New York businessman who is as eager as you are to learn French. You will also meet his congenial teacher, Monsieur Picard, a Frenchman living in New York. You will also meet Mrs. Brown, a university history professor. As Monsieur Picard teaches Mr. Brown, he will also teach you.

So **Bonne Chance** (good luck) and **Bon Voyage** (have a good trip) as you accompany Mr. Brown on the road that leads to a practical knowledge of the French language.

COMMENT ÉTUDIER LE TEXTE—HOW TO STUDY THE TEXT

- Cover up the English text and read the French text silently, referring to the English only when necessary to get the meaning.
- Study the Pronunciation and Spelling Aids and the sections Building Vocabulary and French Expressions that follow the text.
- Then, read the French text aloud, pronouncing carefully.
- Identify new words by doing the exercise Completion of Text.
- Proceed to Grammar Notes, the additional exercises, and the Questionnaire.

Follow the same instructions in subsequent chapters.

Qui est Monsieur Brown?

1. **Monsieur Brown est un homme d'affaires américain.**
2. **Il habite dans une petite ville dans les environs de New-York.**
3. **Il y a six personnes dans la famille Brown: le père, Monsieur Brown; la mère, Madame Brown; deux fils et deux filles. Monsieur Brown est un homme de quarante ans. Madame Brown est une femme de trente-quatre ans qui enseigne l'histoire dans une université située à quelques kilomètres de leur maison.**
4. **Les fils s'appellent[1] Charles et Thomas. Les filles s'appellent Elizabeth et Anne.**
5. **La famille Brown habite dans une maison particulière.**
6. **Dans la maison il y a cinq pièces: le salon, la salle à manger, et trois chambres à coucher. Il y a aussi la cuisine et la salle de bain.**
7. **Le bureau de Monsieur Brown est dans la rue Whitehall.**
8. **Il est au vingtième étage d'un gratte-ciel.**
9. **Tous les lundis, les mardis, les mercredis, les jeudis, et les vendredis, Monsieur Brown prend le train pour aller à son bureau en ville.**
10. **Toute la journée il travaille dans son bureau.**

Who Is Mr. Brown?

1. Mr. Brown is an American businessman.
2. He lives in a small town in the suburbs of New York.
3. There are six persons in the Brown family: the father, Mr. Brown; the mother, Mrs. Brown; two sons and two daughters. Mr. Brown is a forty-year-old man. Mrs. Brown is a thirty-four-year-old woman who teaches history in a university located a few miles from their house.
4. The sons are named Charles and Thomas. The daughters are named Elizabeth and Anne.
5. The Brown family lives in a private house.
6. In the house there are five rooms: the living room, the dining room, and three bedrooms. There are also the kitchen and the bathroom.
7. Mr. Brown's office is on Whitehall Street.
8. It is on the twentieth floor of a skyscraper.
9. On Mondays, Tuesdays, Wednesdays, Thursdays, and Fridays, Mr. Brown takes the train to go to his office in the city.
10. He works in his office the whole day.

[1]Remember: **s,** when linked, has the sound **z. les environs** (lay zahñ-vee-**rawñ**)
NOTE: The French do not count the kitchen or bathroom as rooms in a home.

Pronunciation and Spelling Aids

Practice aloud:

1. **un homme d'affaires américain** (euñ num da-fehr za-may-ree-**kañ**)
2. **dans une petite ville** (dahñ zün puh-teet **veel**)
3. **dans les environs** (dahñ lay zahñ-vee-**rawñ**)
4. **trois chambres à coucher** (trwah shahñbr a koo-**shay**)
5. **il est au vingtième étage** (eel eh toh vañ-tyehm ay-**tazh**)
6. **prend le train** (prahñ luh **trañ**)

Building Vocabulary

In the vocabulary lists, the definite articles **le, la, l'**, and **les** (*the*) are not translated into English. They are not included in the Pronunciation Keys either, with the exception of **l'**, since this abbreviation before a word that begins with a vowel or mute **h** becomes the initial sound of the word.

A. LA FAMILLE (fa-**meey**)—FAMILY

le père (pehr) father
la mère (mehr) mother
le fils (fees) son
la fille (feey) daughter
le frère (frehr) brother
la soeur (seur) sister
l'oncle (lawñkl) uncle
la tante (tahñt) aunt
le cousin (koo-**zañ**) cousin (*m*)
la cousine (koo-**zeen**) cousin (*f*)
l'enfant (lahñ-**fahñ**) child
le garçon (gar-**sawñ**) boy
la jeune fille (zheun **feey**) young woman, girl
le monsieur (muh-**syeu**) gentleman
messieurs (may-**syeu**) gentlemen

la dame (dam) lady
Madame (ma-**dam**) Mrs., Madam
Mademoiselle (md-mwe-**zehl**) Miss, young lady
l'homme (lum) man
la femme (fam) woman
les parents (lay pa-**rahñ**) parents, relatives

B. LES PIÈCES DE LA MAISON (pyehs duh la meh-zawñ) **ROOMS OF THE HOUSE**
le salon (sa-**lawñ**) living room
la chambre à coucher (shahñbr a koo-**shay**) bedroom
la cuisine (küee-**zeen**) kitchen
la salle à manger (sal a mahñ-**zhay**) dining room
la salle de bains (sal duh **bañ**) bathroom

C. LES MOTS INTERROGATIFS (mo zañ-teh-ru-ga-**teef**)—QUESTION WORDS

qui (kee) who?
où (oo) where?
comment (ku-**mahñ**) how?
combien (kawñ-**byañ**) how many?

French Expressions

1. **il y a** (eel **ya**) there is, there are
2. **y a-t-il?** (ya-**teel**) is there? are there?
3. **par coeur** (par **keur**) by heart
4. **toute la journée** (toot la zhoor-**nay**) all day long, the whole day (long)

Exercise No. 1—Completion of Text

To gain the maximum benefit, follow these instructions carefully in all Completion of Text exercises.

Complete each sentence by replacing the English words with the French. Do this from memory where you can.

If you do not remember the words, refer to the French text. There you will find the words in order of their appearance in the conversation.

When you have completed each sentence with the appropriate words, read the complete sentence aloud in French.

It will greatly help your memory if you write down each completed sentence. The correct French words for the Completion of Text exercises are in the Answers section at the end of this book, as well as answers to all other exercises. Check all your answers.

Exemple (ehg-**zahñpl)** Example 1. **Qui est Monsieur Brown?**
 1. (Who) **est Monsieur Brown?**
 2. **C'est un** (businessman) **américain.**
 3. **Il habite une petite** (city).
 4. (There are) **six personnes dans la famille.**
 5. **Monsieur Brown est le** (father).
 6. **Madame Brown est la** (mother).
 7. **Les** (sons) **s'appellent Charles** (and) **Thomas.**
 8. **Les filles** (are named) **Elizabeth** (and) **Anne.**
 9. **Il y a** (five rooms) **dans la maison.**
10. **Il y a aussi une** (kitchen) **et une** (bathroom).
11. **Le** (office) **est dans la Whitehall** (street).
12. (It is) **dans un gratte-ciel.**
13. **Il est au** (twentieth) **étage.**
14. **Monsieur Brown travaille** (all day long)

Grammar Notes

1. GENDER OF NOUNS

Nouns are either of masculine or feminine gender. This is true for nouns representing things (objects, places, ideas) as well as for nouns representing persons.

It is useful to learn the gender of nouns as they occur.

2. PLURAL OF NOUNS

The plural of nouns is usually formed by adding **s** to the singular. The added **s** is not pronounced. If a noun already ends in **s** in the singular, no additional **s** is added. Learn these exceptions as you meet them. Nouns ending in **eau** add **x** to form their plural: **bureau, bureaux**

3. DEFINITE ARTICLE

Note the four ways in which the definite article *the* is expressed in French—**le** (luh), **la** (la), **l'**, or **les** (lay).

Le is used with a masculine singular noun; **la** is used with a feminine singular noun; **l'** is used with any noun that begins with a vowel or **h** (mute);[1] **les** is used with any plural noun, masculine or feminine.

With Singular Nouns

Masculine:	**le père**	**le fils**	**le frère**
Feminine:	**la mère**	**la fille**	**la soeur**
Masculine:	**l'oncle**	**l'homme**	**l'enfant**
Feminine:	**la tante**	**la femme**	**l'enfant**

With Plural Nouns

Masculine:	**les pères**	**les fils**	**les frères**
Feminine:	**les mères**	**les filles**	**les soeurs**
Masculine:	**les oncles**	**les hommes**	**les enfants**
Feminine:	**les tantes**	**les femmes**	**les enfants**

When the **s** of **les** is linked with the following noun, it is pronounced like *z*. Thus:

les enfants (lay zahñ-**fahñ**), **les hommes** (lay **zum**).

NOTE:[1] In all French words beginning with **h,** this letter is silent or mute. However, there are certain words where one does not use elision before the initial **h.** Instead "**l'**," "**le**," "**la**," or "**les**" must be used before such words; the letter is known as aspirate **h.** Note the following examples:

With Singular Nouns

Masculine: **le héros** (ay-**roh**) hero   **le hibou** (ee-**boo**) owl

Feminine: **la halle** (al) covered market   **la harpe** (arp) harp

With Plural Nouns

The **s** of **les** is not linked with the following noun. Thus:

Masculine: **les héros** (lay ay-**roh**)   **les hiboux** (lay ee-**boo**)

Feminine: **les halles** (lay al)   **les harpes** (lay arp)

4. INDEFINITE ARTICLE

Note how the indefinite article *a, an, one* is expressed in French:

With Singular Nouns

Masculine:	**un père**	**un fils**	**un enfant**	**un train**	**un oncle**
Feminine:	**une mère**	**une fille**	**une enfant**	**une rue**	**une tante**

With Plural Nouns

Masculine:	**des pères**	**des fils**	**des enfants**	**des trains**	**des oncles**
Feminine:	**des mères**	**des filles**	**des enfants**	**des rues**	**des tantes**

The indefinite article in French is **un** (euñ) with singular masculine nouns; **une** (ün) with singular feminine nouns. With plural nouns, masculine or feminine; **des** (day), meaning *some* is used.

When the **s** of **des** is linked with the following noun, it is pronounced like "z." Thus:

> **des enfants** (day zahñ-**fahñ**)   **des hommes** (day zum).

As in the case of the definite article **les,** the **s** of **des** is not linked with nouns beginning with aspirate **h.** Thus: **des héros** (day ay-roh)

The word *some* may be omitted in English, but **des** is never omitted in French. Thus:

> **des objets d'art**   some art objects or art objects

Quelques (kehl-kuh) is also used for some, in the sense of a few: **quelques langues** a few languages

NOTE: Use **il** (or **elle**) in a sentence to refer to a previously mentioned person, if what follows is (**est**) an adjective. Nationalities, professions, and religions are considered adjectives for this purpose.

Example: **Il est américain. Elle est professeur.**

But to identify and describe someone in the constructions: **un** or **une** + noun + adjective or **un** or **une** + adjective + noun, **c'est** is used.

Example: **C'est un homme d'affaires américain.**

Exercise No. 2

Replace the English words *the* and *a* by **le, la, l', un,** or **une** as appropriate.

Exemple: **1. La famille Brown habite à New York.**

1. (The) **famille Brown habite à New York.**
2. **New York est** (a) **grande ville.**
3. (The) **gratte-ciel est dans** (the) **rue Whitehall.**
4. (The) **père est Monsieur Brown.**
5. (The) **mère est Madame Brown.**
6. **Anne est** (one) **fille.**
7. **Charles est** (one) **fils.**
8. (The) **cuisine est grande.**
9. (The) **maison est** (a) **maison particulière.**
10. (The) **homme est dans** (the) **salon.**
11. (The) **enfant est dans** (the) **chambre à coucher.**
12. **Il y a** (one) **soeur et** (one) **frère.**

Exercise No. 3

Change the following nouns to the plural, using **les** or **des**. Read the changed phrases aloud, linking the final **s** or **x** when required.

Example: la salle   les salles

                      un train   des trains

1. la chambre
2. la harpe
3. une pièce
4. le fils
5. l'homme
6. un salon
7. l'Américain
8. un étage
9. le bureau
10. une personne
11. l'oncle
12. un/une enfant
13. le héros
14. la rue
15. une avenue

5. SOME COMMON VERB CONSTRUCTIONS

il est (eel **eh**) he is

est-il? (eh-**teel**) is he?

il habite (eel a-**beet**) he lives

habite-t-il? (a-beet-**teel**) does he live?

ils sont (eel-**sawñ**) they are

sont-ils? (sawñ-**teel**) are they?

il prend (eel **prahñ**) he takes

prend-il? (prahñ-**teel**) does he take?

il travaille (eel tra-**vahy**) he works

travaille-t-il? (tra-vahy-**teel**) does he work?

NOTE: When inversion is used to ask a question, **-t-** must be placed between the verb and the following pronoun if the verb ends in a vowel (even final **e**) and the pronoun starts with a vowel.

Example: **habite-t-il?   travaille-t-il?**

Exercise No. 4

Translate into French:

1. Mr. Brown is an American businessman.
2. He lives in New York.
3. There are six persons in the family.
4. He lives in a private house.
5. There are five rooms in the house.
6. Mr. Brown is the father.
7. Mrs. Brown is the mother.
8. The office is on Whitehall Street.
9. Mr. Brown takes the train.
10. He works in the office.

Exercise No. 5—Questionnaire

First read each French question and answer silently, noting the English meaning.

Then read each French question and answer aloud at least twice, without referring to the English.

Questions (kehs-**tyawñ**) et **Réponses** (ray-**pawñs**)

1. **Qui est Monsieur Brown? C'est un homme d'affaires à New-York.**
2. **Est-il américain? Oui, monsieur, il est américain.**
3. **Où habite Monsieur Brown? Il habite dans les environs de New-York.**
4. **Combien de personnes y a-t-il dans sa (*his*) famille? Il y a six personnes dans sa famille.**
5. **Comment les filles s'appellent-elles? Elles s'appellent Elizabeth et Anne.**
6. **Comment les fils s'appellent-ils? Ils s'appellent Charles et Thomas.**
7. **Quelle est la profession de Madame Brown? Elle est professeur.**
8. **Où travaille-t-elle? Elle travaille dans une grande université.**
9. **Combien de pièces y a-t-il dans la maison des Brown? Il y a cinq pièces.**
10. **Y a-t-il aussi une cuisine et une salle de bains? Oui, monsieur, il y a aussi une cuisine et une salle de bains.**
11. **Dans quelle rue est le bureau de Monsieur Brown? Il est dans la rue Whitehall.**
12. **Où travaille-t-il toute la journée? Il travaille dans son bureau.**

Questions and Answers

1. Who is Mr. Brown? He is a businessman in New York.
2. Is he an American? Yes, sir, he is an American.
3. Where does Mr. Brown live? He lives in the suburbs of New York.
4. How many persons are there in his family? There are six persons in his family.
5. What are the daughters' names? They are called (named) Elizabeth and Anne.
6. What are the sons' names? They are called Charles and Thomas.
7. What is Mrs. Brown's profession? She is a professor/teacher.
8. Where does she work? She works in a large university.
9. How many rooms are there in the Browns' house? There are five rooms.
10. Is there also a kitchen and a bathroom? Yes, sir, there is also a kitchen and a bathroom.
11. On what street is Mr. Brown's office? It is on Whitehall Street.
12. Where does he work all day long? He works in his office.

CHAPTER 4

CHAPITRE 4 (QUATRE)

POURQUOI EST-CE QUE M. BROWN ÉTUDIE LE FRANÇAIS?

WHY IS MR. BROWN STUDYING FRENCH?

1. M. Brown est importateur.
2. Il importe des objets d'art et des articles divers de France et du Maroc.
3. Au printemps M. Brown va faire un voyage en France. Il désire rencontrer sa représentante à Paris. Il désire parler français avec elle.
4. Il désire aussi visiter des endroits intéressants en France. Il compte aussi aller au Maroc et peut-être en Corse.
5. M. Brown sait lire un peu le français. Mais il ne peut pas parler français. C'est pourquoi il étudie la langue française.
6. M. Picard est le professeur de M. Brown.
7. M. Picard, un ami de M. Brown, est un Français. C'est un homme de quarante-cinq ans.
8. Tous les mardis et jeudis les deux messieurs ont rendez-vous, presque toujours chez M. Brown. Là ils parlent français.
9. M. Picard est un bon professeur.
10. M. Brown est très intelligent et il apprend rapidement.
11. Pendant la première leçon il apprend par coeur ce dialogue:
12. —Bonjour, M. Picard. Comment allez-vous?—Très bien, merci. Et vous?—Très bien, merci.
13. M. Brown apprend aussi des salutations et des adieux.
14. Bonjour.
15. Bonsoir.
16. Adieu. Au revoir. À tout à l'heure. À bientôt.

1. Mr. Brown is an importer.
2. He imports art objects and various articles from France and from Morocco.
3. In the spring Mr. Brown is going to make a trip to France. He wants to meet his agent in Paris. He wants to speak French with her.
4. He also wants to visit some interesting places (**endroits interessants**) in France. He also expects to go (counts on going) to Morocco and perhaps to Corsica.
5. Mr. Brown knows how to read French a little. But (**Mais**) he cannot speak French. That is why he is studying the French language.
6. Mr. Picard is Mr. Brown's teacher.
7. Mr. Picard, a friend of Mr. Brown, is a Frenchman. He is a forty-five-year-old man.
8. The two gentlemen have an appointment every Tuesday and Thursday, almost always at Mr. Brown's house. There they speak French.
9. Mr. Picard is a good teacher.
10. Mr. Brown is very intelligent and he learns quickly.
11. During the first lesson he learns this dialogue by heart:
12. Good day, Mr. Picard. How are you?—Very well, thank you. And you?—Very well, thank you.
13. Mr. Brown also learns some greetings and some farewells.
14. Good day. (*Also* good morning, good afternoon)
15. Good evening. (*Also* good night)
16. Farewell. Goodbye (See you again). See you in a little while. See you soon.

Pronunciation and Spelling Aids

Practice aloud:

1. importateur (masc.) (añ-pur-ta-**teur**)
2. représentante (fem.) (ruh-pray-zahñ-**tahñt**)
3. des salutations (day sa-lü-tah-**syawñ**)
4. messieurs (may-**syeu**)
5. La France (lah **frahñs**)
6. Le Maroc (luh ma-**ruk**)
7. des adieux (day za-**dyeu**)
8. des objets d'art (day zub-zhay **dar**)
9. des endroits intéressants (day zahñ-drwa zañ-tay-reh-**sahñ**)

Remember: Accent marks can make a difference in pronunciation and/or meaning. For example, the cedilla under a *c* (**ç**) indicates that it is pronounced like an *s*: français (frahñ-**seh**). The word **la** means *the*, but **là** means *there*; **ou** means *or*, but **où** means *where*.

The names of countries, cities, and people are capitalized, but languages and adjectives of nationality are not capitalized: **l'Amérique, l'Américain; l'Italie, l'Italien** (person), **l'italien** (language). Days of the week and months are also written not capitalized: **lundi** (Monday), **mardi** (Tuesday), **janvier** (January).

Building Vocabulary

A. SYNONYMS (WORDS OF LIKE MEANING)

le professeur
professor, teacher in a university, college, or secondary school

le maître (mehtr), **la maîtresse** (meh-trehs)
teacher in an elementary school

NOTE: Certain professions (**professeur, docteur, médecin**) keep the article **le** even when the person is female.

B. ANTONYMS (WORDS OF OPPOSITE MEANING)

1. **grand** big — **petit** small
2. **bon** good — **mauvais** bad
3. **ici** here — **là** there
4. **rapidement** rapidly — **lentement** slowly
5. **l'importateur** importer — **l'exportateur** exporter

C. QUELQUES LANGUES D'EUROPE (deu-**rup**)—SOME LANGUAGES OF EUROPE

The names of languages are always masculine.

1. **le français** (frahñ-**seh**) French
2. **l'anglais** (ahñ-**gleh**) English
3. **l'espagnol** (ehs-pa-**nyul**) Spanish
4. **l'italien** (ee-ta-**lyañ**) Italian
5. **l'allemand** (lal-**mahñ**) German
6. **le russe** (rüs) Russian

French Expressions

1. **bonjour** (bawñ-**zhoor**) good morning (day)
2. **bonsoir** (bawñ-**swar**) good evening
3. **au revoir** (oh ruh-**vwar**) goodbye; see you again
4. **adieu** (a-**dyeu**) farewell
5. **à bientôt** (a byañ-**toh**) see you soon
6. **à tout à l'heure** (a toot a **leur**) see you in a while
7. **à demain** (a duh-**mañ**) until tomorrow
8. **au printemps** (oh prañ-**tahñ**) in the spring
9. **peut-être** (peu-**tehtr**) perhaps
10. **par coeur** (par **keur**) by heart
11. **c'est pourquoi** (seh poor-**kwa**) that's why
12. **chez** (shay) **M. Brown** at Mr. Brown's house or home
13. **Comment allez-vous?** How are you?
14. **Très bien, merci.** Very well, thank you.

Exercise No. 6—Completion of Text

Follow carefully the instructions given in Chapter 3.

1. (Who) **est M. Brown?**
2. **Il est** (an importer).
3. **Il importe des** (art objects).
4. (In the spring) **il va faire un voyage.**
5. (He wants) **rencontrer sa représentante.**
6. **Il désire** (to speak) **français avec elle.**
7. **Il compte** (also) **aller au Maroc.**
8. (But) **il ne parle pas français.**
9. (That is why) **il étudie la langue.**
10. **M. Picard est** (the teacher) **de M. Brown.**
11. **C'est** (a friend of Mr. Brown).
12. **Les deux messieurs ont** (an appointment).
13. (They speak) **français.**
14. **M. Brown apprend** (rapidly).
15. **Il est** (very intelligent).
16. **M. Picard est** (a good teacher).

Grammar Notes

1. MORE COMMON VERBS

ils sont (eel **sawñ**) they are
sont-ils? (sawñ-**teel**) are they?
il n'est pas (eel neh **pah**) he is not
il va (eel **va**) he goes, is going
va-t-il? (va-**teel**) does he go, is he going?
il parle (eel **parl**) he speaks
parle-t-il? (parl-**teel**) does he speak?
il ne parle pas (eel nuh parl **pah**) he does not speak
il désire (eel day-**zeer**) he wants

il étudie (eel ay-tü-**dee**) he studies
il compte (eel **kawñt**) he expects (counts on)
il apprend (eel a-**prahñ**) he learns
il sait (eel **seh**) he knows, *or* he knows how
ils ont (eel **zawñ**) they have
ont-ils? (awñ-**teel**) have they? (do they have?)
aller (a-**lay**) to go
parler (par-**lay**) to speak
visiter (vee-zee-**tay**) to visit
lire (leer) to read
faire (fehr) to make, to do

2. NEGATIVE VERB FORMS

To form the negative of a verb, place **ne** directly before the verb and **pas** directly after the verb:

il ne parle pas

he does not speak

il ne sait pas

he does not know

Ne becomes **n'** before a verb that begins with a vowel or **h** (mute).

il n'étudie (nay-tü-**dee**) **pas**   **il n'apprend** (na-**prahñ**) **pas**

he does not study   he does not speak

3. QUESTION FORMS

In the simple question form, the verb is inverted and a hyphen is required. Thus:

est-il?   **ont-ils?**   **sait-il?**

is he?   have they?   does he know?

Remember that if the verb ends in **e** or **a,** the letter **t** must be inserted between the verb and the subject pronoun. Thus:

parle-t-il?   **étudie-t-il?**   **va-t-il?**

does he speak?   does he study?   does he go?

Another way of forming a question is by placing **Est-ce que** (ehs **kuh**), literally, Is it that . . . ?, before the subject:

Est-ce que M. Brown apprend?	**Apprend-il?**	**Est-ce qu'ils ont?**	**Ont-ils?**
Is it that Mr. Brown learns?	Does he learn?	Is it that they have?	Have they?
Does M. Brown learn?		Do they have?	

A third way of asking a question is to keep the statement as is, but to raise your voice at the end: **M. Brown compte aller au Maroc?**

More question words: **quand** (kahñ)? when? **pourquoi** (poor-**kwa**)? why?

Exercise No. 7

Supply the missing words (pronouns, correct verb forms) in the following sentences and questions.

Exemple: 1. Qui est M. Brown?

1. **Qui** (is) **M. Brown?**
2. (Is he) **importateur?**
3. (He does not speak) **français.**
4. (Does he speak) **anglais?**
5. (He learns) **rapidement.**
6. (He wants) **faire un voyage.**
7. (He is not studying) **l'espagnol.**
8. (He knows how) **lire le français un peu.**
9. (Have they) **rendez-vous?**
10. (He expects) **visiter Paris.**
11. **Il va** (to make) **un voyage.**
12. **Il ne sait pas** (to speak) **français.**

Exercise No. 8

Matching: select from Column II the word groups that best complete the sentences begun in Column I.

Exemple: 1-d M. Brown désire parler français avec sa représentante à Paris.

<table>
<tr><td align="center">I</td><td align="center">II</td></tr>
<tr><td>1. M. Brown désire parler français</td><td>a. des salutations et des adieux.</td></tr>
<tr><td>2. Il sait lire</td><td>b. de France et du Maroc.</td></tr>
<tr><td>3. Il est très intelligent. C'est pourquoi</td><td>c. chez M. Brown.</td></tr>
<tr><td>4. Il importe des objets d'art</td><td>d. avec sa représentante à Paris.</td></tr>
<tr><td>5. Les deux messieurs ont rendez-vous</td><td>e. de quarante-cinq ans.</td></tr>
<tr><td>6. M. Picard est un homme</td><td>f. un peu le français.</td></tr>
<tr><td>7. M. Brown apprend aussi</td><td>g. il apprend rapidement.</td></tr>
<tr><td>8. Le bureau de M. Brown n'est pas</td><td>h. dans la famille de M. Brown.</td></tr>
<tr><td>9. Il y a six personnes</td><td>i. Charles, Thomas, Elizabeth, et Anne.</td></tr>
<tr><td>10. Les enfants de M. Brown s'appellent</td><td>j. dans la Wall Street.</td></tr>
</table>

Exercise No. 9

Find the corresponding French words in the Reading Text or Building Vocabulary. Write them and say them aloud.

1. French (language)	13. from, of
2. the Frenchman	14. here
3. thank you	15. big
4. also	16. but
5. perhaps	17. where
6. the office	18. good
7. almost	19. bad
8. always	20. with
9. very well	21. some articles
10. rapidly	22. some places
11. a little	23. that is why
12. there	24. How are you?

Exercise No. 10—Questionnaire

Read each French question and answer silently, noting the English meaning. Then, read each French question and answer aloud twice, without referring to the English.

Questions et Réponses

1. **Qui est le professeur? M. Picard est le professeur.**
2. **Parle-t-il français? Oui, monsieur, il parle français.**
3. **Qui est l'homme d'affaires? M. Brown est l'homme d'affaires.**
4. **Parle-t-il français? Non, monsieur, il ne parle pas français.**
5. **Où est le bureau de M. Brown? Il est dans la rue Whitehall.**
6. **Est-il importateur d'automobiles? Non, monsieur, il n'est pas importateur d'automobiles.**
7. **Apprend-il rapidement ou lentement? Il apprend rapidement.**
8. **Quand ces messieurs ont-ils rendez-vous? Ils ont rendez-vous tous les mardis et les jeudis.**
9. **M. Brown est-il intelligent? Oui, il est très intelligent.**
10. **Pourquoi étudie-t-il le français? Parce qu'il désire faire un voyage en France.**

1. Who is the teacher? Mr. Picard is the teacher.
2. Does he speak French? Yes, sir, he speaks French.
3. Who is the businessman? Mr. Brown is the businessman.
4. Does he speak French? No, sir, he does not speak French.
5. Where is Mr. Brown's office? It is on Whitehall Street.
6. Is he an importer of automobiles? No, sir, he is not an importer of automobiles.
7. Does he learn rapidly or slowly? He learns rapidly.
8. When do these gentlemen have an appointment? They have an appointment every Tuesday and Thursday.
9. Is Mr. Brown intelligent? Yes, he is very intelligent.
10. Why is he studying French? Because he wants to make a trip to France.

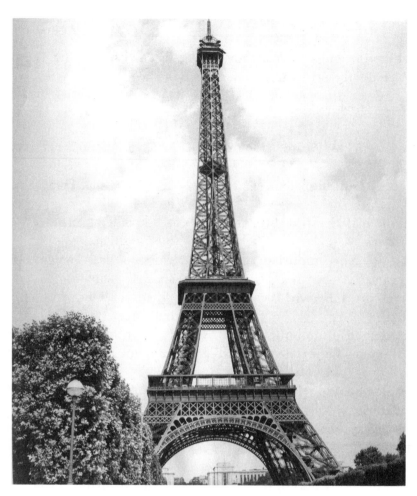

The Eiffel Tower has come to symbolize France.

CHAPITRE 5 (CINQ)

DANS LE SALON DE MONSIEUR BROWN
IN MR. BROWN'S LIVING ROOM

1. C'est mardi le 4 (quatre) janvier, 2005.
2. Il est 8 (huit) heures du soir.
3. M. Brown est assis dans le salon de sa maison. M. Picard est assis près de lui.
4. M. Picard dit à M. Brown:—Il y a beaucoup de choses autour de nous: dans la maison, dans la rue, dans le bureau, dans le parc, dans la ville, et à la campagne.
5. —Aux États-Unis, en Angleterre, et dans les autres pays d'expression anglaise il faut savoir les noms des choses en anglais. En France et dans les autres pays d'expression française il faut savoir les noms des choses en français.
6. —Nous sommes dans le salon de votre maison. Dites-moi, s'il vous plaît, qu'est-ce que c'est que ça?
7. —C'est un piano. Ma femme joue bien du piano. Elle chante bien aussi.
8. —Très bien. Et qu'est-ce qui est sur le piano?
9. —Une lampe et un cahier de musique.
10. —Et qu'est-ce qui est au mur au-dessus du piano?
11. —C'est le portrait de ma femme.
12. —Excellent. Dites-moi, s'il vous plaît, les noms d'autres objets dans le salon, et dites-moi où ils sont.
13. —Avec plaisir. La bibliothèque est près d'une fenêtre. Le miroir est entre les fenêtres. Le bureau est près de la porte. Une chaise est devant le bureau. Sur le bureau il y a un crayon, un stylo, des papiers, et des lettres. Il y a des livres sur la petite table.
14. —Très bien. C'est assez pour aujourd'hui. Au revoir, M. Brown.
15. —À jeudi, M. Picard.

1. It is Tuesday, January 4, 2005.
2. It is 8 o'clock in the evening.
3. Mr. Brown is seated in the living room of his house. Mr. Picard is seated near him.
4. Mr. Picard says to Mr. Brown, There are many things around us: in the house, in the street, in the office, in the park, in the city, and in the country.
5. In the United States, in England, and in other English-speaking countries it is necessary to know the names of things in English. In France and in other French-speaking countries it is necessary to know the names of things in French.
6. We are in the living room of your house. Tell me, please, what is that?
7. It is a piano. My wife plays the piano well. She sings well too.
8. Very good. And what is on the piano?
9. A lamp and a music book.
10. And what is on the wall over the piano?
11. It is the portrait of my wife.
12. Excellent. Tell me, please, the names of other objects in the living room and tell me where they are.
13. With pleasure. The bookcase is near a window. The mirror is between the windows. The desk is near the door. A chair is in front of the desk. On the desk there is a pencil, a fountain pen, some papers, and some letters. There are some books on the little table.
14. Very good. That's enough for today. Goodbye, Mr. Brown.
15. Until Thursday, Mr. Picard.

Pronunciation and Spelling Aids

Practice aloud:

1. **Monsieur Brown est assis dans le salon de sa maison.** (muh-syeu braun eh ta-**see** dahñ luh sa-lawñ duh sa meh-**zawñ**)

   Monsieur Picard est assis près de lui. (muh-syeu pee-kar eh ta-**see** preh duh **lüee**)

2. **en France** (ahñ **frahñs**)
3. **en Angleterre** (ahñ nahñ-gluh-**tehr**)
4. **autour de nous** (oh-toor duh **noo**)

In order to say *in* or *to* a country, use **en** with countries that are of feminine gender (the names end in **e**) and **au** with countries that are of masculine gender (end in letter other than **e**; of course, there are a few exceptions):

en Corse, en Italie   but   **au Maroc, au Canada**

Remember: Final **x** and **s** are linked to the vowel beginning the next word and are pronounced as **z**.

aux États-Unis (oh zay-ta zü-**nee**)

Building Vocabulary

A. DANS LE SALON (dahñ luh sa-**lawñ**)—IN THE LIVING ROOM

1. **le bureau** (bü-**roh**) desk, office
2. **la chaise** (shehz) chair
3. **le cahier de musique** (ka-yay duh mü-**zeek**) music book
4. **le crayon** (kreh-**yawñ**) pencil
5. **la fenêtre** (fuh-**nehtr**) window
6. **la lampe** (lahñp) lamp
7. **la lettre** (lehtr) letter
8. **le miroir** (mee-**rwar**) mirror
9. **le papier** (pa-**pyay**) paper
10. **le piano** (pya-**noh**) piano
11. **la porte** (purt) door
12. **le portrait** (pur-**treh**) portrait
13. **le stylo** (stee-**loh**) pen
14. **la table** (tabl) table
15. **la bibliothèque** (bee-blee-u-**tehk**) bookcase, library

B. SOME COMMON PREPOSITIONS

1. **à** to, at, in, on
2. **en** in, into
3. **de** (duh) of, from
4. **autour de** (oh-**toor** duh) around
5. **avec** (a-**vehk**) with
6. **au-dessus de** (oh-duh-**sü** duh) above, over
7. **près de** (preh duh) near
8. **chez** (shay) at, to the house of
9. **entre** (ahñtr) between
10. **dans** (dahñ) in, inside of
11. **devant** (duh-**vahñ**) before, in front of
12. **derrière** (deh-**ryehr**) behind, in back of
13. **sous** (soo) under
14. **sur** (sür) on, upon

French Expressions

1. **le quatre janvier, deux mil cinq** (luh katr zhahñ-**vyay** duh-meel-**sañk**) January 4, 2005
2. **Il est huit heures** (eel eh üee **teur**) It is 8 o'clock
3. **Beaucoup de choses** (boh-koo duh **shohz**) many things
4. **Il faut** (eel **foh**) It is necessary
5. **Dites-moi** (deet-**mwa**) Tell me.
6. **Qu'est-ce que c'est que ça?** (kehs kuh seh kuh **sa**) What is that?
7. **Qu'est-ce qui?** (kehs **kee**) What?
8. **Elle joue du piano** (ehl zhoo dü pya-**noh**) She plays the piano.
9. **C'est assez** (seh ta-**say**) That's enough.
10. **Pour aujourd'hui** (poor oh-zhoor-**düee**) for today

Exercise No. 11—Completion of Text

1. **Le monsieur** (is seated) **dans le salon.**
2. **Il y a** (many things) **dans la rue.**
3. (It is necessary to know) **les noms des choses.**
4. **Dites-moi** (What is that)?
5. **Ma femme** (plays) **bien du piano et elle** (sings) **bien aussi.**
6. **Le portrait est** (over the piano).
7. **Un miroir est** (between) **les fenêtres.**
8. **Sur le bureau il y a** (some letters).
9. (That's enough) **pour aujourd'hui.**
10. (Until Thursday), **M. Picard.**

Grammar Notes

1. THE CONTRACTIONS du, des, au, aux ARE DERIVED AS FOLLOWS:

de (of, from) plus **le** (the) becomes **du** (of the, from the)
de (of, from) plus **les** (the) becomes **des** (of the, from the)
à (to, at, in, on) plus **le** (the) becomes **au** (to, at, in, on the)
à (to, at, in, on) plus **les** (the) becomes **aux** (to, at, in, on the)

Où est le bureau *du* commerçant?	Where is the office of the merchant?
Mme Picard est une amie *des* étudiants.	Mrs. Picard is a friend of the students.
M. Picard parle *au* chauffeur.	Mr. Picard is speaking to the driver.
Le maître parle *aux* parents.	The teacher is speaking to the parents.

de la, de l', à la and **à l'** never contract. Thus:

Le salon de la maison est grand.	The living room of the house is large.
Il sait le nom de l'hôtel.	He knows the name of the hotel.
Charles va à la fenêtre.	Charles is going to the window.
La tante parle à l'oncle.	The aunt is speaking to the uncle.

2. POSSESSION

In French, possession is indicated by a phrase beginning with **de**, never by an apostrophe:

la maison du professeur   the teacher's house, the house of the teacher
l'oncle de Marie   Mary's uncle, the uncle of Mary

Possession may also be expressed by a phrase with the preposition **à**:

À qui est ce bureau?   Whose office is this?
                                               (*Literally:* To whom is this office?)

Ce bureau est au professeur   This is the teacher's office.

Exercise No. 12

Use **du, de l', de la, des; au, à l', à la, aux**, as required. Be sure to say the completed sentences aloud after writing them.

Exemple: 1. Le salon du professeur est grand.

1. **Le salon** (of the) **professeur est grand.**
2. **M. Brown parle** (to the) **professeur.**
3. **M. Picard est le maître** (of the) **garçons.**
4. **C'est un ami** (of the) **docteur.**
5. **Mme Brown va** (to the) **université.**
6. **La jeune fille va** (to the) **porte.**
7. **Le père parle** (to the) **enfants.**
8. **Le portrait est** (on the) **mur.**
9. **Il ne parle pas** (to the) **homme.**
10. **Où est la maison** (of the) **cousins?**

Exercise No. 13

Review Building Vocabulary, Part B; then supply the missing words in French.

Exemple: 1. Au-dessus du piano il y a un portrait.

1. (Above the) **piano il y a un portrait.**
2. **L'automobile est** (near the) **maison.**
3. (On the) **bureau il y a beaucoup de lettres.**
4. **Le miroir est** (above the desk).
5. **Une petite table est** (between the) **fenêtres.**
6. **Il y a des chaises** (around the) **table.**
7. **Qu'est-ce qui est** (behind the) **porte?**
8. **Qu'est-ce qui est** (in front of the) **lampe?**.
9. **Qu'est-ce qui est** (in the) **cuisine?**
10. **M. Brown est** (with) **M. Picard** (in the) **salon.**

Exercise No. 14—Questionnaire

Answer each question in French, using the information in the conversation. Remember to practice by saying the question and answer aloud.

1. **Qui est assis dans le salon?**
2. **Qui est assis près de lui?**
3. **Y a-t-il beaucoup de choses autour de « nous? »**
4. **Madame Brown chante bien?**
5. **Qui joue bien du piano?**
6. **Où est le cahier de musique?**
7. **Où est le portrait de Madame Brown?**
8. **Qu'est-ce qui est près d'une fenêtre?**
9. **Où est le miroir?**
10. **Où est le bureau?**
11. **Qu'est-ce qui est devant le bureau?**
12. **Où est-ce qu'il y a des livres?**

RÉVISION I, CHAPITRES I–5

Première Partie

Each Review Chapter will begin with a summary of the most important words and expressions that have occurred in the chapters being reviewed. Check your memory in these ways:

1. Cover the English words on the right side of the page. Read the French words aloud, one at a time, and give the English meaning. Uncover the English word of the same number if you need to check your response.
2. Now cover the French words. Say the French for each English word. Uncover the French word to check yourself.
3. Write the words, three or four times, that you have had difficulty in remembering.

Review of Words (Révision de Mots)

NOUNS

1. l'ami (m)		1. friend (m)
2. l'amie (f)		2. friend (f)
3. le bureau		3. office, desk
4. les bureaux		4. offices, desks
5. la campagne		5. countryside
6. la chaise		6. chair
7. la chambre à coucher		7. bedroom
8. la chose		8. thing
9. le crayon		9. pencil
10. la cuisine		10. kitchen
11. l'enfant		11. child
12. la famille		12. family
13. la femme		13. wife, woman
14. la fenêtre		14. window
15. la fille		15. daughter, girl
16. la jeune fille		16. girl
17. le garçon		17. boy
18. l'homme		18. man

19. l'homme d'affaires, la femme d'affaires	19. businessman, businesswoman
20. le jour	20. day
21. la lampe	21. lamp
22. la langue	22. language, tongue
23. la leçon	23. lesson
24. la lettre	24. letter
25. le livre	25. book
26. la dame, Madame	26. lady, madam, Mrs.
27. le monsieur, Monsieur	27. gentleman, sir, Mr.
28. les messieurs, Messieurs	28. gentlemen
29. la demoiselle, Mademoiselle	29. young lady, Miss
30. la mère	30. mother
31. le miroir	31. mirror
32. l'oncle	32. uncle
33. le papier	33. paper
34. le père	34. father
35. la personne	35. person
36. la porte	36. door
37. la rue	37. street
38. la salle à manger	38. dining room
39. la salle de bains	39. bathroom
40. le salon	40. living room
41. la soeur	41. sister
42. le stylo	42. pen
43. la tante	43. aunt
44. le voyage	44. voyage, trip
45. la ville	45. city, town

VERBS AND VERB PHRASES

1.	aller	1.	to go
2.	apprendre	2.	to learn
3.	faire	3.	to do, make
4.	lire	4.	to read
5.	parler	5.	to speak
6.	rencontrer	6.	to meet
7.	savoir	7.	to know
8.	il apprend	8.	he learns
9.	elle chante	9.	she sings
10.	il compte	10.	he expects
11.	il demeure	11.	he lives
12.	il désire	12.	he wants
13.	il étudie	13.	he studies
14.	elle joue	14.	she plays
15.	il parle	15.	he speaks
16.	parle-t-il?	16.	does he speak? is he speaking?
17.	il ne parle pas	17.	he does not speak
18.	il prend	18.	he takes
19.	il sait	19.	he knows
20.	il travaille	20.	he works
21.	il va	21.	he goes
22.	va-t-il?	22.	does he go?
23.	il y a	23.	there is (are)
24.	y a-t-il?	24.	is (are) there?
25.	il faut	25.	it is necessary
26.	il est	26.	he is
27.	est-il?	27.	is he?
28.	il n'est pas	28.	he is not
29.	ils ont	29.	they have
30.	dites-moi	30.	tell me

ADJECTIVES

1.	assis	1.	seated
2.	autre	2.	other
3.	intelligent	3.	intelligent
4.	bon	4.	good
5.	divers	5.	various
6.	grand	6.	big, large, tall
7.	intéressant	7.	interesting
8.	mauvais	8.	bad
9.	petit	9.	little, small

10. difficile		10. difficult
11. premier		11. first
12. tous		12. all

ADVERBS

1. aujourd'hui	1. today
2. assez	2. enough, rather
3. bien	3. well
4. aussi	4. also
5. ici	5. here
6. là	6. there
7. lentement	7. slowly
8. peut-être	8. perhaps
9. presque	9. almost
10. rapidement	10. rapidly
11. très	11. very
12. toujours	12. always

PREPOSITIONS

1. à	1. to, at, on
2. au-dessus de	2. over, above
3. autour de	3. around
4. avec	4. with
5. chez	5. at the house of
6. dans	6. in, inside of
7. de	7. of, from
8. derrière	8. behind
9. devant	9. in front of
10. en	10. in, on
11. entre	11. between
12. pour	12. for
13. près de	13. near
14. sous	14. under
15. sur	15. on, upon

QUESTION WORDS

1. qui?	1. who?
2. qui est-ce qui?	2. who (*subject of verb*)?
3. qu'est-ce qui?	3. what (*subject of verb*)?
4. combien de?	4. how much, many?
5. comment?	5. how?

6. où?

7. pourquoi?

8. quand?

9. qu'est-ce que c'est que ça?

6. where?

7. why?

8. when?

9. what is that?

CONJUNCTIONS

1. et

2. ou

3. mais

4. parce que

1. and

2. or

3. but

4. because

French Expressions

1. à demain

2. à bientôt

3. à tout à l'heure

4. au revoir

5. Bonjour.

6. Bonsoir.

7. à la campagne

8. en ville

9. au printemps

10. aux États-Unis

11. c'est assez

12. c'est pourquoi

13. Comment allez-vous?

14. par coeur

15. s'il vous plaît

16. toute la journée

1. until tomorrow

2. see you soon, goodbye

3. see you in a while

4. goodbye

5. Good morning (afternoon).

6. Good evening (night).

7. in the country

8. in (to) the city

9. in the spring

10. in the U.S.

11. that's enough

12. that's why

13. How are you?

14. by heart

15. please

16. all (the whole) day long

Deuxième Partie

Exercise No. 15

Select the antonym (opposite) or counterpart for each word in Group I from Group II.

I	II
1. bon	a. devant
2. oui	b. la campagne
3. ici	c. la fille
4. petit	d. Bonsoir
5. au-dessus de	e. non
6. beaucoup de	f. l'homme
7. le père	g. mauvais

8. derrière
9. Bonjour
10. le garçon
11. la ville
12. la femme

h. grand
i. là
j. au-dessous de
k. peu de
l. la mère

Exercise No. 16

Complete the following sentences in French.

1. **M. Brown travaille** (all day).
2. **Dites-moi,** (please).
3. (Perhaps) **il est au bureau.**
4. (Good evening), **monsieur.**
5. **M. Brown va** (to the city).
6. (That is why) **il étudie le français.**

7. How are you?
8. (Where) **habite-t-il?**
9. What is this?
10. (Who) **est professeur?**
11. (What) **est au mur?**
12. (When) **va-t-il en ville?**

Exercise No. 17

Select the group of words in Column **II** that best completes each sentence begun in Column **I**.

Exemple: 1-d Dans la famille Brown il y a six personnes.

I

1. **Dans la famille Brown**
2. **La maison de M. Brown**
3. **M. Brown prend le train**
4. **Il étudie le français**
5. **Il travaille toute la journée**
6. **Il sait lire un peu le français**
7. **Il apprend rapidement**
8. **Pendant la première leçon**
9. **Tous les mardis et jeudis**
10. **La femme de M. Brown chante bien**
11. **M. Brown va faire un voyage**

II

a. il apprend les salutations et les adieux.
b. et elle joue bien du piano.
c. parce qu'il est très intelligent.
d. il y a six personnes.
e. en France et peut-être au Maroc.
f. est dans les environs de New York.
g. mais il ne parle pas français.
h. dans son bureau.
i. pour arriver à son bureau en ville.
j. les deux messieurs ont rendez-vous.
k. parce qu'il désire voyager en France.

Exercise No. 18

Complete these sentences in French.

1. **L'automobile est** (in front of the house).
2. **Les chaises sont** (around the table).
3. **La bibliothèque est** (near the door).
4. **M. Brown est assis** (behind the desk).
5. **La lampe est** (on the piano).
6. (The boy's books) **sont sur la petite table.**
7. (The girl's mother) **est en ville.**
8. (The children's teacher) **est français.**
9. **Le portrait de Madame Brown est** (on the wall).
10. (To whom/Whose) **est l'automobile?**

Exercise No. 19

Translate into French:

1. Who is Mr. Brown?
2. He is an American businessman.
3. Where does he live?
4. He lives in the suburbs of New York.
5. Why is he learning French?
6. He wants to take a trip to France.
7. Who is his (**son**) teacher?
8. His teacher is Mr. Picard.
9. Why does he learn rapidly?
10. He learns rapidly because he is intelligent.
11. How many children are there in the Browns' family?
12. There are four children.
13. How many rooms are there in Mr. Brown's house?
14. There are five rooms, a bathroom, and a kitchen.

Dialogue 1

Read each dialogue silently several times, using the English translation to make certain of the meaning. Practice the French text aloud many times. Follow this procedure with all dialogues.

Où est la rue Scribe?
(oo eh la rü **skreeb?**)

Where is Scribe street?

1. **Pardon, monsieur, où est la rue Scribe?**
2. **Continuez tout droit, mademoiselle.**
3. **Est-ce que c'est loin?**
4. **Non, mademoiselle, c'est à trois rues d'ici.**
5. **Merci beaucoup, monsieur.**
6. **Il n'y a pas de quoi, mademoiselle.**

1. Pardon me, sir, where is Scribe street?
2. Continue straight ahead, Miss.
3. Is it far?
4. No, Miss. It's three blocks from here.
5. Thank you very much, sir.
6. Don't mention it (you're welcome), miss.

Dialogue 2

Où s'arrête l'autobus? (oo sa-reht **lu-toh-büs?**)	Where does the bus stop?
1. S'il vous plaît, monsieur, où s'arrête l'auto-bus, le 52?	1. Please, sir, where does the number 52 bus stop?
2. Il s'arrête au coin là-bas, mademoiselle.	2. It stops at the corner over there, Miss.
3. Merci beaucoup, monsieur.	3. Thank you so much, sir.
4. Il n'y a pas de quoi.	4. You're welcome.

Exercise No. 20—Lecture (Reading Selection)

How to Read the Lectures

1. Read the passage silently from beginning to end to get the meaning as a whole.
2. Reread the passage, looking up any words you may have forgotten in the French-English dictionary at the end of this book. For the few new words in these reading selections, their meaning is given in footnotes at the end of the passage.
3. Read the passage silently a third time, as well as aloud. Then translate it and check your translation with the one given in the answers section of the appendix.
4. Follow this procedure in all succeeding *lectures*.

MONSIEUR BROWN APPREND LE FRANÇAIS

Monsieur Brown est un homme d'affaires américain qui importe des objets d'art de France. C'est pourquoi il désire faire un voyage en France au printemps. Il désire parler avec sa représentante. Il désire aussi visiter des endroits intéressants en France. Mais il ne sait pas parler français.

Monsieur Brown a un bon professeur. C'est un Français qui habite à New York et qui s'appelle Monsieur Picard. Tous les mardis et jeudis le professeur prend le train pour aller chez son élève.[1] Là les deux messieurs parlent français. Monsieur Brown est très intelligent et il apprend rapidement. Pendant la première leçon, par exemple, il apprend par coeur les salutations et les adieux. Il sait déjà[2] dire bonjour, comment allez-vous? à bientôt, et à demain. Il sait déjà dire en français les noms de beaucoup de choses qui[3] sont dans son salon, et il sait répondre[4] aux questions, "Qu'est-ce que c'est que ça?" et "Où est. . . . ?" Monsieur Picard est très satisfait des progrès[5] de son élève et il dit,—Très bien. C'est assez pour aujourd'hui. à bientôt.

NOTES: [1] **chez son élève**—to the home of his student. [2] **déjà**—already. [3] **qui**—that, which. [4] **répondre (à)** —to reply, answer. [5] **très . . . progrès**—very satisfied with the progress.

CHAPITRE 6 (SIX)

LES VERBES SONT IMPORTANTS AUSSI
VERBS ARE IMPORTANT TOO

1. M. Brown et M. Picard sont assis dans le salon chez M. Brown. M. Picard commence à parler. M. Brown écoute le professeur avec attention.
2. —Vous savez déjà que les noms des choses et des personnes sont importants. Mais les verbes sont importants aussi. Il n'est pas possible de former une phrase sans verbes. Il n'est pas possible non plus de bavarder sans verbes.
3. Nous allons étudier des verbes d'usage courant. Je vais vous poser des questions. Vous allez répondre aux questions.
4. Si vous ne savez pas la réponse, dites, s'il vous plaît, "Je ne sais pas."
5. —Très bien, dit M. Brown. Je vais dire, "Je ne sais pas," si je ne sais pas la réponse.
6. —Est-ce que vous êtes homme d'affaires?
7. —Oui, monsieur, je suis homme d'affaires; je suis importateur d'objets d'art et d'autres articles de France et du Maroc.
8. —Et pourquoi est-ce que vous étudiez le français?
9. —J'étudie le français parce que je désire faire un voyage en France pour rendre visite à ma représentante à Paris. Je désire parler en français avec elle. Elle ne parle pas anglais.
10. —Comptez-vous visiter d'autres pays?

1. Mr. Brown and Mr. Picard are seated in the living room at Mr. Brown's house. Mr. Picard begins to speak. Mr. Brown listens to the teacher attentively.
2. You already know that the names of things and of persons are important. But verbs are important too. It is not possible to make a sentence without verbs. It is not possible to chat without verbs either.
3. We are going to study some commonly used verbs. I am going to ask you some questions. You are going to reply to the questions.
4. If you don't know the answer, please say, "I don't know."
5. Very well, says Mr. Brown. I am going to say, "I don't know," if I don't know the answer.
6. Are you a businessman?
7. Yes, sir, I am a businessman; I am an importer of art objects and other artifacts from France and from Morocco.
8. And why are you studying French?
9. I am studying French because I want to make a trip to France in order to pay a visit to my agent in Paris. I want to speak with her in French. She does not speak English.
10. Do you intend to visit other countries?

11. —Je compte visiter aussi le Maroc et peut-être la Corse.	11. I expect to visit Morocco too and perhaps Corsica.
12. —Quand est-ce que vous partez en voyage?	12. When are you leaving on your trip?
13. —Je pars le 31 (trente et un) mai.	13. I am leaving on the 31st of May.
14. —Est-ce que vous allez voyager en bateau?	14. Are you going to travel by boat?
15. —Non, je vais voyager en avion parce que c'est plus rapide.	15. No, I am going to travel by plane because it's quicker.
16. —Combien coûte le voyage?	16. How much does the trip cost?
17. —Je ne sais pas. Je vais prendre des renseignements demain et je vais retenir ma place.	17. I don't know. I am going to get information tomorrow and I'll make a reservation.
18. —Excellent, monsieur. Vous apprenez le français rapidement.	18. Excellent, sir. You are learning French rapidly.
19. —Merci. Vous êtes trop aimable.	19. Thank you. You are too kind.
20. —Pas du tout. C'est la vérité. Eh bien, ça suffit pour aujourd'hui. À bientôt.	20. Not at all. It's the truth. Well, that's enough for today. See you soon.
21. —À jeudi prochain.	21. Until next Thursday.

Pronunciation and Spelling Aids

Practice aloud:

1. **attention** (a-tahñ-**syawñ**)
2. **nous allons étudier** (noo za-lawñ zay-tü-**dyay**)
3. **je ne sais pas** (zhuh nuh seh **pah**)
4. **je suis importateur** (zhuh süee zañ-pur-ta-**teur**)
5. **d'autres articles** (doh-truh zar-**teekl**)

Building Vocabulary

A. QUELQUES PAYS D'EUROPE (kehl-kuh pay-ee deu-**rup**)—SOME COUNTRIES IN EUROPE

1. **l'Angleterre** (lahñ-gluh-**tehr**) England
2. **la Belgique** (behl-**zheek**) Belgium
3. **l'Allemagne** (lal-**man**-yuh) Germany
4. **la France** (frahñs) France
5. **l'Espagne** (leh-**span**-yuh) Spain
6. **l'Italie** (lee-ta-**lee**) Italy
7. **la Suisse** (süees) Switzerland
8. **la Russie** (rü-**see**) Russia

B. LES PAYS DE L'AMÉRIQUE DU NORD (pay-yee duh la-may-reek dü **nur**)—COUNTRIES OF NORTH AMERICA

1. **les États-Unis** (leh zay-ta zü-**nee**) United States
2. **le Mexique** (mehk-**seek**) Mexico (masc.)
3. **le Canada** (ka-na-**da**) Canada
4. **aux États-Unis** (oh zay-ta zü-**nee**) in or to the United States
5. **au Mexique** in or to Mexico
6. **au Canada** in or to Canada

Reminder: Names of countries, like other nouns, are of feminine or masculine gender. If its name ends in **e**, the country is feminine; otherwise it is masculine.

Example: **la France, la Suisse, l'Italie** (f); **le Portugal, le Danemark** (m)
Exceptions: **le Mexique, le Zaïre** (za-**eer**)

Use **en** before feminine names of countries, to express *to* or *in*.

Je vais en France (zhuh veh zahñ **frahñs**).	I am going to France.
Je suis en Italie (zhuh suee zahñ ee-ta-**lee**).	I am in Italy.

Use **au** to express *to* and *in* before masculine names of countries.

Je vais au Canada (zhuh veh zoh ka-na-**da**).	I go to Canada.
Je suis au Japon (zhuh suee zoh zha-**pawñ**).	I am in Japan.

Use **aux** before plural names of countries.

Je vais aux États-Unis (zhuh veh zoh zay-ta-zu-**nee**).	I am going to the United States.
Je suis aux Philippines (zhuh suee zoh fee-lee-**peen**).	I am in the Philippines.

The names of continents are all feminine. They follow the same rule, with regard to accompanying prepositions, as do countries.

Je vais en Afrique (zhuh veh zahñ a-**freek**).
Je suis en Asie (zhuh suee zahñ a-**zee**).

French Expressions

1. **pas . . . non plus** (nawñ **plü**) not . . . either
2. **d'usage courant** (dü-zazh koo-**rahñ**) of common usage, commonly used
3. **poser des questions** (pu-zay day kes-**tyawñ**) to ask questions
4. **rendre visite à** (rahñdr vee-**zeet** a) to pay a visit to
5. **en bateau** (ahñ ba-**toh**) by boat
6. **en avion** (ahñ na-**vyawñ**) by airplane
7. **prendre des renseignements** (prahñdr day rahñ-seh-nyuh-**mahñ**) to get information
8. **bavarder** (ba-var-**day**) to chat, to gossip
9. **retenir une place** (ruh-tuh-neer ün **plas**) to reserve a seat
10. **pas du tout** (pah dü **too**) not at all
11. **Ça (**or **cela) suffit** (sah *or* suh-lah sü-**fee**) that's enough

Exercise No. 21—Completion of Text

1. **Les verbes** (are important), **monsieur.**

2. **Nous allons étudier** (some verbs).
3. (Why) **étudiez-vous le français?**
4. (Because) **je désire rendre visite à ma représentante.**
5. **Je désire parler** (with her).
6. **Je compte visiter** (other countries).
7. **Allez-vous voyager** (by boat or by plane)?
8. (How much) **coûte le voyage?**
9. **Vous apprenez** (very rapidly).
10. (That's enough for today.)

Grammar Notes

1. ABOUT VERB ENDINGS

The infinitive is the basic or neutral form (the "title") of the verb. In English it is expressed by *to* plus the verb: *to* speak, *to* learn, etc.

The infinitives of French verbs end in **-er, -ir, -re,** or **-oir.** Thus:

parler, to speak

apprendre, to learn

partir, to leave

savoir, to know

That part of the verb that remains after the ending is removed is called the stem. Thus: **parl-, part-, apprend-,** and **sav-** are the stems of **parler, partir, apprendre,** and **savoir.**

The verb **parler,** *to speak,* is a regular **-er** verb. Learn the present tense of the verb, noting carefully the endings that are added to the stem **parl-** to accompany the different pronouns.

2. PRESENT TENSE OF parler, *to speak*—REGULAR -er VERB, FIRST CONJUGATION

je parle (parl)	I speak	**nous parlons** (par-lawñ)	we speak
tu parles (parl)	you speak	**vous parlez** (par-lay)	you speak
il parle (parl)	he speaks	**ils parlent** (parl)	they (*m*) speak
elle parle (parl)	she speaks	**elles parlent** (parl)	they (*f*) speak

a. The endings of a regular **-er** verb in the present tense are:

Singular: **-e -es -e**

Plural: **-ons -ez -ent**

The endings are silent except for **-ons** and **-ez.**

b. The pronoun **vous** (voo), like the English *you*, is used both in the singular and plural. It is the plural of **tu** and also the plural of **vous**. The singular **vous** is the polite form of address among people who do not have a close relationship. Examples:

Parlez-vous français, monsieur?	Do you speak French, sir?
Vous parlez bien, mesdames.	You speak well, ladies.

The pronoun **tu** (tü) is used in addressing a relative or a friend. In general, all young people use **tu** among themselves. **Tu** is also used when talking to a child or to an animal. It is known as the familiar form of address. Study the following examples:

Tu parles trop haut, mon enfant.	You speak too loudly, my child.
Paul, veux-tu étudier avec moi?	Paul, do you want to study with me?

When abroad in a French-speaking country, it is a good idea for Americans to use the formal, **vous** with all acquaintances, except very close friends, and children.

c. The present tense may be translated in three ways:

I speak, I am speaking, I do speak; you speak, you are speaking, you do speak, etc.

3 THE IMPERATIVE OR COMMAND FORMS OF VERBS LIKE PARLER.

parle, mon enfant (speak, my child); **parlons** (let us speak); **parlez, monsieur** or **messieurs** (speak, sir or gentlemen)

Imperative verb forms sound and are spelled the same as the corresponding present tense of **tu**, **nous** and **vous** forms. As in English, the pronouns are dropped. An exception: the familiar singular is (**tu**) written **parle**, rather than **parles**.

4. THE INTERROGATIVE

As you have already noted, there are three ways of forming a question: 1) by raising your voice at the end of a statement; 2) by placing **Est-ce que?** (The literal *Is it that?* is not translated) before the subject of the sentence; or 3) by placing the subject after the verb (inverted form of question). The inverted form is rarely used with **je**. There is no difference in meaning between the forms.

Question with **est-ce que**	Inverted form of question	English
Est-ce que je parle?		Do I speak?
Est-ce que tu parles?	**Parles-tu?**	Do you *(fam.)* speak?
Est-ce qu'il parle?	**Parle-t-il?**	Does he speak?
Est-ce qu'elle parle?	**Parle-t-elle?**	Does she speak?
Est-ce que nous parlons?	**Parlons-nous?**	Do we speak?
Est-ce que vous parlez?	**Parlez-vous?**	Do you speak?
Est-ce qu'ils parlent?	**Parlent-ils?**	Do they *(m or m+f)* speak?
Est-ce qu'elles parlent?	**Parlent-elles?**	Do they *(f)* speak?

Note the three ways of forming a question when there is a noun subject:

M. Brown est professeur?	Mr. Brown is a teacher?
Est-ce que M. Brown est professeur?	Is Mr. Brown a teacher?
M. Brown est-il professeur?	Mr. Brown, is he a teacher?

5. THE NEGATIVE: ne . . . pas

The negative is formed by placing **ne** before the verb and **pas** after the verb. See examples:

Il *ne* parle *pas* anglais.	He does not speak English.
Est-ce qu'il *ne* parle *pas* anglais?	Does he not speak English?
Ne *parle-t-il* pas *anglais?*	Does he not speak English?
Ne *parlez pas* trop haut.	Do not speak too loudly.

6. OTHER REGULAR -er VERBS LIKE parler

The vast majority of verbs in French are regular **-er** verbs like **parler**. You are already familiar with the following:

bavarder to chat	**je bavarde,** etc.
compter to expect, intend	**je compte,** etc.
commencer to begin	**je commence,** etc.
coûter to cost	**il coûte**
désirer to want	**je désire,** etc.
écouter to listen	**j'écoute,** etc.
étudier to study	**j'étudie,** etc.
habiter to live, reside	**j'habite,** etc.
importer to import	**j'importe,** etc.
jouer to play	**je joue,** etc.
travailler to work	**je travaille,** etc.
visiter to visit	**je visite,** etc.

Exercise No. 22

Complete each of the following verbs with the correct ending:

Exemple: j'étudie

1. j'étudi _____
2. ils ne parl _____ pas
3. nous compt _____
4. elles désir _____
5. je travaill _____
6. habit _____ -vous?
7. il écout _____
8. il ne coût _____ pas
9. nous travaill _____
10. vous étudi _____
11. elles bavard _____
12. elle ne visit _____ pas
13. vous commenc _____
14. import _____ -t-il?
15. Qui parl _____ ?
16. Les enfants jou _____

Exercise No. 23

Change the following sentences into the negative:

Exemple: Henri ne joue pas bien du piano.

1. Henri joue bien du piano.
2. Paul étudie le français.
3. Nous parlons espagnol.
4. Ils écoutent avec attention.
5. Mes enfants, jouez dans le salon.
6. Elle désire aller en Europe.
7. Qui étudie l'anglais?
8. Nous travaillons toute la journée.
9. Elle compte aller au Maroc.
10. Vous travaillez bien.

Exercise No. 24

Practice aloud the following brief dialogues:

1. —Parlez-vous français, Jean?

   —Oui, monsieur, je parle français.

   —Marie parle-t-elle français?

   —Non, monsieur, elle ne parle pas français.

2. —Qui joue du piano?

   —Annette joue du piano.

   —Ne joues-tu pas du piano, Michelle?

   —Non, je ne joue pas du piano.

3. —Est-ce que les garçons étudient la leçon?

—Non, il n'étudient pas la leçon.

—Est-ce qu'ils jouent dans la rue?

—Oui, ils jouent dans la rue.

4. —Qui est le professeur de M. Brown?

—M. Picard est son professeur.

—Est-il français?

—Oui, il est français.

Exercise No. 25—Questionnaire

1. Où est-ce que les messieurs sont assis?
2. Qui commence à parler?
3. Qui écoute avec attention?
4. Qui pose les questions?
5. Qui est-ce qui répond aux questions?
6. Est-ce que les verbes sont importants?
7. M. Brown importe-t-il des objets d'art?
8. Pourquoi étudie-t-il le français?
9. Quels pays (which countries) est-ce qu'il compte visiter?
10. Est-ce qu'il va voyager en bateau ou en avion?
11. Est-ce que M. Brown apprend rapidement ou lentement?

CHAPTER 7

CHAPITRE 7 (SEPT)

LA FAMILLE DE M. BROWN

MR. BROWN'S FAMILY

1. C'est jeudi, le 17 janvier. Il est huit heures du soir.
2. M. Picard sonne à la porte chez M. Brown. La bonne ouvre la porte et dit:—Entrez, monsieur. Passez au salon, s'il vous plaît.
3. Dans le salon M. Brown est seul. Il attend M. Picard. Sa femme n'est pas avec lui au salon aujourd'hui. Elle est dans la chambre de leur fille Anne. Quand M. Picard arrive, M. Brown dit:—Bonsoir. Comment allez-vous?
4. —Comme ci, comme ça. Et vous?
5. —Quant à moi, ça va très bien, mais ma fille Anne est malade. Elle est enrhumée.
6. —J'en suis désolé. Avez-vous d'autres enfants?
7. —Oui. J'ai quatre enfants, deux garçons et deux filles. Nous sommes six dans notre famille.
8. —Comment vos enfants s'appellent-ils?
9. —Ils s'appellent Charles, Thomas, Elizabeth, et Anne.
10. —Quel âge ont-ils?
11. —Charles a dix ans. Il est l'aîné. Thomas a huit ans. Elizabeth a six ans. Anne est la cadette. Elle a cinq ans.
12. —Ils vont tous à l'école excepté Anne.
13. Les deux messieurs bavardent un peu plus. Ensuite M. Brown invite M. Picard à visiter son bureau lundi prochain à midi et demi. M. Picard accepte l'invitation avec plaisir.
14. À neuf heures M. Picard dit:—À bientôt.
15. M. Brown répond:—À lundi à midi et deme.

1. It is Thursday, January 17. It is eight o'clock in the evening.
2. Mr. Picard rings the doorbell of Mr. Brown's house. The maid opens the door and says, Come in, sir. Please go into the living room.
3. In the living room Mr. Brown is alone. He is waiting for Mr. Picard. His wife is not with him in the living room today. She is in the room of their daughter Anne. When Mr. Picard arrives, Mr. Brown says, Good evening. How are you?
4. So so. And you?
5. As for me, I'm fine, but my daughter Anne is ill. She has a cold.
6. I'm very sorry to hear it. Have you any other children?
7. Certainly. I have four children, two boys and two girls. There are six of us in our family.
8. What are your children's names?
9. Their names are Charles, Thomas, Elizabeth, and Anne.
10. How old are they?
11. Charles is ten years old. He is the oldest. Thomas is eight years old. Elizabeth is six years old. Anne is the youngest. She is five years old.
12. They all go to school except Anne.
13. The two gentlemen talk a while longer. Then Mr. Brown invites Mr. Picard to visit his office the following Monday at half past twelve. Mr. Picard accepts the invitation with pleasure.
14. At 9 o'clock Mr. Picard says, "So long."
15. Mr. Brown answers, "Until Monday at half past twelve."

Pronunciation and Spelling Aids

Practice aloud:

1. **passez au salon** (pa-say zoh sa-**lawñ**)
2. **quand il arrive** (kahñ teel a-**reev**)
3. **comme ci, comme ça** (kum see kum **sa**)
4. **elle est enrhumée** (ehl eh tahñ-rü-**may**)
5. **d'autres enfants** (doh-truh zahñ-**fahñ**)
6. **lundi prochain** (leuñ-dee pru-**shañ**)
7. **l'aîné** (leh-**nay**)
8. **la cadette** (la ka-**deht**)

Final **d** when linked with the next word is pronounced as *t*. Thus:

quand il (kañ **teel**)   **apprend-il** (a-prahñ-**teel**)

The accent marks "^" and "`" sometimes indicate a difference in meaning, *not* in pronunciation. Thus:

sur = on   **à** = to, at, on
sûr = sure   **a** (as in **il a**) = has.

Building Vocabulary

Most French words ending in -**tion** and -**sion** (syawñ) have corresponding English words ending in *-tion* and *-sion*. They are always feminine. They are pronounced somewhat differently in French.

la nation	la situation
la prononciation	l'obligation
la continuation	l'invention
l'expression	la concession
l'élection	l'observation
l'attention	l'invitation
la direction	la révolution
la profession	l'obsession

Generally adverbs in English are formed by adding -ly to the adjective. In French they are formed by adding -**ment** to the feminine form of the adjective.

rapide	**rapidement**	rapidly	**certaine**	**certainement**	certainly
lente	**lentement**	slowly	**probable**	**probablement**	probably
facile	**facilement**	easily	**générale**	**généralement**	generally

French Expressions

1. **comme ci, comme ça** so so
2. **quant à moi** (kahñ ta **mwa**) as for me
3. **Ça va très bien.** I'm fine. *(Literally:* It's going very well)
4. **Elle est enrhumée.** She has a cold.
5. **J'en suis désolé.** I'm sorry to hear about it.
6. **bien sûr** (byañ **sür**) surely, certainly
7. **Quel âge avez-vous?** How old are you?
8. **J'ai quinze ans.** I am fifteen years old.

9. **Comment s'appellent-ils?** What are their names?

10. **Ils s'appellent . . .** Their names are . . .

Exercise No. 26—Completion of Text

1. **La bonne** (opens) **la porte.**
2. **Elle dit—**(Enter, sir.)
3. (Go) **au salon,** (please).
4. (My daughter) **Anne est malade.**
5. (Have you) **d'autres enfants?**
6. **Bien sûr.** (I have) **quatre enfants.**
7. (We are) **six dans notre famille.**
8. **Charles est** (the oldest).
9. **Il a** (ten years).
10. **Anne est** (the youngest).
11. (They chat/talk) **un peu plus.**
12. **M. Picard** (accepts) **l'invitation.**

Grammar Notes

1. PRESENT TENSE OF avoir, *to have*—IRREGULAR VERB

j'ai (zhay)	I have	**nous avons** (noo za-vawñ)	we have
tu as (tü a)	you have	**vous avez** (voo za-**vay**)	you have
il a (eel a)	he has	**ils ont** (eel **zawñ**)	they (m) have
elle a (ehl a)	she has	**elles ont** (ehl **zawñ**)	they (f) have

Interrogative (have I, am I having, etc.?)

est-ce que j'ai? (ai-je)[1]	avons-nous?
as-tu?	avez-vous?
a-t-il?	ont-ils?
a-t-elle?	ont-elles?

Negative (I have not, I do not have, etc.)

je n'ai pas	nous n'avons pas
tu n'as pas	vous n'avez pas
il n'a pas	ils n'ont pas
elle n'a pas	elles n'ont pas

Negative-Interrogative:	**N'a-t-il pas?**	Has he not?
	N'ont-ils pas?	Have they not?

NOTE I. With the verb **avoir,** the inverted form is sometimes used with **je.**

Est-ce que j'ai? *or* **Ai-je?** Do I have? or Have I?

Exercise No. 27

Complete the following in French with the correct form of **avoir:**

1. **Combien d'enfants** (have you)?
2. (I have) **six enfants.**
3. **Combien de filles** (has she)?
4. (She has) **trois filles.**
5. (Do you have) **les livres, Jean et Paul?**
6. (We do not have) **les livres.**
7. **Anne,** (have you) **le miroir?**
8. (I do not have) **le miroir.**
9. **Les jeunes filles** (have they) **la balle?**
10. (They do not have) **la balle.**
11. **Qui** (has) **quatre enfants?**
12. **Mme Picard** (has) **quatre enfants.**
13. **Quel âge** (have) **vous?**
14. (I have) **dix ans.**

2. PRESENT TENSE OF aller, *to go*—IRREGULAR VERB

je vais (zhuh **vay**)	I go	**nous allons** (noo za-lawñ)	we go
tu vas (tü **va**)	you go	**vous allez** (voo za-**lay**)	you go
il va (eel **va**)	he goes	**ils vont** (eel **vawñ**)	they go
elle va (ehl **va**)	she goes	**elles vont** (ehl **vawñ**)	they go

Interrogative (do I go? etc.)

est-ce que je vais?
vas-tu?
va-t-il?
va-t-elle?

allons-nous?
allez-vous?
vont-ils?
vont-elles?

Negative (I do not go, etc.)

je ne vais pas
tu ne vas pas
il ne va pas
elle ne va pas

nous n'allons pas
vous n'allez pas
ils ne vont pas
elles ne vont pas

Negative-Interrogative:

Ne va-t-il pas?
Ne vont-ils pas?

Does he not go? Isn't he going?
Do they not go? Aren't they going?

NOTE: The verb **aller** is frequently used to indicate future time, more precisely an immediate future. Thus:

Je vais faire un voyage en France.
Ils vont apprendre le français.

I am going to (I shall) take a trip to France.
They are going to (will) learn French.

Exercise No. 28

Complete the following in French with the correct form of **aller**:

1. **Où** (is he going)?
2. (He is going) **à l'hôtel.**
3. (Are you going) **à la campagne?**
4. **Non,** (we are going) **en Europe.**
5. **Les enfants** (do they go) **à l'école?**
6. **Qui** (is going) **faire visite à sa représentante?**
7. **Où** (are you going), **mon enfant?**
8. **M. Brown** (is going) **faire un voyage en France.**
9. (Are you going) **visiter l'Espagne?**
10. (We are not going) **visiter l'Espagne.**
11. **Où** (are you going), **mes enfants?**
12. (We are going) **au parc.**
13. How are you?
14. I am fine.

3. PRESENT TENSE OF être, *to be*—IRREGULAR VERB

je suis (zhuh **süee**)	I am	**nous sommes** (noo **sum**)	we are
tu es (tü **eh**)	you are	**vous êtes** (voo **zeht**)	you are
il est (eel **eh**)	he is	**ils sont** (eel **sawñ**)	they are
elle est (ehl **eh**)	she is	**elles sont** (ehl **sawñ**)	they are

Interrogative (am I?, etc.)

est-ce que je suis? (Suis-je)[1]	**sommes-nous?**
es-tu?	**êtes-vous?**
est-il?	**sont-ils?**
est-elle?	**sont-elles?**

Negative (I am not, etc.)

je ne suis pas	**nous ne sommes pas**
tu n'es pas	**vous n'êtes pas**
il n'est pas	**ils ne sont pas**
elle n'est pas	**elles ne sont pas**

Negative-Interrogative:

N'est-il pas? Is he not?   **Ne sommes-nous pas?** Are we not?

NOTE: With the verb **être,** the inverted form is sometimes used with **je. Est-ce que je suis?** or **Suis-je?** Am I?

Exercise No. 29

Complete the following in French with the correct form of **être**:

1. **Qui** (is) **dans le bureau?**
2. **M. Brown** (is) **dans le bureau.**
3. **Où** (is) **Mme Brown?**
4. **Elle** (is) **dans le salon.**
5. **M. Picard,** (is he) **anglais?**
6. **Non, il** (is not) **anglais.**
7. (Are you) **un Français?**
8. **Non,** (I am) **un Américain.**
9. **Où** (are) **les enfants?**
10. (They are) **dans la rue.**
11. **Les messieurs** (are they) **assis?**
12. (They are) **assis dans le salon.**
13. (Are you) **professeurs, mesdames?**
14. Non, **(we are not)** professeurs.

Exercise No. 30—Questionnaire

1. **Qui sonne à la porte?**
2. **Qui est-ce qui ouvre la porte?**
3. **Où est-ce que M. Brown attend M. Picard?**
4. **Qui est malade?**
5. **Est-elle enrhumée?**
6. **Combien d'enfants M. Brown a-t-il?**
7. **Combien de personnes y a-t-il dans sa famille?**
8. **Comment les enfants s'appellent-ils?**
9. **Quel âge a Charles?**
10. **Les enfants vont-ils à l'école?**
11. **Qui est-ce que** (whom) **l'homme d'affaires invite à visiter son bureau?**
12. **Est-ce que le professeur accepte l'invitation?**

CHAPITRE 8 (HUIT)

AU BUREAU DE M. BROWN
AT MR. BROWN'S OFFICE

1. Le bureau de M. Brown est au vingtième étage d'un gratte-ciel. Il n'est pas grand mais il est confortable. Par deux grandes fenêtres on peut voir en bas la Rue Whitehall. Aux murs gris il y a des posters et une grande carte de France.

2. Sur le bureau de M. Brown il y a beaucoup de papiers. Près de la porte il y a un petit bureau avec un ordinateur individuel. Entre les deux fenêtres il y a une longue table. Sur la table il y a des journaux, des revues, et un cendrier.

3. M. Brown est assis à son bureau quand M. Picard arrive. Il va à la porte pour saluer son professeur.

4. —Bonjour, M. Picard. Je suis très content de vous voir.

5. —Bonjour, M. Brown. Comment allez-vous?

6. —Très bien, merci.

7. —Votre bureau est très beau. J'aime bien cette carte de France, et ces posters. Quelles jolies couleurs! À propos, M. Brown, la leçon continue! Qu'est-ce que vous voyez sur ce poster-là?

8. —Je vois le ciel et le soleil, un château blanc sur une colline, avec un toit rouge et beaucoup de cheminées.

9. —De quelle couleur est le soleil?

10. —Il est jaune et il est immense.

11. —De quelles couleurs sont le ciel, les cheminées et la colline?

---

1. Mr. Brown's office is on the twentieth floor of a skyscraper. It is not large but it is comfortable. Through two large windows one can see Whitehall Street below. On the gray walls there are some (decorative) posters and a large map of France.

2. On Mr. Brown's desk there are many papers. Near the door is a small desk with a personal computer. Between the two windows there is a long table. On the table there are some newspapers, magazines, and an ash tray.

3. Mr. Brown is seated at his desk when Mr. Picard arrives. He goes to the door to greet his teacher.

4. Good afternoon (day), Mr. Picard. I am very glad to see you.

5. Good afternoon (day), Mr. Brown. How are you?

6. Very well, thank you.

7. Your office is very beautiful. I like this map of France and these posters. What pretty colors! By the way, Mr. Brown, the lesson continues! What do you see on that poster?

8. I see the sky and the sun, a white castle on a hill, with a red roof and many chimneys.

9. What color is the sun?

10. It is yellow and it is immense.

11. What colors are the sky, the chimneys, and the hill?

12. —Le ciel est bleu. Les cheminées sont noires. La colline est verte.
13. —Mon Dieu, il est déjà une heure! C'est assez de couleurs! Je commence à avoir faim. Et vous? N'avez-vous pas faim?
14. —Eh bien, moi aussi, j'ai faim. Pas loin d'ici il y a un bon restaurant.
15. —Tant mieux! Allons-y!

12. The sky is blue. The chimneys are black. The hill is green.
13. My goodness! It's already one o'clock. That's enough of colors! I'm beginning to be hungry. And you? Aren't you hungry?
14. Well, me too, I am hungry. Not far from here there is a good restaurant.
15. Fine! Let's go!

Pronunciation and Spelling Aids

Practice aloud:

1. **deux grandes fenêtres** (deu grahñd fuh-**nehtr**)
2. **des posters** (des pu-**stehr**)
3. **un ordinateur individuel** (ün ur-dee-na-**teur** añ-dee-vee-**dü**-el)
4. **quelles jolies couleurs** (kehl zhu-lee koo-**leur**)
5. **beaucoup de cheminées** (boh-koo duh shuh-mee-**nay**)
6. **pas loin d'ici** (pah lwañ dee-**see**)

Building Vocabulary

SOME COMMON ADJECTIVES

blanc (blahñ) **blanche** *f.* (blahñsh) white
bleu (bleu) blue
noir (nwar) black
vert (vehr) green
violet (vyuh-**lay**) **violette** *f.* (vyuh-**leht**) violet, purple
bon (bawñ) **bonne** *f.* (buhn) good
mauvais (mu-**veh**) bad
beau (boh) **belle** *f.* (behl) beautiful, handsome
joli (zhu-**lee**) pretty
grand (grahñ) big
petit (puh-**tee**) small
long (lawñ) **longue** *f.* (lawñg) long
court (koor) short
riche (reesh) rich
haut (oh) high

gris (gree) gray
jaune (zhohn) yellow
orange (uh-**rañzh**) orange
rose (rohz) pink
rouge (roozh) red
bas (bah) low **basse** *f.* (bahs)
pauvre (pohvr) poor
facile (fa-**seel**) easy
jeune (zheun) young
vieux (vyeu) old **vieille** *f.* (vyehy)
difficile (dee-fee-**seel**) difficult
malade (ma-**lad**) sick
important (añ-pur-**tahñ**) important
intéressant (añ-tay-reh-**sahñ**) interesting
assis (a-**see**) seated

French Expressions

1. **on peut voir** (awñ peu **vwar)** one can see
2. **à propos** (a pru-**poh)** by the way
3. **j'aime bien** (zhehm **byañ)** I like
   j'aime beaucoup (zhehm boh-**koo)** I like very much, I love
4. **de quelle couleur** (duh kehl koo-**leur)** (of) what color
5. **Il est une heure.** (eel eh tü **neur)** It is one o'clock.
6. **tant mieux** (tahñ **myeu)** good, fine, so much the better
7. **avoir faim** (a-vwar **fañ)** to be hungry.
8. **J'ai faim** (zhay **fañ)** I am hungry.
9. **Mon Dieu!** (mawñ **dyeu)** Goodness! (My God!)
10. **moi aussi** (mwa oh-**see)** me (I) too

NOTE: use of the verb **avoir** in items 7 and 8: literally, *to have hunger*

Exercise No. 31—Completion of Text

1. **Il y a deux** (large) **fenêtres.**
2. (One can) **voir la rue.**
3. **Sur la table il y a des** (newspapers).
4. **M. Brown** (is seated) **à son bureau.**
5. **Je suis content** (to see you).
6. (I like) **cette carte**
7. (I see) **un château blanc.**
8. (What color) **est le ciel?**
9. **Le ciel est** (blue).
10. (Goodness!) **Il est une heure.**
11. (Not far from here) **il y a un restaurant.**
12. (Good! Let's go there.)

Grammar Notes

1. AGREEMENT OF ADJECTIVES

Adjectives have masculine, feminine, and plural forms, and must agree with (match) the number and gender of the nouns they accompany. Study the following examples which illustrate such agreement, noting especially the feminine and plural forms of adjectives.

le père intelligent	le crayon noir	le stylo bleu
la mère intelligent *e*	la table noir *e*	la carte bleu *e*
les pères intelligent *s*	les crayons noir *s*	les stylos bleu *s*
les mères intelligent *es*	les tables noir *es*	les cartes bleu *es*
un exemple facile	l'homme riche	le mur gris
une question facile	la femme riche	la carte gris *e*
les exemples facile *s*	les hommes riche *s*	les murs gris
les questions facile *s*	les femmes riche *s*	les cartes gris *es*

a. To make an adjective feminine, add a silent **e** to the masculine, unless the masculine already ends in **e** (such as in **riche, facile, rouge, jaune**). See unusual feminine forms (for example, **blanche, longue**) in Building Vocabulary.

b. To make an adjective plural, add **-s** to the singular, unless the singular adjective already ends in **-s** or **-x** (such as in **gris, assis, vieux**).

2. POSITION OF ADJECTIVES

In French, adjectives generally come *after* the nouns they modify. A few common adjectives, however, are exceptions: they come *before* the noun. Among adjectives that come befoe the noun:

bon good	**jeune** young
meilleur better	**vieux** old
mauvais bad	**joli** pretty
grand big, tall	**long** long
petit small	**haut** high, loud (**h** aspiré)
beau beautiful	**gros** big, thick
un bon livre	**une jeune femme**
la grande station	**un long voyage**
les petits enfants	**les hautes collines**

If the adjective is used after some form of the verb **être,** *to be,* the adjective must agree with the subject of the sentence in gender and number. For example:

Anne est très belle. Charles est très beau.

Exercise No. 32

Replace the English words in parentheses with the correct form of the adjective in French. Remember to read aloud the completed sentences:

Exemple: 1. Madame Brown est assise dans le salon.

1. **Mme Brown est** (seated) **dans le salon.**
2. **Les** (little) **enfants jouent dans le parc.**
3. **Mme Brown est une femme** (intelligent).

4. **J'aime bien les** (pretty) **couleurs.**
5. **M. Brown a un bureau** (comfortable).
6. **Le château est situé sur une** (high) **colline.**
7. **Les murs du bureau sont** (gray).
8. **Tous les élèves sont** (intelligent).
9. **As-tu un** (good) **stylo?**
10. **Anne et Elizabeth sont** (pretty).
11. **Il y a beaucoup de** (large) **parcs à Paris.**
12. **Où sont les** (old) **livres?**
13. **Il y a une** (beautiful) **carte au mur.**
14. **Le ciel est-il** (red) **ou** (blue)?
15. **Les cheminées sont-elles** (black)?
16. **Son grand-père est très** (old).

NOTE: Some plural nouns may include both masculine and feminine persons, such as **élèves,** *pupils;* **étudiants,** *students;* **enfants,** *children.* In that case, the agreeing adjective is in the masculine plural. The plural pronoun that includes both masculine and feminine persons is **ils.**

3. SOME IRREGULAR ADJECTIVES

a. Note the feminine forms.

le bon livre	**le beau château**
la *bonne* **revue**	**la** *belle* **maison**
les bons livres	**les beaux châteaux**
les *bonnes* **revues**	**les** *belles* **maisons**

le long crayon	**le papier blanc**
la *longue* **table**	**la chaise** *blanche*
les long crayons	**les papiers blancs**
les *longues* **tables**	**les chaises** *blanches*

b. The adjective **tout** and the interrogative adjective **quel.** Study the forms and meanings:

tout le livre the whole book	**quel frère?** which, what brother?
toute la salle the whole room	**quelle soeur?** which, what sister?
tous les livres all the books	**quels frères?** which, what brothers?
toutes les salles all the rooms	**quelles soeurs?** which, what sisters?

Exercise No. 33

Complete in French with the correct form of the adjective:

Exemple: 1. Madame Picard est une belle femme.

1. **Madame Picard est une** (beautiful) **femme.**   2. **Marie est une** (good) **fille.**

3. **Les filles de M. Brown sont très** (intelligent).
4. **Elles ont beaucoup de** (good) **amies.**
5. **Voyez-vous les maisons** (white)?
6. **Où est la** (long) **table?**
7. (The whole) **salon est** (beautiful).

8. (Which) **homme parle anglais?**
9. **De** (what) **couleur est le mur?**
10. (Which) **cendriers sont sur le bureau?**
11. **M. Brown travaille** (all) **la journée.**
12. **Où sont** (all) **les journaux?**

Exercise No. 34

Translate into French; read aloud the changed sentences.

1. Mr. Brown's office is very comfortable.
2. The windows of the office are large.
3. There are some posters on the walls.
4. There are some French newspapers on the table.
5. The sky on the poster is blue.

6. The sun is yellow.
7. How are you, Mr. Brown?
8. Very well, thank you.
9. I am hungry.
10. I too.

Exercise No. 35—Questionnaire

1. Où est le bureau de M. Brown?
2. Est-ce que le bureau est grand?
3. Est-ce qu'il est confortable?
4. Où est-ce qu'il y a des posters?
5. Où est-ce qu'il y a beaucoup de papiers?
6. Où est-ce qu'il y a un petit bureau?
7. Où est-ce qu'il y a une longue table?

8. De quelle couleur est le soleil sur le poster?
9. De quelle couleur sont les cheminées?
10. De quelle couleur est la colline?
11. Est-ce que le ciel est bleu?
12. De quelle couleur est le château?
13. Est-ce que le toit est rouge ou jaune?
14. Est-ce que M. Brown a faim?

NOTE: Remember that, in any question containing **est-ce que,** the word order is the same as in most statements: the subject first, then the verb.

CHAPITRE 9 (NEUF)

M. BROWN SALUE UN AMI

MR. BROWN GREETS A FRIEND

1. M. Dupont, un ami de M. Brown, habite maintenant à New York. Il parle bien le français parce que ses parents sont canadiens et il faut étudier la langue à l'école.
2. Il sait que son ami M. Brown apprend le français. Il désire voir si son ami fait des progrès dans ses études. Donc il entre un jour dans le bureau de M. Brown et commence à¹ parler français.
3. —Comment ça va?
4. —Très bien, merci. Et vous?
5. —Pas mal, merci. À propos, vous apprenez le français, n'est-ce pas?
6. —Bien entendu. J'apprends à¹ parler, à lire et à écrire le français.
7. —Vous trouvez le français difficile à¹ apprendre?
8. —Mais non. Le français n'est pas difficile à¹ apprendre. J'aime beaucoup la langue française et je l'étudie² avec enthousiasme.
9. —Comment s'appelle votre professeur de français?

1. Mr. Dupont, a friend of Mr. Brown, lives in New York. However, he speaks French well because his parents are Canadians.
2. He knows that his friend Mr. Brown is learning French. He wants to see whether his friend is making progress in his studies. Thus, he enters Mr. Brown's office one day and begins to speak French.
3. How's it going?
4. Very well, thank you. And you?
5. Not bad, thank you. By the way, you are learning French, aren't you (isn't that so)?
6. Of course. I am learning to speak, read and write French.
7. Do you find French difficult to learn?
8. No. French is not difficult to learn. I like the French language very much and I'm studying it enthusiastically.
9. What's the name of your French teacher?

NOTE: ¹After certain verbs such as **apprendre** and **commencer, à** is placed immediately before the infinitive which follows. Similarly, the infinitive is preceded by **à** after certain adjectives, for example **difficile** and **facile.** Exemple: **La carte du Métro est facile à comprendre.** See Grammar Notes in this chapter. ²**le (l'),** *him, it;* **la (l')** *her, it;* and **me,** *me,* are direct object pronouns, which usually precede the verb. See explanations in chapter 15.

10. —M. Picard. C'est un professeur excellent, et de jour en jour je parle, je lis, et j'écris le français de mieux en mieux. J'apprends les mots et les expressions de la vie quotidienne. Je comprends M. Picard quand il parle français, et il me[2] comprend également. Le français me plaît beaucoup.

11. —Mon ami, vous parlez français à merveille.

12. —Merci. Vous êtes trop aimable.

13. —Pas du tout. C'est la vérité. Mes amis me disent que vous allez faire un voyage en France cet été. C'est vrai?

14. —Oui. J'espère partir au printemps, vers la fin de mai. Je vais voyager en avion. Je voudrais arriver en France le plus tôt possible.

15. —Alors, bon voyage! Et bonne chance! Au revoir.

16. —Au revoir.

10. Mr. Picard. He is an excellent teacher, and day by day I speak, read, and write better and better. I am learning words and expressions from daily life. I understand Mr. Picard when he speaks French and he understands me as well. I like French very much.

11. My friend, you speak French wonderfully.

12. Thanks. You are too kind.

13. Not at all. It is the truth. My friends tell me that you are going to take a trip to France this summer. Is that true?

14. Yes. I hope to leave in the spring, toward the end of May. I am going to travel by plane. I want to arrive in France as soon as possible.

15. Well then, have a good trip. And good luck! See you again.

16. Goodbye.

Pronunciation and Spelling Aids

Practice aloud:

1. **Il parle bien français.** (eel parl byañ frahñ-**seh**)
2. **Ses parents sont canadiens.** (say pa-rahñ sawñ ka-na-**dyañ**)
3. **Dupont** (dü-**pawñ**)
4. **donc** (dawñk)
5. **vers** (vehr)
6. **C'est un professeur excellent** (seh teuñ pru-feh-seur eh-skay-**lañ**)
7. **je prends** (prahñ), **ils prennent** (prehn)

Building Vocabulary

ANTONYMS
1. **apprendre** to learn / **enseigner** to teach
2. **partir** to leave / **arriver** to arrive
3. **beaucoup de choses** many things / **peu de choses** few things
4. **poser une question** to ask a question / **répondre à une question** to answer a question
5. **loin d'ici** far from here / **près d'ici** near here
6. **le professeur** the professor, teacher / **l'étudiant(e)** the student

7. **le maître, la maîtresse** the teacher / **l'élève** the pupil
8. **il est assis** he is seated / **il est debout** he is standing
9. **voici** here is (are) / **voilà** there is (are)

French Expressions

1. **faire des progrès** (fehr day pru-**greh**) to make progress
2. **voici** (vwa-**see**) here is, are
3. **n'est-ce pas** (nehs **pah**) is it not true? Translated in various ways: isn't that so? isn't he (she, it)? aren't you? don't you?
4. **de jour en jour** (duh zhoor ahñ **zhoor**) day by day
5. **de mieux en mieux** (duh myeu zahñ **myeu**) better and better
6. **à merveille** (a mehr-**vehy**) wonderfully
7. **pas du tout** (pah dü **too**) not at all
8. **le plus tôt possible** (luh plü toh **puseeble**) as soon as possible
9. **bon voyage** (bawũ vwa-**yazh**) (have a) nice trip
10. **bonne chance** (bun **shahñs**) good luck

Exercise No. 36—Completion of Text

1. (His parents) **sont canadiens.**
2. (His friend) **fait des progrès.**
3. (Here is) **leur**(= their) **conversation.**
4. **Vous apprenez le français,** (aren't you)?
5. (I am learning) **à parler français.**
6. **Le français** (is not difficult) **à apprendre.**
7. (I am studying) **diligemment.**
8. (I like French) (*Literally:* French pleases me) **beaucoup.**
9. **Vous parlez français** (wonderfully).
10. (I understand) Mr. Picard.
11. (You are) **trop aimable.**
12. (Not at all). **C'est** (the truth).

Grammar Notes

NOTE: In French, the word *to* is included in infinitives (**lire,** *to* read; **écrire,** *to* write; etc.) and is translated as such into English. However, as we see in this chapter, **à** is added between some verbs and an infinitive following, for instance **apprendre,** *to learn;* **enseigner,** *to teach;* **commencer,** *to begin.* Similarly, an infinitive is introduced by **à** following certain adjectives, for example **difficile,** *difficult,* and **facile,** *easy.* Sometimes *to* is expressed by **de** after a verb or adjective. Observe the following examples:

Tu commences à voir la vérité. You (fam.) begin to see the truth.

Je refuse de le faire. I refuse *to* do it.

Il est content de danser avec moi. He is happy *to* dance with me

1. PRESENT TENSE OF vendre, *to sell*—REGULAR -re VERB, OFTEN CALLED THE THIRD CONJUGATION

I sell, you sell, etc.

je vends (vahñ)	**nous vendons** (vahñ-**dawñ**)
tu vends (vahñ)	**vous vendez** (vahñ-**day**)
il, elle, on vend (vahñ)	**ils, elles vendent** (vahñd)

The endings of regular **-re** verbs in the present tense are:

Singular: **-s -s**   Plural: **-ons -ez -ent**

Imperative: **vends** sell; **vendons** let us sell; **vendez** sell

Other regular **-re** verbs conjugated like **vendre** are:

attendre *to wait for (to await)*, **j'attends**, etc.   **perdre** *to lose*, **je perds**, etc.
entendre *to hear*, **j'entends**, etc.   **rendre** *to give back, to return (an item)* **je rends**, etc.
descendre *to go down, to descend*, **je descends**, etc.   **répondre** *to answer*, **je réponds**, etc.

2. PRESENT TENSE OF prendre, *to take*; lire, *to read*; écrire, *to write*, IRREGULAR -re VERBS.

These are **-re** verbs with irregular conjugations:

I take, you take, etc.   *I read, you read, etc.*   *I write, you write, etc.*

je prends	**nous prenons**	**je lis**	**nous lisons**	**j'écris**	**nous écrivons**
tu prends	**vous prenez**	**tu lis**	**vous lisez**	**tu écris**	**vous écrivez**
il prend	**ils prennent**	**il lit**	**ils lisent**	**il écrit**	**ils écrivent**
elle prend	**elles prennent**	**elle lit**	**elles lisent**	**elle écrit**	**elles écrivent**

Imperative: **prends** take; **prenons**, let us take; **prenez**, take
             lis, read; **lisons**, let us read; **lisez**, read
             écris, write; **écrivons**, let us write; **écrivez**, write

Other verbs like **prendre** are:

apprendre *to learn*—**j'apprends, nous apprenons, ils apprennent**

comprendre *to understand*—je comprends, nous comprenons, ils comprennent

surprendre *to surprise*—je surprends, nous surprenons, ils surprennent

Other verbs like **lire** are: **élire**, *elect;* **relire**, *reread.*

Other verbs like **écrire** are: **décrire**, *describe;* **inscrire**, *to register.*

Irregular verbs most frequently used in French will be introduced gradually in the conversation texts and Grammar Notes of the chapters to follow. A summary of these irregular verbs will appear at the end of this book.

Exercise No. 37

Translate these short dialogues. Then practice them aloud. They will help you get a feel for the correct use of the new verbs in this chapter

1. —**Apprenez-vous le français?**
   —**Oui, monsieur, j'apprends le français.**
   —**Est-ce que Charles apprend le français?**
   —**Non, il n'apprend pas le français.**

2. —**Est-ce que tu écris une lettre?**
   —**Je n'écris pas de** (any) **lettre.**
   —**Qu'est-ce que tu écris?**
   —**J'écris les exercices de français.**

3. —**Qu'est-ce que tu lis?**
   —**Je lis un journal français.**
   —**Qu'est-ce qu'Anne lit?**
   —**Elle lit une revue française.**

4. —**Comprenez-vous votre professeur quand il parle rapidement?**
   —**Non, madame, mais nous comprenons le prof quand il parle lentement.**

5. —**Qu'est-ce que M. Brown vend?**
   —**Il vend des objets d'art.**
   —**Vend-il en gros** (wholesale) **ou en détail** (retail)**?**
   —**Il vend seulement (only) en gros.**

6. —**Qui est-ce que M. Brown attend?**
   —**Il attend M. Picard.**
   —**Où est-ce qu'il l'attend?**
   —**Il l'attend dans le salon** (waits for *him*).

Exercise No. 38

Complete these sentences in French with the correct form of the verb indicated:

Exemple: 1. Nous vendons notre automobile.

1. (We are selling) **notre automobile.**
2. (You, sir, are learning) **à parler français.**
3. (I understand) **le professeur.**
4. (The parents read) **les journaux français.**
5. (Are you returning) **les livres à la bibliothèque?**
6. (I take) **le train en ville.**
7. (They [fem.] are not taking) **le train.**
8. (We answer) **à toutes les questions.**
9. **Qui** (reads) **l'espagnol?**
10. (You do not understand) **la leçon ?**
11. (Let us write) **des lettres.**
12. **Les Américains** (are electing) **un nouveau Président.**
13. **Que** (do they sell)?
14. (Read) **cette lettre, s'il vous plaît.**
15. (She is registering) **sa fille au lycée.**
16. (Do you hear) **le maître?**

Exercise No. 39—Questionnaire

1. Qui habite New-York?
2. Est-ce que M. Dupont parle bien le français?
3. Est-ce que ses parents sont Américains?
4. Qu'est-ce que M. Dupont sait?
5. Où est-ce qu'il entre un jour?
6. Qui est-ce que (whom) M. Dupont salue en français?
7. Qui apprend à parler, à lire et à écrire le français?
8. Comment M. Brown étudie-t-il?
9. Comment s'appelle son professeur de français?
10. Est-ce un bon professeur?
11. Est-ce que M. Brown comprend quand M. Picard parle français?
12. Quels mots et quelles expressions M. Brown apprend-il?
13. Qui va faire un voyage en France?
14. Quand est-ce qu'il espère partir?

Première Partie

Review of Words (Révision de Mots)

NOUNS

1. l'an	1. year
2. l'avion	2. airplane
3. le bateau	3. boat
4. les bateaux	4. boats
5. la bonne	5. maid
6. la carte	6. map
7. le cendrier	7. ashtray
8. le château	8. castle
9. les châteaux	9. castles
10. le ciel	10. sky
11. la couleur	11. color
12. l'élève	12. pupil
13. l'endroit	13. place
14. les environs	14. suburbs
15. l'étage	15. story, floor
16. l'été	16. summer
17. l'étudiant(e)	17. student
18. le journal	18. newspaper
19. les journaux	19. newspapers
20. le mot	20. word
21. le nom	21. name
22. le plaisir	22. pleasure
23. le printemps	23. spring
24. la revue	24. magazine
25. le soleil	25. sun
26. le toit	26. roof
27. le travail	27. work
28. la vérité	28. truth
29. la vie	29. life
30. le voyage	30. trip

VERBS

1.	aimer	1.	to like, love
2.	s'appeler	2.	to be named
3.	il s'appelle	3.	his name is
4.	bavarder, causer	4.	to chat, talk
5.	commencer	5.	to begin
6.	coûter	6.	to cost
7.	chanter	7.	to sing
8.	demeurer	8.	to live, dwell
9.	demander	9.	to ask
10.	désirer	10.	to want
11.	écouter	11.	to listen
12.	entrer (dans)	12.	to enter
13.	espérer	13.	to hope
14.	étudier	14.	to study
15.	jouer	15.	to play
16.	poser	16.	to ask (question)
17.	regretter	17.	to regret, to be sorry
18.	saluer	18.	to greet
19.	sonner	19.	to ring
20.	travailler	20.	to work
21.	voyager	21.	to travel
22.	répondre	22.	to answer
23.	vendre	23.	to sell
24.	dire	24.	to say, tell
25.	écrire	25.	to write
26.	voir	26.	to see
27.	partir	27.	to leave
28.	je sais	28.	I know
29.	ils prennent	29.	they take
30.	je vais dire	30.	I am going to say

ADJECTIVES

1.	blanc (*m*)	1.	white
2.	blanche (*f*)[1]	2.	white (*f*)
3.	bleu	3.	blue
4.	gris	4.	gray
5.	jaune	5.	yellow
6.	rouge	6.	red
7.	vert	7.	green

NOTE: [1]If adjectives are irregular, the masculine and feminine forms are given.

8. beau (bel)[1]	8. beautiful
9. belle (*f*)	9. beautiful (*f*)
10. bon	10. good
11. bonne (*f*)	11. good (*f*)
12. confortable	12. comfortable
13. difficile	13. difficult
14. facile	14. easy
15. joli	15. pretty
16. jeune	16. young
17. long	17. long
18. longue (*f*)	18. long (*f*)
19. malade	19. sick
20. pauvre	20. poor
21. prochain	21. next
22. riche	22. rich
23. quel homme	23. which man
24. quelle femme	24. which woman
25. quels garçons	25. which boys
26. quelles filles (*f*)	26. which girls
27. tout le mur	27. the whole wall
28. toute la cuisine	28. the whole kitchen
29. tous les journaux	29. all the newspapers
30. toutes les revues	30. all the magazines

NOTE: [1]**Bel** is used only before a masculine noun beginning with a vowel or **h** (mute). Thus:

un beau portrait   **un bel ami**   **un bel hôtel**   **une belle amie**

ADVERBS

1. déjà	1. already
2. ensuite	2. then
3. trop	3. too much, too many
4. demain	4. tomorrow
5. vite	5. quickly, fast
6. le plus vite	6. most quickly, fastest

PREPOSITIONS

1.	après	1.	after
2.	par	2.	by, through
3.	pour	3.	for, in order to
4.	loin de	4.	far from

CONJUNCTIONS

1.	cependant	1.	however
2.	donc	2.	therefore, thus
3.	si	3.	if, whether
4.	que	4.	that

French Expressions

1.	à propos	1.	by the way
2.	à merveille	2.	wonderfully
3.	bien sûr	3.	surely, of course
4.	bon voyage	4.	have a good trip
5.	bonne chance	5.	good luck
6.	comme ci, comme ça	6.	so so
7.	eh bien	7.	well
8.	mon Dieu!	8.	goodness!
9.	De quelle couleur est-il?	9.	What color is it?
10.	de jour en jour	10.	day by day
11.	de mieux en mieux	11.	better and better
12.	tant mieux	12.	so much the better
13.	en avion	13.	by plane
14.	moi aussi	14.	I too, me too
15.	pas du tout	15.	not at all
16.	demander des renseignements	16.	to ask for information
17.	poser des questions	17.	to ask questions
18.	répondre aux questions	18.	to answer questions
19.	partir en voyage	19.	to leave on a trip
20.	le plus tôt possible	20.	as soon as possible
21.	quant à moi	21.	as for me
22.	Elle est enrhumée.	22.	She has a cold.
23.	voici	23.	here is (are)
24.	J'ai faim.	24.	I am hungry.
25.	Quel âge avez-vous?	25.	How old are you?
26.	n'est-ce pas?	26.	is it not so; isn't it? etc.

Exercise No. 40

Select the words in Column II which best complete each sentence begun in Column I:

Exemple: 1-c Je suis importateur d'objets d'art de la France et du Maroc.

I	II
1. Je suis importateur d'objets d'art	a. dites, "Je ne sais pas."
2. Je ne comprends pas bien	b. nous allons faire des progrès de jour en jour.
3. Si vous ne savez pas la réponse	c. de la France et du Maroc.
4. M. Picard dit, "Je le regrette beaucoup,"	d. pas loin d'ici.
5. Ils vont en avion parce que	e. quand le professeur parle rapidement.
6. Si nous étudions diligemment	f. du voyage.
7. Quand j'ai faim	g. parce que l'enfant est enrhumée.
8. Il y a un bon restaurant	h. "Comment ça va?"
9. Son ami salue M. Brown et dit,	i. c'est le plus vite.
10. Je ne sais pas le prix	j. je vais au restaurant.

Exercise No. 41

Answer each of the following questions in complete sentences, using the suggested words in the answer. Make the adjectives agree with their nouns in number and gender.

Exemple: De quelle couleur sont les toits? (blanc) Ils sont blancs.

1. Quelle langue parlez-vous? (français)
2. Où demeurent-ils? (aux États-Unis)
3. Qui a faim? (Nous)
4. De quelles couleurs est la revue? (blanc et noir)
5. De quelle couleur sont les maisons? (rouge)
6. Quel âge avez-vous? (quinze ans)
7. Qui pose des questions? (les professeurs)
8. Qui répond aux questions? (nous)
9. Qui est-ce que M. Brown attend? (son ami)
10. Qu'est-ce que vous écrivez? (des lettres)

Exercise No. 42

Complete each verb with the correct ending:

1. nous travaill _____
2. elles apprenn _____
3. vous ne sav _____ pas
4. tu écri _____
5. ils lis _____
6. je ne comprend _____ pas
7. il étudi _____
8. vous pren _____
9. elles attend _____
10. vous ne répond _____ pas
11. Lis _____ !
12. N'attend _____ pas, M. Picard.

Exercise No. 43

Answer each of the following questions in the affirmative and negative singular:

Exemple: 1. Oui, monsieur, j'ai faim. Non, madame, je n'ai pas faim.

1. Avez-vous faim?
2. Êtes-vous enrhumé?
3. Étudiez-vous la leçon?
4. Attendez-vous le professeur?
5. Comptez-vous voyager en France?
6. Apprenez-vous à écrire le français?
7. Lisez-vous la revue?
8. Écrivez-vous la lettre?
9. Comprenez-vous les questions?
10. Acceptez-vous l'invitation?
11. Commencez-vous à lire?
12. Répondez-vous à la question?

Exercise No. 44

You are already acquainted with the following question pronouns:

Persons	*Things*
1. **qui** *or* **qui est-ce qui?** who? *(subject of verb)*	3. **qu'est-ce qui?** what? *(subject of verb)*
2. **qui** *or* **qui est-ce que?** whom? *(object of verb or with a preposition)*	4. **que** *or* **qu'est-ce que?** what? *(object of verb)*

Supply the correct question pronouns in the French sentences which follow. Remember: **que** becomes **qu'** if the next word begins with a vowel or **h** (mute).

Question pronouns containing **est-ce que** are followed by the regular word order *(subject—verb)*.

1. (Who) **sait parler français?**
2. (Whom) **voyez-vous tous les jours?**
3. (Whom) **M. Picard voit le mardi et le jeudi?**
4. **Avec** (whom) **Madame Brown parle-t-elle?**
5. **À** (whom) **parlez-vous?**
6. (What) **M. Brown apprend?**
7. (What) **apprenez-vous?**
8. (Who) **va faire un voyage en France?**
9. (What) **est sur le toit de la maison?**
10. (What) **lisez-vous?**
11. (What) **les enfants lisent?**
12. (What) **est au mur au-dessus du piano?**

Dialogue I

Quel autobus faut-il prendre?[1]	What bus should I take?
1. **Excusez-moi, monsieur, quel autobus faut-il prendre pour l'Étoile? (pour le Quai Voltaire?) (pour la Place Vendôme?)**	1. Excuse me, sir, which bus do I take for the Étoile? (for the Quai Voltaire?) (for the Place Vendôme?)
2. **Prenez l'Autobus 52,**[2] **etc. Il s'arrête ici-même, au coin.**	2. Take the 52 bus, etc. It stops right here at the corner.
3. **Merci beaucoup, monsieur.**	3. Thank you very much, sir.
4. **De rien, monsieur.**	4. Don't mention it, sir.

NOTE: [1]*Lit.* What bus is it necessary to take?   [2]**cinquante-deux.**

Dialogue 2

Quel autobus va à . . .?	Which bus goes to . . . ?
1. Excusez-moi, monsieur, pouvez-vous me dire quel autobus va à l'Opéra? (au Jardin du Luxembourg?) (au Louvre?)	1. Excuse me, sir, can you tell me which bus goes to the Opera? (the Luxembourg Gardens?) (the Louvre?)
2. Je regrette. Je ne suis pas d'ici, monsieur. Je ne sais pas. Mais cet agent au coin va certainement vous le dire.	2. I'm sorry. I am not from here, sir. I don't know. But that policeman at the corner will certainly tell you.
3. Merci beaucoup, monsieur. Je vais lui[1] demander.	3. Thank you very much, sir. I am going to ask him.

NOTE: [1]**Lui,** *him,* is an indirect object pronoun; it usually precedes the verb. It replaces a masculine or a feminine noun.

Exercise No. 45—Lecture I

DEUX AMIS DE M. BROWN

M. Brown sait déjà les noms de tous les objets dans sa maison. Maintenant il commence à étudier les verbes parce qu'il désire apprendre à lire, à écrire, et à parler en français. Il désire aussi apprendre les nombres en français. Comme[1] il désire rendre visite à[2] sa représentante à Paris, qui ne parle pas anglais, il désire apprendre à parler français le plus tôt possible. Donc il lui faut[3] beaucoup de pratique avec des personnes qui parlent bien le français. Heureusement, il a deux amis français qui sont dans les affaires[4] près de son bureau dans la rue Whitehall.

Un jour M. Brown rend visite à ces messieurs français. Les deux messieurs écoutent avec attention pendant que[5] M. Brown cause avec eux[6] en français. Après dix minutes de conversation, les messieurs posent beaucoup de questions à leur[7] ami, et ils sont très contents de ses[8] progrès.

NOTE: [1]**comme,** as. [2]**rendre visite à,** to pay a visit to. [3]Therefore he needs (*Lit.* It is necessary to him.) [4]**être dans les affaires,** to be in business. [5]**pendant que,** while. [6]**eux,** them. [7]**leur,** their. [8]**ses,** his.

Exercise No. 46—Lecture 2

M. BROWN EST MALADE

Jeudi le vingt-deux avril à neuf heures du soir M. Picard arrive à la maison de son élève, M. Brown. Le fils aîné,[1] un garçon de dix ans, ouvre la porte, et salue le professeur poliment. Ils entrent dans le salon où d'habitude[2] M. Brown attend son professeur.

Mais ce soir il n'est pas là. Mme Brown n'est pas là non plus. M. Picard est très surpris, et il demande au garçon,—Où est ton papa? Le fils répond tristement[3]—Papa est malade. Il est au lit[4] parce qu'il est très enrhumé.

Le professeur est un peu ennuyé,[5] mais il dit seulement—Quel dommage![6] Eh bien, la semaine prochaine nous allons étudier deux heures. À mardi prochain, alors. Au revoir, mon petit. Le garçon répond,—Au revoir, monsieur.

NOTE: [1]**le fils ainé,** the oldest son. [2]**d'habitude,** usually. [3]**tristement,** sadly. [4]**au lit,** in bed. [5]**ennuyé,** annoyed. [6]**Quel dommage!,** What a pity!

CHAPITRE 10 (DIX)

DANS LA SALLE À MANGER
IN THE DINING ROOM

1. M. Brown et M. Picard sont assis dans la salle à manger chez M. Brown. Sur la table il y a deux tasses et soucoupes, deux verres, des cuillers à thé, des fourchettes, un couteau, un pot à lait, un sucrier, et un plat avec une tarte aux fruits. Les deux messieurs prennent du café avec des gâteaux.
2. M. Brown dit,—Comment trouvez-vous ces tasses et ces soucoupes?
3. —Je les (them) trouve charmantes, répond M. Picard. Cette tasse blanche ornée de fleurs bleues est de Limoges, n'est-ce pas?
4. —En effet, oui. La porcelaine fine de Limoges est célèbre. Il y a plusieurs régions en France connues pour leurs produits céramiques et chaque région a son style individuel.
5. —Et ce gai petit pot à lait jaune avec des dessins verts, d'où vient-il?
6. —Ce pot à lait est de Vallauris, en Provence. C'est une ville célèbre pour sa poterie. La petite ville de Biot, près de Vallauris, est aussi un centre de l'industrie céramique.
7. —Il y a d'autres régions en France connues pour leurs produits céramiques, n'est-ce pas?
8. —Oui, c'est vrai. Il y a surtout la Bretagne. La poterie bretonne est très jolie. La poterie de Normandie est aussi jolie.

1. Mr. Brown and Mr. Picard are seated in the dining room at Mr. Brown's house. On the table there are two cups and saucers, two glasses, some teaspoons, some forks, a knife, a milk pitcher, a sugar bowl, and a plate with a fruit tart. The two gentlemen are having coffee with some cakes.
2. Mr. Brown says, "How do you like these cups and saucers?"
3. "I find them charming," answers Mr. Picard. "This white cup decorated with blue flowers is from Limoges, isn't it?"
4. "Yes, indeed. The fine porcelain of Limoges is famous. There are several districts in France known for their ceramic products and each district has its individual style."
5. "And this bright little milk pitcher, yellow with green designs, where does this come from?"
6. "This milk pitcher is from Vallauris, in Provence. It is a town famous for its pottery. The little town of Biot, near Vallauris, is also a center of the ceramic industry."
7. "There are other regions in France known for their ceramic products, aren't there?"
8. "Yes, that's so. There is above all Brittany. Breton pottery is very lovely. The pottery of Normandy is also pretty."

9. —Je vois que vous connaissez bien votre métier, dit M. Picard.
10. —Eh bien, oui, il le faut, dit M. Brown.
11. —C'est vrai, répond M. Picard. En tout cas, je vois ici beaucoup de beaux échantillons de l'industrie céramique française.
12. —Bien sûr. Comme vous dites, c'est mon métier. J'ai aussi des échantillons de poterie ordinaire pour la cuisine. Cette poterie est généralement très simple en couleur unie, tout en marron, comme ce plat-là près de vous.
13. —C'est un plat simple, mais beau.
14. —Voulez-vous encore une tasse de café? Un peu de cette tarte aux fruits?
15. —Merci. Tout est délicieux.

9. "I see that you know your trade very well," says Mr. Picard.
10. "Well, yes; it is necessary," says Mr. Brown.
11. "That's true," answers Mr. Picard. "At any rate, I see here many fine samples of the French ceramic industry."
12. "Of course. As you say, it's my trade. I also have some samples of everyday pottery for kitchen use. This pottery is usually very simple and in one color, all in brown, like that dish near you."
13. "It is a simple dish, but handsome."
14. "Do you want another cup of coffee? A little of this fruit tart?"
15. "Thank you. Everything is delicious."

Pronunciation and Spelling Aids

Practice aloud:

1. **Limoges** (lee-**muzh**)
2. **Vallauris** (va-loh-**rees**)
3. **Provence** (pruh-**vahñs**)
4. **Normandie** (nur-mahñ-**dee**)
5. **Bretagne** (bruh-tahn-**yuh**)
6. **bretonne** (bruh-**tun**)
7. **l'industrie céramique** (lañ-dü-stree say-ra-**meek**)
8. **leurs produits** (leur pru-**düee**)
9. **son style individuel** (sawñ steel añ-dee-vee-dü-**ehl**)
10. **tout est délicieux** (too teh day-lee-**syeu**)

Building Vocabulary

Dans la salle à manger (dahñ la sal a mahñ-**zhay**)

1. **le plat** (pla) platter
2. **la tasse** (tas) cup
3. **la soucoupe** (soo-**koop**) saucer
4. **le couteau** (koo-**toh**) knife
5. **la fourchette** (foor-**sheht**) fork
6. **la cuiller** (küee-**yehr**) spoon
7. **la cuiller à soupe** (soop) soupspoon
8. **la cuiller à thé** (tay) teaspoon
9. **le pot à lait** (pu ta **leh**) milk pitcher
10. **le sucrier** (sü-kree-**ay**) sugar bowl
11. **le verre** (vehr) (drinking) glass
12. **manger** (mahñ-**zhay**) to eat; **on mange** (awñ **mahñzh**) one eats
13. **les échantillons** (m.) (ay-shahñ-tee-**yawñ**) samples, examples

French Expressions

1. **c'est vrai** (seh **vray**) certainly, that's true
2. **comment trouvez-vous?** (ku-mahñ troo-vay-**voo**) How do you like (*Lit.* find)?
3. **surtout** (sür-**too**) above all, especially
4. **en tout cas** (ahñ too **kah**) at any rate. in any case

5. **il le faut** (eel luh **foh**) it is necessary
6. **d'ordinaire** (dur-dee-**nehr**) usually
7. **encore une tasse** (akñ-kur ün **tas**) one more cup
8. **autre** (oh-**tr** *or* oh-**truh**) other, i.e., a different one

Exercise No. 47—Completion of Text

1. (They are having) **du café avec des gâteaux.**
2. **Comment trouvez-vous** (these cups)?
3. **Cette tasse est ornée de** (blue flowers).
4. **La poterie fine de Limoges est** (famous).
5. (Each region) **a son style individuel.**
6. **La poterie bretonne est** (very pretty).
7. **La poterie de Normandie est** (also pretty).
8. (You know) **bien votre métier.**
9. (That's true), **répond M. Picard.**
10. **Je vois** (many) **beaux échantillons.**
11. (As you say), **c'est mon métier.**
12. (It's a simple dish), **dit M. Picard.**
13. **Voulez-vous** (another cup) **de café?**
14. **Merci.** (Everything) **est délicieux.**

Grammar Notes

1. THE VERBS **dire,** *to say,* **voir,** *to see*

I say, you say, etc.		*I see, you see, etc.*	
je dis (dee)	**nous disons** (dee-**zawñ**)	**je vois** (vwa)	**nous voyons** (vwa-**yawñ**)
tu dis (dee)	**vous dites** (deet)	**tu vois** (vwa)	**vous voyez** (vwa-**yay**)
il dit (dee)	**ils disent** (deez)	**il voit** (vwa)	**ils voient** (vwa)
elle dit (dee)	**elles disent** (deez)	**elle voit** (vwa)	**elles voient** (vwa)

Imperative			*Impératif*		
dis	**disons**	**dites**	**vois**	**voyons**	**voyez**

Exercise No. 48

Practice these questions and answers aloud:

1. **Que dites-vous? Je dis:—Non.**

2. **Que dit-il? Il dit:—Oui.**
3. **Que dit-elle? Elle dit:—C'est vrai.**
4. **Que disent-elles? Elles disent:—Ce n'est pas vrai.**
5. **Dites-moi où vous demeurez. Je demeure dans cette rue.**
6. **Qu'est-ce que tu vois au mur? Je vois une carte de France.**
7. **Voyez-vous le château sur une colline? Nous le voyons.**
8. **Voit-il son ami Jean le dimanche? Non, il ne le voit pas le dimanche; il le voit le samedi.**
   (on, every Saturday)

Exercise No. 49

Translate into French:

1. We say.
2. I see.
3. He does not say.
4. He says.
5. Does he say?
6. What do you say?
7. What do you see?
8. They see.
9. Do you (**tu**) see?
10. I do not see.
11. They are saying.
12. What are they saying?
13. She does not see.
14. Let's see.
15. Tell me.

2. THE DEMONSTRATIVE ADJECTIVE ce, cet, cette, ces—*this* or *that*, *these* or *those*.

a. **ce** (*this, that*) is used before masculine singular nouns.

cet is used, not **ce**, before *masculine* singular nouns beginning with a vowel or mute **h**.
cette (*this, that*) is used before feminine singular nouns.
ces (*these, those*) is used before all nouns in the plural.
Study the following sentences. They show the various forms of the demonstrative adjective **ce**.

Ce garçon apprend le français.
This (that) boy is learning French.
Cet article est de France.
This (that) article is from France.
Cet homme est professeur.
This (that) man is a teacher.

Cette jeune fille est ma soeur.
This (that) girl is my sister.
Ces garçons apprennent le français.
These (those) boys are learning French.
Ces jeunes filles sont mes soeurs.
These (those) girls are my sisters.

b. **-ci** (contraction of **ici** *here*) and **-là** (*there*) are added to the end of the noun when it is important to distinguish between *this* and *that*, or *these* and *those*, (if the meaning is not clear without them).

ce pot-ci this pot
ce pot-là that pot
cette tasse-ci this cup

cette tasse-là that cup
ces plats-ci these dishes
ces plats-là those dishes

Exercise No. 50

Complete the following expressions in French:

1. (that) **amie-là**
2. (these) **couteaux-ci**
3. (that) **portrait-là**
4. (those) **plats-là**
5. (this) **tasse-ci**
6. (that) **étudiant-là**
7. (those) **mots-là**
8. (this) **fleur-ci**
9. (these) **échantillons-ci**
10. (this) **homme-ci**
11. (these) **revues-ci**
12. (that) **ami-là**

3. OTHER USES OF c'est, *this is* **or** *it is,* instead of **il est, elle est.**

a. **c'est** is used before an adjective when the adjective refers to a thought already expressed in a sentence, and not to a single noun. Thus:

M. Potter étudie le français. C'est vrai. It's (*That's*) true.

b. **c'est** is used for **il (elle) est** and **ce sont** is used for **ils (elles) sont,** when a modified noun or a proper noun follows:

C'est une ville célèbre. It is (*This is*) a famous town.
Ce sont des portraits de mes enfants. They (*these, those*) are portraits of my children.
C'est M. Picard. It's Mr. Picard.

Exercise No. 51

Practice these common **c'est** expressions aloud:

1. **C'est assez.** It's enough.
2. **C'est bon.** It's good.
3. **C'est mauvais.** It's bad.
4. **C'est bien.** It's (That's) all right.
5. **C'est ça (cela).** That's it. That's right. O.K.
6. **C'est ceci.** This is it.
7. **Ce n'est rien.** It's nothing.
8. **C'est facile.** It's easy.
9. **C'est difficile.** It's hard.
10. **C'est ici.** It's here.
11. **C'est là.** It's there.
12. **C'est près d'ici.** It's near here.
13. **C'est loin d'ici.** It's far from here.
14. **Ce n'est pas loin.** It's not far.

Exercise No. 52—Questionnaire

1. Où M. Picard et M. Brown sont-ils assis?
2. Qu'est-ce qu'ils prennent?
3. Que dit M. Brown?
4. D'où est la tasse blanche?
5. Quelle porcelaine est célèbre?
6. D'où est le petit pot à lait?
7. Pourquoi la ville de Vallauris est-elle célèbre?
8. Où est la ville de Vallauris?
9. Est-ce que la poterie de la Bretagne est jolie?
10. Qui connaît bien son métier?
11. Qu'est-ce que M. Brown a pour la cuisine?
12. La poterie ordinaire, est-elle simple ou ornée?
13. Est-ce que M. Brown offre encore une tasse de café?
14. Qu'est-ce que M. Picard dit?

CHAPITRE 11 (ONZE)

LES NOMBRES, TOUJOURS LES NOMBRES

NUMBERS, ALWAYS NUMBERS

1. —M. Brown, vous savez déjà que les noms de choses et de personnes sont importants. Vous savez qu'il n'est pas possible de former une phrase sans verbes.
2. —Oui, je le sais, M. Picard.
3. —Eh bien, monsieur, il y a une catégorie de mots qui est tout aussi importante que celle de noms et de verbes. En effet, il est difficile d'imaginer notre civilisation moderne sans ces mots. Pouvez-vous deviner à quoi je pense?
4. —Je crois que oui. Vous voulez dire les nombres.
5. —Vous avez raison. Pouvez-vous expliquer comment les nombres sont indispensables pour la vie moderne?
6. —Certainement, rien de plus facile. Nous avons besoin de nombres pour le commerce.
7. —Ha, ha! L'homme d'affaires pense tout de suite au commerce. Néanmoins, sans argent les nombres ne valent pas grandchose, n'est-ce pas?
8. —En évidemment, nous avons besoin de nombres pour désigner les dates, les heures, la température; pour exprimer les quantités et les mesures; pour téléphoner; pour la radio; pour toutes les sciences; et pour des milliers d'autres choses.

1. Mr. Brown, you already know that the names of things and of persons are important. You know that it is not possible to make a sentence without verbs.
2. Yes, I know Mr. Picard.
3. Well, sir, there is a class of words that is just as important as nouns and verbs. In fact, it is difficult to imagine our modern civilization without these words. Can you guess what I am thinking of?
4. I think so. You mean numbers.
5. You are right. Can you explain how numbers are indispensable to modern life?
6. Certainly. Nothing could be easier. We need numbers for business.
7. Ha, ha! The businessman thinks immediately of business. However, without money, numbers are not worth much, are they?
8. In truth (*In fact*), we need numbers to indicate dates, the hours (of the day), the temperature; to express quantities and measurements; to telephone; for the radio; for all the sciences, and for thousands of other things.

9. —Les nombres, toujours les nombres. Oui, M. Brown, les nombres sont essentiels. Cependant, il est nécessaire non seulement de connaître les nombres mais aussi de savoir les employer correctement et rapidement dans la vie quotidienne.

10. —Vous avez raison. Je vais faire tout mon possible pour comprendre et employer les nombres correctement.

11. —En attendant, je veux vous (to you) dire que vous avancez rapidement dans vos études.

12. —Vous êtes trop aimable, M. Picard.

13. —Pas du tout. C'est la vérité. Eh bien, c'est assez pour aujourd'hui. Au revoir.

14. —Au revoir, monsieur. À jeudi prochain.

9. Numbers, always numbers. Yes, Mr. Brown, numbers are essential. However, it is necessary not only to know the numbers but also to know how to use them correctly and rapidly in daily life.

10. You are right. I am going to do all I can to understand and use them correctly.

11. Meanwhile, I want to tell you that you are progressing rapidly in your studies.

12. You are too kind, Mr. Picard.

13. Not at all. It's the truth, Well, enough for today. Goodbye.

14. Goodbye, sir. Until next Thursday.

Pronunciation and Spelling Aids

Practice aloud. Stress slightly only the key syllables in heavy type.

Il y a une catégorie de mots
qui est tout aussi importante
que les noms et les verbes.

(Eel ya ün ka-tay-gu-ree duh **moh**
kee eh too toh-see añ-pur-**tahñt**
kuh lay nawñ zay lay **vehrb**.)

Building Vocabulary

RELATED WORDS

1. **vrai** true, **la vérité** truth
2. **répondre** to answer, **la réponse** the answer
3. **étudier** to study, **l'étude** the study
4. **savoir** to know, **le savant** scientist, scholar
5. **connaître** to know, **la connaissance** knowledge
6. **le commerce** commerce, trade, **le (la) commerçant(e)** merchant
7. **civiliser** to civilize, **la civilisation** civilization
8. **le jour** day, **le journal** daily newspaper

French Expressions

1. **aussi bien que** (oh-see bjañ **kuh**) as well as
2. **en effet** (ahñ nay-**feh**) in fact
3. **penser à** (pahñ-say **a**) to think of. **À quoi**[1] **pensez-vous?** (a kwa pahñ-say **voo**) What are you thinking about?

NOTE: [1]The interrogative pronoun **quoi?** *what?* is used after prepositions: **à quoi? de quoi? dans quoi? avec quoi?**, etc., and is not used to replace persons.

4. **Je crois que oui.** (zhuh krwa kuh **wee**) I think so. **Je crois que non.** I think not.
5. **Vous voulez dire** (voo voo-lay **deer**) You mean (*Lit.* You wish to say)
6. **avoir raison** (a-vwah reh-**sawñ**) to be right (*Lit.* to have reason) **Vous avez raison** You are right.
7. **avoir besoin de** (a-vwar buh-zwañ **duh**) to need (*Lit.* to have need of) **Vous avez besoin d'argent.** You need money.
8. **tout de suite** (too duh **süeet**) at once
9. **pas du tout** (pah dü **too**) not at all
10. **rien de plus facile** (ryañ duh plü fa-**seel**) nothing could be easier
11. **d'ailleurs** (dah-**yeur**) besides
12. **d'accord** (da-**kur**) okay, agreed
13. **entendu** (ahñ-tahñ-**dü**) understood, agreed
14. **bien entendu** (bjañ ahñ-tahñ-**dü**) of course

Exercise No. 53—Completion of Text

1. (You know) **déjà les noms des choses.**
2. **Cette catégorie de mots est tout** (as important as) **les noms et les verbes.**
3. **Pouvez-vous deviner** (of what) **je pense?**
4. (I think so). **Vous** (mean) **les nombres.**
5. (You are right). **Les nombres** (are indispensable).
6. (We need) **de nombres pour le commerce.**
7. (Without money) **les nombres ne valent pas** (much).
8. (In the meantime), **je veux vous dire que** (you are progressing rapidly) **dans vos études.**
9. (It is) **la vérité.**
10. Until next Thursday.

Grammar Notes

1. PRESENT TENSE OF THE VERBS **vouloir**, *to wish, want* and **pouvoir**, *to be able*

I wish, want, you wish, want, etc.

je veux (veu)
tu veux (veu)
il, elle veut (veu)
nous voulons (voo-**lawñ**)
vous voulez (voo-**lay**)
ils, elles veulent (veul)

I can (am able) you can, etc.

je peux (peu) or **je puis**
tu peux (peu)
il, elle peut (peu)
nous pouvons (poo-**vawñ**)
vous pouvez (poo-**vay**)
ils, elles peuvent (peuv)

Exercise No. 54

Translate into French

1. (I want) **savoir**.
2. (I am able) **deviner**.
3. (Do you want) **manger**?
4. (Can you) **jouer**?
5. (We wish) **étudier**.

6. (We are not able) **attendre**.
7. (They do not want) **travailler**.
8. (Are you able) **travailler**?
9. (Does he wish) **comprendre**?
10. (Is she able) **apprendre**?

2. LES NOMBRES DE 1 (UN) À 69 (SOIXANTE-NEUF)

1. **un** (euñ) **une** (ün)
2. **deux** (deu)
3. **trois** (trwah)
4. **quatre** (katr)
5. **cinq** (sañk)
6. **six** (sees)
7. **sept** (seht)
8. **huit** (üeet)
9. **neuf** (neuf)
10. **dix** (dees)
11. **onze** (awñz)
12. **douze** (dooz)
13. **treize** (trehz)
14. **quatorze** (ka-turz)
15. **quinze** (kañz)
16. **seize** (sehz)
17. **dix-sept** (dee-seht)
18. **dix-huit** (dee-züeet)
19. **dix-neuf** (deez-neuf)
20. **vingt** (vañ)

21. **vingt et un** (vañ tay **eun**)
22. **vingt-deux** (vañt-**deu**)
23. **vingt-trois** (vañ-**trwah**)
24. **vingt-quatre** (vañt-**katr**)
25. **vingt-cinq** (vañt-**sank**)
26. **vingt-six** (vañt-**sees**)
27. **vingt-sept** (vañt-**seht**)
28. **vingt-huit** (vañt-**üeet**)
29. **vingt-neuf** (vañt-**neuf**)
30. **trente** (trahñt)
31. **trente et un**
32. **trente-deux**
40. **quarante** (ka-**rahnt**)
41. **quarante et un**
50. **cinquante** (sañ-**kahnt**)
51. **cinquante et un**
60. **soixante** (swa-**sahnt**)
65. **soixante-cinq**
69. **soixante-neuf**

NOTE: The final consonants of 5, 6, 8, 10 are silent before words beginning with a consonant.

cinq livres (sañ **leevr**)
six plumes (see **plüm**)

huit lettres (üee **lehtr**)
dix choses (dee **shohz**)

Exercise No. 55

Write the numbers in French. Then read each expression aloud.

Exemple: a. (30) trente mots français

a. 30 mots français
b. 10 leçons faciles
c. 50 bonnes phrases
d. 49 affiches françaises
e. 16 maisons blanches
f. 38 femmes anglaises

g. 17 beaux garçons
h. 15 tables longues
i. 62 papiers verts
j. 68 hommes riches
k. 24 grandes villes
l. 13 plumes noires

Exercise No. 56

Write each arithmetical expression in French. Then read each expression aloud.

NOTE: $+$ = **et** $-$ = **moins** $\times$ = **fois** $\div$ = **divisé par** make = **font, égalent**

Exemples: $4 + 6 = 10$ quatre et six font dix

$20 \div 5 = 4$ vingt divisé par cinq égalent quatre

a. $2 + 6 = 8$
b. $10 + 7 = 17$
c. $7 \times 8 = 56$
d. $9 \times 7 = 63$
e. $19 - 8 = 11$
f. $18 - 6 = 12$
g. $60 \div 10 = 6$
h. $69 \div 3 = 23$

Exercise No. 57

Read each question aloud in French. Answer it aloud in a complete French sentence.

Exemple: 1. Il y a sept jours dans une semaine.

1. Combien de jours y a-t-il dans une semaine?
2. Combien de mois y a-t-il dans une année?
3. Combien d'heures y a-t-il dans une journée?
4. Combien de minutes y a-t-il dans une heure?
5. Combien de secondes y a-t-il dans une minute?
6. Combien de jours y a-t-il dans le mois de septembre?
7. Combien d'étudiants y a-t-il dans la classe? (36 étudiants)
8. Quel âge avez-vous? (17 ans)
9. Quel âge a Louis? (19 ans)
10. Combien d'automobiles y a-t-il dans le garage? (15 automobiles)

Exercise No. 58—Questionnaire

1. Qu'est-ce que M. Brown sait déjà?
2. Quelle catégorie de mots est aussi importante que les noms et les verbes?
3. De quoi avons-nous besoin pour le commerce?
4. À quoi est-ce que l'homme d'affaires pense tout de suite?
5. Avons-nous besoin des nombres pour téléphoner?
6. Qui veut comprendre et employer les nombres correctement?
7. Comment est-ce que M. Brown avance dans ses études?
8. Dites à haute voix (aloud) en français les nombres 10, 20, 30, 40, 50, 60.

CHAPITRE 12 (DOUZE)

LE SYSTÈME MONÉTAIRE DE FRANCE
FRENCH MONEY, PAST AND PRESENT

1. —Dans notre dernière conversation nous avons dit qu'il est difficile d'imaginer notre civilisation moderne sans les nombres, c'est à dire, sans mathématiques. Il est difficile également d'imaginer de faire un voyage sans mathématiques.

2. —Savez-vous combien de fois on fait usage des mathématiques en voyage?

3. —Je crois que oui. On fait usage des maths pour changer de l'argent, pour acheter des billets, pour payer ses repas et sa note d'hôtel, pour faire peser ses bagages, pour estimer les distances, pour faire des achats dans les grands magasins, dans les boutiques et aux marchés.

4. —Connaissez-vous le système monétaire de France?

5. —Absolument!, Je le connais à fond. Je suis importateur d'articles français, n'est-ce pas? Mais en fait, le système monétaire est très différent aujourd'hui, depuis l'adoption de l'euro par douze pays en Europe, la France comprise.

6. —Alors, M. Brown, je vois bien que vous êtes au courant de ce changement qui date du premier janvier, 2002. Avant cette date, chaque pays avait (had) sa propre unité monétaire. En France, c'était (was) le franc.

1. In our last conversation we said that it is difficult to imagine our modern civilization without numbers, that is to say, without mathematics. It is equally difficult to imagine taking a trip without mathematics.

2. Do you know how many times one makes use of mathematics on a trip?

3. I think so. One makes use of math in order to change money, to buy tickets, to pay for one's meals and hotel bill, to weigh luggage, to estimate distances, to make purchases in department stores, in shops and at the markets.

4. Are you familiar with the monetary system of France?

5. Absolutely! I know it thoroughly. I am an importer of French things, am I not? But in fact, the monetary system is very different today, since the adoption of the euro by 12 countries in Europe, France included.

6. So, Mr. Brown, I see that you are aware of this change which began January first, 2002. Before that date, each country had its own currency. In France, this was the franc.

7. —Il n'y a pas très longtemps. Et je me rappelle que le dollar des États-Unis valait entre cinq et six francs.

8. —Maintenant il y a des euro et des cent au lieu de francs et centimes. Un euro vaut approximativement un dollar 25 cents. De l'autre côté, si on a un dollar, on reçoit à peu près 80 (quatre-vingt) cent, c'est-à-dire, quatre-vingt pourcent d'un euro.

9. —C'est ça. Imaginez que vous voulez changer 100 dollars en euro à un bureau d'échange ou à une banque. Combien d'euro allez-vous recevoir?

10. —C'est facile. On va me donner presque 80 euro, moins de petits frais de service.

11. —Correcte! Continuons: ensuite vous allez à la gare. Vous voulez acheter deux billets de chemin de fer. Chaque billet coûte 20 (vingt) euros et vous donnez 50 (cinquante) euros à l'employé du guichet. Combien d'euros est-ce qu'il vous rend en monnaie?

12. —Il me rend 10 (dix) euros. Deux fois 20 font 40; et 50 moins 40 font 10 euros. Mais, Monsieur, laissons ces problèmes de notre enfance!

13. —Vous avez raison. Mais, dans notre prochaine conversation, nous allons continuer à discuter ce sujet, et pratiquer les nombres. Usage rend maître.

7. It hasn't been that long. And I remember that the U.S. dollar was worth between five and six francs.

8. Now there are euros and cents instead of francs and centimes. A euro is worth approximately $1.25. On the other hand, if one has a dollar, one receives nearly 80 cents, that is, 80 percent of a euro.

9. That's right. Imagine that you want to change (exchange) 100 dollars into euros at an exchange bureau or at a banque. How many euros are you going to receive?

10. That's easy. They'll give me almost 80 euros, minus any service costs.

11. Correct! Let's continue: next you go to the railroad station. You want to buy two train tickets. Each ticket costs 20 euros and you give the ticket agent 50 euros. How many euros does he give you back in change?

12. He gives me back 10 euros. Two times 20 is 40; and 50 minus 40 makes 10 euros. But, Sir, let's leave these problems from our childhood!

13. You're right. But in our next conversation we will continue to discuss other aspects of this subject and practice numbers. Practice makes perfect.

NOTE: The relative value of the U.S. dollar and the European euro often changes. The examples in these chapters are for the purpose of language study, not economics.

Pronunciation and Spelling Aids

Practice aloud:

1. **l'unité monétaire** (lü-nee-tay mu-nay-**tehr**)
2. **civilisation** (see-vee-lee-zah-**syawñ**)
3. **mathématiques** (ma-tay-ma-**teek**)
4. **boutiques** (boo-**teek**)
5. **les billets** (leh bee-**yeh**)

6. **un million** (añ meel-**yawñ**)
7. **chemin de fer** (shuh-mañ duh **fehr**)
8. **le guichet** (luh gee-**shay**)

Building Vocabulary

The word **l'argent**, *money* (it also means *silver*), is used for any kind of money. **Les billets** are (money) *bills* (or [*transportation*] *tickets*) and **la monnaie** means *coins*, and also the *currency* of a country. **En monnaie** means *in change*; **le porte-monnaie** is *the change purse.*

ANTONYMS AND RELATED WORDS
1. **vendre** to sell; **acheter** to buy; **je vends** I sell; **j'achète** I buy
2. **le vendeur, la vendeuse** (*f*) salesperson; **l'acheteur, l'acheteuse** (*f*) buyer; or **le client, la cliente,** customer; **l'achat** (*m*), purchase; **la vente,** sale
3. **donner** to give; **recevoir** to receive
4. **emprunter** to borrow; **rendre** to give back; **prêter** to lend; **rembourser** to pay back
5. **vrai** true; **faux** false
6. **Vous avez raison.** You are right. **Vous avez tort.** You are wrong.

French Expressions

1. **c'est à dire** (seh ta **deer**) that is to say
2. **combien de fois** (kawñ-byañ duh **fwa**) how many times
3. **à peu près** (a peu-**preh**) about, nearly
4. **changer de l'argent** (shahñ-zhay duh lar-**zhahñ**) to change money, exchange currency
5. **payer ses repas** (pay-yay seh ruh-**pa**) to pay for one's meals
6. **faire peser les bagages** (fehr puh-zay lay ba-**gazh**) to have the baggage weighed
7. **faire des achats** (deh za-**sha**) to go shopping
8. **c'est ça** (seh **sa**) that's right.
9. **Usage rend maître** (ü-zazh rahñ **mehtr**). Practice makes perfect.

Exercise No. 59—Completion of Text

1. (How many times) **fait-on usage des mathématiques** (on a trip)?
2. (One) **fait usage des maths** (in order to buy tickets).
3. **Nous faisons des achats** (in department stores).
4. (Are you familiar with) **le système monétaire de la France?**
5. (I know it) **à fond.**
6. **Le dollar** (is worth) **à peu près 80 cent** (d'un euro).
7. **Je vais recevoir** (about) **80 euro.**
8. (You want to purchase) **deux billets de chemin de fer.**
9. (You give) **50 euro à l'employé du guichet.**
10. (He gives me back) **10 euros en monnaie.**

Grammar Notes

1. **PRESENT TENSE OF faire,** *to make* or *to do* (**Qu'est-ce que tu fais?** = *What are you doing? What do you do?*) and **croire,** *to believe, to think*

I make or I do, you make or you do, etc.

je fais (feh)
tu fais (feh)
il, elle fait (feh)
nous faisons (fuh-**zawñ**)
vous faites (feht)
ils, elles font (fawñ)

I believe or I think, you believe, etc.

je crois (krwah)
tu crois (krwah)
il, elle croit (krwah)
nous croyons (krwah-**yawñ**)
vous croyez (krwah-**yay**)
ils, elles croient (krwah)

Imperative

fais   **faisons**   **faites**

Imperative

crois   **croyons**   **croyez**

Exercise No. 60

Practice aloud in French. Then, translate into English.

1. Que faites-vous?
   J'écris une lettre.
2. Qu'est-ce que Jean fait?
   Il joue du piano.
3. Qu'est-ce que Marie fait?
   Elle étudie la leçon de français.
4. Qu'est-ce que les filles font?
   Elles font des achats.

5. Que fais-tu, mon enfant?
   Je joue à la balle.
6. Qu'est-ce que M. Martin fait?
   Il fait peser les bagages.
7. Croyez-vous cette histoire (story)?
   Je ne la crois pas.
8. Est-ce que votre ami la croit?
   Il ne la croit pas non plus.

2. LES NOMBRES DE 70 (SOIXANTE-DIX) À 1000 (MILLE)

70 soixante-dix	89 quatre-vingt-neuf
71 soixante et onze	90 quatre-vingt-dix
72 soixante-douze	91 quatre-vingt-onze
73 soixante-treize	92 quatre-vingt-douze
74 soixante-quatorze	93 quatre-vingt-treize
75 soixante-quinze	94 quatre-vingt-quatorze
76 soixante-seize	95 quatre-vingt-quinze
77 soixante-dix-sept	96 quatre-vingt-seize
78 soixante-dix-huit	97 quatre-vingt-dix-sept
79 soixante-dix-neuf	98 quatre-vingt-dix-huit
80 quatre-vingts (katr-**vañ**)	99 quatre-vingt-dix-neuf
81 quatre-vingt-un	

NOTE: In some French-speaking countries—Belgium and Switzerland, for example—the numbers 70, 80, and 90 are called, respectively, **septante, octante,** and **nonante.** There, 71 is **septante et un,** 72 is **septante-deux,** etc.; 91 is **nonante et un;** 70th is **septantième,** and so on.

100 **cent** (sahñ)
101 **cent un** (sahñ **euñ**)
102 **cent deux** (sahñ **deu**)
200 **deux cents** (deu **sahñ**)
345 **trois cent quarante-cinq**
1000 **mille** (meel)
2000 **deux mille**

a. Numbers between 1000 (**mille**) and one million (**un million**) are formed as in English. Thus:

987,896 **neuf cent quatre-vingt-sept mille huit cent quatre-vingt-seize**

b. **et** is used in 21, 31, 41, 51, 61, 71; never in 81, 91, 101.

c. **quatre-vingts** and **cents** (**deux cents**) drop the s if another number follows them. Thus:

(83) **quatre-vingt-trois**   (945) **neuf cent quarante-cinq**

d. **mille** never takes an s.

deux mille 2000

Exercise No. 61

Write out the numbers in French:

Exemple: 18,942 **dix-huit mille neuf cent quarante-deux**

a. 400
b. 1000
c. 753
d. 1,974
e. 95
f. 77
g. 86
h. 71
i. 670
j. 14,586

Exercise No. 62

Practice the following table aloud:

$1.00 Un dollar américain vaut	80 cent (.8 euro)
$2.00 Deux dollars américains valent	un euro, 60 cent
$3.00 Trois dollars américains valent	deux euro, 40 cent
$4.00 Quatre dollars américains valent	trois euro, 20 cent
$5.00 Cinq dollars américains valent	quatre euro
$100.00 Cent dollars américains valent	quatre-vingts euro

Exercise No. 63—Questionnaire

1. Pourquoi M. Brown connaît-il le système monétaire de France?
2. Quelle est la date du changement à l'euro en Europe?
3. Quelle unité monétaire existait en France avant l'euro?
4. Combien de pays européens ont adopté l'euro?
5. À ce moment, quelle unité monétaire—le dollar ou l'euro—vaut plus?
6. Est-ce que les questions de M. Picard sont difficiles ou faciles?
7. Quel proverbe exprime la philosophie de M. Picard, le professeur?

CHAPITRE 13 (TREIZE)

LES NOMBRES DANS LA VIE QUOTIDIENNE

NUMBERS IN DAILY LIFE

1. —Continuons notre étude de l'usage des mathématiques en voyage.

1. Let us continue our study of the uses of mathematics on a trip.

2. —Nous dînons au restaurant. Nous sommes quatre. Les repas coûtent: 43 (quarante-trois) euro, 39 (trente-neuf) euro, 41 (quarante et un) euro, et 47 (quarante-sept) euro. Nous laissons quinze pour cent comme pourboire. Combien est l'addition pour tout le monde? Et combien le pourboire?

2. We are dining in a restaurant. We are four. The meals cost: 43 euros, 39 euros, 41 euros, and 47 euros. We leave 15% for a tip. What is the total bill for everybody? And how much is the tip?

3. —L'addition pour tout le monde monte à 170 (cent soixante-dix) euro, le pourboire à 25 euro, cinquante cent.

3. The bill for everybody amounts to 170 euros, the tip to 25 euros, 50 cents.

4. —Très bien. Continuons. Je suis à la gare et je porte une valise très lourde. Je la fais peser. Elle pèse 30 (trente) kilos. Comment est-ce que je peux calculer le poids de la valise en livres?

4. Very good. Let us continue. I am at the railroad station and I am carrying a very heavy suitcase. I have it weighed. It weighs 30 kilos. How can I calculate the weight of the suitcase in pounds?

5. —Ce n'est pas difficile. Un kilo equivaut à 2,2 (deux virgule deux) livres. On multiplie 30 (trente) par 2,2. La valise pèse 66 (soixante-six) livres.

5. It is not difficult. One kilo is equal to 2.2 pounds. You multiply 30 by 2.2. The suitcase weighs 66 pounds.

6. —Correct. En France et dans les autres pays de l'Europe continentale on ne compte pas les distances en milles mais en kilomètres. Savez-vous changer les kilomètres en milles?

6. Correct. In France and in the other countries of continental Europe one does not figure distance in miles but in kilometers. Do you know how to change kilometers into miles?

Note: In French, the words **euro** and **cent** do not add s in the plural; in English, they do.

7. —Certainement. Je divise par huit et je multiplie par cinq. Ainsi, quatre-vingts kilomètres équivalent à cinquante milles. C'est facile, n'est-ce pas?

8. —Vous calculez vite et bien. Encore un problème, le dernier: vous entrez dans une boutique. Vous achetez une paire de chaussures pour vous-même à 150 (cent cinquante) euro; deux paires de chaussures pour votre femme à 165 (cent soixante-cinq) euro chacune; et une ceinture en cuir pour chacun de vos quatre enfants à 30 (trente) euro chacune. Quel est le montant de tous vos achats?

9. —600 (six cent) euro. Si je donne à la vendeuse deux billets de 500 (cinq cent) euro je vais recevoir 400 (quatre cents) euro en monnaie.

10. —Parfait. Assez de mathématiques pour aujourd'hui. Jeudi nous allons parler des heures de la journée. C'est un sujet très important.

11. —Bien sûr. Je compte sur une conversation intéressante.

12. —À propos, M. Brown, je ne peux pas arriver avant huit heures et demie jeudi prochain.

13. —Ça va. Mieux vaut tard que jamais.

14. —Bien dit! Au revoir, M. Brown.

15. —Au revoir. A jeudi, M. Picard.

7. Certainly. I divide by eight and I multiply by five. Thus 80 kilometers are equal to 50 miles. It's easy, isn't it?

8. You figure fast and well. One more problem, the last one: you go into a shop. You buy a pair of shoes for yourself at 150 euros; two pairs of shoes for your wife at 165 euros each; and a leather belt for each of your four children at 30 euros each. What is the total price of all your purchases?

9. 600 euros. If I give the salesgirl two 500-euro bills, I am going to receive 400 euros in change.

10. Perfect. Enough mathematics for today. On Thursday we are going to talk about the time of day. It is a very important subject.

11. Certainly. I am expecting an interesting conversation.

12. By the way, Mr. Brown, I cannot arrive before 8:30 next Thursday.

13. That's all right. Better late than never.

14. Well said. Goodbye, Mr. Brown.

15. Goodbye. Until Thursday, Mr. Picard.

Pronunciation and Spelling Aids

Practice aloud:

1. **les problèmes d'arithmétique** (pru-blehm da-reet-may-**teek**)
2. **les autres pays** (lay zoh-truh pay-**yee**)
3. **l'addition** (la-dee-**syawñ**)
4. **le restaurant** (rehs-toh-**rahñ**)
5. **la ceinture** (sañ-**tür**)
6. **parfait** (par-**feh**)
7. **la virgule** (veer-**gül**)
8. **je multiplie** (mül-tee-**plee**)

In French a comma (**virgule**) is used instead of a period to set off decimals. Thus:

2,2 (deux virgule deux) instead of 2.2.

Building Vocabulary

WEIGHTS AND MEASURES

In France and in Europe generally, the metric system of weights and measures is used. Instead of the yard and inch, the meter (39.4 inches) and centimeter (2.54 cms equal 1 inch) are used; instead of pounds, the kilogram or kilo (2.2 pounds) is used.

NOTE: la livre = pound, **le livre** = book

French Expressions

1. **comme pourboire** (poor-**bwar**) as a tip
2. **tout le monde** (too luh **mawñd**) everybody
3. **en monnaie** (ahñ mu-**neh**) in change
4. **Mieux vaut tard que jamais.** (myeu voh tar kuh zha-**meh**) Better late than never.

Grammar Notes

1. **PRESENT TENSE OF savoir,** *to know (how)* and **connaître,** *to know, to be acquainted, familiar with*

I know (how), you know (how), etc.

je sais (seh)
tu sais (seh)
il sait (seh)
elle sait (seh)
nous savons (sa-**vawñ**)
vous savez (sa-**vay**)
ils savent (sav)
elles savent (sav)

I know (am acquainted with, etc.)

je connais (ku-**neh**)
tu connais (ku-**neh**)
il connaît (ku-**neh**)
elle connaît (ku-**neh**)
nous connaissons (ku-nehs-**sawñ**)
vous connaissez (ku-nehs-**say**)
ils connaissent (ku-**nehs**)
elles connaissent (ku-**nehs**)

a. **savoir,** *to know* or *to know how* (with or without **comment**) means to know facts, rules, etc. In general this verb implies mental action, memory.

b. **connaître** means *to know* in the sense of to be acquainted with, to be familiar with persons or things. In general this verb implies knowing through the senses—hearing, seeing, etc.

Vous savez les noms des choses. You know the names of things.

Il sait lire le français. He knows how to read French.

Je sais où cet homme travaille. I know where that man works.

Je connais cet homme. I know (am acquainted with) that man.

Nous connaissons cette rue. We know (are familiar with) this street.

Exercise No. 64

Complete these sentences with the correct form of **savoir** or **connaître** as appropriate.
1. (Do you know) **les noms de ces choses?**
2. (We know) **cet homme.**
3. (We do not know) **où il demeure.**
4. (He knows how) **écrire le français.**
5. (I know) **qui est ici.**
6. (They do not know) **cette région de la France.**
7. (I know) **les enfants de M. Picard.**
8. (Do you know how) **changer kilomètres en milles?**
9. (Do they know) **les musées de Paris?**
10. **Que veulent-elles** (to know)?

2. POSSESSIVE ADJECTIVES

You are already familiar with most of the possessive adjectives. Here is a summary of the forms and meanings of all of them.

	Masc. Singular	Fem. Singular	Masc. Plural	Fem. Plural
my	**mon frère**	**ma soeur**	**mes frères**	**mes soeurs**
your	**ton oncle**	**ta tante**	**tes oncles**	**tes tantes**
his, her	**son fils**	**sa fille**	**ses fils**	**ses filles**
our	**notre salon**	**notre rue**	**nos salons**	**nos rues**
your	**votre crayon**	**votre plume**	**vos crayons**	**vos plumes**
their	**leur bureau**	**leur maison**	**leurs bureaux**	**leurs maisons**

a. Possessive adjectives agree in number and gender with the nouns they precede.

b. **ton, ta, tes** (your) like **tu** (you) are used only in addressing children, pets, relatives, or close friends.

c. **son, sa, ses** mean either *his* or *her*, depending on the gender and number of the noun following **son, sa,** or **ses.**

Sa soeur *His* or *her* sister

Son frère *His* or *her* brother

Ses cousins *His* or *her* cousins (all masculine or mixed)

Ses cousines *His* or *her* cousins (all feminine)

d. **mon, ton, son** are used instead of **ma, ta, sa**, before feminine nouns beginning with a vowel or h (mute). Thus:

mon amie (*f*)   **ton école** (*f*)   **son histoire** (*f*)

Exercise No. 65

Complete these sentences with the correct form of **mon, (ma, mes), ton, (ta, tes)**, etc.:
1. (Our) **conversations sont très intéressantes.**
2. **Je vais payer** (my) **note d'hôtel.**
3. **Continuons** (our) **étude des numéros.**
4. (Their) **valises sont très lourdes.**
5. **M. Brown est un de** (his) **amis.**
6. **Où sont** (your) **bagages, monsieur?**
7. **Achetez-vous une paire de gants pour** (your) **femme?**
8. (His) **professeur est M. Picard.**
9. (His) **femme joue du piano.**
10. (Their) **enfants vont à l'école.**
11. **Nous sommes six dans** (our) **famille.**
12. **Qui est** (her) **professeur?**
13. **Aimes-tu** (your) **maître,** (my) **enfant?**
14. **Où est** (his) **bureau?**
15. **Je ne connais pas** (their) **professeur.**

Exercise No. 66

Write out in French the numbers in the following table. Then read the table aloud.

Exemples: Dix kilos équivalent (ay-kee-val) **à 22 (vingt-deux) livres. Seize kilomètres équivalent à dix milles.**

10 kilos = 22 livres	16 kilomètres = 10 milles
20 kilos = 44 livres	32 kilomètres = 20 milles
30 kilos = 66 livres	48 kilomètres = 30 milles
40 kilos = 88 livres	64 kilomètres = 40 milles
50 kilos = 110 livres	80 kilomètres = 50 milles
100 kilos = 220 livres	160 kilomètres = 100 milles

Exercise No. 67—Questionnaire

1. Où est-ce que vous dînez?
2. Combien est l'addition pour tout le monde?
3. Qu'est-ce que vous laissez comme pourboire dans un bon restaurant?
4. Où portez-vous une valise très lourde?
5. Combien de kilos pèse-t-elle? Combien de livres pèse-t-elle?
6. Comment est-ce qu'on compte les distances en France, en milles ou en kilomètres?
7. Qui sait changer les kilomètres en milles?
8. Combien de paires de chaussures est-ce que M. Brown achète dans une boutique?
9. Quel est le sujet de la prochaine conversation?
10. De quel proverbe M. Brown fait-il usage?

CHAPITRE 14 (QUATORZE)

QUELLE HEURE EST-IL?

WHAT TIME IS IT?

PREMIER DIALOGUE

1. —L'heure! Tout le monde veut savoir: Quelle heure est-il? À quelle heure est-ce que l'avion arrive? À quelle heure est-ce que le train part? À quelle heure est-ce que les examens commencent? À quelle heure est-ce que le film commence? À quelle heure est-ce que la séance commence? et des milliers d'autres questions.

2. M. Brown, je vais jouer le rôle de l'employé de guichet à la gare. Vous allez jouer le rôle d'un voyageur qui désire acheter un billet et qui demande des renseignements. Commençons.

3. —Bonjour, monsieur. Un billet pour Chartres, s'il vous plaît.

4. —Oui, monsieur. Première ou deuxième classe?

5. —Première classe, s'il vous plaît. C'est combien?

6. —Onze euro pour un billet d'aller.

7. —Donnez-moi un billet d'aller et retour, s'il vous plaît. Je désire partir lundi.

8. —Voici votre billet. Ça fait vingt-deux euros.

9. —Merci, monsieur. À quelle heure est-ce que le train part et à quelle heure est-ce qu'il arrive à Chartres?

1. The time! Everyone wants to know: "What time is it? At what time does the plane arrive? At what time does the train leave? At what time do the examinations begin? At what time does the film begin? At what time does the performance begin?" And thousands of other questions.

2. Mr. Brown, I am going to play the role of the ticket agent at the railroad station. You are going to play the role of a traveler who wants to buy a ticket and is asking for information. Let us begin.

3. Good day, sir. One ticket to Chartres, please.

4. Yes, sir. First or second class?

5. First class, please. It's how much?

6. For a one-way ticket, 11 euros.

7. Please give me a round-trip ticket. I wish to leave on Monday.

8. Here is your ticket. That makes 22 euros.

9. Thank you, sir. At what time does the train leave, and at what time does it arrive at Chartres?

10. —Il y a plusieurs trains par jour pour Chartres. Vous avez un bon train à quinze heures quarante-cinq, qui arrive à seize heures cinquante-cinq.	10. There are several trains a day for Chartres. You have a good train at 15:45 (a quarter to four), which arrives at 16:55 (five minutes to five).
11. —Merci beaucoup, monsieur.	11. Thank you very much, sir.
12. —À votre service, monsieur.	12. At your service, sir.
13. —Excellent, M. Brown. Vous jouez votre rôle à merveille.	13. Excellent, Mr. Brown. You play your part wonderfully.

NOTE: The French often use the 24-hour clock for official times and schedules. Thus, **quatre heures moins le quart** would be reported as **quinze heures quarante-cinq** to assure the greatest accuracy. See explanation after Grammar Notes.

DEUXIÈME DIALOGUE

1. —Maintenant, je joue le rôle d'un employé au cinéma. Vous demandez des renseignements sur les séances. Voulez-vous commencer, s'il vous plaît?	1. Now I am playing the role of the ticket seller at the movies. You are asking for information about the performances. Will you begin, please?
2. —Dites-moi, s'il vous plaît, quelles sont les heures des séances?	2. Please tell me, when are the showtimes?
3. —Il y a trois séances. La première commence à quatre heures vingt de l'après-midi, la deuxième à six heures cinquante, et la troisième à neuf heures dix du soir.	3. There are three showings. The first one begins at 4:20 in the afternoon, the second at 6:50 and the third at 9:10 in the evening.
4. —Y a-t-il des actualités?	4. Is there a newsreel?
5. —Mais oui. Vingt minutes avant le film.	5. Yes indeed. Twenty minutes before the picture.
6. —Quel est le prix des billets?	6. What is the price of the tickets?
7. —Les billets coûtent six euros. Si vous arrivez de bonne heure vous allez avoir de bonnes places.	7. The tickets cost six euros. If you come early you will get good seats.
8. —Donnez-moi deux billets pour la troisième séance, s'il vous plaît.	8. Give me two tickets for the third showing, please.
9. —Les voici. Merci bien.	9. Here they are. Thank you very much.
10. —Admirable. Je répète: vous jouez votre rôle à merveille.	10. Admirable. I repeat: you play your part wonderfully.

Pronunciation and Spelling Aids

Practice aloud:

1. **L'heure! Tout le monde veut savoir: Quelle heure est-il?**
2. **Vous demandez des renseignements sur les séances.**
3. **des milliers d'autres questions.**

1. (**Leur!** Too luh mawñd veu sa-**vwar,** kehl leur eht-**teel?**)
2. (Voo duhmahñ-day day rahñ-sehn-yuh-mahñ sür lay say-**ahñs**)
3. (day mee-lyay dohtr kehs-**tyawñ**)

Remember: **ll** (double L) after the letter **i** is usually pronounced like *y*:

fille (feey)   **billet** (bee-**yay**)   **merveille** (mehr-**vehy**)   **Marseille** (mar-**sehy**)

Important exceptions:

1. **ll** is pronounced like *ly* in **million** (mee-**lyawñ**), **milliers** (mee-**lyay**)
2. **ll** is pronounced like *l* in **mille** (meel), **ville** (veel), **tranquille** (trahñ-**keel**)

Building Vocabulary

A. EXPRESSIONS OF APPROVAL AND PRAISE

1. **admirable** (ad-mee-**rabl**) splendid
2. **excellent** (ehk-seh-**lahñ**) excellent
3. **très bien** (treh **byañ**) very good
4. **c'est ça** (seh **sa**) right, that's right
5. **correct(e)** (ku-**rehkt**) correct
6. **parfait** (par-**feh**) perfect
7. **c'est bien** (seh **bya**) that's good
8. **c'est exact** (seh tayg-**zakt**) that's so
9. **c'est vrai** (seh **vray**) that's true
10. **à merveille** (a mehr-**vehy**) wonderfully

B. RAILROAD TRAVEL TERMS

1. **la gare** the railroad station
2. **À quelle heure est-ce que le train part pour . . . ?** At what time does the train leave for . . . ?
3. **À quelle heure est-ce que le train arrive à (de) . . . ?** At what time does the train arrive at (from) . . . ?
4. **Le train arrive (part) à sept heures du matin.** The train arrives (leaves) at 7 A.M.
5. **un billet de première (deuxième) classe** a first (second) class ticket
6. **un billet d'aller** (*or* **billet simple**) a one-way ticket

7. **un billet d'aller et retour** a round-trip ticket
8. **Quel est le prix de la place?** *or* **Combien coûte la place?** What is the fare?
9. **plusieurs trains par jour** several trains a day
10. **payer les billets** to pay for the tickets
11. **En voiture!** All aboard!
12. **la salle de bagages** baggage room
13. **un wagon-lit** sleeping car
14. **un wagon-restaurant** dining car

French Expressions

1. **demander des renseignements** to ask for information
2. **jouer le rôle** to play the role
3. **mais oui** (meh **wee**) yes indeed, of course
4. **mais non** of course not
5. **de bonne heure** (duh bu-**neur**) early
6. **les voici** (lay vwa-**see**) here they are
7. **les voilà** there they are

Exercise No. 68—Completion of Text

1. (At what time) **est-ce que le film commence?**
2. (The first showing) **commence à** (4:30 p.m.).
3. **Il y a des milliers** (of other questions).
4. **Où est** (the railroad station)?
5. **Vous êtes un voyageur qui** (asks for information).
6. **Donnez-moi** (a round trip ticket).
7. **À quelle heure** (does the train leave)?
8. (Does it arrive) **à neuf heures du matin?**
9. **Venez** (early) **si vous désirez de bonnes places.**
10. (Here they are).
11. (Many thanks, sir).
12. (At your service), **monsieur.**

Grammar Notes

1. PRESENT TENSE OF partir, *to leave* and sortir, *to go out*

I leave, you leave, etc.

		I go out, you go out, etc.	
je pars (par)	nous partons (par-**tawñ**)	je sors (sur)	nous sortons (sur-**tawñ**)
tu pars (par)	vous partez (par-**tay**)	tu sors (sur)	vous sortez (sur-**tay**)
il part (par)	ils partent (part)	il sort (sur)	ils sortent (surt)
elle part (par)	elles partent (part)	elle sort (sur)	elles sortent (surt)

Imperative			*Imperative*		
pars	partons	partez	sors	sortons	sortez

Other verbs like **partir** and **sortir** are:

servir to serve **je sers, tu sers, il sert, nous servons, vous servez, ils servent;**
sentir to feel, smell **je sens, tu sens, il sent, nous sentons, vous sentez, ils sentent;**
dormir to sleep **je dors, tu dors, il dort, nous dormons, vous dormez, ils dorment.**

Exercise No. 69

Complete these sentences by writing the correct forms of **partir, sortir, dormir, sentir, servir.** Then read the completed sentences aloud:

1. **Le train** (leaves) **à sept heures.**
2. **À quelle heure** (do you leave)?
3. (We sleep) **jusqu'à** (*until*) **huit heures.**
4. **Elle** (does not sleep) **bien.**
5. **Madame Brown** (serves) **le café.**
6. (Do you smell) **le parfum?**
7. (I do not smell) **le parfum.**
8. **À quelle heure** (do they go out) **de la maison?**
9. (I go out) **du bureau à cinq heures.**
10. (Do not sleep) **jusqu'à neuf heures.**

2. TIME OF DAY

Quelle heure est-il? What time is it?
Il est midi. It is noon.
Il est une heure. It is 1 o'clock.
Il est deux heures. It is 2 o'clock.
Il est trois heures. It is 3 o'clock.
Il est minuit. It is midnight.
Il est une heure et demie. It is half-past one.

Il est deux heures et quart.
It is a quarter past two.
Il est trois heures moins le quart.
It is a quarter to three.
Il est quatre heures dix (minutes).
It is ten minutes past four.
Il est quatre heures moins dix.
It is ten minutes to four.

NOTE: Variations on expressing time: **et,** *and,* is used for time after the hour; **moins,** *less* or *minus,* is used for time before the hour; the word **minutes** may be omitted, but **heures** is never omitted.

Time expressions after the half hour are based on the hour that follows. Thus:

6:40 Il est sept heures moins vingt. It is twenty minutes to seven. However, as in English, you may say: **six heures quarante** (*six forty*).

France uses the 24-hour clock. In timetables and schedules, and sometimes in conversation, time is indicated by 24 hours beginning with midnight. The hours 24.00 (midnight) through 11.59 are A.M. The hours 12.00 (noon) through 23.59 are P.M. Thus:

24.20 **(vingt-quatre heures vingt)** = 12.20 A.M. **(douze heures vingt du matin)**

12.20 **(douze heures vingt)** = 12.20 P.M. **(douze heures vingt de l'après-midi)**

15.20 **(quinze heures vingt)** = 3.20 P.M. **(trois heures vingt de l'après-midi)**

Usually in conversation the following expressions are used to distinguish A.M. from P.M.:

du matin	**de l'après-midi**	**du soir**
in the morning	in the afternoon	in the evening

Exercise No. 70

Write out the time expressions in words. Then read the sentences aloud giving the time in French.

Exemple: 1. Le train de Lyon arrive à sept heures et demie du soir.

1. **Le train de Lyon arrive à** (7.30 P.M.)
2. **Le train arrive à Paris à** (10.15 P.M.)
3. **Le train pour Marseille part à** (6.30 A.M.)
4. **Le train pour Rouen part à** (noon.)
5. **La première séance commence à** (4.30 P.M.)
6. **La deuxième séance commence à** (6.40 P.M.)

7. La troisième séance commence à (9 P.M.)
8. Les actualités commencent à (4.10 P.M.)
9. M. Brown prend le train en ville à (7.45 A.M.) précises.
10. Il arrive en ville à (8.40 A.M.)

Exercise No. 71—Questionnaire

1. Qu'est-ce que tout le monde veut savoir?
2. Qui joue le rôle du voyageur?
3. Qui joue le rôle de l'employé du guichet?
4. Quelle classe de billet est-ce que M. Brown désire?
5. Combien coûte un billet d'aller et retour?
6. Qui joue le rôle de l'employé au cinéma?
7. Qui demande des renseignements?
8. Combien de séances y a-t-il à ce ciné (cinéma)?
9. Pour quelle séance est-ce que M. Brown achète deux billets?
10. Combien paie-t-il pour ces billets?

RÉVISION 3, CHAPITRES 10–14

Première Partie

Révision de Mots

NOUNS

1. l'acheteur, -euse (*f*)	1. buyer
2. l'addition	2. bill, "check" (restaurant)
3. l'argent	3. money, silver
4. les bagages	4. baggage
5. le billet	5. ticket
6. la boutique	6. shop
7. la chaussure	7. shoe
8. le chemin de fer	8. railroad
9. le couteau	9. knife
10. la cuiller	10. spoon
11. l'échantillon	11. sample
12. l'employé, -e (*f*)	12. employee
13. la fleur	13. flower
14. une fois	14. one time, once
15. la fourchette	15. fork
16. le gant	16. glove
17. la gare	17. station
18. le gâteau	18. cake
19. le guichet	19. ticket window
20. l'heure	20. hour, time
21. la livre	21. pound
22. le magasin	22. store
23. le maître, la maîtresse	23. teacher, master; mistress (in elementary school)
24. le marché	24. market
25. la note	25. bill (hotel)
26. le pays	26. country (nation)
27. le plat	27. dish
28. la poche	28. pocket

29. le pot à lait	29. milk pitcher
30. le porte-monnaie	30. purse
31. le prix	31. price, prize
32. la radio	32. radio
33. le repas	33. meal
34. la séance	34. performance, showing
35. la soucoupe	35. saucer
36. le style	36. style
37. le sujet	37. subject
38. la tarte	38. tart, pie
39. la tasse	39. cup
40. le verre	40. glass
41. le vendeur	41. seller
42. le voyageur, la voyageuse	42. traveler

VERBS

1. acheter	1. to buy
2. avancer	2. to progress
3. changer	3. to change
4. continuer	4. to continue
5. dîner	5. to dine
6. donner	6. to give
7. laisser	7. to let
8. manger	8. to eat
9. payer	9. to pay for
10. penser (à)	10. to think (of)
11. peser	11. to weigh
12. porter	12. to carry, wear
13. téléphoner	13. to telephone
14. trouver	14. to find (locate), have opinion about
15. connaître	15. to know
16. nous connaissons	16. we know
17. croire	17. to believe
18. perdre	18. to lose
19. rendre	19. to give back
20. faire	20. to make, to do
21. je fais	21. I make, I do
22. dire	22. to say
23. nous disons	23. we say
24. dormir	24. to sleep
25. partir	25. to leave
26. je pars	26. I leave

27.	sentir	27.	to feel
28.	sortir (de)	28.	to go out (of)
29.	venir	29.	to come
30.	je viens	30.	I come
31.	pouvoir	31.	to be able
32.	je peux	32.	I can
33.	recevoir	33.	to receive
34.	je reçois	34.	I receive
35.	savoir	35.	to know (how)
36.	je sais	36.	I know (how)
37.	valoir	37.	to be worth
38.	il vaut	38.	it is worth
39.	vouloir	39.	to want
40.	je veux	40.	I want

ADJECTIVES

1.	célèbre	1.	famous
2.	chaque	2.	each
3.	charmant	3.	charming
4.	connu	4.	known
5.	délicieux	5.	delicious
6.	délicieuse (f)	6.	delicious (f)
7.	gai	7.	gay, bright
8.	lourd	8.	heavy
9.	ordinaire	9.	ordinary
10.	parfait	10.	perfect
11.	plusieurs	11.	several
12.	précis	12.	exact
13.	premier	13.	first
14.	première (f)	14.	first (f)
15.	vrai	15.	true

ADVERBS

1.	à peu près	1.	about, nearly
2.	comme	2.	as, like, how
3.	correctement	3.	correctly
4.	d'ordinaire	4.	generally, usually
5.	encore	5.	again
6.	encore un	6.	one more
7.	maintenant	7.	now
8.	moins	8.	less
9.	naturellement	9.	naturally

10. presque	10. almost
11. surtout	11. especially
12. tout de suite	12. at once

PREPOSITIONS

1. avant	1. before
2. après	2. after
3. devant	3. in front of
4. derrière	4. behind
5. pour	5. for, in order to
6. vers	6. towards, about (approx.)

French Expressions

1. j'ai besoin de	1. I need
2. j'ai raison	2. I am right
3. vous avez tort	3. you are wrong
4. c'est ça	4. that's correct
5. c'est vrai	5. that's true
6. c'est à dire	6. that is (to say)
7. changer de l'argent	7. to change money
8. Combien de fois?	8. How many times?
9. Je crois que oui	9. I think so
10. Je crois que non	10. I think not
11. en tout cas	11. in any case
12. en effet	12. actually
13. en monnaie	13. in change
14. entendu	14. agreed, understood
15. il faut	15. it is necessary
16. faire des achats	16. to go shopping
17. faire peser	17. to have weighed
18. mais oui (non)	18. indeed yes (no)
19. payer ses repas	19. to pay for one's meals
20. comme pourboire	20. as a tip
21. merci bien	21. many thanks
22. rien de plus facile	22. nothing easier
23. tout le monde	23. everybody
24. Que veut dire . . . ?	24. What does . . . mean?
25. il veut dire . . .	25. it means . . .
26. les voici	26. here they are
27. il n'y a pas de quoi *ou*	27. you're welcome, *or*
28. de rien	28. don't mention it

Deuxième Partie

Exercise No. 72

Select the group of words in Column II which best completes each sentence begun in Column I.

Exemple: 1-f Cette région en France est connue pour ses produits céramiques.

I	II
1. Cette région en France est connue	a. tout de suite au commerce?
2. De quelle région sont	b. que jamais.
3. Est-ce que le commerçant pense	c. dans les grands magasins.
4. Vous savez que l'usage	d. le système monétaire de la France.
5. Mieux vaut tard	e. d'aller et retour.
6. Le voyageur a besoin d'argent	f. pour ses produits céramiques.
7. Nous faisons des achats	g. à quatre heures de l'après-midi.
8. Ils ne connaissent pas	h. ces tasses et ces soucoupes?
9. Donnez-moi un billet	i. pour acheter des billets.
10. La première séance commence	j. rend maître.

Exercise No. 73

Complete these sentences by choosing the most logical expression from those listed in the column on the right. Be sure to use the correct form of the verb.

Exemple: 1. La touriste demande des renseignements.

1. **La touriste** (asks for information).	demander des renseignements
2. (We need) **un porte-monnaie.**	avoir raison / avoir tort
3. **M. Brown** (knows his trade).	avoir faim
4. **Ils veulent** (to change some money).	avoir besoin de
5. **À quoi** (are you thinking)? (Use **tu**)	payer nos repas
6. (Do you like) **bien ce portrait?**	connaître son métier
7. **Je mange quand** (I am hungry).	penser à
8. **Que** (do you mean)?	changer de l'argent
9. (We pay for our meals) **en euro.**	aimer bien
10. (You are right), **M. Brown.**	vouloir dire
11. **J'ai raison, mais** (you are wrong). (Use **tu**)	
12. **De quoi** (do you need)?	

Exercise No. 74

For each word in Group I, select an antonym from Group II:

I	II
1. arriver	a. moins
2. donner	b. acheter
3. plus	c. partir
4. devant	d. derrière
5. trouver	e. enseigner
6. parler	f. l'acheteur
7. vendre	g. perdre
8. apprendre	h. recevoir
9. avant	i. peu de
10. le vendeur	j. j'ai tort
11. beaucoup de	k. écouter
12. j'ai raison	l. après

Exercise No. 75

Answer these questions in the affirmative. Use complete sentences, and use the pronoun **je** in your answers.

Exemple: 1. Oui, monsieur, je pense à mon ami.

1. Pensez-vous à votre ami?
2. Est-ce que vous voulez faire un voyage en France?
3. Pouvez-vous acheter une automobile?
4. Portez-vous les bagages à la gare?
5. Vous partez demain de la ville?
6. Comptez-vous toujours la monnaie?
7. Est-ce que vous dites les nouveaux mots deux fois?
8. Connaissez-vous cet homme-là?
9. Donnez-vous un pourboire au garçon?
10. Savez-vous compter en français?

Exercise No. 76

Answer these questions in complete sentences, this time using the *negative*. Use **nous** in your answers.

Exemple: 1. Non, madame, nous ne posons pas beaucoup de questions.

1. Posez-vous beaucoup de questions?
2. Calculez-vous rapidement en français?
3. Est-ce que vous trouvez cette revue intéressante?
4. Lisez-vous les journaux français?
5. Écrivez-vous bien en français?
6. Dînez-vous au restaurant?
7. Connaissez-vous la ville de Biot?
8. Vous achetez beaucoup de parfum?
9. Avez-vous besoin d'une valise?
10. Savez-vous l'adresse de M. Picard?

DIALOGUE

Une touriste prend des renseignements sur la poterie française

1. —Dites-moi, s'il vous plaît, madame, dans quelles régions de la France peut-on trouver de jolies poteries? Je désire acheter un service à thé: tasses, soucoupes, et assiettes.
2. —Eh bien, chaque région a son style individuel: Limoges, la Bretagne, et la Provence sont toutes connues pour leurs produits céramiques.
3. —Est-ce qu'il faut aller dans ces régions pour trouver de la poterie régionale?
4. —Pas du tout. Vous pouvez acheter de la poterie de toutes les régions ici même à Paris.
5. —Est-ce que ça coûte plus cher ici?
6. —Naturellement, ça coûte plus cher dans une grande ville. Mais vous avez un assortiment bien choisi.
7. —Voulez-vous bien me dire où est-ce qu'on peut acheter de la poterie à Paris?
8. Vous allez trouver le meilleur assortiment dans les grands magasins—aux Galeries Lafayette, au Printemps—et dans les boutiques dans la rue du Paradis.
9. —Merci infiniment, madame.
10. —De rien, mademoiselle.

1. Please tell me, ma'am, in what regions of France can one find beautiful pottery? I want to buy a tea service: cups, saucers, and plates.
2. Well, each region has its own individual style: Limoges, Brittany, and Provence are all well known for their ceramic products.
3. Does one have to go to these regions to find regional pottery?
4. Not at all. You can buy pottery from all regions right here in Paris.
5. Does it cost more here?
6. Of course it costs more in a big city. But you have a well-chosen selection.
7. Will you tell me, please, where one can buy pottery in Paris?
8. You will find the best assortment in the department stores—Galeries Lafayette, Printemps—and in the shops on the rue du Paradis.
9. Thank you so much, ma'am.
10. Don't mention it, miss.

Exercise No. 77—Lecture (Reading)

Read silently, aloud, and try to understand without translating word for word.

LA FAMILLE BROWN FAIT UNE PETITE VISITE À MAMAN.

C'est la première fois que la famille Brown va voir Madame Brown à son bureau. Monsieur Brown a un jour de congé aujourd'hui, il profite de cette occasion pour aller se promener avec les enfants et rendre visite à sa femme à l'université. Monsieur Brown et ses quatre enfants entrent dans un édifice assez impressionant et ils montent par ascenseur au quinzième étage où se trouve le bureau de Madame Brown. Anne, la plus jeune, qui a seulement cinq ans, est très curieuse. Elle pose beaucoup de questions à son père au sujet des étudiants qu'elle voit passer dans les corridors.

Quand ils arrivent au bureau, la mère se lève et dit—Quelle bonne surprise! Que je suis contente de vous voir!

Les enfants admirent tous les objets qu'ils voient dans le bureau: l'ordinateur, les rayons de livres, et aux murs, les diplômes et certificats, une jolie carte mondiale, et surtout les posters. Tout le monde est très content.

Charles, l'aîné, regarde par la grande fenêtre, et il voit le ciel bleu et le soleil qui brille. Sa soeur Anne et lui regardent en bas les automobiles qui passent dans la rue. Du quinzième étage elles paraissent toutes petites.

La visite terminée, toute la famille entre dans un petit restaurant tout près de l'université, car Madame Brown doit être de retour dans une heure pour une autre classe. Ils mangent tous de bon appétit, surtout les enfants, parce qu'ils ont bien faim.

NOTE: se lever, *to get (oneself) up, to stand up:* **je me lève, elle se lève.** Reflexive verbs will be discussed more fully in Chapter 33.

CHAPITRE 15 (QUINZE)

LE CINÉMA

THE MOVIES

1. —M. Brown, vous savez déjà demander des renseignements sur les séances des cinémas. Mais dites-moi, êtes-vous amateur de ciné?
2. —J'aime voir un bon film quelquefois, mais pour la plupart, les films ne m'intéressent pas.
3. —Alors vous préférez le théâtre?
4. —Mais oui. Ma femme et moi nous le préférons. Nous y[1] allons souvent voir une bonne pièce ou une opérette.
5. —Et vos enfants? Est-ce qu'ils préfèrent le théâtre?
6. —Pas du tout! Ils adorent les films policiers qui nous[2] ennuient à mourir.
7. —Est-ce qu'ils connaissent toutes les vedettes de l'écran?
8. —Naturellement. Ils les connaissent bien. Ils connaissent aussi les vedettes de la télévision.
9. — Vous habitez une petite ville dans les environs de New York. Y a-t-il un ciné près de chez vous?
10. —Oui, monsieur, pas loin. Nous y allons à pied dans un quart d'heure à peu près.
11. —Quelles places préférez-vous, les places des premiers rangs, ou les places au fond de la salle?

1. Mr. Brown, you already know how to ask for information about the showtimes of the movies. But tell me, are you a movie fan?
2. Well, I like to see a good picture sometimes, but for the most part films do not interest me.
3. Then you prefer the theater?
4. Oh yes. My wife and I prefer it. We go there[1] often to see a good play or a musical comedy.
5. And your children? Do they prefer the theater?
6. Not at all! They love detective movies that bore us[2] to death.
7. Do they know all the stars of the screen?
8. Of course. They know them well. They also are familiar with the stars of television.
9. You live in a small town on the outskirts of New York. Is there a movie theater near your house?
10. Yes, sir, not far away. We walk there (go on foot) in about fifteen minutes.
11. Which seats do you prefer, the seats in the first rows or the seats at the back of the hall?

12. —Nous préférons les places du quatorzième ou du quinzième rang. De là, on peut bien voir et entendre. De là, la lumière et les mouvements sur l'écran ne font pas mal aux yeux.

13. —Que faites-vous si la plupart des places sont occupées?

14. —Alors, dans ce cas, nous prenons n'importe quelles places libres, devant, au fond, aux côtés. Mais nous n'aimons pas ces places. Donc nous esssayons toujours d'arriver de bonne heure.

15. —Voilà, M. Brown, une autre conversation formidable! Vous avancez très rapidement.

16. —Grâce à vous, M. Picard.

12. We prefer the seats in the fourteenth or fifteenth row. From there, one can see and hear well. From there, the light and the movements on the screen do not hurt the eyes.

13. What do you do if most of the seats are occupied?

14. In that case we take any vacant seats whatsoever, in front, in back, or at the side. But we do not like those seats. Therefore we try always to come early.

15. There you go, another terrific conversation, Mr. Brown! You are progressing very quickly.

16. Thanks to you, Mr. Picard.

NOTES: ¹ **y** = *there*. It usually precedes the verb. ² **nous,** *us*, and **les,** *them*, are object pronouns. They also usually precede the verb.

Pronunciation and Spelling Aids

Practice aloud:

1. **Vous savez demander des renseignements sur les séances des cinémas.**

1. (Voo sa-vay duh-mahñ-day day rahñ-seh-nyuh-**mahñ** sür lay sayahñs day see-nay-**ma**)

2. **Êtes-vous amateur du ciné?**

2. (Eht-voo za-ma-teur dü see-**nay?**)

3. **Ils adorent les films policiers et les opérettes.**

3. (Eel za-dur lay feelm pu-lee-**syay** ay lay zu-pay-**reht**)

Remember **â** = ah, **ô** = oh, **ê** = eh. Thus: **rôle** (rohl) **grâce** (grahs) **êtes-vous** (eht-**voo**)

Building Vocabulary

Words Dealing with the Movies

1. **le cinéma** (see-nay-**ma**) movies, movie theater
2. **le ciné** (short for **cinéma**)
3. **le film** (feelm) film
4. **la séance** (say-**ahñs**) showing, showtime
5. **l'écran** (lay-**krahñ**) screen

6. **la vedette** (vuh-**deht**) movie star
7. **la pièce** (pyehs) play
8. **les actualités** (lay zak-tü-a-lee-**tay**) newsreel
9. **le rôle** (rohl) role
10. **le rang** (rahñ) row
11. **la place** (plas) seat

French Expressions

1. **pour la plupart** for the most part
2. **Ils nous ennuient à mourir.** They bore us to death.
3. **près de chez vous** near your home
4. **à pied** (a **pyay**) on foot
5. **faire mal aux yeux** (oh-**zyeu**) to hurt the eyes
6. **la plupart des places** most of the seats
7. **N'importe** (nañ-**purt**) It doesn't matter.
8. **Grâce à vous.** Thanks to you.
9. **Je vous remercie.** I thank you.

Exercise No. 78—Completion of Text

1. (I like very much to see) **un bon film.**
2. **Les films** (do not interest me).
3. (They adore) **les films policiers.**
4. **Connaissent-ils** (all the screen stars)?
5. (They know them) **bien.**
6. **Y a-t-il un ciné** (near your home)?
7. **Nous y allons** (on foot).
8. (We prefer) **les places des premiers rangs.**
9. (Therefore) **nous arrivons** (early).

Grammar Notes

1. **PRESENT TENSE OF venir,** *to come*

I come, I am coming, you come, you are coming, etc.

je viens (vyañ)	**nous venons** (vuh-**nawñ**)
tu viens (vyañ)	**vous venez** (vuh-**nay**)
il, elle vient (vyañ)	**ils, elles viennent** (vyehn)

Imperative: **viens**, come   **venons**, let's come   **venez**, come
Like **venir**: **revenir**, *to come back*   **devenir**, *to become*

Exercise No. 79

Translate each verb into French. Read each sentence aloud.

1. (I am coming) **aujourd'hui.**
2. (They do not come) **de bonne heure.**
3. **Qui** (is coming) **avec vous?**
4. **Les petits garçons** (come) **avec leurs pères.**
5. (Come) **ici, mes enfants.**
6. (Are you coming) **à sept heures?**
7. (We are coming back) **de bonne heure ce soir.**
8. **Quand** (is he coming back)?
9. (She is not coming) **ici ce matin.**
10. **M. Martin, à quelle heure** (are you coming)?
11. **Que voulez-vous** (to become)?
12. (I want to become) **professeur.**

2. DIRECT OBJECT PRONOUNS

Study the following sentences. They illustrate the direct object pronouns. You are already familiar with most of them.

1. **M. Picard *me* connaît.**
2. **Il *te* connaît aussi, Anne.**
3. **Qui *vous* apprend à parler français?**
4. **M. Picard *nous* apprend à parler français.**
5. **Qui salue M. Picard? M. Brown *le* salue.**
6. **Connaissez-vous Mlle Picard? Je ne *la* connais pas.**
7. **Avez-vous le journal français? Nous ne *l'*avons pas.**
8. **Connaissent-ils les vedettes de l'écran? Oui, ils *les* connaissent bien.**

1. Mr. Picard knows me.
2. He knows you also, Anne.
3. Who is teaching *you* to speak French?
4. Mr. Picard is teaching *us* to speak French.
5. Who greets Mr. Picard? Mr. Brown greets *him*.
6. Do you know Miss Picard? I do not know *her*.
7. Do you have the French newspaper? We do not have *it*.
8. Do they know the screen stars? Yes, they know *them* well.

The direct object pronouns are:

me (m') me	**nous** us	**le (l')** him, it	**les** them
te (t') you (fam.)	**vous** you	**la (l')** her, it	

me and **te** become **m'** and **t'**, and **le** and **la** become **l'**, when they precede a verb beginning with a vowel or **h** (mute).

Object pronouns precede the verb *except* in the affirmative imperative when they follow the verb and are joined to it by a hyphen. In the negative imperative the object pronouns precede the verb:

Prenez la fleur. Prenez-la.
Take the flower. Take it.

Ne prenez pas la fleur. Ne la prenez pas.
Do not take the flower. Do not take it.

me when used after the verb in the affirmative imperative becomes **moi.**

Dites-moi. Écoutez-moi. Tell *me.* Listen to *me.*

3. THE USE of **y,** *there*

The word **y,** *there,* is used to indicate a place already mentioned. Like the object pronouns it always precedes the verb, except in the affirmative imperative.

Quand est-ce que M. Brown va en France?	When is Mr. Brown going to France?
Il *y* va au printemps.	He is going *there* in the spring.
Allons-*y* avec lui.	Let's go *there* with him.

Exercise No. 80

Read each question. Write each answer filling in the correct object pronoun in French. Finally, read the questions and complete answers aloud.

1. Achetez-vous les billets?	1. Oui, je (them) achète.
2. Connaissez-vous cette rue?	2. Non, nous ne (it) connaissons pas.
3. Est-ce que Jeanne attend son ami, Louis?	3. Oui, elle (him) attend dans le salon.
4. Les enfants adorent-ils les vedettes de l'écran?	4. Certainement! Ils (them) adorent.
5. Préfèrent-ils le premier rang?	5. Non, ils ne (it) préfèrent pas.
6. Comment trouvez-vous cette tasse?	6. Je (it) trouve charmante.
7. Allez-vous visiter M. Brown?	7. Nous allons (him) visiter ce soir.
8. Est-ce que le professeur m'attend?	8. Bien sûr, il (you) attend.
9. Qui vous attend au ciné?	9. Notre ami (us) attend.
10. Qui vous apprend à parler français?	10. M. Picard (us) apprend à parler français.
11. Vont-ils au ciné à pied ou en autobus?	11. Ils (there) vont en autobus.
12. Demeure-t-il dans cette maison-là?	12. Oui, il (there) demeure.
13. Quand allez-vous nous aider?	13. Nous allons (you) aider demain.
14. Est-ce que les films vous intéressent?	14. Non, ils ne (me) intéressent pas.
15. Est-ce que tu m'aimes, maman?	15. Je (you) aime beaucoup, mon enfant.

Exercise No. 81—Questionnaire

1. Qui sait demander des renseignements?
2. Qu'est-ce que M. et Mme Brown préfèrent, le théâtre ou le cinéma?
3. Qu'est-ce que les enfants préfèrent?
4. Est-ce que les enfants connaissent les vedettes de l'écran?
5. Le ciné est-il près de la maison de M. Brown ou loin de sa maison?
6. Quelles places préfèrent-ils au ciné?
7. Est-il possible de bien voir et entendre de là?
8. Est-ce qu'ils arrivent de bonne heure ou en retard (late)?

CHAPITRE 16 (SEIZE)

QUELQUES DATES DE L'HISTOIRE MODERNE DE FRANCE

SOME DATES IN MODERN FRENCH HISTORY

1. —M. Brown, vous connaissez bien les nombres. Je vois que vous savez les employer correctement et rapidement. Voyons si vous connaissez les nombres en forme de dates.

2. —Avec plaisir, M. Picard. J'aime bien les examens en français.

3. —C'est pourquoi vous apprenez vite. Je vais citer quelques dates de l'histoire de France et vous allez citer un événement important pour chacune.

4. —Bon. Commençons.

5. —Le quatorze juillet, 1789. (mil sept cent quatre-vingt-neuf)

6. —Que vous êtes gentil! C'est facile: la prise de la Bastille au début de la Révolution française.

7. —Très bien. Ensuite: 1815. (mil huit cent quinze)

8. —C'est sans aucun doute Napoléon. Voyons. C'est la bataille de Waterloo, n'est-ce pas?

9. —Correct. 1870. (mil huit cent soixante-dix)

10. —Ah, c'est une date triste pour la France: la défaite de l'armée dans la guerre franco-prussien.

11. —Voici une date victorieuse: 1918. (mil neuf cent dix-huit.)

12. —La victoire del Alliés à la fin de la première guerre mondiale.

1. Mr. Brown, you know the numbers well. I see that you know how to use them correctly and rapidly. Let us see if you know the numbers in the form of dates.

2. With pleasure, Mr. Picard. I like tests in French.

3. That's why you learn quickly. I am going to mention some dates in the history of France and you will name an important event for each one.

4. Good. Let's begin.

5. July 14, 1789.

6. How kind you are! That's easy: the capture of the Bastille at the beginning of the French Revolution.

7. Very good. Next: 1815.

8. That's Napoleon, no doubt. Let's see. It's the battle of Waterloo, isn't it?

9. Correct. 1870.

10. Ah, that's a sad date for France: the defeat of the army in the Franco-Prussian war.

11. Here is a victorious date: 1918.

12. The victory of the Allies at the end of World War I.

NOTE: **Mille,** *thousand,* is shortened to **mil** in dates.

13. —Finissons l'examen. Encore une date, la dernière: 1944. (mil neuf cent quarante-quatre.)
14. —C'est une date glorieuse pour les Parisiens: la libération de Paris à la fin de l'occupation Nazi.
15. —Merveilleux, M. Brown. Je vois que vous connaissez très bien l'histoire de France
16. —Mais, M. Picard, je n'ai pas passé seize ans en classe pour rien. D'ailleurs, j'ai une femme qui est professeur d'histoire et qui parle un peu français, et un professeur qui m'apprend à aimer la France.
17. —C'est vous maintenant qui êtes trop aimable.
18. — Pas du tout. C'est la vérité.

13. Let's finish the test. One more date, the last: 1944.
14. That is a glorious date for Parisians: the liberation of Paris at the end of the Nazi occupation.
15. Marvellous, Mr. Brown. I see that you know the history of France very well.
16. Well, Mr. Picard, I didn't spend sixteen years in school for nothing. Besides, I have a wife who is a history professor and who speaks French a little and a teacher who teaches me to love France.
17. Now it is you who flatter me.
18. Not at all. It's the truth.

Pronunciation and Spelling Aids

Practice aloud:

1. Voyons si vous connaissez les nombres en forme de dates.
2. Avec plaisir, Monsieur Picard.
3. J'aime bien les questionnaires en français.

1. (Vwa-yawñ see voo ku-neh-say lay nawñ-br ahñ furm duh **dat**)
2. (A-vehk pleh-**zeer**, muh-syeu pee-**kar**)
3. (Zhehm byañ lay kehs-tyu-nehr ahñ frahñ-seh)

This poster depicts a French soldier during World War I.

Vocabulary Building

A. LES MOIS DE L'ANNÉE (lay mwah duh la-nay)—THE MONTHS OF THE YEAR

janvier (zhañ-**vyay**) January	**juillet** (zhüee-**yeh**) July
février (fay-vree-**ay**) February	**août** (oo) August
mars (mars) March	**septembre** (sehp-**tahñbr**) September
avril (a-**vreel**) April	**octobre** (uk-**tubr**) October
mai (meh) May	**novembre** (nu-**vahñbr**) November
juin (zhwañ) June	**décembre** (day-**sahñbr**) December

B. L'AN, L'ANNÉE, LE JOUR, LA JOURNÉE

L'année and **la journée** are used instead of **l'an** and **le jour** when one emphasizes the duration of time or one has in mind the events that take place during the year or during a day. **L'an et le jour** by contrast are used when one is emphasizing these periods of time as units or as a more exact amount of time. Observe the differences:

J'étudie toute la journée (toute l'année).	I study all day (all year) long.
But: **Je vais rester trois jours à Paris.**	I am going to stay in Paris for three days.
M. Brown a trente-cinq ans.	Mr. Brown is 35 years old.

Exercise No. 82—Completion of Text

1. (You know how) **employer correctement les nombres.**
2. **Vous allez citer** (an important event).
3. Let's begin.
4. (How) **vous êtes gentil!**
5. **L'an 1870 est** (a sad date) **pour la France.**
6. **Voici** (a victorious date).
7. (Let us finish) **le questionnaire.**
8. **Vous connaissez l'histoire de France** (as well as) **son système monétaire.**
9. (Besides), **j'ai un bon professeur.**
10. (He teaches me) **à aimer la France.**
11. (It is you) **qui êtes trop aimable.**
12. (Not at all.) **C'est la vérité.**

French Expressions

1. **Comme vous-êtes gentil!** How nice you are!
2. **sans doute** (sahñ doot) without doubt
3. **en classe** (ahñ klahs) in school, in class
4. **Il m'apprend à aimer la France.** He teaches me to love France. **Apprendre** may mean either *to learn* or *to teach.*

Grammar Notes

1. PRESENT TENSE OF finir *to finish*—REGULAR -ir VERB (also known as the second conjugation)

I finish, you finish, etc.

je finis (fee-**nee**)	**nous finissons** (fee-nee-**sawñ**)
tu finis (fee-**nee**)	**vous finissez** (fee-nee-**say**)
il, elle finit (fee-**nee**)	**ils, elles finissent** (fe-**nees**)

Imperative: **finis** finish, **finissons** let us finish, **finissez** finish

Interrogative: **Finit-il?** Does he finish?

Negative: **Il ne finit pas.** He does not finish.

Negative Interrogative: **Ne finit-il pas?** Is he not finishing?

2. SOME COMMON REGULAR -ir VERBS CONJUGATED LIKE finir

bâtir	to build	je bâtis	tu bâtis	il bâtit	nous bâtissons, etc.
choisir	to choose	je choisis	tu choisis	il choisit	nous choisissons, etc.
obéir	to obey	j'obéis	tu obéis	il obéit	nous obéissons, etc.
punir	to punish	je punis	tu punis	il punit	nous punissons, etc.
remplir	to fill	je remplis	tu remplis	il remplit	nous remplissons, etc.
rougir	to turn red or to blush	je rougis	tu rougis	il rougit	nous rougissons, etc.
saisir	to seize	je saisis	tu saisis	il saisit	nous saisissons, etc.

Exercise No. 83

Write the correct form of the verbs indicated. Read each completed sentence aloud in French.

1. **À quelle heure** (do you finish) **le dîner?**
2. (We finish) **notre dîner à sept heures.**
3. **Quelle place** (do you choose)?
4. (I choose) **une place dans le premier rang.**
5. **Pourquoi est-ce que le maître** (punishes) **Jacques?**
6. **Parce qu'** (he does not obey).
7. **Les enfants** (are building) **une petite maison.**
8. (Fill) **ma tasse de café, s'il vous plaît.**
9. (They are not finishing) **leurs exercises.**
10. **Elle** (is filling) **son stylo d'encre** (*ink*) **bleue.**
11. (Let us choose) **nos places maintenant.**

3. ORDINAL NUMBERS

1st **premier** (*m*) (pruh-**myay**)
1st **première** (*f*) (pruh-**myehr**)
2nd **deuxième** (deu-**zyehm**)
3rd **troisième** (trwa-**zyehm**)
4th **quatrième** (ka-**tryehm**)
5th **cinquième** (sañ-**kyehm**)
6th **sixième** (see-**zyehm**)
7th **septième** (seh-**tyehm**)
8th **huitième** (üee-**tyehm**)
9th **neuvième** (neu-**vyehm**)
10th **dixième** (dee-**zyehm**)
21st **vingt-et-unième**
last **dernier** (*m*) **dernière** (*f*)

Ordinal numbers are formed by adding **-ième** to the cardinal numbers, with the exception of **premier**, *first*. If the cardinal number has a final **e**, this letter is dropped before adding **-ième** (**quatrième**); **u** is added after **q** (**cinquième**) and a final **f** changes to **v** (**neuvième**). Second (suh-**gawñ**) is used instead of **deuxième** for the *second* of only two.

Exercise No. 84

Complete in French. Then, read your results aloud.

1. **la** (first) **leçon**
2. **la** (third) **place**
3. **le** (fourteenth) **chapitre**
4. **la** (fifth) **semaine**
5. **le** (twelfth) **jour**
6. **le** (first) **mois**
7. **la** (last) **classe**
8. **la** (ninth) **rue**
9. **les** (last) **rangs**

4. DATES

a. **Quel jour du mois sommes-nous aujourd'hui?** *or* **Quel jour du mois est-ce aujourd'hui?**

What is today's date?

C'est aujourd'hui le vingt mai.

Today is May 20.

b. le 1ᵉʳ (premier) janvier 2005 (deux mil cinq) January 1, 2005

le 2 (deux) juin 1990 (dix-neuf cent quatre-vingt-dix) June 2, 1990

le 14 (quartorze) juillet 1789 (mil sept cent quatre-vingt-neuf) July 14, 1789

premier is used for the first day of the month. For the other days the cardinal numbers **deux, trois,** etc., are used.

In dates **mil** is used instead of **mille** for thousand. As in English dates, **dix-neuf cent** (nineteen hundred), etc., may be used instead of **mil neuf cent** (one thousand nine hundred), etc.

Exercise No. 85

Write out the following dates in full. Read each date aloud in French.

Exemple: le 4 juillet 1776

le quatre juillet, mil sept cent (*or* dix-sept cent) soixante-seize

1. le 18 avril 1775
2. le 12 octobre 1492
3. le 22 février 1809
4. le 1ᵉʳ mai 1956

Exercise No. 86—Questionnaire

1. Pourquoi est-ce que M. Brown apprend vite?
2. Qu'est-ce que M. Picard va citer?
3. Qu'est-ce que M. Brown va citer?
4. Quel événement important M. Brown cite-t-il pour 1789?
5. Quel événement important cite-t-il pour 1815?
6. Est-ce que 1870 est une date triste ou une date glorieuse pour la France?
7. Quel événement est-ce que M. Brown cite pour 1918?
8. Est-ce que 1944 est une date glorieuse ou une date triste pour les Parisiens?

CHAPITRE 17 (DIX-SEPT)

QUESTIONS SUR LA GÉOGRAPHIE DE FRANCE

QUESTIONS ABOUT FRENCH GEOGRAPHY

1. —M. Brown, aujourd'hui voyons si vous connaissez la géographie de France aussi bien que son histoire. Vous permettez que je vous pose quelques questions?

2. —Certainement. Est-ce que je vais recevoir un prix si mes réponses sont correctes?

3. —Non, M. Brown. Ce n'est pas une émission de télé. Commençons avec la question la plus facile. La ville de Paris est située sur quel grand fleuve?

4. —C'est vraiment trop facile. Sur la Seine.

5. —Et quel port très important est situé à l'embouchure de la Seine?

6. —C'est Le Havre, grand marché de café, coton, et sucre. La plus grande partie du commerce entre la France et l'Amérique du Nord passe par ce port.

7. —Quel est le fleuve le plus long de France?

8. —Voyons. Est-ce le Rhône?

9. —Non. La Loire est le fleuve le plus long de France. Mais, il n'est pas beaucoup plus long que le Rhône, une centaine de kilomètres plus ou moins.

10. —En tout cas, il est bien plus petit que notre Mississippi.

11. —Oh décidément. Le Mississippi est plus long et plus large que la Loire. Savez-vous quelle est la plus haute montagne de France?

12. —Ça oui, je sais, le Mont Blanc.

---

1. Mr. Brown, today let us see if you know French geography as well as its history. Will you permit me to ask you a few questions?

2. Certainly. Am I going to receive a prize if my answers are correct?

3. No, Mr. Brown. This is not a TV program! Let's begin with the easiest question. The city of Paris is situated on what great river?

4. That is really too easy. On the Seine.

5. And what very important port is situated at the mouth of the Seine?

6. It is Le Havre, an important market for coffee, cotton, and sugar. Most of the trade between France and North America passes through this port.

7. What is the longest river in France?

8. Let's see. Is it the Rhône?

9. No. The Loire is the longest river in France. But it is not very much longer than the Rhône, a hundred kilometers, more or less.

10. In any case, it is much smaller than our Mississippi River.

11. Oh definitely. The Mississippi is longer and wider than the Loire. Do you know which is the highest mountain in France?

12. That I do know: Mont Blanc.

Pronunciation and Spelling Aids

Practice aloud:

1. **Voyons si vous connaissez la géographie de France aussi bien que son histoire.**

   1. Vwa-yawñ see voo ku-neh-say la zhay-u-gra-fee duh **frahñs** oh-see byañ kuh sawñ nees-twar.

2. **Vous permettez que je vous pose quelques questions?**

   2. Voo pehr-meh-**tay** kuh zhuh voo pohz kehl-kuh kehs-**tyawñ?**

NOTE: When **si** (in the meaning *if*) is followed by **il** it shortens to **s'il**.

Building Vocabulary

RELATED WORDS

1. **grand** great, large, **la grandeur** greatness, size
2. **haut** high, **la hauteur** height
3. **long** long, **la longueur** length
4. **large** wide, **la largeur** width

5. **visiter** to visit, **le visiteur** visitor
6. **porter** to carry, **le porteur** porter
7. **compter** to count, **le, la comptable** accountant

French Expressions

1. **pas tout à fait** (pah too ta **feh**) not quite, not completely
2. **en tout cas** (ahñ too **kah**) in any case
3. **ni moi non plus** (nee mwa nawñ **plü**) neither do I
4. **pas encore** (pah zahñ-**kur**) not yet
5. **alors** (a-**lur**) well, then, in that case, and so.
6. **voilà** (vwa-**la**) is used in the sense of *there is* or *there are* (pointing); also as an exclamation translated in various ways: *there! there now! that's that! behold!* etc.

Exercise No. 87—Completion of Text

1. (Let us see) **si vous connaissez** (French geography).
2. **Vous permettez** (that I ask you) **quelques questions?**
3. **Vous n'allez pas** (to receive a prize).
4. **Le Havre** (is situated) **à l'embouchure de la Seine.**
5. **C'est un grand marché de** (coffee, cotton and sugar).
6. **Quel est** (the longest river) **de France.**
7. **Il n'est pas** (much longer than) **le Rhône.**
8. **Il est** (smaller than) **le Mississippi.**
9. **Le Mont Blanc est** (the highest mountain) **de France.**
10. **Le Mont Blanc n'est pas** (higher than) **le Mount McKinley.**
11. **Je sais** (that you are right).
12. **L'examen** (is finished).

Grammar Notes

1. PRESENT TENSE of mettre, *to put*

I put, you put, etc.

je mets (meh)	*nous mettons (meh-tawñ)*
tu mets (meh)	*vous mettez (meh-tay)*
il, elle met (meh)	*ils, elles mettent (meht)*

Imperative: **mets** *put,* **mettons** *let us put,* **mettez** *put*

Verbs similar to **mettre** are: *permettre,* to permit; *admettre,* to admit; *remettre,* to put back; *soumettre,* to submit (to demands)

Exercise No. 88

Translate into French:

1. I am putting
2. Who submits?
3. Why do you put?
4. What do you (**tu**) put?
5. We are not submitting
6. They do not put
7. I do not admit
8. Does he permit?
9. Why do you permit?
10. Put it back.
11. Does he not permit?
12. Permit me

2. COMPARISON OF ADJECTIVES AND ADVERBS

Observe the positive (initial statement), comparative, and superlative forms of the adjectives **grand** and **diligent,** and of the adverb **vite:**

La Seine est un *grand* **fleuve.**
Le Rhin est *plus grand* **que la Seine.**
La Volga est *le plus grand* **fleuve d'Europe.**

The Seine is a *large* river.
The Rhine is *larger* than the Seine.
The Volga is *the largest* river in Europe.

Louise est très *diligente.*
Marie est **moins diligente** *que Louise.*
Anne est l'élève **la moins diligente** *de cette classe.*

Louise is very *diligent.*
Marie is less diligent *than Louise.*
Anne is the least diligent *pupil in this class.*

Le vélo marche **vite.**
Le scooter marche *plus vite* **que le vélo.**
La moto marche *le plus vite* **de tous.**

The bicycle travels fast.
The scooter travels *faster* than the bicycle.
The motorcycle travels *fastest* of all.

Positive	Comparative	Superlative
grand tall, big, great	**plus grand** taller	**le plus grand** tallest
diligent diligent	**moins diligent** less diligent	**le moins diligent** least diligent
vite fast	**plus vite** faster	**le plus vite** fastest

The comparative form of an adjective or adverb is made by placing **plus** (*more*) or **moins** (*less*) before the modifier. The superlative of an adjective is formed by placing the definite article (**le, la,** or **les**) before the comparative. Only **le** is used to form the superlative of an adverb.
See above: *La moto marche le* **plus vite.**
The superlative of the adjective may be preceded by the possessive instead of the definite article, **le meilleur ami, ma meilleure amie,** best friend, my best friend.
As in English, the superlative form of an adjective may stand alone as a noun: **le meilleur des amis,** the best of friends.
After a superlative use **de** not **dans** for *in.*
la montagne la plus haute d'Europe the highest mountain *in* Europe.

3. EXPRESSIONS OF COMPARISON

When unequals are compared **que** is used for *than,* except with numbers; then **de** is used.

La Loire est *plus longue que* **le Rhône.**	The Loire is *longer than* the Rhone.
Ce tour coûte *plus (moins) de* **cent dollars.**	This tour costs *more (less) than* $100.

When equals are compared **aussi** + adjective or adverb + **que** (*as . . . as*) is used. After a negative construction.**si . . . que** is used instead of **aussi . . . que.**

M. Brown connaît l'histoire de France *aussi bien que* **sa géographie.**	Mr. Brown knows the history of France *as well as* its geography.
Bernard n'est *pas si grand que* **Robert.**	Bernard is *not as tall as* Robert.

4. SOME IRREGULAR COMPARISONS

Adjectives	Adverbs
bon (bonne) good	**bien** well
meilleur better	**mieux** better
le meilleur the best	**le mieux** best
mauvais bad	**mal** badly
pire (or **plus mauvais**) worse	**pis** (**plus mal**) worse
le pire (or **le plus mauvais**) the worst	**le pis** (**le plus mal**) worst

The comparative and superlative forms of **bon** and **mauvais,** as well as the articles immediately before them, must agree in gender and number with the subjects of the sentence.

Additional expressions: **tant mieux** so much the better, **tant pis** too bad

Exercise No. 89

Translate the following sentences. Read them aloud in French three times.

1. Les films français sont-ils *meilleurs* que les films américains?
2. Quelques-uns sont *meilleurs,* d'autres sont *pires (plus mauvais).* En France et aux Etáts Unis on peut voir *les meilleurs* et aussi *les pires (plus mauvais)* films. En général j'aime *mieux* les films français.
3. Robert chante *mal.* Richard chante *pis (plus mal)* que Robert. Mais Bernard chante *le pis (le plus mal)* de tous.
4. Herbert écrit *bien,* mais vous écrivez *mieux* que lui. Renée écrit *le mieux* de tous.
5. Où fait-on *la meilleure* porcelaine?—On la fait à Limoges.
6. *Mieux* vaut tard que jamais.

Exercise No. 90

Complete the French sentences so that they correspond fully to the English. Read each completed French sentence aloud.

Exemple: 1. **Les verbes sont aussi importants que les noms.**

1. The verbs are as important as the nouns.
2. Marguerite is nicer than Suzanne.
3. I have the best pen.
4. The black ink is not as good as the blue.
5. Isabel is taller than Julie.
6. John is the most hardworking boy in the class.
7. Anne is the youngest child in the family.
8. I find French more interesting than Spanish.
9. Which is the longest river in France?
10. London is the largest city in the world.
11. The Loire is longer than the Rhine.
12. Why do you answer so badly?
13. We like the best films.
14. I have the worst pen.
15. This watch costs more than fifty dollars.

1. Les verbes sont ___ importants ___ les noms.
2. Marie est ___ aimable ___ Suzanne.
3. J'ai ___ plume.
4. L'encre noire n'est pas ___ bonne ___ la bleue.
5. Isabelle est ___ que Julie.
6. Richard est l'élève ___ de la classe.
7. Anne est la ___ enfant de la famille.
8. Je trouve le français ___ l'espagnol.
9. Quel est le fleuve ___ de France?
10. Londres est ___ du monde.
11. La Loire est ___ longue ___le Rhin.
12. Pourquoi répondez-vous si ___ ?
13. Nous aimons les ___ films.
14. J'ai la ___ plume.
15. Cette montre coûte ___ cinquante dollars.

NOTE: With the superlative, the usual place of the adjective in a sentence must be kept.

un garçon intelligent
un jeune enfant

le garçon le plus intelligent
le plus jeune enfant

Exercise No. 91—Questionnaire

1. Avec quelle question facile est-ce que M. Picard commence?
2. Où est situé le port du Havre?
3. Le port du Havre est-il un grand marché?
4. Quel fleuve est plus long et plus large que la Loire?
5. Quelle montagne est plus haute, le Mont Blanc ou le Mount McKinley?
6. M. Dupont est un homme de quarante-cinq ans. Il a $100,000 (cent mille dollars). Mme Millet est une femme de cinquante ans. Elle a $80,000 (quatre-vingt mille dollars).
   M. Arnaud est un homme de soixante ans. Il a $50,000 (cinquante mille dollars).

   a. Quelle personne est le plus jeune des trois?
   b. Quelle personne est le plus âgée des trois?

c. Est-ce que Mme Millet est plus âgée que M. Dupont?
d. Quel individu est le plus riche?
e. Quel individu est le moins riche?
f. Est-ce que Mme Millet est aussi riche que M. Dupont?

CHAPITRE 18 (DIX-HUIT)

LA JOURNÉE DE M. BROWN

MR. BROWN'S DAY

1. —M. Brown, est-ce que je peux vous demander comment vous passez une journée typique?
2. —Certainement. Quand c'est une journée de travail, je me lève à six heures et demie. Je me lave et je m'habille dans une demi-heure, plus ou moins. Vers sept heures je me mets à table pour prendre mon petit déjeuner.
   Ma femme, qui est matinale aussi, se lève de bonne heure et nous prenons ensemble le petit déjeuner. Naturellement cela me plaît beaucoup. Nous avons une bonne occasion de parler des enfants et d'autres choses qui nous intéressent.
3. —Que prenez-vous au petit déjeuner?
4. —Je prends du (some) jus d'orange, du café, des petits pains et des oeufs. Parfois je mange des crêpes au lieu d'oeufs.
5. —Je vois que vous aimez un copieux petit déjeuner. Et ensuite?
6. —À sept heures et demie je suis prêt à partir pour prendre le train. Parfois les enfants se lèvent de bonne heure pour m'embrasser avant mon départ.
7. —À quelle heure arrivez-vous au bureau?
8. —J'y arrive à neuf heures à peu près. Au bureau je lis mon courrier, je parle au téléphone avec certains clients, et je fais d'autres choses qu'un homme d'affaires doit faire.

1. Mr. Brown, may I ask you how you spend a typical day?
2. Certainly. When it's a workday, I get up at six-thirty. I wash and dress in half an hour, more or less. At about seven, I sit down at the table to have my breakfast.
   My wife, who is also any early riser, gets up early and we have breakfast together. Naturally that pleases me very much. We have a good opportunity to talk about the children and other things that interest us.
3. What do you eat for breakfast?
4. I have (some) orange juice, coffee, rolls, and eggs. Sometimes I eat pancakes instead of eggs.
5. I see that you like a substantial breakfast. And afterward?
6. At seven-thirty I am ready to leave to take the train. Sometimes the children get up early to kiss me before my departure.
7. At what time do you arrive at the office?
8. I arrive at about nine o'clock. In the office I read my mail, I talk on the telephone to various clients, and I do other things that a businessman has to do.

9. —Et quand est-ce que vous déjeunez?

9. And when do you have lunch?

10. —Presque toujours à une heure. Il me faut à peu près vingt minutes pour manger.

10. Almost always at one. I need about twenty minutes to eat.

11. —C'est très peu de temps. En France vous allez voir que les habitudes des repas sont tout autres. Le Français passe beaucoup plus de temps à table. Mais parlons de cela une autre fois. Qu'est-ce que vous mangez au déjeuner?

11. That is very little time. In France you will see that meal habits are very different. The Frenchman spends much more time at meals. But let us speak about that some other time. What do you have for lunch?

12. —D'habitude je prends un sandwich, un café et un dessert—une pomme cuite ou une tarte.

12. Usually I have a sandwich, coffee, and some dessert—a baked apple or a piece of pie.

13. —Qu'est-ce que vous faites après le déjeuner?

13. What do you do after lunch?

14. —Il y a souvent des clients qui viennent me voir. De temps en temps je sors pour voir d'autres clients.

14. Often some clients come to see me and from time to time I go out to see other clients.

15. —À quelle heure finissez-vous votre journée?

15. At what time do you finish your day's work?

16. —À cinq heures précises je quitte le bureau. J'arrive chez moi vers sept heures moins le quart. Je fais un bout de toilette, je joue un peu avec les enfants et puis nous nous mettons à table pour dîner.

16. At five o'clock sharp I leave the office. I arrive home at about a quarter to seven. I wash up a bit, play a little with the children, and then we sit down at the table to have dinner.

17. —Vous devez être fatigué après une journée pareille.

17. You must be tired after such a day.

18. —Je pense bien que oui, répond M. Brown.

18. "I should think so," answers Mr. Brown.

NOTE: The idea *some* is expressed in French by **de la, du, de l'** and **des.** This usage is fully treated in the next chapter.

Pronunciation and Spelling Aids

Practice aloud:

1. **je me lève** (zhuh muh **lehv**)
2. **je me lave** (zhuh muh **lav**)
3. **je m'habille** (zhuh ma-**beey**)
4. **je me mets à table** (zhuh muh meh za **tabl**)
5. **Je prends du café** (zhuh prahñ dü ka-**fay**)
6. **des petits pains** (day puh-tee **pañ**)
7. **des oranges** (day zu-**rahñzh**)
8. **des oeufs** (day **zeu**)

Building Vocabulary

A. **Les repas** (lay ruh-**pah**)—Meals
1. **le déjeuner** (day-zheu-**nay**) lunch

2. **déjeuner** *or* **prendre le déjeuner** to have lunch
3. **le petit déjeuner** breakfast (usually coffee, tea, or hot chocolate with bread or croissants)
4. **le dîner** dinner; **dîner** to dine
5. **le souper** supper

B. **Quelques vivres** (veevr)—Some foods

1. **le pain** bread; **du pain** some **bread**
2. **l'oeuf** (leuf) egg; **des oeufs** (day **zeu**) some eggs
3. **le petit pain** roll
4. **le café** coffee; **du café** some coffee
5. **la crêpe** pancake
6. **le beurre** butter; **du beurre** some butter
7. **le lait** milk; **du lait** some milk
8. **la pomme** apple
9. **le gâteau (les gâteaux)** the cake(s)
10. **la crème** cream; **de la crème** some cream
11. **la viande** meat; **de la viande** some meat
12. **le jus d'orange** orange juice
13. **la soupe** soup
14. **le légume** vegetable

French Expressions

1. **Cela me plaît.** That pleases me *or* I like that.
2. **Il me faut 20 minutes.** I need 20 minutes.
3. **de temps en temps** at times, from time to time
4. **Je fais un bout de toilette.** I wash up a bit.
5. **Je pense bien que oui.** I should think so.
6. **se mettre à table** to sit down at the table
7. **le copieux petit déjeuner** substantial breakfast

Exercise No. 92—Completion of Text

1. **Comment passez-vous** (a typical day)?
2. **Je me lève** (at six-thirty).
3. **Je suis** (an early riser).
4. **Ma femme se lève** (early).
5. (What do you eat) **au petit déjeuner?**
6. **Je prends** (coffee, rolls, and eggs).
7. (At times) **les enfants se lèvent de bonne heure.**
8. **J'arrive** (at the office) **à neuf heures.**
9. **Je lis** (my mail) **et je dicte** (the answers).

10. (What do you do) **après le déjeuner?**
11. **Des clients viennent souvent** (to see me).
12. **À quelle heure** (do you finish) **votre journée?**
13. (I leave) **le bureau à cinq heures.**
14. (We sit down) **à table.**

Grammar Notes

1. PRESENT TENSE OF THE REFLEXIVE VERB se laver, *to wash oneself, to get washed*

I wash myself, you wash yourself, etc.

je me lave (lav)	I wash myself
tu te laves (lav)	you wash yourself
il se lave (lav)	he washes himself
elle se lave (lav)	she washes herself
nous nous lavons (la-**vawñ**)	we wash ourselves
vous vous lavez (la-**vay**)	you wash yourselves
ils se lavent (lav)	they wash themselves
elles se lavent (lav)	they wash themselves

Interrogative:
Vous lavez-vous? or **Est-ce que vous vous lavez?**
Do you wash yourself? Are you getting washed?

Negative:
Je ne me lave pas.
I am not washing myself.

The reflexive pronouns are: **me**, *myself;* **te**, *yourself;* **nous**, *ourselves;* **vous**, *yourself, yourselves;* **se**, *himself, herself, itself, oneself* and *themselves*. The different reflexive pronouns must accompany reflexive verbs; they agree in gender and number with the subject of the verb.

Like all object pronouns the reflexive pronouns always precede the verb except in the affirmative imperative when they follow it. Note that in this case **te** becomes **toi** when it comes after the verb.

Imperative (Affirmative)
Lave-toi (*fam.*). Wash yourself ("wash up").
Lavons-nous. Let's wash ourselves.
Lavez-vous. Wash yourself (yourselves).

Imperative (Negative)
Ne te lave pas. Do not wash yourself.
Ne nous lavons pas. Let's not wash ourselves.
Ne vous lavez pas. Do not wash yourself (yourselves).

2. SOME COMMON REFLEXIVE VERBS

Note that the French reflexive verb is not always translated by a reflexive verb in English.

1. **s'appeler** *to be called, named*
2. **s'amuser** *to have a good time, to have fun*
3. **se lever** *to get up, to rise (from sleep)*
4. **s'asseoir** (sa-**swar**) *to sit down*
5. **se mettre à** *to sit down at*
6. **se mettre debout** *to stand up*
7. **se porter** *to feel* (health)
8. **se coucher** *to go to bed*
9. **s'habiller** *to get dressed*
10. **se promener** *to go for a walk, ride*
11. **se souvenir de** *to remember*
12. **se demander** *to wonder*
13. **se dépêcher** *to hurry*
14. **s'ennuyer** *to be bored*

Exercise No. 93

Complete each French sentence by inserting the correct reflexive pronoun. Read the completed sentences aloud.

Exemple: 1. M. Brown va se mettre à table.

1. Mr. Brown is going to sit down at the table.
2. He gets up at seven o'clock.
3. He washes (himself) and dresses (himself).
4. At what time do you go to bed?
5. How do you feel? (How are you?)
6. She is not feeling well.
7. My mother is feeling better today.
8. We have a good time at the movies.
9. What is your name? (How do you call yourself?)
10. What are their names?
11. My name is Albert.
12. Dress yourself quickly, Anne.
13. Do not get up late, children.
14. I do not go to bed before 10 o'clock.
15. The children do not want to get up.

1. M. Brown va ___ mettre à table.
2. Il ___ lève à sept heures.
3. Il ___ lave et ___ habille.
4. A quelle heure ___ couchez-vous?
5. Comment ___ portez-vous?
6. Ma mère ne___ porte pas bien.
7. Elle___ porte mieux aujourd'hui.
8. Nous ___ amusons au ciné.
9. Comment ___ appelez-vous?
10. Comment ___ appellent-ils?
11. Je ___ appelle Albert.
12. Habille ___ vite, Anne.
13. Ne ___ levez pas tard, mes enfants.
14. Je ne ___ couche pas avant dix heures.
15. Les enfants ne veulent pas ___ lever.

Exercise No. 94

Translate the questions and answers. Read the questions and answers aloud several times. Verify your comprehension in the answer section, as needed.

1. —Comment vous appelez-vous?
   — Je m'appelle Albert.
2. —À quelle heure est-ce que vous vous levez?
   —Je me lève à sept heures du matin.

3. —À quelle heure est-ce que vous vous couchez?
    —Je me couche à onze heures du soir.
4. —Est-ce que vous vous habillez vite?
    —Je m'habille très vite.
5. —Comment vous portez-vous?
    —Je me porte bien, merci.
6. —Comment est-ce que votre père se porte?
    —Il ne se porte pas bien. Il est enrhumé.
7. —À quelle heure est-ce que M. Brown se met à table?
    —Il se met à table à sept heures du soir.
8. —Est-ce que les garçons s'amusent bien en jouant au baseball?
    —Ils s'amusent très bien.

Exercise No. 95—Questionnaire

1. À quelle heure est-ce que M. Brown se lève?
2. Ensuite que fait-il?
3. En combien de temps s'habille-t-il?
4. Que fait-il à sept heures à peu près?
5. Est-ce que sa femme se lève de bonne heure?
6. Est-ce qu'ils déjeunent ensemble?
7. Qu'est-ce qu'il mange au petit déjeuner?
8. Qu'est-ce qu'il mange parfois au lieu d'oeufs?
9. À quelle heure est-il prêt à partir?
10. À quelle heure arrive-t-il à son bureau?
11. À quelle heure prend-il son déjeuner?
12. Qu'est-ce qu'il mange au déjeuner?
13. Quelles personnes viennent le voir l'après-midi?
14. À quelle heure est-ce qu'il finit sa journée?

CHAPITRE 19 (DIX-NEUF)

LA VIE DANS LA BANLIEUE
LIFE IN THE SUBURBS

1. —Maintenant je suis bien renseigné sur votre journée en ville. Mais je suis toujours curieux. Dites-moi, M. Brown, comment passez-vous le temps chez vous dans la banlieue où vous demeurez?

2. —Comment je passe mon temps? Eh bien, c'est très simple. Vous savez déjà que je rentre assez tard. Nous ne terminons pas notre dîner bien avant huit heures et demie. Alors, pendant la semaine de travail, il ne nous reste pas trop de temps pour de grandes entreprises.

3. —Tout de même, vous vous permettez quelques distractions, le cinéma, par exemple.

4. —Évidemment. Mais d'habitude nous restons sagement chez nous, en famille. Pourtant, nous ne restons pas des heures devant la télévision. Nous bavardons, nous lisons et nous faisons la guerre aux enfants quand ils ne veulent pas se coucher.

5. —Et quant aux achats, est-ce que vous et madame pouvez faire votre marché commodément?

6. —Oh, tout à fait. Tout près de chez nous il y a un supermarché où l'on peut acheter non seulement des fruits, des légumes, du lait, du fromage, du beurre, du café, des conserves de toutes sortes, de la viande, des bonbons et des gâteaux, mais aussi des bas et des casseroles.

7. —Tout de même, vous n'y trouvez pas de pardessus.

1. Now I am well informed about your day in town. But I am still curious. Tell me, Mr. Brown, how do you pass the time at home in the suburbs where you live?

2. How do I pass my time? Well, it's very simple. You know already that I get home rather late. We don't finish our dinner much before 8:30. So, during the work week, there is not too much time left for big projects.

3. All the same, you do allow yourselves some entertainment, the movies, for example.

4. Obviously. But usually, we stay quietly at home with the family. However, we don't spend hours in front of the television. We talk, we read, and we do battle with the children when they don't want to go to bed.

5. And as for shopping, are you and Mrs. Brown able to do your marketing conveniently?

6. Oh, entirely. Very near us there is a supermarket where you can buy not only fruit, vegetables, milk, cheese, butter, coffee, all sorts of canned goods, meat, candy, and cakes, but also stockings and saucepans.

7. All the same, you don't find overcoats there.

8. —Pas encore. Mais nous avons un quartier commerçant très important. Plusieurs grands magasins de New York ont des succursales qui nous fournissent presque tout ce qu'il nous faut.

9. —Vous avez de la chance.

10. —Et le plus beau de l'affaire c'est qu'on peut toujours stationner, on n'est pas bousculé, et on peut parler à son aise avec les vendeurs.

11. —Et les enfants, sont-ils contents à l'école?

12. —Si on peut jamais dire qu'un enfant est content à l'école, alors oui, ils sont contents. Ils aiment bien leurs maîtres d'école et ils ont de bons camarades.

13. —Vous faites si bien la propagande pour la banlieue que j'ai envie de déménager!

14. —Venez donc! Vous serez le bienvenu!

8. Not yet. But we have a very large business section. Several New York department stores have branches which supply us with almost everything we need.

9. You're lucky.

10. And the best part of it is that we can always park, we're not pushed around, and we can talk comfortably with the salesmen.

11. And the children, are they happy at school?

12. If one can ever say that a child is happy at school, then yes, they are happy. They like their teachers, and they have good friends.

13. You do such good advertising for the suburbs that I feel like moving.

14. Come on, then. You will be very welcome.

NOTE: on is an indefinite personal pronoun that takes the third person singular form of the verb (like **il** and **elle).** It can be translated as *one, you, we, they,* or *people,* depending on the context. It is very commonly used, especially in the spoken language.

On is often replaced by **l'on** after **et, ou, où, que, à qui, à quoi, si,** for sound value only. Contrast:

Où on peut acheter.   **Où l'on peut acheter.**

Pronunciation and Spelling Aids

Practice aloud:

Maintenant je suis bien renseigné sur votre journée en ville.

(Mañt-nahñ zhuh süee byañ rahñ-seh-**nyay** sur vutr zhoor-nay ahñ **veel.)**

Mais je suis toujours curieux.

(Meh zhuh süee too-zhoor kür-**yeu.)**

Dites-moi, Monsieur Brown, comment passez-vous le temps chez vous dans la banlieue où vous demeurez?

(Deet-mwa muh-syeu Brown, ku-mawñ pah-say voo luh **tahñ** shay voo dahñ la bahñ-**lyeu** oo voo duh-meu-**ray?)**

Building Vocabulary

Some fruits and vegetables

la banane (ba-**nan**) banana

le citron (see-**trawñ**) lemon

la fraise (frehz) strawberry

la framboise (fram-**bwaz**) raspberry

l'orange (*f*) (lu-**rahñzh**) orange

la poire (pwar) pear

la pêche (pehsh) peach

la pomme (pum) apple

la tomate (tu-**mat**) tomato

les raisins (*m*) (reh-**zañ**) grapes

les raisins secs (sehk) raisins

Quelques fruits et légumes

l'artichaut (*m*) (ar-tee-**shoh**) artichoke

l'aubergine (*f*) (oh-behr-**zheen**) eggplant

la betterave (beh-**trahv**) beet

la carotte (ka-**rut**) carrot

les champignons (*m*) (shahñ-pee-**nyawñ**) mushrooms

le chou (shoo) cabbage

les épinards (*m*) (lay zay-pee-**nar**) spinach

les petits pois (pwa) green peas

les haricots (lay za-ree-**koh**) beans

l'oignon (*f*) (lu-**nyawñ**) onion

la pomme de terre (pum duh **tehr**) potato

la salade (sa-**lad**) lettuce, salad

French Expressions

1. **tout de même** (too duh **mehm**) all the same, nevertheless
2. **en famille** (ahñ fa-**meey**) with the family
3. **faire son marché** to do one's marketing
4. **le plus beau de l'affaire** the best part of it all
5. **être à son aise** to be at one's ease, comfortable
6. **j'ai envie de** (zhay ahñ-**vee** duh) I want, have a mind to
7. **être le bienvenu** (byañ-vuh-**nü**) to be welcome

Exercise No. 96—Completion of Text

1. **Je suis** (well informed).
2. (All the same) **vous vous permettez quelques distractions.**
3. (We remain) **sagement chez nous.**
4. **Vous pouvez faire** (your marketing) **commodément.**
5. **On achète au supermarché** (fruits, vegetables, milk, butter, cheese and coffee).
6. **On y achète aussi** (stockings and saucepans).
7. **On peut toujours** (park).
8. **On peut parler** (at one's ease).

9. **Les enfants ont** (good friends)
10. I feel like moving.

Grammar Notes

1. SOME OR ANY

Observe in the following sentences how *some* or *any* is expressed in French.

1. **J'achète** *du* **jus d'orange.**
2. **Je prends** *de la* **crème.**
3. **Avez-vous** *de l'***argent?**
4. **M. Brown importe** *des* **objets d'art.**

1. I buy (*some*) orange juice.
2. I take (*some*) cream.
3. Do you have (*any*) money?
4. Mr. Brown imports (*some*) art objects.

The idea *some* or *any* preceding a noun is usually expressed in French by **de** plus the definite article, that is: **du, de l', de la** or **des.** This construction is called the *partitive* because it indicates *part* but not all of the thing or things.

The words *some* and *any* are often omitted in English but the corresponding words in French are almost never omitted.

2. OMISSIONS OF THE DEFINITE ARTICLE IN THE PARTITIVE

The partitive (*some* or *any*) is usually expressed by **de** without the definite article a) after a negative verb; b) when an adjective precedes the noun.

Je n'achète pas *de* **café,** *de* **crème ou (ni)** *d'***oeufs.**

M. Brown importe *de* **beaux objets d'art.**

I am not buying (*any*) coffee, (*any*) cream, or (nor) (*any*) eggs.

Mr. Brown imports (*some*) beautiful art objects.

Exercise No. 97

In these sentences substitute the French words for *some* or *any* (**du, de l', de la, des** or **de**):

1. **Comme déjeuner je prends** (some) **café et** (some) **jus d'orange.**
2. **Voulez-vous** (some) **lait,** (some) **beurre et** (some) **oeufs?**
3. **N'avez-vous pas** (any) **porcelaine de Limoges?**
4. **Les enfants mangent** (some) **gâteaux.**
5. **Préférez-vous** (some) **crêpes au lieu des oeufs?**
6. **M. Brown ne vend pas** (any) **automobiles.**
7. **Comme dîner M. Brown prend** (some) **soupe,** (some) **viande et** (some) **légumes.**

8. **Est-ce qu'il y a** (any) **bons restaurants près d'ici?**
9. **Je veux acheter** (some) **encre rouge.**
10. **Les enfants ont** (some) **bons camarades.**

Remember to practice the new structures by reading aloud the completed sentences.

3. THE PARTITIVE PRONOUN en (some of it, any of it, etc.)

You are familiar with the word **en** as a preposition:

En été il fait chaud.	It is warm in summer.
Ils voyagent en France.	They are traveling in France.
Répétez ces mots en français.	Repeat these words in French.

Now, study the use of the pronoun **en** in the following sentences:

Voulez-vous du sucre?	Do you want some sugar?
Merci. J'*en* ai déjà.	Thanks. I have *some* (*of it*) already.
As-tu des stylos?	Have you any pens?
Moi, je n'*en* ai pas. Mais Louis *en* a trois.	I haven't *any* (*of them*). But Louis has three (*of them*).
Achetez-vous des oeufs?	Are you buying eggs?
Oui, j'*en* achète deux douzaines.	Yes, I am buying two dozen (*of them*).
A-t-il beaucoup d'argent?	Does he have a lot of money?
Non. Il n'*en* a qu'un peu.	No, he has only a little (*of it*).

en is used as a pronoun meaning *some* or *any;* **en** may be translated as *some, any, some of it, any of it, some of them, any of them, one.*

In English the above words will be either expressed or understood. However, in French, **en** must not be omitted. Compare the French with the English translation.

Voici des gâteaux.	Here are some cakes.
N'*en* prenez pas trop.	Don't take too many (*of them*).

Like the object pronouns, **en** precedes the verb except in the affirmative imperative.

Voici des gâteaux.	Here are some cakes.
Prenez-*en*. N'*en* prenez pas.	Take *some.* Do not take *any* (*of them*).

Exercise No. 98

Read each question, silently and aloud. Then give the indicated answer in French.

Exemple: 1. Oui, nous en vendons beaucoup.

1. Vendez-vous beaucoup de porcelaine?
2. Achète-t-elle des conserves?
3. Avez-vous un pardessus?
4. Voici de la soupe.
5. Les pommes ne sont pas mûres (ripe).
6. Combien d'élèves a-t-il?
7. Prenez quelques poires.
8. Ont-ils assez de livres?

1. Yes, we sell a good deal of it.
2. Yes, she is buying some.
3. No, I haven't one.
4. Take some.
5. Do not eat any (of them).
6. He has thirty (of them).
7. Thanks. I don't want any.
8. Yes, they have enough (of them).

Exercise No. 99—Questionnaire

1. Qui est toujours curieux?
2. Qu'est-ce que M. Picard sait déjà?
3. À quelle heure est-ce que la famille Brown termine souvent son dîner?
4. Pourquoi les parents font-ils la guerre aux enfants?
5. Où est-ce que Monsieur et Madame Brown font leurs achats?
6. Qu'est-ce qu'on peut acheter au supermarché?
7. Qu'est-ce qu'on ne trouve pas (encore) au supermarché?
8. Est-ce que les grands magasins de New York ont des succursales dans la banlieue?
9. Qui est-ce que les enfants aiment à l'école?
10. Qui a envie de déménager à la banlieue?

RÉVISION 4, CHAPITRES 15–19

Première Partie

NOUNS

1.	l'amateur	1.	follower, enthusiast
2.	le beurre	2.	butter
3.	le ciné	3.	movies
4.	le cinéma	4.	movies
5.	le côté	5.	side
6.	le cours	6.	course
7.	la date	7.	date
8.	le départ	8.	departure
9.	le petit déjeuner	9.	breakfast
10.	le déjeuner	10.	lunch
11.	le dîner	11.	dinner
12.	le film	12.	film, movie
13.	la glace	13.	ice cream
14.	l'histoire	14.	history, story
15.	la lumière	15.	light
16.	la montagne	16.	mountain
17.	l'oeil (les yeux)	17.	eye (eyes)
18.	l'oeuf	18.	egg
19.	le pain	19.	bread
20.	le petit pain	20.	roll
21.	la plupart de	21.	the majority, most of
22.	la pomme	22.	apple
23.	le porteur	23.	porter
24.	le programme	24.	program
25.	le rang	25.	row
26.	le fleuve	26.	river
27.	le (la) sténo	27.	stenographer
28.	le téléphone	28.	telephone
29.	la télévision	29.	television
30.	la viande	30.	meat
31.	la voiture	31.	car, carriage

VERBS

1.	adorer	1.	to adore
2.	aider	2.	to help
3.	déjeuner	3.	to have breakfast or lunch
4.	embrasser	4.	to kiss
5.	ennuyer	5.	to bore, annoy
6.	féliciter	6.	to congratulate
7.	intéresser	7.	to interest
8.	remercier	8.	to thank
9.	préférer	9.	to prefer
10.	rester	10.	to remain, stay
11.	mettre	11.	to put
12.	je mets	12.	I put
13.	permettre	13.	to permit
14.	finir	14.	to finish
15.	nous finissons	15.	we finish
16.	bâtir	16.	to build
17.	choisir	17.	to choose
18.	obéir	18.	to obey
19.	punir	19.	to punish
20.	remplir	20.	to fill
21.	saisir	21.	to seize
22.	mourir	22.	to die
23.	venir	23.	to come
24.	il vient	24.	he comes
25.	devenir	25.	to become
26.	revenir	26.	to come back
27.	s'amuser	27.	to enjoy oneself
28.	je m'amuse	28.	I'm having fun
29.	s'appeler	29.	to be called
30.	il s'appelle	30.	his name is
31.	se coucher	31.	to go to bed
32.	s'habiller	32.	to dress oneself
33.	se laver	33.	to wash oneself
34.	se lever	34.	to get up
35.	levez-vous	35.	get up
36.	se reposer	36.	to rest

ADJECTIVES

1.	fatigué	1.	tired
2.	gentil (ille f.)	2.	kind, nice

3. glorieux (i.e., use *f.*)	3. glorious
4. occupé	4. busy
5. pareil (eille *f.*)	5. like, similar
6. quelconque	6. any whatsoever
7. terminé	7. finished
8. triste	8. sad

ADVERBS

1. alors	1. well, then, so
2. ensemble	2. together
3. d'ailleurs	3. besides
4. exactement	4. exactly
5. parfois	5. at times
6. puis	6. then
7. seulement	7. only
8. souvent	8. often
9. toujours	9. always

PREPOSITIONS

1. au lieu de	1. instead of
2. jusqu'à (+ noun)	2. up to, until
3. pendant	3. during
4. sans	4. without

French Expressions

1. attraper un rhume	1. to catch (a) cold
2. être le bienvenu	2. to be welcome
3. bien entendu	3. of course
4. à l'heure	4. on time
5. de bonne heure	5. early
6. n'importe	6. it doesn't matter
7. se mettre à table	7. to sit down at the table
8. ni moi non plus	8. neither do I
9. pas encore	9. not yet
10. cela me plaît	10. that pleases me, I like that
11. rester (être) debout	11. to stand, stay standing
12. de temps en temps	12. from time to time
13. (pas) tout à fait	13. (not) quite
14. tout de même	14. all the same
15. voilà	15. there is (are)
16. en tout cas	16. in any case

Exercise No. 100

Select the group of words in list II which best completes each sentence begun in list I:

I	II
1. **Les enfants de M. Brown connaissent**	a. que je me lève de bonne heure.
2. **Du quatorzième rang**	b. M. Brown prend du jus d'orange.
3. **Le quatorze juillet 1789 est la date**	c. à sept heures du soir.
4. **M. Brown connaît l'histoire de France**	d. et moi nous déjeunons ensemble.
5. **La Loire est le fleuve**	e. on peut bien voir et entendre.
6. **"Je suis matinal" veut dire**	f. de la prise de la Bastille.
7. **Toute la famille se met à table**	g. le plus long de la France.
8. **Pour arriver à son bureau M. Brown voyage**	h. aussi bien que son système monétaire.
9. **Pour commencer le petit déjeuner**	i. toutes les vedettes de l'écran.
10. **Il me plaît beaucoup que ma femme**	j. en voiture, par train et par le métro (subway).

Exercise No. 101

Translate the English words in parentheses into French:
1. **La Loire est** (the longest river) **de la France.**
2. **Londres est** (bigger than) **Paris.**
3. **Philippe est** (more tired than) **moi.**
4. **Je ne suis pas** (as tall as) **mon frère.**
5. **Le Mont Blanc n'est pas** (higher than) **le Mount McKinley.**
6. **Le Mont Everest est** (the highest mountain) **du monde.**
7. **Lundi est** (the first day) **de la semaine.**
8. **January 30, 1988.**
9. **Annette est la plus jeune** (in the family).
10. **Georges est** (my best friend).

Exercise No. 102

Translate the following brief dialogues. Practice them aloud. Note the various ways in which the partitive is used:

1. —Pour votre petit déjeuner prenez-vous du café ou du chocolat?—Je ne prends ni l'un ni l'autre. Je bois un verre d'eau.
2. —Désirez-vous de la crème et du sucre dans votre café?—Je désire de la crème mais je ne désire pas de sucre.
3. —Qu'est-ce qu'on mange comme petit déjeuner en France?—On mange très peu; en général des petits pains[1] et du café.
4. —Que mange-t-on le matin comme déjeuner aux États-Unis?—D'ordinaire on commence avec du jus d'orange. Puis on mange une céréale quelconque, une tranche de pain grillé ou des oeufs.

Les Américains sont aussi très friands (**fond**) de crêpes avec du sirop. Bien entendu il y a aussi du café, du thé ou du lait à boire.

NOTE [1]**des** (not **de**) **petits pains,** because **petits pains,** like **petits pois,** is considered to be a (two-part) noun, not an adjective plus noun.

Exercise No. 103

Read each French question. Then make your answer in French correspond to the English answer that follows the question, using object and reflexive pronouns.

Exemple: 1. Oui, je les invite.

1. **Invitez-vous vos amis à dîner chez vous?**
2. **Préférez-vous le ciné?**
3. **Est-ce que les enfants connaissent les vedettes du ciné?**
4. **Est-ce que vous nous attendez?**
5. **Vous levez-vous de bonne heure?**
6. **À quelle heure est-ce que vous vous couchez?**
7. **Les enfants s'habillent-ils rapidement le matin?**
8. **Comment vous appelez-vous?**
9. **À quelle heure finissez-vous vos examens?**
10. **Finissent-ils maintenant le travail?**

1. Yes, I am inviting them.
2. No, I do not prefer it.
3. Yes, they know them well.
4. Yes, we are waiting for you.
5. No, I get up late.
6. We go to bed at 11 o'clock.
7. Yes, they dress themselves very quickly.
8. My name is Albert Martin.
9. We finish them at 4 o'clock in the afternoon.
10. Yes, they are finishing it now.

Exercise No. 104

Complete these sentences by choosing the correct expression from those listed in the right column. Be sure to use the correct form of the verbs and adjectives: attention to gender and number.

1. **Elle doit être** (tired) **après une journée** (such).
2. (They sit down to table) **à sept heures.**
3. (They are standing) **devant la maison.**
4. **Les messieurs** (are seated) **dans le salon.**
5. (From time to time) **nous prenons du chocolat** (instead of) **café.**
6. **Nous ne voulons pas** (to catch cold).
7. **Je vois** (the majority of) **mes clients le matin.**
8. **Le train arrive rarement** (on time).
9. (We are) **toujours** (welcome) **chez M. Brown.**
10. **Nous nous levons** (early); **ils se lèvent** (late).

a. **au lieu de**
b. **pareil (eille f.)**
c. **tard**
d. **fatigué**
e. **la plupart de**
f. **de bonne heure**
g. **de temps en temps**
h. **attraper un rhume**
i. **se mettre à table**
j. **être le bienvenu**
k. **être debout**
1. **être assis**
m. **à l'heure**

Dialogue

On visite le marché aux puces

Nous sommes près d'un étalage de couvertures de lit.	*We are near a display of bedspreads.*
L'Acheteur: *Combien coûte cette couverture blanche brodée en bleu?*	Customer: *How much does this white bedspread embroidered in blue cost?*
Le Vendeur: Elle coûte quatre-vingt-dix euro.	*Salesman:* It costs ninety euros.
L'Acheteur: *C'est beaucoup trop. Je vais vous donner soixante-cinq.*	Customer: *That's much too much. I'll give you sixty-five.*
Le Vendeur: Mais monsieur, vous n'y pensez pas! Regardez ce travail, comme il est fin. Regardez la qualité du drap. Enfin, ça va lentement aujourd'hui: Je vous la laisse à quatre-vingt-cinq.	Salesman: But sir, you don't mean it! Look at this fine work. Look at the quality of the cloth. Well, things are slow today. I'll let you have it for eighty-five.
L'Acheteur: *C'est toujours beaucoup. Je vous donne soixante-dix euro.*	Customer: *It's still high. I'll give you seventy euros.*
Le Vendeur: Mais regardez, monsieur, comme elle est grande. Elle est assez grande pour un lit à deux places. Donnez-moi quatre-vingt-deux.	Salesman: But look, sir, how big it is. It is big enough for a double bed. Give me eighty-two.
L'Acheteur: *Je dors dans un lit à une place. Je suis célibataire. Je ne vais pas me marier. Je vous donne soixante-quinze.*	Customer: *I sleep in a single bed. I am a bachelor. I am not going to get married. I'll give you seventy-five.*
Le Vendeur: Impossible, monsieur. Je suis marié, moi, et j'ai des enfants à nourrir. Quatre-vingts euro. C'est mon dernier prix.	Salesman: *Impossible, sir. I am married and I have children to feed. Eighty euros. That's my final price.*
L'Acheteur: *Bon, d'accord. Voici, monsieur.*	*Customer:* Good, agreed. Here you are, sir.
Il donne au vendeur quatre-vingts euro et il s'en va avec la couverture blanche brodée en bleu. C'est la coutume de marchander au marché aux puces, et tous les deux hommes sont contents.	He gives the salesman four hundred francs and he leaves with the white bedspread embroidered in blue. It is the custom to bargain at the flea market, and both men are pleased.

NOTE: **s'en aller** means *to go away:* **je m'en vais, tu t'en vas, il s'en va, nous nous en allons, vous vous en allez, ils s'en vont.** (**en** is usually not translated in this verb)

Lecture

Exercise No. 105—
Une Visite au paquebot (ocean liner) Queen Elizabeth II

C'est samedi. M. Brown se lève à huit heures, et il regarde par la fenêtre. Le ciel est bleu. Le soleil brille. Il dit à sa femme:—Aujourd'hui allons visiter le paquebot Queen Elizabeth II qui est arrivé ce matin. J'ai de la marchandise à bord. Nous allons avoir une belle occasion pour visiter le bateau.

—Très bien, dit Mme Brown.

À neuf heures ils partent en voiture et dans une heure à peu près ils arrivent au quai. À l'entrée ils voient un groupe de garçons qui mangent des glaces et qui causent en français.

M. Brown dit bonjour aux garçons et il parle un peu avec le plus proche. Voici la conversation.

—Bonjour, jeune homme! Êtes-vous français?
—Non, monsieur, je suis américain.
—Mais vous parlez très bien le français.
—Eh bien, ces garçons qui travaillent sur le paquebot sont mes amis, et ils m'apprennent à parler correctement. Ce sont mes professeurs. D'ailleurs, j'étudie le français au lycée et tous les jours je lis quelques pages de français. À propos, êtes-vous français?
—Non, je suis américain comme vous, et comme vous j'étudie le français. Mais moi je n'ai qu'un seul professeur.
—Ah bon. Mais vous parlez très bien.
—Merci. Au revoir et bonne chance.
—Au revoir, monsieur.
M. Brown rejoint sa femme qui l'attend en souriant, et ils se remettent en route pour la visite au paquebot.
—Il est sympathique, ce garçon, dit M. Brown à sa femme. Et puis il traduit la phrase "He's a likeable boy," pour voir la réaction de sa femme.

CHAPITRE 20 (VINGT)

QUEL MAUVAIS TEMPS!
WHAT BAD WEATHER!

1. Il pleut à verse. La bonne ouvre la porte de la maison de M. et Mme Brown. M. Picard entre.

2. La bonne dit:—Bonsoir, M. Picard. Quel mauvais temps! Entrez, entrez. Vous êtes trempé. Donnez-moi votre imperméable et votre chapeau, s'il vous plaît. Mettez votre parapluie dans le porte-parapluies. Vous pouvez laisser vos caoutchoucs ici à l'entrée.

3. M. Picard répond:—Merci, mademoiselle. Maintenant ça va mieux. Il pleut à verse, mais il ne fait pas froid. Je suis sûr que je ne vais pas attraper un rhume. Est-ce que M. Brown est là?

4. —Oui, oui, monsieur. Il vous attend dans le salon. Le voilà lui-même.

5. —Bonsoir, M. Picard. Je suis très content de vous voir, mais par un temps pareil on ne doit pas sortir. Venez dans la salle à manger et prenez une tasse de thé au rhum pour vous réchauffer un peu.

6. —Merci beaucoup, M. Brown. À vrai dire, j'ai un peu froid. Une tasse de thé au rhum fera mon affaire, et pendant que nous prenons le thé nous allons discuter le temps qu'il fait. C'est un sujet de conversation très courant et tout à fait à propos.

1. It is pouring. The maid opens the door of the Browns' house. Mr. Picard comes in.

2. The maid says, Good evening, Mr. Picard. What bad weather! Come in, come in. You are soaking wet. Give me your raincoat and your hat. Put your umbrella in the umbrella stand. You can leave your rubbers here in the hall.

3. Mr. Picard answers, Thank you. Now I feel better. It's pouring, but it's not cold. I am sure that I shall not catch cold. Is Mr. Brown at home?

4. Yes, sir, yes. He is waiting for you in the living room. There he is (himself).

5. Good evening, Mr. Picard. I am very glad to see you, but in weather like this one should not go out. Come into the dining room and drink a cup of tea with rum to warm yourself a bit.

6. Thank you very much, Mr. Brown. Actually, I am a little cold. A cup of tea with rum will suit me fine, and while we drink the tea we will discuss the weather. It is a very common topic of conversation and quite appropriate.

7. Les messieurs entrent dans la salle à manger en parlant d'un ton animé. Ils s'assoient et la bonne leur apporte un plateau de deux tasses et deux soucoupes, une théière pleine de thé chaud, un sucrier, et des cuillers à thé. Elle met le plateau sur la table avec une bouteille de rhum qu'elle va chercher au buffet. Puis elle sort de la salle à manger.

8. —Permettez-moi de vous servir, M. Picard, dit M. Brown. Il verse le thé dans les tasses avec une portion libérale de rhum pour chacun.

9. Pendant qu'ils prennent le thé au rhum les messieurs continuent à parler d'un ton animé.

10. Dehors il pleut toujours.

7. The gentlemen go into the dining room chatting in animated voices. They sit down and the maid brings them a tray with two cups and two saucers, a teapot full of hot tea, a sugar bowl, and some teaspoons. She puts the tray on the table with a bottle of rum which she locates in the buffet. Then she leaves the dining room.

8. Allow me to serve you, Mr. Picard, says Mr. Brown. He pours tea into the cups, with a generous portion of rum for each.

9. While they are drinking the tea with rum the gentlemen continue to speak in animated voices.

10. Outside it is still raining.

Pronunciation and Spelling Aids

Practice aloud:

Bonsoir, M. Picard. Je suis très content de vous voir; mais par un temps pareil on ne doit pas sortir.

(Bawñ-swar, muh-syeu pee-**kar**. zhuh süee treh kawñ-tahñ duh voo **vwar**; may par euñ tahñ pa-ray awñ nuh dwa pah sur-**teer**.)

Venez dans la salle à manger et prenez une tasse de thé au rhum pour vous réchauffer.

(Vuh-nay dahñ la sal a mahñ-**zhay** ay pruh-nay zün tahs duh tay oh **rum** poor voo ray-shoh-**fay**.)

Building Vocabulary

A. **QUEL TEMPS FAIT-IL?** (kehl tahñ feh-**teel?**) What's the weather?

1. **Il fait beau.** (eel feh **boh**)
2. **Il fait mauvais.** (moh-**veh**)
3. **Il fait (très) chaud.** (shoh)
4. **Il fait (très) froid, frais.** (frwah, freh)
5. **Il fait du vent.** (dü **vahñ**)
6. **Il pleut. Il neige. Le soleil brille.** (eel **pleu.** eel **nehzh.** luh su-ley **breey**)
7. **La pluie (la neige) tombe.** (la plüee, la nehzh **tawñb**)
8. **Il pleut à verse.** (eel pleu ta **vehrs**)
9. **Avez-vous froid? J'ai froid.**
10. **Avez-vous chaud? Je n'ai pas chaud.**

1. It's beautiful (weather).
2. It's bad (weather).
3. It is (very) hot.
4. It is (very) cold, cool.
5. It is windy.
6. It is raining. It is snowing. The sun is shining.
7. Rain (snow) is falling.
8. It's pouring.
9. Are you cold? I am cold.
10. Are you warm? I am not warm.

NOTE: The French use the verb **faire** (make, do) in talking about what the weather *does*, instead of the English What *is* the weather? It *makes* (**fait**) warm, cold—not It *is* warm, cold, etc. They also use the verb **avoir,** *to have*, in describing whether they personally are warm or cold: I *have* warm(th), I *have* cold, not I *am* warm, I *am* cold.

B. CLOTHING FOR VARIOUS KINDS OF WEATHER

le **pardessus** (par-duh-**sü**) overcoat

l'**imperméable** (lañ-pehr-may-**ah**-bl) raincoat

le **chandail** (shahñ-**dahy**) cardigan, le **pullover** sweater

le **gilet** (zhee-**lay**) vest

le **parapluie** (pa-ra-**plüee**) umbrella

les **caoutchoucs** (kow-**tchoo**) rubbers, galoshes

French Expressions

1. **Quel mauvais temps!** (kehl sal **tahñ**) What bad weather!
2. **attraper un rhume** (a-tra-pay euñ **rum**) to catch (a) cold
3. **le voilà** there he (it) is
4. **Une tasse de thé fera mon affaire.** A cup of tea will suit me.
5. **en causant** while chatting
6. **lui-même** he himself
7. **elle-même** she herself
8. **moi-même** I myself

Exercise No. 106—Completion of Text

1. **La bonne dit:—** (What bad weather!)
2. (Come in, come in.) **Vous êtes** (soaking wet).
3. **Donnez-moi** (your raincoat).
4. (Put) **votre parapluie dans le porteparapluies.**
5. **Maintenant,** (I feel better).
6. **Je ne vais pas** (to catch cold).
7. **Par un temps pareil** (one should not go out).
8. (Come) **à la salle à manger.**
9. **La bonne** (brings them) **un plateau.**
10. (Drink) **une tasse de thé au rhum.**
11. (Permit me) **de vous servir.**
12. **Dehors,** (it continues to rain).

Grammar Notes

1. THE PRESENT TENSE OF ouvrir, *to open*

(Despite the ending of the infinitive, **ouvrir** is conjugated like a regular **–er** verb.)

I open, you open, etc.

j'**ouvre** (zhoovr)
tu **ouvres** (oovr)
il, elle **ouvre** (oovr)

nous **ouvrons** (oo-vrawñ)
vous **ouvrez** (oo-vray)
ils, elles **ouvrent** (oovr)

Like ouvrir are: **couvrir**, *to cover;* **découvrir**, *to discover;* **offrir**, *to offer*

1. **Charles *me* fait un cadeau.**

2. **Ton père *t'*achète un chandail.**
3. **Qui *vous* apprend le français?**
4. **M. Picard *nous* apprend le français.**
5. **Voilà M. Brown. Qui *lui* parle?**
6. **Voilà Mme Brown. Qui *lui* parle?**
7. ***Nous* leur *apportons les parapluies.***

1. Charles is giving *me* a gift. (*Lit.,* making [offering] a gift to me)
2. Your father is buying (*for*) *you* a sweater.
3. Who is teaching (*to*) *you* French?
4. Mr. Picard is teaching (*to*) *us* French.
5. There is Mr. Brown. Who is speaking *to him?*
6. There is Mrs. Brown. Who is speaking *to her?*
7. We are bringing (*to*) *them* the umbrellas.

2. COMPARISON OF THE DIRECT OBJECT PRONOUNS WITH THE INDIRECT OBJECT PRONOUNS.

Direct	*Indirect*
me, m' me	**me, m'** (to) me
te, t' you (fam.)	**te, t'** (to) you (fam.)
le, l' him, it; **la, l'** her, it	**lui** (to) him, (to) her
nous us	**nous** (to) us
vous you	**vous** (to) you
les them	**leur** (to) them

The direct and indirect objects are identical except in the third person. Direct: **le** (him), **la** (her), **les** (them). Indirect: **lui** (to him, to her), **leur** (to them).

Like the direct object, the indirect object precedes the verb except in the affirmative imperative.

Donnez-*lui* le livre. Give *him* the book.

Ne *lui* donnez pas le livre. Do not give *him* the book.

NOTE: demander means *to ask* or *ask for something.* The person asked is the indirect object. The thing asked or asked for is the direct object. This is true in many of the above verbs.

M. Picard demande à M. Brown (lui demande) le nom de son représentant.

Mr. Picard asks Mr. Brown (asks him) the name of his agent.

Exercise No. 107

Complete the French sentences with the missing indirect objects. Read aloud. Remember **lui** means *to him* or *to her;* **leur** means *to them.* (In English, we often consider the word *"to"* to be understood in this structure; thus, note most of the following parts of this exercise.)

Exemple: 1. Je ne lui prête pas d'argent.

1. I am not lending *him* any money.
2. They are bringing *us* some candy.
3. We are teaching *her* French.

4. The maid is serving *them* some tea.
5. He is showing *them* the samples.
6. Are you sending *her* a gift?
7. She is buying *me* a pair of rubbers.
8. Do not speak *to her.*
9. Bring the umbrella back *to him.*
10. They are asking *us* for our tickets.
11. Give *us* more time.
12. Return my fountain pen *to me,* please.
13. You may repeat my words *to them.*
14. I am going to introduce my friend *to her.*
15. Do not sell *him* your bicycle.

1. Je ne ___ prête pas d'argent.
2. Ils ___ apportent des bonbons.
3. Nous ___ enseignons (*or* apprenons) le français.
4. La bonne ___ sert du thé.
5. Il ___ montre les échantillons.
6. ___ envoyez-vous un cadeau?
7. Elle ___ achète une paire de caoutchoucs.
8. Ne ___ parlez pas.
9. Rapportez- ___ le parapluie.
10. Ils ___ demandent nos billets.
11. Donnez- ___ plus de temps.
12. Rendez- ___ mon stylo, s'il vous plaît.
13. Vous pouvez ___ répéter mes mots.
14. Je vais ___ présenter mon ami.
15. Ne ___ vendez pas votre bicyclette.

Exercise No. 108—Questionnaire

Answer in complete sentences. As usual, practice both questions and answers aloud.

1. **Quel temps fait-il quand M. Picard arrive chez M. Brown?**
2. **Qui ouvre la porte?**
3. **Où est-ce que M. Picard met son parapluie?**
4. **Où est-ce qu'il laisse ses caoutchoucs?**
5. **Où est-ce que les deux messieurs entrent?**
6. **Qu'est-ce qu'ils prennent dans la salle à manger?**
7. **Qu'est-ce que la bonne met sur la table?**
8. **Et après, que fait-elle?**

Even in rainy weather, the French love to spend time in ourdoor cafés.

CHAPITRE 21 (VINGT ET UN)

LE CLIMAT EN FRANCE
THE CLIMATE IN FRANCE

1. Les deux messieurs sont toujours assis dans la salle à manger. Ils bavardent toujours en prenant le thé au rhum. Dehors il continue à pleuvoir. M. Picard n'a plus froid.

2. M. Picard dit:— Le climat des États-Unis et celui de la France sont quelque peu différents. Ici à New York nous avons un climat qui va d'un extrême à l'autre.

3. —C'est vrai. En été il fait chaud; quelquefois il fait très chaud. En hiver il fait froid; parfois il fait très froid, de temps en temps il neige. Au printemps il commence à faire beau, mais il pleut souvent comme ce soir. Parfois il fait froid pendant des semaines quand tout à coup il fait chaud. Quelle saison préférez-vous, M. Picard?

4. —Je préfère l'automne. L'air est frais et vif. Le ciel est lumineux. Le soleil brille de tout son éclat. Et vous, M. Brown, quelle saison préférez-vous?

5. — Je préfère le printemps quand petit à petit tout devient vert. Mais parlons plutôt du climat de la France. Est-ce qu'il y a en France une différence marquée entre les saisons?

6. —Pour la plupart, oui, assez marquée; mais nous n'avons pas des extrêmes de chaleur et de froid.

7. —Cela doit être beaucoup plus agréable.

1. The two men are still sitting in the dining room. They are still chatting while drinking the tea with rum. Outside it continues to rain. Mr. Picard is no longer cold.

2. Mr. Picard says, The climate of the United States and that of France are somewhat different. Here in New York we have a climate that goes from one extreme to the other.

3. That's true. In summer it is hot; sometimes it is very hot. In winter it is cold; at times it is very cold, and it snows now and then. In spring it begins to be nice, but it often rains like tonight. Sometimes it stays cold for weeks when suddenly it gets hot. Which season do you prefer, Mr. Picard?

4. I prefer the autumn. The air is cool and crisp. The sky is clear. The sun shines brilliantly. And you, Mr. Brown, which season do you prefer?

5. I prefer the spring when little by little everything becomes green. But let us talk rather about the climate of France. Is there a marked difference in France among the seasons?

6. For the most part, yes, quite marked; but we don't have extremes of heat and cold.

7. That must be much nicer.

8. —Pas tout à fait. Il est vrai qu'à Paris par exemple il fait rarement très très froid en hiver. Mais par contre, il pleut beaucoup, il fait du vent, le ciel est gris pâle, et on commence à se demander,—Le printemps ne revient-il jamais?

9. —Ah oui, le printemps à Paris est célèbre.

10. —Vous qui préférez le printemps, vous allez être heureux à Paris. Au printemps il fait presque toujours beau. Le ciel est bleu clair avec de gros nuages blancs; les grands platanes des boulevards commencent à feuiller; l'air est doux, embaumé. Toute la ville sourit.

11. —Mais vous faites un poème, M. Picard!

12. —Ce n'est pas pour rien que le printemps à Paris est célèbre.

13. —Tant mieux pour moi, car je compte partir au mois de mai. Et les autres saisons?

14. —Il est déjà tard. Laissons le reste pour la semaine prochaine.

8. Not quite. It is true that in Paris for example it is rarely extremely cold in winter. But on the other hand, it rains a great deal, it is windy, the sky is a pale gray and one begins to wonder, Is spring never coming again?

9. Ah yes, spring in Paris is famous.

10. You who prefer the spring will be happy in Paris. In spring the weather is almost always nice. The sky is blue with thick white clouds; the tall sycamores on the boulevards begin to leaf out, the air is mild and balmy. The whole city smiles.

11. But you're composing a poem, Mr. Picard!

12. It's not for nothing that spring in Paris is famous.

13. All the better for me, as I expect to leave in May. And the other seasons?

14. It is already late. Let us leave the rest for next week.

Pronunciation and Spelling Aids

Practice aloud:

Les deux messieurs sont toujours assis dans la salle à manger.

(Lay deu may-syeu sawñ too-zhoor **za-see** dahñ la sal a mahñ-**zhay**.)

Ils bavardent toujours en prenant le thé au rhum.

(Eel ba-vard too-zhoor ahñ pruh-nahñ luh tay oh **rum**.)

Dehors il continue à pleuvoir.

(Duh-ur eel kawñ-tee-nü a pleu-**vwar**.)

Monsieur Picard n'a plus froid.

(Muh-syeu pee-kar na plü **frwah**.)

Building Vocabulary

A. LES QUATRE SAISONS (*f*)

le printemps (prañ-**tahñ**) spring

l'été (lay-**tay**) (*m*) summer

l'automne (loh-**tun**) (*m*) autumn

l'hiver (lee-**vehr**) (*m*) winter

au printemps in spring

en été in summer

en automne in autumn

en hiver in winter

B. RELATED WORDS

1. différent, la différence
2. intelligent, l'intelligence (f)
3. diligent, la diligence
4. évident, l'évidence (f)
5. content, le contentement
6. intéressant, l'intérêt (m)

French Expressions

1. **tout à coup** (toot ta **koo**) all of a sudden
2. **de tout son éclat** (ay-**kla**) in all its brilliance
3. **petit à petit** little by little
4. **pour la plupart** for the most part
5. **par contre** (par **kawñtr**) on the other hand
6. **se demander** to wonder (*Lit.* to ask oneself)

Exercise No. 109—Completion of Text

1. **Ils causent** (while drinking) **le thé au rhum.**
2. **Dehors il continue** (to rain).
3. **En été** (it is hot).
4. **En hiver** (it is very cold).
5. **Au printemps** (it often rains).
6. (I prefer) **l'automne.**
7. **Quelle saison** (do you prefer)?
8. **Mais** (let us talk rather) **du climat de la France.**
9. **Nous n'avons pas ces extrêmes** (of heat and of cold).
10. **Cela** (ought) **être plus agréable.**
11. **Au printemps** (the weather is fine) **à Paris.**

Grammar Notes

1. PRESENT TENSE OF devoir, *to owe, to be obliged to, to have to;* recevoir, *to receive*

I owe, am obliged to, have to, etc.

je dois (dwa)	nous devons (duh-vawñ)
tu dois (dwa)	vous devez (duh-vay)
il doit (dwa)	ils doivent (dwav)
elle doit (dwa)	elles doivent (dwav)

I receive, you receive, etc.

je reçois	nous recevons
tu reçois	vous recevez
il reçoit	ils reçoivent
elle reçoit	elles reçoivent

Like **recevoir: apercevoir,** *to perceive;* **décevoir,** *to disappoint*

The verb **devoir** is a very important verb with various shades of meaning. It expresses the idea of *must, ought, should,* in the sense of duty or obligation, as well as *must* in the sense of *is supposed to, is probably.*

Exercise No. 110

In the following sentences note the various meanings of **devoir**. Repeat each French sentence aloud five times.

1. Nous leur devons vingt dollars.	1. We owe them twenty dollars.
2. M. Brown doit à M. Picard ses grands progrès dans l'étude du français.	2. Mr. Brown owes his great progress in the study of French to Mr. Picard.
3. Les élèves doivent faire leurs devoirs tous les jours.	3. The pupils must (ought to, have to) do their homework every day.
4. Le train doit arriver à six heures.	4. The train should arrive (is due) at six o'clock.
5. Le climat de France doit être plus agréable que celui de notre pays.	5. The climate of France must be (is probably) more agreeable than that of our country.
6. Cela doit être vraiment beau.	6. That must be really beautiful.
7. Par un temps pareil on ne doit pas sortir.	7. One must (should) not go out in such weather.
8. Vous devez être fatigué après une journée pareille.	8. You must be tired after such a day.

2. SOME NEGATIVE EXPRESSIONS

You have learned that the negative *not* is expressed in French by **ne** before the verb and **pas** after the verb. Thus:

Je *ne* sais *pas.* Est-ce que vous *ne* savez *pas? Ne* savez-vous *pas?*

Study in the following sentences other negative expressions that also have two parts:

1. Le professeur *n'*est *pas encore* ici.	1. The teacher is *not yet* here.
2. Ces élèves *ne* sont *jamais* en retard.	2. These pupils are *never* late.
3. M. Martin *ne* me doit *rien.*	3. Mr. Martin owes me *nothing.*
4. Nous *ne* pouvons *pas* aller *non plus.*	4. We can *not* go *either.*
5. Est-ce que vous *n'*avez *que* cinq dollars?	5. Do you have *only* five dollars?
6. Ils *ne* viennent *plus* ici.	6. They do *not* come here *any more.*
7. Elle *ne* sait *ni* parler *ni* écrire le français.	7. She can *neither* speak *nor* write French.
8. Il *ne* connaît *personne* à Paris.	8. He does *not* know anybody in Paris. (He knows *nobody* in Paris.)

Negative expressions usually have two parts, **ne** before the verb and the rest of each expression after it. Learn:

1. **ne . . . pas encore** not yet
2. **ne . . . jamais** never, not ever
3. **ne . . . rien** nothing, not anything
4. **ne . . . pas . . . non plus** not . . . either

5. **ne . . . que** only
6. **ne . . . plus** no longer, not anymore
7. **ne . . . ni . . . ni** neither . . . nor
8. **ne . . . personne** nobody, not anybody

NOTE: The word **jamais** used without **ne** means ever. For example:

Lisez-vous *jamais* les journaux français?

Do you *ever* read the French newspapers?

Negatives drop the **ne** when used without a verb.

Que faites-vous? *Rien.*

What are you doing? *Nothing.*

Quand le voyez-vous? *Jamais.*

When do you see him? *Never.*

Est-ce que Jean est ici? *Pas encore.*

Is John here? *Not yet.*

Je ne l'aime pas. Ni moi *non plus.*

I don't like him. *Neither* do I.

Qui est là? *Personne.*

Who is there? *Nobody.*

Exercise No. 111

Complete each French sentence with the correct negative. Read each sentence aloud twice.

Example: 1. Je ne sais rien de cette affaire.

1. I know nothing about that matter.
2. The examination is not yet finished.
3. We never travel in winter.
4. They do not like detective films either.
5. He says nothing and he does nothing.
6. Don't you want to take a trip to France?

7. She is no longer satisfied with her TV set.
8. I am not working either.
9. We have nothing to say to you.
10. I have only one notebook.
11. What you are bringing me? Nothing.
12. Is the lesson finished? Not yet.
13. Is spring never coming?
14. We have neither the time nor the money.

1. **Je ___ sais ___ de cette affaire.**
2. **L'examen ___ est ___ terminé.**
3. **Nous ___ voyageons ___ en hiver.**
4. **Ils ___ aiment ___ les films policiers ___ .**
5. **Il ___ dit ___ et il ___ fait___ .**
6. **___ voulez-vous ___ faire un voyage en France?**
7. **Elle ___ est ___ contente de sa télévision.**
8. **Je ___ travaille ___ .**
9. **Nous ___ avons ___ à vous dire.**
10. **Je ___ ai ___ un cahier.**
11. **Qu'est-ce que vous m'apportez? ___ .**
12. **La leçon est-elle finie? ___ .**
13. **Le printemps ___ vient-il ___ ?**
14. **Nous ___ avons ___ le temps ___ l'argent.**

Exercise No. 112—Questionnaire

1. De quoi les messieurs parlent-ils?
2. Est-ce que le climat en France est pareil à (similar to, like) celui des États-Unis?
3. Quel temps fait-il en été à New York?
4. Quelle saison M. Picard préfère-t-il?
5. Et M. Brown quelle saison préfère-t-il?
6. Y a-t-il une différence marquée entre les saisons en France?
7. Comment est l'hiver à Paris?
8. Comment est le printemps à Paris?

CHAPITRE 22 (VINGT-DEUX)

LE CLIMAT EN FRANCE (SUITE)
THE CLIMATE IN FRANCE (CONT'D)

1. —Ce soir nous allons continuer à parler du climat en France.
2. —Vous savez maintenant que le climat de Paris n'est pas très agréable en hiver. C'est pour cela que ceux qui ont les moyens quittent Paris en hiver pour aller en Suisse ou à la Côte d'Azur.
3. —Est-ce que le climat de Suisse en hiver est moins sévère que celui de Paris?
4. —Au contraire, il est plus sévère, mais il est beaucoup plus agréable.
5. —Il n'y a pas d'hiver sur la Côte d'Azur?
6. —L'hiver est doux. Presque tous les jours le soleil brille. Il fait bon. En été il fait plus chaud, mais il y a toujours une jolie brise de mer. Au fait, ce climat ressemble un peu à celui de la Floride.
7. —Ah bon. Mais ne fait-il jamais froid?
8. — Il fait frais pendant la nuit. Il faut se mettre un lainage quelconque. Mais il ne fait jamais très froid sauf dans les montagnes.
9. —Est-ce vrai qu'on peut nager le matin et faire du ski l'après-midi sur la Côte d'Azur?
10. —Mais oui. Ceux qui sont jeunes et forts le font tout le temps. De la plage on peut voir les grandes montagnes des Alpes Maritimes couvertes de neige. Elles sont à une distance de quatre-vingts kilomètres à peu près.

1. This evening we are going to continue to talk about the climate of France.
2. Now you know that the climate of Paris in winter is not very pleasant. That is why those who have the means leave Paris in winter to go to Switzerland or to the Riviera.
3. Is the climate of Switzerland in winter less severe than that of Paris?
4. On the contrary, it is more severe, but it is much nicer.
5. There's no winter on the Riviera?
6. The winter is mild. Nearly every day the sun shines. The weather is fine. In summer it's warmer, but there is always a nice sea breeze. In fact, this climate resembles somewhat that of Florida.
7. Oh, I see. But isn't it ever cold?
8. It is cool during the night. One must put on some woolen garment or other. But it is never very cold except in the mountains.
9. Is it true that you can go swimming in the morning and skiing in the afternoon on the Riviera?
10. Yes, indeed. Those who are young and strong do it all the time. From the beach you can see the high mountains of the Maritime Alps covered with snow. They are at a distance of about eighty kilometers.

11. —Ah, cela doit être vraiment beau!

12. —C'est un coin délicieux. Si vous avez le temps de faire un saut jusqu'à Nice ou Cannes vous allez être enchanté de votre visite.

13. —Merci bien pour le bon conseil. Je vais essayer de faire ce petit voyage au mois du juin.

14. —Vous n'allez pas le regretter, je vous assure.

11. That must be really beautiful!

12. It is a delightful spot. If you have the time to take a hop to Nice or Cannes you will be delighted with your visit.

13. Thank you for the good advice. I shall try to make that little trip in the month of June.

14. You won't be sorry, I assure you.

Pronunciation and Spelling Aids

Practice aloud:

L'hiver est doux. Presque tous les jours le soleil brille. Il fait bon.

(Lee-vehr eh **doo**. Prehsk too lay zhoor luh sulehy **breey**. Eel feh bawñ.)

En été il fait plus chaud, mais il y a toujours une jolie brise de mer.

(Ahñ nay-tay eel feh plü **shoh**, met zeel ya too-zhoor zün zhu-lee breez duh **mehr**.)

Building Vocabulary

ANTONYMS

1. **agréable** agreeable
   désagréable disagreeable
2. **doux** mild, soft, gentle
   sévère severe, harsh
3. **toujours** always, still
   ne . . . jamais never
4. **souvent** often
   rarement rarely
5. **devant** in front of
   derrière behind
6. **avant** before
   après after
7. **entrer dans** to enter
   sortir de to leave
8. **l'entrée** entrance
   la sortie exit

French Expressions

1. **au contraire** on the contrary
2. **au fait** in fact
3. **faire du ski** to go skiing
4. **être enchanté de** to be delighted with
5. **essayer de faire** to try to do (make, take)
6. **il faut partir** one must (it is necessary to) leave

7. **il faut avoir** one must (it is necessary to) have

Exercise No. 113—Completion of Text

1. **Ce soir** (we are going to continue) **à parler du climat en la France.**
2. **Le climat en hiver à Paris est** (very disagreeable).
3. **Ceux** (who have the means) **quittent Paris en hiver.**
4. (Isn't there any winter) **sur la Côte d'Azur?**
5. (It is never cold) **sauf dans les montagnes.**
6. (It is necessary to put on) **un lainage quelconque.**
7. **On peut** (swim in the morning).
8. (One can see) **les grandes montagnes.**
9. **Cela** (must be) **vraiment beau.**
10. (If you have the time) **faites un saut jusqu'à Nice.**

Grammar Notes

DEMONSTRATIVE PRONOUNS

Compare the demonstrative pronouns (**celui, celle, ceux, celles**) with the demonstrative adjectives (**ce, cette, ces**) in the following sentences:

Demonstrative adjectives	Demonstrative pronouns
Ce (this) **docteur-ci est une Française.**	**Celui-ci** (this one) **est anglais.**
Ce (that) **docteur-là est américain.**	**Celui-là** (that one) **est un Italien.**
Cette (this) **fleur-ci est pour Louise.**	**Celle-ci** (this one) **est pour Marie.**
Cette (that) **fleur-là est pour Anne.**	**Celle-là** (that one) **est pour Jeanne.**
Ces (these) **docteurs-ci sont françaises.**	**Ceux-ci** (these) **sont anglais.**
Ces (those) **docteurs-là sont américains.**	**Ceux-là** (those) **sont italiens.**
Ces (these) **fleurs-ci sont pour Louise.**	**Celles-ci** (these) **sont pour Marie.**
Ces (those) **fleurs-là sont pour Anne.**	**Celles-là** (those) **sont pour Jeanne.**

The Demonstrative Pronoun Chart

Singular	*Plural*
Masculine: **celui** *this (one), that (one)*	**ceux** *these, those*
Feminine: **celle** *this (one), that (one)*	**celles** *these, those*

The demonstrative adjectives (**ce, cet, cette, ces**) are always followed by a noun. The demonstrative pronouns (**celui, celle, ceux, celles**) are never followed by a noun. **Ce** and **cet** are both masculine demonstrative adjectives; **cet** is used before a noun beginning with a vowel or mute **h**.

Ce livre, cet étudiant, cet homme

The demonstrative pronouns have the same gender and number as the nouns for which they stand.

Le climat de la France, et *celui* **de l'Italie.**	The climate of France and *that* of Italy.
Ceux *(= les gens)* **qui ont les moyens quittent Paris en hiver**	*Those* who have the means leave Paris in winter.

-**ci** and -**là** are used for emphasis or clarity. Omit -**ci** and -**là** before **de** and before a relative pronoun (**qui** or **que**).

ceci, cela (ça) this, that

ceci and **cela** or **ça** mean *this thing* or *that thing* or they may refer to whole ideas or statements.

Ceci est un rasoir électrique.	This is an electric razor.
Cela est un rasoir de sûreté.	That is a safety razor.
Cela est vrai (faux).	That is true (false).
Ça ne fait rien.	That doesn't matter.
N'oubliez pas ceci: Le commerçant français n'est pas pressé.	Do not forget this: The French merchant is not in a hurry.

Exercise No. 114

Translate these brief exchanges. Practice them aloud.

1. — Quelle poterie préférez-vous, celle de Vallauris ou celle de Biot?—Je préfère celle de Biot.
2. — Quel chapeau aimez-vous mieux, celui-ci ou celui-là?—J'aime mieux celui-là.
3. —Quel climat est plus doux, celui de la France ou celui du Canada?—Celui de la France est plus doux.
4. —Comment trouvez-vous (= *quelle est votre opinion de*) ces robes?—J'aime bien celle-ci. Je trouve les couleurs de celle-là trop éclatantes.
5. —Quelles places préférez-vous, celles des premiers rangs ou celles du fond?—Nous préférons celles des premiers rangs.
6. —Quelle sorte de mouchoirs allez-vous acheter?—Je vais acheter ceux qui sont à meilleur marché.

Exercise No. 115

Complete with the correct form of the demonstrative pronoun:

Example: 1. Les montagnes du Canada sont plus hautes que *celles* de l'Europe.

1. **Les montagnes du Canada sont plus hautes que** (those) **de l'Europe.**
2. **Les fleuves de l'Amérique du Sud sont plus longs que** (those) **de l'Europe.**
3. **Ce pot au lait-ci est de Limoges,** (that one) **est de Biot.**
4. **Ces tasses et ces soucoupes-ci sont de la France,** (those) **sont du Mexique.**
5. **Ces robes-ci sont meilleur marché que** (those).
6. **Ces problèmes-ci** (*m*) **sont plus difficiles que** (those).
7. **Lequel (= which one) est votre parapluie,** (this one) **ou** (that one)?
8. **Laquelle (= which one) est votre place,** (this one) **ou** (that one)?
9. **Le climat de la France est plus doux que** (that) **de la Suisse.**
10. **Ma femme et moi, nous déjeunons ensemble.** (That) **me plaît beaucoup.**

Exercise No. 116—Questionnaire

1. **Pourquoi est-ce que ceux qui ont les moyens quittent Paris en hiver?**
2. **Où vont-ils?**
3. **Comment est l'hiver sur la Côte d'Azur?**
4. **Comment est l'été sur la Côte d'Azur?**
5. **Où est-ce qu'on peut nager le matin et faire du ski l'après-midi?**
6. **Qu'est-ce qu'on peut voir de la plage?**
7. **Quel temps fait-il pendant la nuit?**
8. **Où fait-il très froid?**
9. **À quelle distance les montagnes sont-elles de la plage?**
10. **Quand est-ce que M. Brown va essayer de faire ce petit voyage?**

Paris winters can be very cold. Bundled-up pedestrians pass by these chairs in the park.

CHAPITRE 23 (VINGT-TROIS)

LA BONNE CUISINE FRANÇAISE

GOOD FRENCH COOKING

1. —Vous savez, sans doute, M. Brown, que la bonne cuisine française est un des plus grands plaisirs du touriste en France.

2. —Je le sais bien, M. Picard. Je peux même dire que je la connais un peu, la cuisine française. Quand j'ai des clients importants, je les invite à déjeuner dans un des bons restaurants français ici à New York. Et cela arrive assez souvent.

3. —La cuisine française nous fait cadeau de beaucoup d'expressions d'usage courant en anglais; par exemple: à la carte, bouillon, consommé, purée, sauté, au gratin, café, petits fours, hors d'oeuvres, soufflé, et beaucoup d'autres. À propos, M. Brown, vous êtes dans l'importation. Quand vous serez à Paris, faites une liste de vos plats préférés, et ramenez un bon livre sur la cuisine française, en français, bien entendu.

4. —Quelle bonne idée! Mais la cuisine française n'est-elle pas compliquée?

5. —Pas vraiment. Il y a certains plats célèbres qui sont très compliqués, mais il n'y a rien de mystérieux dans la bonne cuisine française. Je vais vous dire les trois secrets.

6. —Pour commencer, tout ce qui entre dans un plat doit être de bonne qualité: le beurre, les oeufs, la viande, les légumes, tout enfin; ensuite, il faut avoir le goût et l'amour de la cuisine; et après, du beurre, du beurre, et encore du beurre.

1. Most probably you know, Mr. Brown, that good French cooking is one of the greatest pleasures of the tourist in France.

2. I know it well, Mr. Picard. I can even say that I am fairly familiar with French cooking. When I have important customers, I invite them to have lunch at one of the good French restaurants here in New York. And this happens quite often.

3. French cooking gives us (*has "gifted" us with*) many expressions well-accepted in English; for example: à la carte, bouillon, consommé, purée, sauté, au gratin, café, petits fours, hors d'oeuvres, soufflé, and many others. By the way, Mr. Brown, you are in the import business. When you are in Paris, make a list of your favorite dishes and bring back a good French cookbook—in French of course.

4. What a good idea! But isn't French cooking complicated?

5. Not really. There are certain famous dishes which are very complicated but there is nothing mysterious in good French cooking. I am going to tell you the three secrets.

6. First, everything that goes into a dish must be of good quality: the butter, the eggs, the meat, the vegetables, everything, in short; then, one must have a taste for and a love of cooking; then, butter, butter, and more butter.

7. —Merci pour les trois secrets. Je vais les raconter tout de suite à ma femme.
8. —Voilà un mari modèle!
9. —M. Picard, j'ai un appétit de loup! Voulez-vous manger un morceau avec moi?
10. —Avec plaisir, M. Brown.

7. Thank you for the three secrets. I am going to tell them immediately to my wife.
8. There's a model husband!
9. Mr. Picard, I'm as hungry as a wolf (Eng.: bear, horse)! Will you have a bite with me?
10. With pleasure, Mr. Brown.

Pronunciation and Spelling Aids

Practice aloud:

Vous savez, sans doute, Monsieur Brown, que la bonne cuisine française est un des plus grands plaisirs du touriste en France.

(Voo sa-vay, sahñ **doot,** muh-syeu Brown kuh la bun küee-zeen frahñ-**seh** zeh teuñ day plü grahñ pleh-**zeer** dü too-reest ahñ **frahñs.**)

Building Vocabulary

A. SOME FRENCH COOKING EXPRESSIONS ADOPTED IN ENGLISH

1. **le bouillon** (boo-**yawñ**) broth
2. **le consommé** (kawñ-su-**may**) clear soup
3. **la purée** (pü-**ray**) whipped vegetables
4. **sauté** (soh-**tay**) fried
5. **au gratin** (oh gra-**tañ**) dressed with bread crumbs or cheese, and browned in the oven
6. **les petits fours** (puh-tee-**foor**) small cakes
7. **hors d'oeuvres** (ur-**deuvr**) appetizers served at the beginning of a meal

B. SOME FRENCH SPECIALTIES THAT ARE NOT DIFFICULT TO PREPARE

1. la soupe à l'oignon (soop a lu-**nyawñ**) **onion soup**
2. le poulet Marengo (poo-leh ma-rañ-**goh**) **chicken Marengo**
3. le boeuf bourguignon (beuf boor-ghee-**nyawñ**) **beef stew Burgundy style**
4. la blanquette de veau (blahñ-keht duh **voh**) **veal stew in cream sauce**
5. les haricots verts (lay a-ree-koh **vehr**) **green beans** (**note** h aspiré)
6. les épinards à la crème (lay zay-peenar a la **krehm**) **creamed spinach**
7. les petits pois à la française (puh-tee pwa a la frahñ-**sehz**) **peas with lettuce and onions (in the French style)**
8. la poire Hélène (pwar ay-**lehn**) **poached pear with chocolate sauce**
9. les fraises Chantilly (frehz shahñtee-**yee**) **strawberries with whipped cream**
10. la crème Chantilly (krehm shahñ-tee-**yee**) **whipped cream**

French Expressions

1. **cela arrive** that happens
2. **assez souvent** quite often
3. **faire cadeau de** to make a gift of, to give
4. **beaucoup d'autres** many others
5. **Quelle bonne idée!** What a good idea!
6. **rien de mystérieux** nothing mysterious
7. **tout ce qui** everything that

Exercise No. 117—Completion of Text

1. **Je connais un peu la** (good French cooking).
2. **C'est** (one of the greatest pleasures) **du touriste.**
3. **J'invite des clients importants** (to have lunch).
4. (That happens) **assez souvent.**
5. **La cuisine française** (makes us a gift) **de beaucoup d'expressions.**
6. (Bring back) **un bon livre sur la cuisine française.**
7. (I am going to tell you) **les trois secrets.**
8. (. . . all that) **entre dans un plat doit être** (of good quality).
9. (One must have) **l'amour de la cuisine.**
10. **Et après** (butter, butter, and more butter).

Grammar Notes

1. PRESENT TENSE of envoyer, *to send*

I send, you send, etc.

j'envoie **(zhahñ-vwa)**	nous envoyons **(noo zahñ-vwa-yawñ)**
tu envoies **(tü ahñ-vwa)**	vous envoyez **(voo zahñ-vwa-yay)**
il envoie **(eel ahñ-vwa)**	ils envoient **(eel zahñ-vwa)**
elle envoie **(ehl ahñ-vwa)**	elles envoient **(ehl zahñ-vwa)**

Imperative: envoie **send** envoyons **let us send**

envoyez **send**

Like envoyer: renvoyer, *to send back*

2.INDEPENDENT PRONOUNS USED AFTER PREPOSITIONS

a. Note carefully the personal pronouns used after prepositions. They are called *independent* pronouns because they are usually independent of the verb. They are sometimes called *emphatic* or *disjunctive* pronouns.

après *moi* **after** *me*	près de *nous* **near** *us*
sans *toi* **without** *you*	loin de *vous* **far from** *you*
avec *lui* **with** *him*	excepté *eux* **except** *them* (*m*)
pour *elle* **for** *her*	derrière *elles* **behind** *them* (*f*)

b. Note the independent pronouns with the preposition **chez:**

chez moi **at my house (home)**	chez nous **at our house (home)**
chez toi **at your house (home)**	chez vous **at your house (home)**
chez lui **at his house (home)**	chez eux (*m*) **at their house (home)**
chez elle **at her house (home)**	chez elles (*f*) **at their house (home)**

c. The independent pronouns with the preposition **à** after **est** and **sont** indicate possession.

Ce chapeau est à moi	This hat is mine (belongs to me)
(à toi, à lui, à elle)	(yours, his, hers)
Ces chaises sont à nous	These chairs are ours
(à vous, à eux, à elles)	(yours, theirs, m, theirs, f)

Exercise No. 118

Complete the following in French:

1. **Voulez-vous aller** (with me)?
2. **Cette carte est** (for you), **mon enfant.**
3. **Ils vont dîner** (at my house).
4. **Nous restons** (at home) **en famille.**
5. **Mlle Martin n'est pas** (at her house).
6. **L'avion va partir** (without them, *m*).
7. **Il est assis** (near her).
8. **Il y a beaucoup de choses** (around us).
9. **Ces places-ci sont** (ours).
10. **Ces places-là sont** (theirs, *f*).

3. OTHER USES OF THE INDEPENDENT PRONOUNS

a. When the pronoun stands alone, a one-word answer (verb is understood):

Qui a un appétit de loup?	**Who's as hungry as a wolf?**
Moi. Toi. Lui. Elle.	**I. You. He. She.**
Nous. Vous. Eux. Elles.	**We. You. They (*m*). They (*f*).**

b. For emphasis and in double pronoun subjects:

Moi, j'aime le théâtre. **or** Quant à moi	**I *like the theater. or As for me, I . . .***
Lui et moi, nous étudions le français.	**He and I (we) are studying French.**

c. With c'est and ce sont:

C'est moi. **It is I. (In conversation: It's me.)**	C'est nous. **It is we. (us)**
C'est toi. **It is you.**	C'est vous. **It is you.**
C'est lui (elle). **It is he (she).**	Ce sont eux (elles). **It is they.**

NOTE: Ce sont **is used with** eux **and** elles.

d. In the affirmative imperative, me becomes moi and te becomes toi.

Dites-moi où vous demeurez.	**Tell me where you live.**
Lève-toi, mon enfant.	**Get up, child.**
But: Ne me dites pas. Ne te lève pas.	**Do not tell me. Do not get up.**

Exercise No. 119

Complete the following in French:

1. **Qui fait de grands progrès dans ses études?** (He). (She).
2. (I), **j'aime le français; elle aime l'anglais.**
3. **Qui frappe** (knocks) **à la porte? C'est** (me). **C'est** (we). **Ce sont** (they, *m*).
4. **Habille-**(yourself), **Louise.**
5. **Envoyez-**(me) **les fleurs.**
6. **Vous venez plus tard que** (he).
7. (She and I), **nous allons au théâtre.**
8. **Qui étudie diligemment?** (I).

9. **Est-ce que ce stylo-ci est** (yours)?
10. **Non, c'est** (his).

Exercise No. 120—Questionnaire

1. Quel est un des plus grands plaisirs du touriste en France?
2. Est-ce que M. Brown connaît la cuisine française?
3. De quoi la cuisine française nous fait-elle cadeau?
4. Qu'est-ce que M. Brown doit faire à Paris?
5. Est-ce que la cuisine française est compliquée?
6. Quel est le troisième secret de la bonne cuisine?
7. Est-ce que M. Brown va les raconter à sa femme?
8. Qui est un mari modèle?
9. Qui a un appétit de loup?
10. Qui va manger un morceau avec M. Brown?

Première Partie

NOUNS

1.	l'amour	1.	love
2.	l'appétit	2.	appetite
3.	le boeuf	3.	beef
4.	le cadeau	4.	gift
5.	le climat	5.	climate
6.	le coin	6.	corner
7.	le conseil	7.	advice
8.	le dessert	8.	dessert
9.	les épinards	9.	spinach
10.	les fraises	10.	strawberries
11.	les haricots verts	11.	green beans
12.	l'hiver	12.	winter
13.	l'imperméable	13.	raincoat
14.	le légume	14.	vegetable
15.	la mer	15.	sea
16.	la neige	16.	snow
17.	les moyens	17.	means
18.	le parapluie	18.	umbrella
19.	le pardessus	19.	overcoat
20.	le plateau	20.	tray
21.	la pluie	21.	rain
22.	la poire	22.	pear
23.	le poulet	23.	chicken
24.	le reste	24.	remainder
25.	la saison	25.	season
26.	la sortie	26.	exit
27.	la soupe	27.	soup
28.	le thé	28.	tea
29.	le veau	29.	veal
30.	la visite	30.	visit

VERBS

1. apporter	1. to bring
2. briller	2. to shine
3. casser	3. to break
4. chercher	4. to look for
5. envoyer	5. to send
6. j'envoie	6. I send
7. essayer	7. to try
8. frapper	8. to knock
9. nager	9. to swim
10. neiger	10. to snow
11. oublier	11. to forget
12. quitter	12. to leave, quit
13. raconter	13. to tell about
14. réchauffer	14. to warm
15. tomber	15. to fall
16. verser	16. to pour, spend
17. couvrir	17. to cover
18. je couvre	18. I cover
19. devenir	19. to become
20. je deviens	20. I become
21. pleuvoir	21. to rain
22. il pleut	22. it is raining
23. sourire	23. to smile
24. je souris	24. I smile
25. ramener	25. to bring back

ADJECTIVES

1. agréable	1. agreeable
2. clair	2. clear
3. couvert	3. covered
4. enchanté	4. delighted
5. faux (fausse *f*)	5. false
6. plein	6. full
7. pâle	7. pale
8. préféré	8. preferred
9. pressé	9. in a hurry
10. sale	10. nasty, dirty
11. trempé	11. soaked
12. sûr	12. sure
13. vif (vive *f*)	13. brisk, lively

ADVERBS

1. dehors	1. outside
2. plutôt	2. rather
3. tôt	3. soon
4. tard	4. late
5. plus tôt	5. sooner
6. plus tard	6. later

PREPOSITIONS

1. à côté de	1. at the side of
2. au lieu de	2. instead of
3. sauf	3. except

NEGATIVES

1. ne . . . pas	1. not
2. ne . . . jamais	2. never
3. ne . . . pas encore	3. not yet
4. ne . . . plus	4. no longer, no more
5. ne . . . rien	5. nothing
6. ne . . . que	6. only
7. ne . . . personne	7. nobody

French Expressions

1. cela arrive	1. that happens
2. assez souvent	2. quite often
3. par contre	3. on the other hand
4. petit à petit	4. little by little
5. il pleut à verse	5. it is pouring
6. quel sale temps!	6. what nasty weather!
7. ça va mieux	7. I feel better
8. tout à coup	8. all of a sudden
9. moi-même	9. myself
10. lui-même	10. himself
11. elle-même	11. herself
12. le, la voilà	12. there he, she (it) is

Deuxième Partie

Exercise No. 121

From Group II select the opposite of each word in Group I:

I	II
1. tôt, bientôt	a. beaucoup de temps
2. vieux, ancien	b. ne . . . jamais
3. peu de temps	c. tard
4. perdre	d. vrai
5. occupé	e. trouver
6. envoyer	f. jeune, nouveau
7. agréable	g. libre
8. toujours	h. rarement
9. faux	i. recevoir
10. tout	j. pas encore
11. souvent	k. désagréable
12. déjà	1. rien

Exercise No. 122

Complete the following sentences in French:

1. **Quand il fait froid** (I am cold).
2. **Quand il fait chaud** (I am warm).
3. **En été** (it is warm).
4. **Au printemps** (it rains a great deal).
5. **En automne** (it is cool).
6. **En hiver** (it is cold).
7. **Quand il pleut je porte** (a raincoat).
8. **Quand il neige** (I wear an overcoat).
9. **La pluie** (is falling).
10. **J'aime bien** (all the seasons).

Exercise No. 123

Select the group of words in Column II which best completes each sentence begun in Column I.

I	II
1. Moi, je préfère le climat de la France,	a. quelque chose du climat de la France.
2. Prenez du thé au rhum	b. préparer quelques bons plats français.
3. Je vais vous dire	c. arriver à cinq heures de l'après-midi.
4. C'est vrai que l'hiver	d. mais elle préfère celui de la Suisse.
5. Prenez un parapluie	e. mais celles-là sont libres.
6. Les deux messieurs entrent dans le salon	f. pour vous réchauffer.
7. Ces places-ci sont occupées,	g. à Paris est souvent désagréable.
8. Il n'est pas difficile de	h. en causant d'un ton animé.
9. Je vais ramener	i. parce qu'il pleut à verse.
10. Le train de Lyon doit	j. un bon livre sur la cuisine française.

Exercise No. 124

Complete the answer to each question with the correct direct or indirect object pronoun in French:

1. Qu'est-ce que la bonne dit à M. Brown?
2. Qu'est-ce que M. Picard donne à la bonne?
3. Est-ce que M. Brown attend M. Picard?
4. Est-il content de voir M. Picard?
5. Pourquoi est-ce que M. Picard prend une tasse de thé?
6. Qu'est-ce que M. Brown dit à M. Picard?
7. Préférez-vous les films policiers?
8. Quand allez-vous quitter la ville?
9. Qui vous invite à déjeuner?
10. Qu'est-ce que vous donnez aux enfants?

1. Elle (to him) dit:—Quel mauvais temps!
2. Il (to her) donne son parapluie.
3. Oui, il (him) attend.
4. Il est content de (him) voir.
5. Il (it) prend pour (himself) réchauffer.
6. Il lui dit:—Permettez-(me) de (you) servir.
7. Nous ne (them) préférons pas.
8. Je vais (it) quitter l'été prochain.
9. Mon ami Charles (me) invite à déjeuner.
10. Je (to them) donne un ballon de football.

Exercise No. 125

Translate the English sentences using the negative indicated. ne must precede the verb.

1. (ne ___ personne) I do not know anybody.
2. (ne ___ jamais) We never eat meat.
3. (ne ___ que) I have only one teacher.

4. (ne ___ plus) She no longer wants that hat.
5. (ne ___ pas encore) Joan does not go to school yet.
6. (ne ___ pas ___ non plus) I am not tired either.
7. (ne ___ plus) We have no more (de) time.
8. (ne ___ rien) Why do you say nothing?
9. (ne ___ ni ___ ni) We have neither the time nor the money.

Dialogue

Au Restaurant

1. —Bonjour, monsieur. Voici la carte.
2. —Merci. Qu'est-ce qu'il y a de bon aujour-d'hui?
3. —Nous avons un très bon dîner à prix fixe aujourd'hui: soupe à l'oignon, entrecôte aux pommes, tomates farcies, salade, fromage et une belle tarte aux pêches.
4. —Qu'est-ce qu'il y a de bon à la carte?
5. —Je vous recommande le canard. C'est de l'extra.
6. —Très bien. J'aime beaucoup le canard. Apportez-moi pour commencer la soupe à l'oignon.
7. —Très bien, monsieur. Voulez-vous un légume? Le canard est garni de pommes sautées.
8. —Non, merci. Pas de légumes. Une salade, c'est tout.
9. —Bien, monsieur. Voulez-vous un fromage?
10. —Ça oui. Comment est le camembert? Est-il bien fait?
11. —Il est au point, monsieur, un délice!
12. —Très bien. Avec ça un café bien fort.
13. —Et comme boisson?
14. —Une demi-bouteille de Pommard.
15. —Très bien, monsieur. Tout de suite.
16. —Le repas terminé, M. Brown dit:— Garçon, l'addition, s'il vous plaît.
17. —Voici, monsieur.
18. —Est-ce que le service est compris?

1. Good day, sir. Here is the menu.
2. Thank you. What is there that's good today?
3. We have a very good fixed-price dinner today: onion soup, steak with potatoes, stuffed tomatoes, salad, cheese, and a fine peach tart.
4. What is there that's good à la carte?
5. I recommend the duck. It is especially good.
6. Very good. I like duck very much. Bring me the onion soup to begin with.
7. Very good, sir. Do you want a vegetable? The duck is garnished with sautéed potatoes.
8. No, thank you. No vegetables. A salad, that's all.
9. Good, sir. Do you want cheese?
10. That, yes. How is the camembert? Is it ripe?
11. It is just right, sir, a treat!
12. Very good. With that, a cup of good strong coffee.
13. And what will you drink? (and as a beverage?)
14. A half bottle of Pommard.
15. Very good, sir. Right away.
16. At the end of the meal Mr. Brown says: "Waiter, the check, please."
17. Here you are, sir.
18. Is the service charge included?

19. —Oui, monsieur, voyez-vous, là, en bas.	19. Yes, sir, see, there, at the bottom.
20. —Merci.	20. Thank you.
21. —Merci bien, monsieur.	21. Thank you very much, sir.

NOTES: In many cafés and restaurants, there will be a lunch or dinner **à prix fixe,** which for a more reasonable, set price, diners will receive three or four courses, with only one or a limited set of choices for each course.

Service compris is a custom by which a certain percentage tip is already built into the price of a meal; diners are free to add to this tip if they felt that their waiter or waitress was exceptionally good.

Exercise No. 126—Lecture

Un programme exceptionnel au cinéma

To read silently and aloud with proper intonation; try to understand as much as possible without looking up vocabulary.

Ce soir M. et Mme Brown vont au cinéma. Ils n'aiment pas la plupart des films de Hollywood, surtout les "Westerns" dans lesquels les "cowboys" tirent des coups de feu sur tout le monde et galopent sans cesse. Les films policiers ne les intéressent pas non plus.

Mais ce soir il y a un programme exceptionnel dans un théâtre qui est tout près de chez eux. Le film s'appelle "Un Voyage en France." C'est un film de reportage sur le pays que M. Brown va visiter dans quelques mois. Il y a des scènes qui représentent l'histoire de la France, d'autres qui montrent ses paysages, ses rivières, ses montagnes, ses grandes villes, etc. C'est-à-dire que c'est un film très intéressant pour les touristes.

Les Brown arrivent au théâtre à huit heures et demie. Presque toutes les places sont prises, donc ils doivent s'asseoir au troisième rang. Ceci ne plaît pas à M. Brown parce que les mouvements sur l'écran lui font mal aux yeux. Heureusement ils peuvent changer de place après un quart d'heure et ils se mettent au treizième rang.

Les Brown aiment beaucoup ce film. Ils le trouvent passionnant.

En sortant du théâtre M. Brown dit à sa femme,—Sais-tu, Alice, je crois que je me tirerai bien d'affaire en France. J'ai compris presque tout ce qu'on a dit.

CHAPITRE 24 (VINGT-QUATRE)

LES FRANÇAIS

THE FRENCH PEOPLE

1. —M. Picard, je vais vous poser quelques questions sur les Français. Êtes-vous prêt? Voulez-vous encore un cigare?

2. —Merci, M. Brown. Je suis bien à mon aise. Continuez, s'il vous plaît.

3. —Pour commencer, est-ce que les Français se ressemblent plus ou moins, ou est-ce qu'ils diffèrent en caractère selon la géographie du pays?

4. —Je vais vous dire tout de suite, M. Brown, que les Français sont français partout. Mais il est vrai qu'il y a de très grandes différences entre les Français, non seulement à cause de la géographie, mais aussi à cause de leurs métiers.

5. —Dites-moi, M. Picard, quelles sont quelques-unes de ces différences?

6. —Eh bien, pour commencer, au nord-ouest, nous avons les pêcheurs et les marins de la Bretagne, plus souvent en mer que chez eux; très dévots, et très dévoués à leur eau de vie, le Calvados. Ensuite, les fermiers de la Normandie, ronds et railleurs. Et après, les ouvriers des mines et des usines du nord-est, débrouillards et syndiqués.

7. —Tout cela, seulement pour commencer? M. Picard, nous allons rester ici toute la nuit!

1. Mr. Picard, I am going to ask you a few questions about the French people. Are you ready? Do you want another cigar?

2. Thank you, Mr. Brown. I am very comfortable. Continue, please.

3. To begin with, are the French people more or less alike (resemble each other), or do they differ in character according to the geography of the country?

4. I'll tell you at once, Mr. Brown, that the French are French everywhere. It is true that there are some very great differences among all the French, not only because of the geography but also because of their occupations.

5. Tell me, Mr. Picard, what are some of these differences?

6. Well, to begin with, in the northwest we have the fishing people and sailors of Brittany, more often at sea than at home; very devout—and very devoted to their brandy, Calvados! Next, the farmers of Normandy, rotund and fond of bantering. And then the workers in the mines and factories of the northeast, resourceful and unionized.

7. All this, just to begin? Mr. Picard, we're going to be here all night!

8. —Je crois que nous n'avons pas besoin de continuer. Vous comprenez par exemple, que les gens du Midi, bavards et blagueurs, ne ressemblent pas trop au montagnards taciturnes de l'Auvergne.

9. —Sans connaître trop les détails, je peux comprendre cela.

10. —Mais, malgré toutes ces différences, ils sont tous français; c'est-à-dire, qu'ils aiment beaucoup discuter, surtout les questions politiques; qu'ils n'ont pas peur des idées; qu'ils sont fiers de leur tradition de démocratie, de belles-lettres, de philosophie, et de science; et finalement qu'ils aiment tous la bonne cuisine et le bon vin.

11. —Je les aime déjà sans les connaître.

12. —Si c'est comme ça à présent, qu'est-ce qui va se passer au mois de juin pendant votre visite?

13. —Ça va être un roman d'amour, M. Picard!

8. I think that we don't need to go on. You realize for example, that the people of the Midi (southern France), talkative and jokers, don't resemble the taciturn mountaineers of Auvergne.

9. Without knowing too many details, I can understand that.

10. But in spite of all these differences, they are all French; that is to say, that they love to discuss, especially questions of politics; that they are not afraid of ideas; that they are proud of their tradition of democracy, of literature, of philosophy, and of science; and finally that they all love good cooking and good wine.

11. I like them already without knowing them.

12. If it's like that now, what will happen in the month of June during your visit?

13. It's going to be a love story, Mr. Picard!

Pronunciation and Spelling Aids

Practice aloud:

Monsieur Picard, je vais vous poser quelques questions sur les Français.

(Muh-syeu pee-**kar**, zhuh veh voo pohzay kehl-kuh kehst-**yawñ** sur lay frahñ-**seh**.)

Êtes-vous prêt? Voulez-vous un autre cigare?

(Eht-voo **preh**?) (Voo-lay-voo euñ nohtr see-**gar**?)

Building Vocabulary

A. POINTS OF THE COMPASS

le nord (nur) north

le sud (süd) south

l'est (lehst) east

l'ouest (lwehst) west

B. QUELQUES LOCUTIONS DE FUMERIE SOME SMOKING TERMS

le cigare (see-**gar**) cigar

la cigarette (see-ga-**reht**)

l'allumette (la-lü-**meht**) match

la pipe (peep) pipe

le tabac (ta-**ba**) tobacco, tobacco store

le cendrier (sahñ-dree-**ay**) ashtray

défense de fumer (day-fahñs duh fü-**may**) no smoking

C. DES OUVRIERS (*m*), ouvrières (*f*) SOME WORKING MEN, WOMEN, LABOURERS

le pêcheur (peh-**sheur**) fisherman

le marin (ma-**rañ**) sailor

le fermier (fehr-**myay**) farmer

le cuisinier (küee-zee-**nyay**) cook

le camionneur truck driver

le mécanicien mechanic

les ouvriers des mines et des usines (lay-zoo-vree-ay day **meen** ay day zü-**zeen**) mine and factory workers

le couturier (koo-tü-rj-**ehr**) dressmaker, designer

French Expressions

1. **avoir peur de** (a-vwar **peur** duh) to be afraid of
2. **se passer** (suh pah-**say**) to happen
3. **se passer de** to do without
4. **Qu'est-ce qui se passe?** What's happening?
5. **Qu'est-ce qui arrive?** What is happening?

Exercise No. 127—Completion of Text

1. **Je vais vous poser** (a few) **questions.**
2. **Êtes-vous** (ready)?
3. **Je suis** (very comfortable).
4. (They are alike) **plus ou moins.**
5. **Mais les Français sont Français** (everywhere).
6. **Il y a de grandes différences** (as you say).
7. **Quelles sont** (some of these) **différences?**
8. (The fishing people and sailors) **sont très dévots.**
9. (The farmers) **sont ronds et railleurs.**
10. (The mine workers) **sont syndiqués.**
11. (We don't need) **de continuer.**
12. **Les gens du Midi** (do not resemble) **les montagnards.**
13. **Ils aiment beaucoup** (to discuss).

Grammar Notes

1. REFLEXIVE VERBS WITH RECIPROCAL MEANING

The reflexive pronouns are sometimes translated *each other* or *one another*. This use is known as the reflexive with reciprocal meaning.

Les Français se ressemblent plus ou moins.	French people resemble each other more or less.
Nous nous rencontrons tous les jeudis.	We meet each other (one another) every Thursday.

If the meaning is not clear from the reflexive construction, **l'un (une) l'autre** and **les uns (unes) les autres** are added after the verb.

Nous nous aimons l'un l'autre.	We love one another.
Elles se font des cadeaux les unes aux autres.	They give gifts to each other.

2. VERBS AFTER PREPOSITIONS

In English the present participle of a verb (= verb + ing) is used after prepositions. In French the infinitive of the verb is used after any preposition (except **en**) to express the same idea. Examples:

Sans connaître les détails je le comprends.	Without knowing the details I understand (it).
Avant de sortir il met son pardessus.	Before leaving he puts on his overcoat.

After the preposition **en** the French do use the present participle. In this case **en** is translated by *while, on, by, upon, in,* or is not translated at all.

Ils entrent dans la salle à manger en bavardant d'un ton animé.	They enter the dining room (while) chatting in an animated tone.
En sortant de la gare ils appellent un taxi.	(On, upon) leaving the station, they call a taxi.

3. FORMATION OF THE PRESENT PARTICIPLE

All French verbs, except **être, avoir,** and **savoir,** form the present participle by dropping the ending **-ons** from the **nous** form of the present tense and adding **-ant.** Thus:

nous donnons	donnant	**nous vendons**	vendant	**nous finissons**	finissant
we give	giving	we sell	selling	we finish	finishing
nous voyons	voyant				
we see	seeing				

nous avons	ayant	nous sommes	étant	nous savons	sachant
we have	having	we are	being	we know	knowing

NOTE: Be sure to distinguish the pronunciation of the endings **-ons** (awñ) and **-ant** (ahñ).

Exercise No. 128

Write the **nous** form of the present tense, then the present participle of the following verbs. Use the verb summary chart at the end of this book if you need assistance:

Exemple: aller, nous allons, allant

1. étudier
2. venir
3. lire
4. acheter
5. vouloir
6. dire
7. choisir
8. finir
9. bâtir
10. connaître
11. apprendre
12. appeler
13. compter
14. dormir
15. mettre
16. faire
17. avoir
18. être

4. quelque, quelqu'un

quelque *some (plural* quelques *some, any, a few)* is an adjective and therefore modifies a noun: *so, there must be agreement in number.*

Voulez-vous quelque chose?	Do you want something?
Je vais poser quelques questions.	I am going to ask a few questions.

quelqu'un, quelqu'une, *somebody, anybody* (plural **quelques-uns, quelques-unes** *some, a few, several*) is a pronoun and therefore is not followed by a noun.

Quelqu'un sait la verité.	Somebody knows the truth.
Quelques-uns de ces élèves apprennent le français.	Some of these pupils are learning French.
Je connais quelques-unes de ces différences.	I know some of these differences.

Exercise No. 129

Complete these sentences with the correct form of **quelque** or **quelqu'un**.

1. Il y a (somebody) **dans la cuisine.**
2. **Nous achetons** (a few) **légumes.**
3. (Some) **de ces messieurs sont Français.**
4. (Some) **de ces dames sont Anglaises.**
5. **Quelles sont** (some) **de ces différences?**
6. **Nous apprenons** (some) **locutions françaises.**
7. **J'ai** (some) **livres pour vous.**
8. **Nous avons** (a few) **cadeaux pour maman.**
9. **Voulez-vous** (some) **de ces poires?**
10. **Est-ce que vous attendez** (somebody)?

Exercise No. 130—Questionnaire

1. Qu'est-ce que M. Brown va faire?
2. Qu'est-ce que M. Brown demande pour commencer?
3. A l'opinion de M. Picard, est-ce qu'il y a de très grandes différences entre tous les Français?
4. Pourquoi y a-t-il des différences entre les Français?
5. Comment sont les pêcheurs de la Bretagne?
6. Comment sont les gens du Midi?
7. Est-ce qu'ils ressemblent aux montagnards de l'Auvergne?
8. Est-ce que les Français aiment bien discuter?
9. De quoi les Français sont-ils fiers?
10. Qu'est-ce qu'ils aiment tous?

CHAPITRE 25 (VINGT-CINQ)

L'ART ET LA MODE

ART AND FASHION

1. M. Brown vient de recevoir une grande caisse de marchandise que M. Picard est en train d'admirer.
2. —Ce sont des échantillons de riches étoffes de soie de Lyon, de beaux tissus de lin, de velours, et de laine. Regardez, M. Picard, cette belle étoffe de laine de la maison Dior pour un manteau de dame.
3. —Tiens! Christian Dior? Mais n'est-il pas couturier?
4. —Certainement. Un des plus connus. Les grandes maisons de couture font le commerce non seulement des robes et des manteaux, mais aussi de la lingerie, des parfums, des gants, des bas, et des tissus. Et qui sait si l'année prochaine ils ne vont pas offrir des éviers de cuisine en couleurs assorties, et parfumés!
5. —M. Brown, je crois que vous n'aimez pas la mode.
6. —J'aime beaucoup les belles choses telles que ces jolies étoffes en couleurs magnifiques; mais la mode, c'est quelque chose d'autre.
7. —Pourtant, la couture est un art, n'est-ce pas? Et vous êtes un connaisseur des arts.
8. —C'est vrai, mais je préfère les beaux-arts: la peinture, la sculpture, l'architecture. Je compte beaucoup sur le plaisir de visiter le Musée du Louvre pour voir l'art des grands maîtres. J'espère aussi visiter les musées de l'art moderne.

1. Mr. Brown has just received a large case of merchandise that Mr. Picard is admiring.
2. These are samples of rich silk materials from Lyons, and of beautiful linen, velvet and woolen fabrics. Look, Mr. Picard, at this fine woolen material from the house of Dior for a lady's coat.
3. Well, well! Christian Dior? But isn't he a dress designer?
4. Certainly. One of the best known. The big dressmaking houses do business not only in dresses and coats, but also in lingerie, perfume, gloves, stockings, and fabrics; and who knows if next year they won't offer perfumed kitchen sinks in assorted colors!
5. Mr. Brown, I think that you don't like fashion.
6. I love beautiful things such as these lovely fabrics in magnificent colors; but fashion, that's another matter.
7. And yet, dressmaking is an art, isn't it? And you are a connoisseur of the arts.
8. That's true, but I prefer the fine arts: painting, sculpture, architecture. I am looking forward to the pleasure of visiting the Louvre Museum to see the art of the great masters. I hope also to visit the museums of modern art.

9. —Vous êtes un homme d'affaires tout à fait exceptionnel. Vous vous intéressez à toutes sortes de choses: l'art, l'histoire, les belles-lettres. Je vous admire.

10. —Et moi, je vous admire aussi. Vous êtes un professeur tout à fait exceptionnel.

11. —Bon. Formons une société d'estime mutuelle!

12. —D'accord. Prochaine réunion de la société: mardi à huit heures.

13. —Entendu. Au revoir, co-sociétaire.

14. Ils se serrent la main.

9. You are a very unusual businessman. You take an interest in all sorts of things, art, history, great literature. I admire you.

10. And I admire you too. You are a very special teacher.

11. Good. Let us form a mutual admiration society!

12. Okay. Next meeting of the society: Tuesday at eight o'clock.

13. Agreed. Goodbye, fellow-member.

14. They shake hands.

Pronunciation and Spelling Aids

Practice aloud:

M. Brown vient de recevoir une grande caisse de marchandise que M. Picard est en train d'admirer.

(Muh-syeu Brown vyañ duh ruh-suh-**vwar** ün grahñd kehs duh mar-shahñ-**deez** kuh muh-syeu pee-kar eh tahñ **trañ** dad-mee-**ray**.)

Remember: **é** is pronounced **ay**, and **è**, **eh**; **e** before a double consonant is pronounced **eh**:

j'appelle (zha-**pehl**) **je jette** (zhuh **zheht**)

Building Vocabulary

A. LES VÊTEMENTS (**veht-mahñ**)—CLOTHES

les bas (bah) stockings

la blouse (blooz) blouse

la ceinture (sañ-**tür**) belt

le chapeau (sha-**poh**) hat

le complet (kawñ-**pleh**) suit (man's)

le costume tailleur (tah-**yeur**) suit (woman's)

le foulard (foo-**lar**) small scarf

les gants (gahñ) gloves

la jupe (zhüp) skirt

les chaussettes (*f.*) (shoh-**seht**) socks

la chaussure (shoh-**sür**) shoe

la chemise (shuh-**meez**) shirt

la cravate (kra-**vat**) necktie

le manteau (mahñ-**toh**) coat

le pantalon (pahñ-ta-**lawñ**) pants, trousers

le mouchoir (moo-**shwar**) handkerchief

la robe (rub) dress

B. NOUN COMBINATIONS

In English we can put two nouns together, the first one usually serving as an adjective, e.g. *a silk dress, a wool coat, a school teacher,* etc. This is not done in French, which uses instead two nouns connected by **de** (of), as in clothing fabrics or other combinations:

une robe de soie a silk dress

un manteau de laine a wool coat

une ceinture de cuir a leather belt

des tissus de lin linen fabrics

un chapeau de velours velvet hat

l'étoffe de coton cotton cloth

le maître d'école school teacher

la classe de français French class

l'Opéra de Paris the Paris Opera

les rues (*f.*) **de New-York** New York streets

French Expressions and Examples

1. **venir de** + *infinitive* to have just (done something)
2. **venir de recevoir** to have just received
3. **il vient de recevoir** he has just received
4. **nous venons d'écrire** we have just written
5. **ils viennent de dîner** they have just dined
6. **être en train de** + *infinitive* to be in the act of (doing something)
7. **nous sommes en train de manger** we are (in the process of) eating
8. **il est en train d'admirer** he is admiring
9. **ils font le commerce de** they do business in
10. **c'est quelque chose d'autre** that's something else, another matter
11. **compter sur le plaisir de** + *infinitive* to look forward to
12. **je compte sur le plaisir de faire votre connaissance** I look forward to meeting you
13. **se serrer la main** to shake hands
14. **nous nous serrons la main** we shake hands

Exercise No. 131—Completion of Text

1. **Il** (has just received) **des échantillons.**
2. **M. Picard** (is admiring) **les étoffes de soie.**
3. **Les maisons de couture font le commerce** (not only) **des robes** (but also) **de la lingerie, etc.**
4. **Je crois** (that you do not like) **la mode.**
5. **La couture est un art** (isn't it?)
6. **Je préfère** (the fine arts).
7. painting, sculpture, and architecture.
8. (I look forward) **de visiter le Musée du Louvre.**
9. **Vous êtes un homme d'affaires** (very special, exceptional).
10. I admire you.

Grammar Notes

VERBS WITH INTERNAL SPELLING CHANGES

acheter, to buy	**préférer,** to prefer	**appeler,** to call, or **s'appeler** to call oneself, be named
j'achète	je préfère	j'appelle
tu achètes	tu préfères	tu appelles
il, elle achète	il, elle préfère	il, elle appelle
nous achetons	nous préférons	nous appelons
vous achetez	vous préférez	vous appelez
ils, elles achètent	ils, elles préfèrent	ils, elles appellent

These verbs are conjugated like regular **-er** verbs. There are, however, slight changes in the spelling of the stem before the silent verb endings corresponding to the pronouns **je, tu, il, elle, on, ils,** and **elles** or those noun subjects in the third person singular or plural (ex. **le professeur, Marie, les géns, les couturières**)

Like **acheter** above, the **e** in the stem becomes **è** before silent endings **-e, -es, -ent.**

lever, *to raise,* **se lever,** *to get up*	je (me) lève	tu (te) lèves	il, elle (se) lève
	nous (nous) levons	vous (vous) levez	ils, elles (se) lèvent

Like **préférer,** (**é** in the stem becomes **è** before the silent endings **-e, -es, ent**

espérer, *to hope*	j'espère	tu espères	il, elle espère
	nous espérons	vous espérez	ils, elles espèrent
célébrer, *to celebrate*	je célèbre	tu célèbres	il, elle célèbre
	nous célébrons	vous célébrez	ils, elles célèbrent
répéter, *to repeat*	je répète	tu répètes	il, elle répète
	nous répétons	vous répétez	ils, elles répètent

Like **appeler** or **s'appeler** (consonant of stem doubles before silent endings)

jeter, *to throw*	je jette	tu jettes	il, elle jette
	nous jetons	vous jetez	ils, elles, jettent

Exercise No. 132

Complete each sentence using the correct French verb form:

1. (She is buying) quelques-uns de ces fichus.
2. (Do you like) les mouchoirs de soie?
3. Non, (I prefer) les mouchoirs de lin.
4. (Let us repeat) cette phrase.
5. (I hope) voir tout cela.
6. À quelle heure (do you get up)?
7. (I get up) à sept heures du matin.
8. En France on (celebrates) le 14 juillet.
9. Le fils aîné (is named) Charles.
10. Les enfants (are throwing) la balle.
11. Le maître (calls) les élèves.
12. (I am repeating) le poème.

Exercise No. 133—Questionnaire

1. Qu'est-ce que M. Brown vient de recevoir?
2. Que fait M. Picard?
3. Qu'est-ce qu'il y a dans la grande caisse?
4. De quelle maison est la belle étoffe de laine?
5. Qu'est-ce que M. Picard croit au sujet de M. Brown et la mode?
6. De quoi est-ce que M. Brown est amateur?
7. Qu'est-ce que M. Brown va voir au Musée du Louvre?
8. Qu'est-ce qu'il espère visiter aussi?
9. À quoi M. Brown s'intéresse-t-il?
10. Qu'est-ce que les messieurs vont former?

CHAPITRE 26 (VINGT-SIX)

LES JOURS DE FÊTE EN FRANCE

FRENCH HOLIDAYS

1. —Ce soir parlons des jours de fête en France. Cela va nous égayer un peu, car il fait du vent et il pleut.
2. —Volontiers. Je sais bien que le quatorze juillet on célèbre la prise de la Bastille, et que c'est la grande fête nationale. Mais dites-moi, M. Picard, comment est-ce qu'elle est célébrée?
3. —Partout en France, le quatorze juillet est célébré dans les rues. Tout le monde est dans la rue. À Paris chaque quartier a sa troupe de musiciens. On danse toute la journée et presque toute la nuit. On vend des crêpes, des gauffres, des glaces, et toutes sortes de friandises. Il y a les petits chevaux de bois, les Guignols pour les enfants, et naturellement les buvettes pour les grands.
4. —J'espère voir tout cela et même danser dans les rues au mois de juillet. Et comment le Noël est-il célébré?
5. —M. Brown, je dois vous corriger. Noël est bien masculin, mais on dit *la* Noël, pas *le* Noël, parce que c'est *la fête de Noël* qu'on veut dire.
6. —Merci. Je recommence. Comment est-ce qu'on célèbre la Noël?
7. —Eh bien, on la célèbre en dormant!
8. —Comment?

1. This evening let's talk about the holidays in France. This will cheer us up a bit, for it's windy and raining.
2. Gladly. I know that on the fourteenth of July they celebrate the taking of the Bastille and that it's the big national holiday. But tell me, Mr. Picard, how is it celebrated?
3. Everywhere in France the fourteenth of July is celebrated in the streets. Everybody is in the street. In Paris each district has its band of musicians. They dance all day and nearly all night. They sell crêpes, waffles, ice cream, and all sorts of treats. There are the small carousels, puppet shows for the children, and naturally, bars for the grown-ups.
4. I hope to see all this and even to dance in the streets in July. And how is Christmas celebrated?
5. Mr. Brown, I must correct you. *Noël* is masculine all right, but we say *la Noël*, not *le Noël*, because it is *la fête de Noël* that is meant.
6. Thank you. I begin again. How is Christmas celebrated?
7. Well, it is celebrated by sleeping!
8. What?

9. —Oui, monsieur, c'est ça. On dort parce qu'on a réveillonné toute la nuit. La veille de Noël correspond à la veille du jour de l'An, ici aux États-Unis. Naturellement les bons viveurs ne manquent pas de saisir l'occasion de réveillonner deux fois.

10. —Et quand est-ce que les enfants reçoivent leurs cadeaux, si tout le monde dort?

11. —Le jour de l'An est le jour des cadeaux, qu'on appelle les étrennes. C'est une fête de réunion de famille. On tient table ouverte. On peut même dire qu'on tient auberge!

12. —Ça doit être très agréable. Y a-til d'autres grandes fêtes en France?

13. —Pendant la quinzaine de Pâques, on va à la campagne si c'est possible. À l'Assomption (le Quinze-Août) tout le monde quitte Paris. La ville est morte pour la journée.

14. —Tiens! Ça doit être intéressant à voir!

15. —Oui. Mais il n'y reste personne pour le voir. Seulement un chien par-ci par-là, au coin un agent mécontent, et le silence.

9. Yes, sir, that's right. People sleep because they have been celebrating all night. Christmas Eve corresponds to New Year's Eve here in the United States. Naturally, pleasure-seekers don't miss the opportunity to celebrate twice.

10. And when do the children receive their presents, if everyone is sleeping?

11. New Year's Day is the day for gifts, which are called *étrennes*. It is a holiday for family gatherings. People keep open house. One can even say that they keep open inn!

12. That must be very pleasant. Are there other big holidays in France?

13. During the Easter fortnight, people go to the country if it's possible. During the Feast of the Assumption (the 15th of August) everybody leaves Paris. The city is dead for the day.

14. Well, well! That must be interesting to see.

15. Yes. But nobody remains there to see it. Only a dog here and there, at the corner a disgruntled policeman, and silence.

Pronunciation and Spelling Aids

Practice aloud:

Ce soir parlons des jours de fête de la France.

(Suh swar par-lawñ day zhoor duh **feht** duh la frahñs.)

Cela va nous égayer un peu, car il fait du vent et il pleut.

(Suh-la va noo zay-geh-yay un peu, kar eel feh dü vahñ ay ell **pleu**.)

Remember: The letter **c** before **e** or **i** is pronounced like the *s* in *see*. Before **a**, **o** or **u**, the letter **c** is hard like a *k*. However, if **c** has a cedilla beneath it— **ç**—, it is then pronounced like the *s* in *see*. For example: **commencer** (ku-mahñ-**say**), **commençons** (ku-mahñ-**sawñ**), but **cacarder** (ka-kar-**day**), *honk like a goose.*

The letter **g**, before **e** or **i**, is pronounced *zh*. Before **a**, **o**, or **u**, the letter **g** is hard like *g* in *gate*. Examples: in **manger** (mahñ-**zhay**), the letter **e** is added between the stem and the ending **–ons**, thus **mangeons** (mahñ-**zhawñ**), to maintain the softer sound of **g** throughout the conjugation. However, **gargouille** (gar-**gweej**), *gargoyle*, has the harder **g** sound.

Building Vocabulary

la Noël (nu-ehl) Christmas

le jour de l'An New Year's Day

Pâque Passover

Pâques Easter

la veille (vehy) de Noël Christmas Eve

le quatorze juillet Bastille Day

Joyeux Noël Merry Christmas

Bonne Année Happy New Year

L'Assomption (le Quinze-Août) Feast of the Assumption

French Expressions

1. **tout le monde** everybody
2. **les étrennes** New Year's gifts
3. **On tient table ouverte.** People keep open house.
4. **toute la nuit** all night
5. **vouloir dire** to mean
6. **Qu'est-ce que ça veut dire?** What does that mean?

Exercise No. 134—Completion of Text

1. **Le quatorze juillet est** (the big national holiday).
2. (People celebrate) **la prise de la Bastille.**
3. (Everybody) **est dans la rue.**
4. **On danse** (all day) **et presque** (all night).
5. **Il y a** (the puppet shows) **pour les enfants.**
6. **Comment la Noël est-elle** (celebrated)?
7. **On la célèbre** (sleeping).
8. (New Year's Day) **est le jour des cadeaux.**
9. **On appelle ces cadeaux** (New Year's gifts).
10. **On tient** (open house).
11. **Cela** (must be) **très agréable.**
12. (Everybody leaves Paris) **le Quinze-Août.**
13. **On voit seulement un chien** (here or there).

Grammar Notes

1. Present Tense of **tenir,** *to hold, to keep.* The present tense of **tenir** is exactly like that of **venir.**

I hold, you hold, etc.

I come, you come, etc.

je tiens (tyañ)	nous tenons (tuh-nawñ)	je viens	nous venons
tu tiens (tyañ)	vous tenez (tuh-nay)	tu viens	vous venez
il tient (tyañ)	ils tiennent (tyehn)	il vient	ils viennent
elle tient (tyañ)	elles tiennent (tyehn)	elle vient	elles viennent

Other verbs like **tenir** are: détenir, *to detain;* retenir, *to reserve, to hold back;* obtenir, *to obtain;* appartenir à, *to belong to;* contenir, *to contain;* soutenir, *to support.*

2. MORE VERBS WITH SPELLING CHANGES, commencer, *to begin;* manger, *to eat*

I begin, you begin, etc.

		I eat, you eat, etc.	
je commence	nous commençons	je mange	nous mangeons
tu commences	vous commencez	tu manges	vous mangez
il, elle commence	ils, elles commencent	il, elle mange	ils, elles mangent

Verbs whose infinitives end in **-cer** must add a cedilla under the **c** before the ending **-ons** in order to keep the **c** soft, like s: **commençons** (ku-mahñ-sawñ). Verbs whose infinitives end in **-ger** must add an **e** after the **g** before the ending **-ons** to keep the **g** soft (zh). (Later, you will learn that the same spelling changes occur when these verbs are in other tenses, such as **l'imparfait**)

Other verbs like **commencer** are: **placer**, *to place;* **recommencer**, *to begin over or again;* **prononcer**, *to pronounce;* **avancer**, *to advance,* **agacer**, to irritate, aggravate. Other verbs like **manger** are: **juger**, *to judge;* **bouger**, *to move;* **changer**, *to change;* **songer**, *to dream, to think;* **plonger**, *to dive;* **voyager**, *to travel.*

Exercise No. 135

Complete each sentence with the correct French verb phrase:

1. (He is holding) **le livre mais il ne le lit pas.**
2. (We are obtaining/getting) **des tissus fins.**
3. (I am not reserving) **les places.**
4. **Les jour de l'An, on** (keeps open house).
5. (We begin to work) **à neuf heures.**
6. **Où** (do we change) **de train?**
7. **Comment** (do you pronounce) **ce mot?**
8. (We pronounce it) **"Noël"** (nu-ehl).
9. (We do not eat) **de viande le matin.**
10. **Sur la Côte d'Azur** (we swim) **tous les jours.**
11. (We are correcting) **nos fautes.**
12. Let us begin again.

3. THE PRONOUN on, *one, people, we, they, you.*

on is an indefinite subject pronoun. It takes the third person singular form of the verb (like il and elle). Note the various ways on is translated.

on dit *one says, people say, we say, you say, they say, it is said.*

On danse toute la journée. *They (people) dance all day.*

In everyday spoken language, **on** is frequently used instead of **nous** for we. For example: **Tu viens? On va prendre un café en bas.** Are you coming? We are going to have a coffee downstairs. **Maman, quand est-ce-qu'on va manger?** Mommy, when are we going to eat?

Often on is used instead of a passive construction:

Ici on parle français.	French is spoken here. (Here one speaks French.)
On célèbre la fête de Noël.	Christmas is celebrated. (One celebrates Christmas.)

4. ne . . . personne, *nobody, no one, not anybody;* ne . . . rien, *nothing, not anything*

When used as objects of the verb, in complete sentences, **personne** *and* **rien**, *like other negatives* (ne . . . **pas**, ne . . . **jamais**, *etc.*) *require* **ne** *before the verb.*

Je ne vois personne.	I do not see anybody. (I see nobody)
Je ne vois rien.	I do not see anything. (I see nothing)

When used as subjects, **personne** *and* **rien** *are followed by* **ne**.

Personne ne sait où il demeure.	Nobody knows where he lives.
Rien ne me plaît aujourd'hui.	Nothing pleases me today.

When **personne** *and* **rien** *are used without a verb, usually as a one-word answer to a question,* **ne** *is omitted.*

Qui est chez vous? Personne.	Who is at your house? Nobody.
Que fait-il? Rien.	What is he doing? Nothing.

D. The negative ne . . . **personne** must not be confused with the noun **la personne**.

Je ne connais pas cette personne-là.	I don't know that person.

Exercise No. 136

Complete each sentence in French:

1. **Ici** (one) **parle français.**
2. **Ici** (nobody) **parle anglais.**
3. (People) **danse dans les rues.**
4. **Nous n'avons** (nothing).
5. **Il ne reste** (nobody) **dans la ville.**
6. **Il n'y a** (nothing) **à voir.**
7. **Que voulez-vous?** (Nothing.)
8. **Qui veut ces billets?** (Nobody)
9. **Il n'aime** (anybody).
10. (Nobody) **l'aime.**

Exercise No. 137—Questionnaire

1. **De quoi est-ce que les messieurs vont parler ce soir?**
2. **Où est-ce qu'on célèbre le quatorze juillet?**
3. **Qu'est-ce qu'on fait dans les rues?**
4. **Qu'est-ce qu'on vend dans les rues?**
5. **Qu'y a-t-il pour les enfants?**
6. **Faut-il dire** *la Noël* **ou** *le Noël* **quand on veut dire "la fête de Noël"?**
7. **Pourquoi est-ce qu'on dort la journée de Noël?**
8. **Quand est-ce que les enfants reçoivent leurs cadeaux?**
9. **Comment appelle-t-on les cadeaux du jour de l'An?**
10. **Comment est la ville le jour de l'Assomption (le Quinze-Août)?**

CHAPITRE 27 (VINGT-SEPT)

QUELS ENDROITS VOULEZ-VOUS VISITER?

WHAT PLACES DO YOU WISH TO VISIT?

1. —Vous allez bientôt partir pour la France, M. Brown. Avez-vous décidé quels endroits vous voulez visiter?

2. —Je ne pense à rien d'autre, et je lis beaucoup dans ma collection de guides.

3. —J'irai à Paris par avion. Je visiterai ce qu'il y a d'intéressant dans la ville, dans les environs de la ville, et ailleurs en France.

4. —C'est un projet ambitieux. Pour voir ce qu'il y a d'intéressant à Paris il vous faudra dix ans.

5. —Je ferai mon possible pour faire l'impossible. À Paris je compte visiter la Cathédrale de Notre-Dame. Au Musée du Louvre, j'irai voir la Vénus de Milo, la Mona Lisa et la salle de la céramique grecque. Vous voyez que je m'intéresse toujours à la céramique.

6. —En sortant du Louvre, je passerai par le Jardin des Tuileries jusqu'à la Place de la Concorde et puis je continuerai dans l'Avenue des Champs Élysées jusqu'à la Place de l'Étoile. Là je prendrai un taxi pour me promener au Bois de Boulogne. Je reviendrai par Passy pour visiter la Tour Eiffel . . .

7. —Ah bon, je comprends! Vous verrez tout, voilà! Mais vous m'étonnez. Vous connaissez Paris mieux que moi.

1. Soon you are going to leave for France, Mr. Brown. Have you decided what places you want to visit?

2. I am thinking about nothing else and I am reading a lot in my collection of guidebooks.

3. I'll travel by plane to Paris. I'll visit what there is of interest in the city, in the outskirts of the city and elsewhere in France.

4. It's an ambitious project. To see what there is of interest in Paris you'll need ten years.

5. I'll do everything possible to do the impossible. In Paris I expect to visit Notre Dame Cathedral. At the Louvre Museum I'll go to see the Venus de Milo, the Mona Lisa, and the Greek pottery room. You see that I'm always interested in ceramics.

6. Leaving the Louvre, I shall pass through the Tuileries garden to the Place de la Concorde and then I'll continue on the Champs Èlysées up to the Place Charles de Gaulle. From there I'll take a taxi to ride around the Bois de Boulogne. I'll come back by way of Passy to visit the Eiffel Tower and. . . .

7. Ah, now I understand. You'll see everything, that's it! But you surprise me. You know Paris better than I.

8. —Ah non, M. Picard. Pas tout à fait. Je connais le Paris des guides. Mais il me semble qu'à Paris tout me sera familier.

9. —C'est une chose qui arrive à tout le monde. On se sent chez soi à Paris. Et qu'est-ce que vous comptez visiter dans les environs de la ville?

10. —Dans les environs j'irai visiter Versailles, surtout les jardins.

11. —Il faut y aller le quatorze juillet pour voir jouer les fontaines et le feu d'artifice.

12. —Ah, très bien. Je n'y manquerai pas. Je veux voir aussi le château de Chantilly. Et puis Fontainebleau, et puis Sens, Senlis. . . .

13. —Oh la, la! Laissons les environs, ou nous n'en sortirons jamais. Et après?

14. —Après, je ferai un grand cercle pour visiter la Normandie, surtout le Mont-Saint-Michel, où je mangerai trois omelettes, la spécialité du Mont. Puis je visiterai la Bretagne, et en revenant à Paris, les châteaux de la Loire.

15. —Et quand irez-vous à la Côte d'Azur?

16. —Tout de suite après j'irai à la Côte d'Azur, pour me tremper dans la mer et dans le soleil, et je reviendrai à Paris par la route des Alpes. Que pensez-vous de tout cela?

17. —Ce que j'en pense? J'ai grande envie de vous accompagner! Mais ce n'est pas possible.

18. —Quel dommage, M. Picard.

8. Oh no, Mr. Picard. Not quite. I know the Paris of the guidebooks. But it seems to me that in Paris everything will be familiar.

9. It's a thing that happens to everybody. One feels at home in Paris. And what do you intend to visit on the outskirts of the city?

10. On the outskirts I'll go to visit Versailles, especially the gardens.

11. You must go there July 14 to see the fountains turned on and the fireworks.

12. Ah, very good. I won't miss it. I also want to see the chateau at Chantilly. Then Fontainebleau, and then Sens, Senlis. . . .

13. Oh la la! Let's leave the outskirts or we'll never get out of them. And after?

14. Afterward, I'll make a large circle to visit Normandy, especially Mont St. Michel, where I'll eat three omelettes, the specialty of the Mont. Then I shall visit Brittany, and on the way back to Paris, the chateaux of the Loire valley.

15. And when will you go to the Riviera?

16. Immediately after, I'll go to the Riviera, to soak myself in the sea and sun, and I'll come back to Paris by way of the Alps. What do you think of all that?

17. What do I think of it? I have a great desire to accompany you! But that isn't possible.

18. What a pity, Mr. Picard.

Pronunciation and Spelling Aids

Practice aloud:

Vous allez bientôt partir pour la France, Monsieur Brown.

(Voo za-lay byañ-toh par-teer poor la **frahñs**, muh-syeu Brown.)

Avez-vous decidé quels endroits vous voulez visiter?

(A-vay **voo** day-see-day kehl zahñ-drwa voo voo-lay **vee-zee-tay?**)

Je ne pense à rien d'autre.

(Zhuh nuh pahñs a ryañ **dohtr.**)

C'est un projet ambitieux.

(Seh teuñ pru-zheh ahñ-bee-**syeu.**)

Building Vocabulary

Expressions indicating future time:

1. **demain** (duh-**mañ**) tomorrow
2. **après-demain** after tomorrow
3. **le mois prochain** (pru-**shañ**) next month
4. **lundi (mardi) prochain** next Monday (Tuesday)
5. **la semaine prochaine** (suh-mehn pru-**shehn**) next week
6. **l'année prochaine** (la-nay pru-**shehn**) next year

French Expressions

1. **Il vous faudra dix ans.** You will need ten years.
2. **Je ferai mon possible.** I shall do my best, everything I can.
3. **d'abord** first, at first
4. **chez soi** at home
5. **se promener** to go for a walk, drive, sail, etc.
6. **Je me promène en voiture (sur l'eau).** I go for a drive (for a sail).
7. **Je n'y manquerai pas.** I won't miss it.
8. **J'ai envie de vous accompagner.** I feel like going with you.

Grammar Notes

1. THE FUTURE TENSE

What *shall or will* happen, **parler, finir, vendre**

I shall speak, you will speak, etc.	*I shall finish, etc.*	*I shall sell, etc.*
je parlerai (par-luh-**ray**)	**je finirai**	**je vendrai**
tu parleras (par-luh-**ra**)	**tu finiras**	**tu vendras**
il parlera (par-luh-**ra**)	**il finira**	**il vendra**
elle parlera (par-luh-**ra**)	**elle finira**	**elle vendra**
nous parlerons (par-luh-**rawñ**)	**nous finirons**	**nous vendrons**
vous parlerez (par-luh-**ray**)	**vous finirez**	**vous vendrez**
ils parleront (par-luh-**rawñ**)	**ils finiront**	**ils vendront**
elles parleront (par-luh-**rawñ**)	**elles finiront**	**elles vendront**
parlera-t-il? will he speak?	**finira-t-il?** will he finish?	**vendra-t-il?** will he sell?

The personal endings of the future tense of all verbs are: **-ai, -as, -a, -ons, -ez, -ont.** They are exactly like the present tense ending of the verb avoir.

To form the future tense, add the future endings to the infinitive:
parler, je parler-ai, etc.   **finir, je finir-ai,** etc.   **ouvrir, j'ouvrir-ai,** etc.

If the infinitive ends in -re, drop the final e before adding the future endings:

vendre je vendr-ai, etc.   *apprendre j'apprendr-ai,* etc.   *lire je lir-ai,* etc.

2. **SOME VERBS WITH AN IRREGULAR FUTURE—IN A NUMBER OF COMMON VERBS THERE IS A CHANGE IN THE INFINITIVE BASE TO WHICH THE FUTURE ENDINGS ARE ADDED. AMONG THESE VERBS ARE:**

avoir to have	aur-
être to be	ser-
aller to go	ir-
voir to see	verr-
venir to come	viendr-
faire to do, make	fer-
pouvoir to be able	pourr-
falloir to be necessary	faudr-

j'aurai	tu auras	il aura	nous aurons, etc.
je serai	tu seras	il sera	nous serons, etc.
j'irai	tu iras	il ira	nous irons, etc.
je verrai	tu verras	il verra	nous verrons, etc
je viendrai	tu viendras	il viendra	nous viendrons, etc.
je ferai	tu feras	il fera	nous ferons, etc.
je pourrai	tu pourras	il pourra	nous pourrons, etc.

il faut it is necessary   **il faudra** it will be necessary

Exercise No. 138—Completion of Text

1. (I shall travel) **en avion.**
2. (I shall visit) **ce qu'il y a d'intéressant.**
3. **Il vous** (will be necessary) **dix ans.**
4. (I shall do) **mon possible.**
5. (I shall go) **voir d'abord la Vénus de Milo.**
6. (I shall pass) **par le jardin des Tuileries.**
7. **Là** (I shall take) **un taxi.**
8. (I shall return) **par Passy.**
9. **Vous connaissez Paris** (better than I).
10. **À Paris tout me** (will be) **familier.**
11. **C'est une chose** (which happens to everybody).
12. **On se sent** (at home) **à Paris.**

Exercise No. 139

Translate each exchange. Read each aloud in French several times.

1. —Où irez-vous l'été prochain?

   —J'irai en France.

   —Quand partirez-vous de New York?

   —Je partirai le 31 mai.

2. —Combien de temps passerez-vous en France?

   —J'y passerai trois mois.

   —Est-ce que vous voyagerez en avion ou en bateau?

   —Je voyagerai en avion.

3. —Est-ce que vous ferez un voyage au Maroc?

   —Oui. Je ferai un voyage au Maroc.

   —M. Picard pourra-t-il vous accompagner?

   —Hélas! Il ne pourra pas m'accompagner.

4. —Est-ce que vous verrez votre représentante à Paris?

   —Mais oui. Elle m'attendra à l'aéroport.

   —Combien de temps resterez-vous à Paris?

   —J'y resterai deux semaines.

5. —Est-ce que vous visiterez la Côte d'Azur?

   —Bien entendu, je la visiterai.

   —Quand reviendrez-vous aux États-Unis?

   —Je reviendrai le premier septembre.

Exercise No. 140

Translate:

1. He will visit.
2. I shall travel.
3. We shall go.
4. They will not write.
5. It will be necessary.
6. Will you see?
7. They will not leave.
8. We shall sell.
9. Will he not finish?
10. She will not learn.
11. He will be.
12. Will you come?
13. I shall have.
14. You (**tu**) will not listen.
15. We shall study.
16. I shall not make.
17. Will you be able?
18. Will you go?

Exercise No. 141—Questionnaire

1. M. Brown voyagera-t-il en avion ou en bateau?
2. Qu'est-ce que M. Brown verra au Louvre?
3. En sortant du Louvre par quel jardin passera-t-il?
4. Où prendra-t-il un taxi?
5. Quelle tour visitera-t-il?
6. Où se promènera-t-il?
7. Quel est le Paris que M. Brown connaît?
8. Qu'est-ce qui arrive à tout le monde?
9. Quand est-ce qu'on voit jouer les grandes fontaines à Versailles?
10. M. Brown, que fera-t-il à la Côte d'Azur?
11. Par quelle route est-ce que M. Brown reviendra à Paris?

Première Partie

NOUNS

1. l'allumette	1. match
2. les bas	2. stockings
3. le bois	3. wood
4. le cercle	4. circle
5. le cheval	5. horse
6. les chevaux	6. horses
7. le chien	7. dog
8. le costume	8. costume
9. le couturier	9. dressmaker, dress designer
10. l'eau de vie	10. brandy
11. l'est	11. east
12. l'étoffe	12. fabric
13. le feu	13. fire
14. la fête	14. holiday
15. les gants	15. gloves
16. le jardin	16. garden
17. le lin	17. linen
18. la laine	18. wool
19. le marin	19. sailor
20. la marchandise	20. merchandise
21. la mode	21. fashion
22. le musicien	22. musician (*m*)
23. la musicienne	23. musician (*f*)
24. le nord	24. north
25. l'ouest	25. west
26. l'ouvrier	26. worker
27. le pêcheur	27. fisherman
28. la peinture	28. painting
29. le projet	29. project
30. la robe	30. dress
31. la soie	31. silk
32. la sorte	32. kind, sort
33. le sud	33. south
34. le tissu	34. fabric, cloth
35. le tabac	35. tobacco
36. le vin	36. wine

VERBS

1.	accompagner	1.	to accompany
2.	admirer	2.	to admire
3.	célébrer	3.	to celebrate
4.	corriger	4.	to correct
5.	danser	5.	to dance
6.	décider	6.	to decide
7.	discuter	7.	to discuss
8.	étonner	8.	to astonish
9.	manquer	9.	to lack, miss
10.	se passer	10.	to happen
11.	se passer de	11.	to do without
12.	s'intéresser à	12.	to interest oneself in
13.	se promener	13.	to take a walk or ride
14.	rester	14.	to remain
15.	recommencer	15.	to begin again
16.	regarder	16.	to look at
17.	ressembler à	17.	to resemble
18.	sembler	18.	to seem

ADJECTIVES

1.	ambitieux	1.	ambitious
2.	droit	2.	straight, right
3.	entendu	3.	agreed, understood, heard
4.	fier (fière f)	4.	proud
5.	bavard	5.	talkative
6.	débrouillard	6.	resourceful
7.	mort	7.	dead
8.	mécontent	8.	discontented
9.	parfumé	9.	perfumed
10.	politique	10.	political
11.	prochain	11.	next
12.	tel (telle f)	12.	such

ADVERBS

1.	alors	1.	then, well, so . . .
2.	autre part	2.	elsewhere
3.	bientôt	3.	soon
4.	même	4.	even
5.	partout	5.	everywhere
6.	volontiers	6.	gladly
7.	trop	7.	too much

PREPOSITIONS

1. à cause de	1. because of
2. malgré	2. in spite of, despite
3. selon	3. according to

French Expressions

1. avoir peur (de)	1. to be afraid (of)
2. avoir envie de	2. to want to
3. être en train de	3. to be in the act, or the process, of
4. faire mon possible	4. to do my best
5. faire le commerce	5. to do business
6. penser à	6. to think about
7. venir de + *infinitive*	7. to have just (done something)
8. plus ou moins	8. more or less
9. mieux que moi	9. better than I
10. par ci par là	10. this way and that
11. quelque chose d'autre	11. something else
12. Bien!	12. Well!
13. défense de fumer	13. no smoking
14. Joyeux Noël	14. Merry Christmas
15. Bonne Année	15. Happy New Year
16. encore un (une)	16. one more

Deuxième Partie

Exercise No. 142

Find the words in Group II that correspond to the words in Group I.

I	II
1. the handkerchief	a. le pantalon
2. the overcoat	b. le manteau
3. the suit (man's)	c. le fichu
4. the suit (woman's)	d. la robe
5. the coat, cloak	e. le mouchoir
6. the shawl	f. la jupe
7. the shoes	g. le pardessus
8. the necktie	h. les bas
9. the shirt	i. les chaussures
10. the socks	j. les chaussettes
11. the stockings	k. la ceinture
12. the belt	l. le complet
13. the dress	m. la chemise
14. the trousers	n. le costume tailleur
15. the skirt	o. la cravate

Exercise No. 143

Combine each pair of nouns to form compound nouns and give the meaning of each:

Exemple: 1. le chapeau—le velour le chapeau de velour the velvet hat

1. la ceinture—le cuir
2. la robe—la soie
3. la montre — l'or (gold)
4. la salle—le bain
5. la chemise—la laine
6. le bureau—la poste
7. le voyage—les affaires
8. le cahier—la musique
9. le tissu—le coton
10. le bracelet—l'argent
11. l'objet—l'art
12. le chapeau—la paille (straw)

Exercise No. 144

Answer these questions in complete sentences (in the future tense) with the help of the words in parentheses:

Exemple: 1. J'achèterai une cravate.

1. Qu'est-ce que vous achèterez? (une cravate)
2. Combien coûtera-t-elle? (vingt euros)
3. Où irez-vous l'été prochain? (en France)
4. Quand reviendrez-vous aux États-Unis? (le 31 décembre)
5. À quelle heure vous coucherez-vous? (à minuit)
6. À quelle heure vous lèverez-vous? (à six heures du matin)
7. Que lui direz-vous? (rien)
8. Qui ira avec vous? (personne ne)
9. Combien de temps travaillerez-vous? (toute la journée)
10. Où nous rencontrerons-nous? (à l'entrée du théâtre)

Exercise No. 145

Complete these sentences with the help of the French expressions listed below them. Be sure to change each infinitive to the correct form, corresponding to the subject of the verb.

Exemple: 1. Ils n'ont pas peur d'exprimer leurs idées.

1. (They are not afraid) d'exprimer leurs idées.
2. (We do not need) de continuer.
3. (She intends) de porter son manteau neuf (new).
4. (Do you want to) m'accompagner?
5. (He will do his best) pour vous aider.
6. (Will you go shopping) au Marché aux Puces?
7. (Mr. Brown is opening) la caisse.
8. (Are you afraid) de dire la vérité?

a. avoir peur de
b. avoir besoin de
c. avoir envie de
d. avoir l'intention de
e. faire des achats
f. s'intéresser à
g. se promener
h. faire son possible
i. être en train de

9. **Allez-vous** (to take a ride) **au Bois de Boulogne?**
10. **Vous savez que M. Brown** (is not interested in) **la mode.**

Exercise No. 146

Complete these sentences in French, **mettre** here means *to put on*, **aller bien à** means *to be becoming to, to suit one (well)*.

1. **Je mets** (my hat).
2. **Tu mets** (your coat).
3. **Il met** (his woolen shirt).
4. **Elle met** (her silk dress).
5. **Nous mettons** (our leather belts[1]).
6. **Vous mettez** (your red gloves).
7. **Ils mettent** (their raincoats[1]).
8. **Elles mettent** (their scarves[1]).
9. (This dress) **me va bien.**
10. (This necktie) **lui va bien.**
11. (These gloves) **nous vont bien.**
12. (This skirt) **ne va pas bien à Jeanne.**

NOTE [1]French uses the singular noun. The idea is that each one puts on one item of clothing.

Dialogue 1
Dans l'autobus

1. —Pardon, monsieur, où est-ce que je descends pour aller à l'Hôtel des Postes[1]?

2. —Vous descendez au coin de la rue du Louvre et la rue Étienne-Marcel.
3. —Est-ce que c'est loin d'ici?
4. —Non, madame, pas trop loin.
5. —Quand est-ce que nous y arriverons?
6. —Dans un quart d'heure plus ou moins.
7. —Merci beaucoup, monsieur.
8. —À votre service, madame.

1. Excuse me, sir, where do I get off for the Main Post Office (for the boulevard St.-Michel) (for the Luxembourg Gardens) (for the United States Embassy) (for the Flea Market) (for the railroad station)?

2. You get off at the corner of the rue du Louvre and the rue Étienne-Marcel (etc.).
3. Is it far from here?
4. No, madam, not too far.
5. When will we get there?
6. In about a quarter of an hour.
7. Thank you very much, sir.
8. At your service, madam.

NOTE [1]**Hôtel des Postes,** main post office in Paris; **bureau de poste,** post office

Dialogue 2

Le courrier

1. —M. Brown, vous avez sans doute une grosse correspondance. Y a-t-il une boîte aux lettres dans votre immeuble?	1. Mr. Brown, you probably have much correspondence. Is there a mailbox in your building?
2. —Naturellement. Nous en avons une à chaque étage, où nous jetons nos lettres. Mais nous envoyons les colis postaux au bureau central des postes.	2. Naturally. We have one at each floor where we drop our letters. But we send parcel post packages to the main post office.
3. —Qui est-ce qui les porte?	3. Who takes them?
4. —Le garçon à tout faire. Il nous achète aussi les quantités de timbres dont nous avons besoin, les timbres de poste aérienne, les timbres d'envoi par exprès, etc.	4. The office boy. He also buys us the many stamps that we need, the air mail stamps, the special delivery stamps, etc.
5. —Où est le bureau central des postes?	5. Where is the main post office?
6. —Pas loin d'ici.	6. Not far from here.

Exercise No. 147—Lecture

Read silently and aloud. If you are unable to determine the meaning of new words from the context of the reading, look them up in the dictionary at the back of this book.

L'anniversaire (birthday) de Mme Brown

C'est le vingt-deux mars, l'anniversaire de Mme Brown. Elle a trente-cinq ans au-jourd'hui. Pour célébrer cette fête, la famille Brown va dîner dans un restaurant élégant de la Madison Avenue à New York.

Quand ils entrent dans le restaurant ils voient sur la table réservée pour les Brown un joli panier rempli de roses blanches. Naturellement Mme Brown est tout à fait surprise. Elle remercie et embrasse son cher mari avec empressement.

A la fin d'un dîner exquis Anne, la plus jeune, dit tout bas aux autres enfants,—Maintenant! Et chacun des quatre enfants sort d'en bas de la table une jolie petite boîte. Ce sont des cadeaux pour leur mère.

Anne lui donne un mouchoir de soie; Elizabeth, une blouse de lin; Thomas, une paire de gants; et Charles, un fichu de laine.

La semaine prochaine, M. Brown fait le calcul du compte de cette journée, le voici:

Dîner	cent soixante	$160
Pourboire	vingt-quatre	24
Fleurs	quarante	40
Cadeaux	cent vingt-six	126
		$350

—Quelle coïncidence! dit M. Brown. Trois cent cinquante dollars—dix fois trente-cinq ans!

CHAPITRE 28 (VINGT-HUIT)

M. BROWN ÉCRIT UNE LETTRE À SA REPRÉSENTANTE

MR. BROWN WRITES A LETTER TO HIS AGENT

1. M. Brown et M. Picard sont assis dans le salon chez M. Brown. M. Brown tient deux lettres à la main: une copie de sa lettre à sa représentante et la réponse qui vient d'arriver.
2. —M. Picard, je vais vous lire ma lettre à ma représentante à Paris, Mme Parmentier.
3. —Cela me fera plaisir.
4. M. Brown lit la lettre qui suit:

New-York, le 4 mai 2005
Mme Denise Parmentier
76, rue de Vaugirard
75006 Paris
France
Chère Madame:

J'ai le plaisir de vous informer que je vais bientôt faire un voyage en France. Je partirai en avion de New York le 31 mai à sept heures de l'après-midi et j'arriverai à Charles de Gaulle II à sept heures du matin le premier juin.

J'ai l'intention de rester en France deux mois. Je compte faire un voyage touristique aussi bien que d'affaires. Je passerai trois semaines à peu près à Paris.

Partant de Paris, je ferai quelques excursions pour voir les endroits intéressants en France. J'espère aussi voyager en avion au Maroc et peut-être en Corse.

1. Mr. Brown and Mr. Picard are sitting in the living room at-the Browns'. Mr. Brown has two letters in his hand: a copy of his letter to his agent and the answer which has just arrived.
2. Mr. Picard, I am going to read you my letter to my agent in Paris, Mrs. Parmentier.
3. That will please me.
4. Mr. Brown reads the letter which follows:

New York, May 4, 2005
Mme Denise Parmentier
76 Rue de Vaugirard
Paris 75006
France
Dear Mrs. Parmentier:

I am pleased to inform you that I am soon going to take a trip to France. I shall leave New York by plane May 31 at 7 P.M. and will arrive at Charles de Gaulle II at 7 A.M. June 1.

I intend to remain in France two months. I expect to make it a trip of tourism as well as a business trip. I shall spend about three weeks in Paris.

Leaving Paris, I shall make a few excursions to see places of interest in France. I hope also to fly to Morocco and perhaps to Corsica.

Pendant mon séjour à Paris j'espère pouvoir saisir l'occasion de faire votre connaissance, car j'ai toujours beaucoup apprécié vos dévoués services, qui ont tant contribué à notre réussite.

Je sais que vous êtes très occupée et que vous êtes souvent en voyage. Par conséquent je vous écris d'avance dans l'espoir de pouvoir fixer un rendez-vous. Je vous prie de me faire savoir si j'aurai le plaisir de vous voir à Paris.

Il y a cinq mois que je prends des leçons de français. Cela vous surprendra peut-être. J'espère pouvoir vous parler dans votre belle langue, car depuis quelque temps j'ai des discussions deux fois par semaine avec mon professeur, M. Auguste Picard, un de vos compatriotes.

Dans l'espoir de vous lire bientôt, agréez, madame, l'assurance de ma considération distinguée.

John Brown

5. —Merveilleux, M. Brown. Il n'y pas de faute dans toute la lettre.
6. —M. Picard, je dois vous avouer quelque chose. Il y a un livre qui s'appelle *La Correspondance commerciale.* Ce livre me rend grand service dans tout ce qui regarde les en-têtes, les conclusions, et les formules de politesse. Naturellement, c'est surtout à vous que je dois les plus vifs remerciements.
7. —Vous êtes très aimable. Et maintenant, voulez-vous bien me lire la réponse que vous venez de recevoir de Mme Parmentier?
8. —Avec plaisir, Monsieur. (La suite au Chapitre 29.)

During my stay in Paris I hope to take advantage of the opportunity to meet you personally, for I have always very much appreciated your dedicated services, which have contributed so much to our success.

I know that you are very busy and that you travel a great deal. For that reason I am writing you beforehand in the hope of being able to arrange an appointment. Please let me know if I shall have the pleasure of seeing you in Paris.

I have been studying French for the last five months. This will surprise you perhaps. I hope to be able to speak with you in your beautiful language, because for some time I have been having discussions twice a week with my teacher, M. Auguste Picard, one of your compatriots.

Awaiting your early reply, I remain sincerely yours. (Lit. In the hope of reading you[r letter] soon, accept, madam, the assurance of my marked esteem.)

John Brown

5. Marvelous, Mr. Brown. There is not a single error in the whole letter.
6. Mr. Picard, I must confess something to you. There is a book entitled *Commercial Correspondence.* This book helps me a great deal (does me a great service) in everything that concerns headings, conclusions, and expressions of courtesy. Of course, it's especially to you that I owe the most sincere thanks.
7. You are very kind. And now will you kindly read me the answer which you have just received from Mrs. Parmentier?
8. With pleasure, sir. (Continued in Chapter 29.)

Pronunciation and Spelling Aids

Practice aloud:

J'ai le plaisir de vous informer que je vais bientôt faire un voyage en France.

(Zhay luh pleh-zeer duh voo zañ-fur-**may** kuh zhuh veh byañ-toh fehr euñ vwa-**yazh** ahñ **frahñs**.)

Je partirai de New York en avion le 31 (trente et un) mai à sept heures.

(Zhuh par-tee-ray duh New-York ahñ **na-vyawñ** luh trahñ-tay-euñ **meh** a seh teur.)

Building Vocabulary

Related expressions:

1. **la main** hand
2. **la main droite** the right hand
3. **la main gauche** the left hand
4. **à droite** on, to the right
5. **à gauche** on, to the left
6. **tourner** *or* **prendre la droite (gauche)** to turn to, or take the right (left)
7. **tout droit** straight ahead
8. **à la main** in his or her hand
9. **Ils se serrent la main** they shake hands

NOTE: Often when referring to parts of the body, French uses the definite article instead of the possessive adjectives **mon, ton, son,** etc. Thus:

Il tient deux lettres à la main.

He has two letters in his hand.

Il a un panier sur la tête.

He has a basket on his head.

French Expressions

1. **avoir l'intention de** to intend to
2. **saisir l'occasion** to seize (take advantage of) the opportunity
3. **par conséquent** consequently
4. **d'avance** in advance, beforehand
5. **faire la connaissance de** to make the acquaintance of, to meet
6. **faire savoir** to let know, to inform
7. **deux fois par semaine** twice a week
8. **voulez-vous bien** will you kindly
9. **cela me fera plaisir** that will please me
10. **être occupé** to be busy

Exercise No. 148—Completion of Text

1. **M. Brown a deux lettres** (in his hand).
2. **Voici la réponse qui** (has just arrived).
3. **M. Brown lit la lettre** (which follows).
4. (I shall leave) **le 31 mai.**
5. (I intend) **de rester en France deux mois.**
6. **Je sais que vous êtes** (very busy).
7. (Consequently) **je vous écris d'avance.**
8. (For some time) **je cause** (twice a week) **avec mon professeur.**
9. **Il n'y a pas** (a single mistake) **dans toute la lettre.**
10. (Will you kindly) **me lire la réponse de Mme Parmentier.**

Grammar Notes

1. **PRESENT TENSE OF** suivre, *to follow;* traduire, *to translate*

I follow, you follow, etc.

		I translate, you translate, etc.	
je suis	nous suivons	je traduis	nous traduisons
tu suis	vous suivez	tu traduis	vous traduisez
il, elle suit	ils, elles suivent	il, elle traduit	ils, elles traduisent

Imperative: **suis, suivons, suivez**   *Imperative:* **traduis, traduisons, traduisez**

Like **suivre** is: **poursuivre,** *to pursue.* Like **traduire: conduire,** *to lead, conduct, drive;* **produire,** *to produce;* **construire,** *to construct.*

2. **MORE VERBS WITH IRREGULAR STEMS IN THE FUTURE TENSE:**

tenir	to hold	tiendr-	je tiendrai, etc.
devoir	to owe, to be obliged	devr-	je devrai, etc.
recevoir	to receive	recevr-	je recevrai, etc.
vouloir	to want	voudr-	je voudrai, etc.
valoir	to be worth	vaudr-	il vaudra, etc.
envoyer	to send	enverr-	j'enverrai, etc.
courir	to run	courr-	je courrai, etc.
savoir	to know	saur-	je saurai, etc.

Exercise No. 149

Complete the following sentences in French:

Exemple: 1. Je leur enverrai les journaux français.

1. (I shall send them) **les journaux français.**
2. **Mme Brown** (will receive) **beaucoup de cadeaux.**

3. (They will know) **où me trouver.**
4. (He will not want) **nous accompagner.**
5. **Les enfants** (will run) **pour voir le Guignol.**
6. **Les billets** (will not be worth) **plus de cinq dollars.**
7. (They will owe us) **moins de dix dollars.**
8. (They will hold) **table ouverte.**
9. (Will you translate) **cet exercice?**
10. (We shall not follow) **la mode.**
11. (I shall make) **la connaissance de Mme Parmentier.**
12. (We shall be able) **fixer un rendez-vous.**

3. **Use of depuis, depuis quand, combien de temps, pendant**

When an action that began in the past continues into the present, French uses **depuis** *(since, for)* or **depuis quand?** *(since when?)* or **combien de temps?** *(how long?)*, with the present tense of the verb. English uses the present perfect tense to express the same notion.

Depuis quand est-ce que M. Brown *étudie* **le français?**	Since when *has* Mr. Brown *been studying* French?
Il *étudie* **le français depuis cinq mois.**	He *has been studying (has studied)* French for (since) five months.
Combien de temps y a-t-il que M. Brown *étudie* **le français?**	How long (is it that) *has* Mr. Brown *been studying (has studied)* French?
Il y a cinq mois qu'il *étudie* **le français.**	He *has been studying (has studied)* French for five months.

For future action, French uses **combien de temps?** *(how long?)* and **pendant** *(for, during)* plus the future tense of the verb, as in English.

4. **PENDANT, THE WORD *FOR* IN ENGLISH, IS OFTEN OMITTED IN FRENCH.**

Combien de temps restera-t-il à Paris?	How long will he remain in Paris?
Il y restera (pendant) trois semaines.	He will remain there (for) three weeks.

Exercise No. 150

Complete the following sentences in French and read them aloud:

Exemple: 1. Combien de temps resterez-vous à Paris?

1. (How long) **resterez-vous à Paris?**
2. **Nous resterons à Paris** (during the months) **de juin et juillet.**
3. (Since when) **le connaissez-vous?**
4. **Nous le connaissons** (for ten years).

5. **J'étudie le français** (for two years).
6. **Il écrit des lettres** (for three hours).
7. (How long) **m'attendrez-vous?**
8. (It is three days) **qu'elle est malade.**
9. (Since when have you been living) **dans cette maison?**
10. (We have been living there) **depuis trois ans.**

Exercise No. 151—Questionnaire

Answer the following questions in French:

1. Où est-ce que les messieurs sont assis?
2. Qu'est-ce que M. Brown tient à la main?
3. Qu'est-ce qu'il va lire à M. Picard?
4. Quand est-ce que M. Brown partira de New York?
5. Combien de temps passera-t-il en France?
6. Combien de temps restera-t-il à Paris?
7. Où espère-t-il voyager en avion?
8. Qui est très occupée?
9. De qui est-ce que M. Brown veut faire la connaissance?
10. Pourquoi écrit-il d'avance?
11. Il y a combien de temps que M. Brown prend des leçons de français?

CHAPTER

29

M. BROWN REÇOIT UNE LETTRE

MR. BROWN RECEIVES A LETTER

1. M. Brown a écrit une lettre à sa représentante à Paris. Dans le dernier chapitre il a lu une copie de cette lettre à son professeur, M. Picard. Celui-ci n'a pas trouvé une seule faute dans la lettre. M. Brown a reçu une réponse de sa représentante. Maintenant il la tient à la main et il est en train de la lire.

Cher M. Brown:
J'ai reçu avec beaucoup de plaisir votre lettre du 4 mai dans laquelle[1] vous m'informez que vous allez bientôt faire un voyage en France.
Heureusement je serai à Paris pendant les mois de juin et juillet, et je serai tout à fait à votre disposition.
Je compte sur le plaisir de vous rencontrer à l'aéroport Charles de Gaulle à sept heures du matin le premier juin. J'espère pouvoir rendre votre séjour agréable quant aux distractions aussi bien que profitable quant aux affaires.
C'est avec plaisir que je parlerai en français avec vous et je suis sûre que vous le parlez à la perfection. En vérité vous écrivez le français à merveille. Je veux vous féliciter aussi bien que votre professeur. Comme M. Picard est français, je comprends bien votre connaissance de beaucoup de gallicismes.

1. Mr. Brown has written a letter to his representative in Paris. In the last chapter he read a copy of that letter to his teacher, M. Picard. He did not find a single error in the letter. Mr. Brown has received an answer from his agent. Now he has it in his hand and is reading it.

Dear Mr. Brown:
I received with great pleasure your letter of May 4 in which[1] you inform me that you will soon make a trip to France.

Fortunately I shall be in Paris during the months of June and July, and I shall be entirely at your service.
I am looking forward to meeting you at Charles de Gaulle airport at 7 A.M. June 1. I hope to be able to make your stay pleasant in terms of entertainment as well as profitable in terms of business.
I shall be happy to speak with you in French and I am sure that you speak it perfectly. Indeed, you write French extremely well. I want to congratulate you as well as your teacher. Since M. Picard is French, I understand very well your familiarity with many French idioms.

Dans l'attente de faire votre connaissance, je vous prie de croire, monsieur, à ma parfaite considération.
Denise Parmentier

Looking forward to making your acquaintance, I remain, Sincerely yours, (Lit. I beg you to believe, sir, in my complete esteem)
Denise Parmentier

2. —C'est une gentille lettre, dit M. Picard. Jusqu'à présent vous avez connu Mme Parmentier comme une représentante de toute confiance. Sans doute vous allez voir qu'elle est aussi très sympathique comme un bon nombre de ses compatriotes. Pardonnez-moi si je suis fier des Français, mais vous verrez vous-même.

2. It's a nice letter, says M. Picard. Until now you have known Madam Parmentier as a reliable agent. No doubt, you will see that she is also very likeable, like a good number of her compatriots. Pardon me if I am proud of the French people, but you will see for yourself.

3. —Je suis certain que je serai très content parmi les Français; et le plus beau de l'affaire c'est que je pourrai parler avec eux dans leur propre langue.

3. I am certain that I shall be very happy among the French; and the best part of it is that I'll be able to converse with them in their own language.

4. —C'est certain. Alors, M. Brown, mardi prochain c'est le dernier rendez-vous avant votre départ. Nous nous rencontrerons à votre bureau, n'est-ce pas?

4. That's right. Well, Mr. Brown, next Tuesday is the last meeting before your departure. We'll meet in your office, will we not?

5. —Oui, monsieur. Et vous me donnerez quelques derniers conseils?

5. Yes, sir. And you will give me some final advice?

6. —Avec plaisir, M. Brown.

6. With pleasure, Mr. Brown.

NOTE [1]**lequel (laquelle, lesquels, lesquelles),** which, is a relative pronoun used after prepositions.

Pronunciation and Spelling Aids

Practice aloud:

J'ai reçu avec beaucoup de plaisir votre lettre du 4 (quatre) mai dans laquelle vous m'informez que vous allez bientôt faire un voyage en France.

(Zhay ruh-sü a-vehk boh-koo duh pleh-zeer vutr lehtr dü katr **meh** dahñ la-kehl voo mañ-fur-**may** kuh voo za-lay byañ-toh fehr euñ vwa-yazh ahñ **frahñs**.)

Building Vocabulary

Expressions referring to past time:

1. **hier** (yehr) yesterday
2. **hier soir** yesterday evening
3. **hier matin** yesterday morning
4. **avant-hier** day before yesterday
5. **la semaine dernière** last week
6. **l'année dernière** last year
7. **il y a deux jours (mois, ans)** two days (months, years) ago
8. **il y a huit jours** a week ago
9. **il y a quinze jours** two weeks ago

French Expressions

1. **je compte sur le plaisir de** I look forward to
2. **quant à** in the matter of, in terms of
3. **en vérité** indeed
4. **jusqu'à présent** until now
5. **ma (sa, leur) propre langue** my (his, her; their) own language

Salutations in business letters:

1. **Monsieur; Madame** Dear Sir; Madam
2. **Messieurs; Mesdames** Gentlemen; Ladies
3. **Cher Monsieur A.:** Dear Mr. A.:
4. **Chère Mademoiselle; Madame B.:** Dear Miss; Mrs.; Ms. B.:
5. **À qui de droit:** To Whom It May Concern:

Closings in business letters: Literally translated, the formulas for closing French business letters may sound very flowery to English-speakers' ears, but they are merely the equivalent of Sincerely yours, Yours truly, etc.

1. **Agréez, monsieur, mes salutations distinguées.**
   Accept, sir, my distinguished greetings.
2. **Agréez, monsieur, mes salutations empressées.**
   Accept, sir, my earnest greetings.
3. **Agréez, je vous prie, l'expression de mes salutations les plus distinguées.**
   Accept I beg you, the expression of my most distinguished greetings.
4. **Veuillez agréer, monsieur, mes sincères salutations.**
   Please accept, sir, my sincere greetings.

Exercise No. 152—Completion of Text

1. (He is in the act of reading) **la lettre.**
2. (I have received) **votre lettre du 4 mai.**
3. **Je serai à Paris** (during the months) **de juin et juillet.**
4. (I am looking forward) **de vous rencontrer à l'aéroport.**
5. **C'est avec plaisir** (that I shall speak in French) **avec vous.**
6. **Je veux** (to congratulate you).
7. (You have known) **Mme Parmentier comme une représentante de toute confiance.**
8. **Pardonnez-moi** (if I am proud) **des Français.**
9. (You will see) **vous-même.**
10. (I shall be able) **parler avec eux en français.**

Grammar Notes

1. **Le passé composé:** Conversational past tense (present perfect). What happened, has happened, did happen. Model verbs **parler, finir, vendre, être**

I have spoken, spoke, did speak, etc.

j'ai parlé	nous avons parlé		
tu as parlé	vous avez parlé		
il, elle a parlé	ils, elles ont parlé		

I have not finished, did not finish, etc.

je n'ai pas fini	nous n'avons pas fini
tu n'as pas fini	vous n'avez pas fini
il, elle n'a pas fini	ils, elles n'ont pas fini

I have sold, did sell, etc.

j'ai vendu	nous avons vendu
tu as vendu	vous avez vendu
il a vendu	ils, elles ont vendu

I have been, was, etc.

j'ai été	nous avons été
tu as été	vous avez été
il a été	ils, elles ont été

Interrogative: a-t-il parlé?, avons-nous fini?, avez-vous vendu?, ont-ils été?

Negative interrogative: n'a-t-il pas parlé?, n'avons-nous pas fini? etc.

Like the present perfect tense in English, the conversational past tense in French (**le passé composé**) is formed by means of an auxiliary verb plus the past participle. The auxiliary verb is usually **avoir**, *to have*, but it is sometimes **être**, *to be*. The use of **être** as an auxiliary verb will be discussed in Chapter 32.

2. HOW TO FORM THE REGULAR PAST PARTICIPLE

-er verbs drop **-er** and add **é**

Infinitive		*Past Participle*	
parler to speak	**apporter** to bring	**parlé** spoken	**apporté** brought
trouver to find	**écouter** to listen to	**trouvé** found	**écouté** listened to
demander to ask	**envoyer** to send	**demandé** asked	**envoyé** sent
casser to break	**manger** to eat	**cassé** broken	**mangé** eaten
fermer to close	**porter** to carry	**fermé** closed	**porté** carried

-ir **verbs drop** -ir **and add** -i

Infinitive	*Past Participle*
finir to finish	**fini** finished
choisir to choose	**choisi** chosen
bâtir to build	**bâti** built
obéir to obey	**obéi** obeyed
saisir to seize	**saisi** seized
dormir to sleep	**dormi** slept
sentir to feel	**senti** felt
servir to serve	**servi** served
punir to punish	**puni** punished
remplir to fill	**rempli** filled

-re **verbs drop** -re **and add** –u

Infinitive	*Past Participle*
vendre to sell	**vendu** sold
répondre to answer	**répondu** answered
perdre to lose	**perdu** lost
entendre to hear	**entendu** heard
rendre to give back	**rendu** gave, given back
attendre to wait for	**attendu** waited for

3. SOME IRREGULAR PAST PARTICIPLES

Infinitive	*Past Participle*
connaître to know	**connu** known
lire to read	**lu** read
dire to say	**dit** said
écrire to write	**écrit** written
faire to make	**fait** made
recevoir to receive	**reçu** received

Exercise No. 153

Translate each dialogue into English, after reading it aloud in French.

1. —M. Picard a-t-il posé des questions difficiles à M. Brown?

   —Oui. Il lui a posé des questions difficiles.

—Est-ce que M. Brown a bien[1] répondu?

—Oui, il a bien répondu à toutes les questions.

2. —Quand est-ce que M. Brown a écrit la lettre à sa représentante?

—Il y a aujourd'hui quinze jours qu'il a écrit la lettre.

—À qui a-t-il lu la copie de cette lettre?

—Il a lu la copie à M. Picard.

3. —Est-ce que M. Picard a trouvé beaucoup de fautes dans la lettre?

—Non. Il n'a pas trouvé une seule faute.

—Quel livre a rendu grand service à M. Brown?

—Le livre *La Correspondance commerciale* lui a rendu grand service.

4. —M. Brown a-t-il apprecié les services de Mme Parmentier?

—Oui. Il a toujours[1] apprecié ses services dévoués.

—Qu'est-ce que M. Picard a dit quand M. Brown a fini de lire la lettre?

—Il a dit: C'est une gentille lettre.

NOTE: Most adverbs (**bien, déjà, encore, toujours, souvent,** etc.) precede the past participle. The adverbs **hier, aujourd'hui, demain, ici, là, tôt, tard,** however, follow the past participle.

Il a déjà écrit la lettre.	He has already written the letter.
Il a écrit la lettre hier.	He wrote the letter yesterday.

Exercise No. 154

Complete the following sentences with the past participle of the verb indicated. Read each completed sentence aloud.

Exemple: 1. J'ai reçu votre lettre du 4 mai.

1. J'ai (recevoir) votre lettre du 4 mai.
2. Nous avons (décider) de visiter le Musée du Louvre.
3. Il a toujours (apprécier) vos services devoués.
4. Ces services ont (contribuer) à notre réussite.
5. M. Brown a (vendre) beaucoup d'objets d'art.
6. Nous n'avons pas (écrire) beaucoup de lettres.
7. N'avez-vous pas (lire) tous les guides?
8. Ont-ils (rendre) les livres à la bibliothèque?
9. Avez-vous (faire) la connaissance de votre représentante?
10. Je n'ai pas (entendre) ce qu'il a (dire).
11. Elles n'ont pas encore (finir) l'examen.
12. La bonne a déjà (servir) le thé au rhum.

Exercise No. 155—Questionnaire

1. Qui a écrit une lettre à sa représentante?
2. À qui a-t-il lu une copie de cette lettre?
3. M. Picard a-t-il trouvé beaucoup de fautes dans la lettre de M. Brown?
4. Quand est-ce que Mme Parmentier sera à Paris?
5. Où est-ce qu'elle va rencontrer M. Brown?
6. Dans quelle langue est-ce qu'elle va parler avec lui?
7. Comment est-ce que M. Brown connaissait Mme Parmentier jusqu'à présent?
8. De quoi M. Brown est-il certain?
9. Quand est-ce que les deux messieurs auront leur dernier rendez-vous?
10. Où est-ce qu'ils se rencontreront?
11. Qu'est-ce que M. Picard donnera à M. Brown?

CHAPITRE 30 (TRENTE)

LES DERNIERS CONSEILS DE M. PICARD

MR. PICARD'S FINAL WORDS OF ADVICE

1. Il fait chaud dans la maison de M. Brown. Il n'y a pas un souffle d'air. Par la fenêtre ouverte on entend les bruits de la rue.
2. —Je suis content de quitter la ville, dit M. Brown à M. Picard.
3. —J'ai envie de vous accompagner, répond M. Picard.
4. —Pourrez-vous venir avec moi?
5. —Malheureusement, ce n'est pas possible.
6. —Quel dommage! Eh bien, voulez-vous bien me donner quelques derniers conseils? Est-ce que la vie en France est différente de la vie aux États-Unis?
7. —Oui, M. Brown, les coutumes du pays sont assez différentes. En général on fait les choses avec plus de formalité qu'ici. La question de politesse, il me semble, est d'une valeur profonde; c'est à dire que chaque personne est digne d'être respectée.
8. —C'est vrai, répond M. Brown.
9. —J'ai remarqué que les affaires se traitent en France avec plus de formalité qu'aux États-Unis. Les gens d'affaires aiment bien bavarder un peu avant d'entamer une affaire. Ils désirent se connaître les uns les autres.
10. —Je serai très content en France.
11. —Il faudra vous habituer à un train de vie moins agité. En général la vie en France est plus tranquille.

1. It is hot in Mr. Brown's house. There is not a breath of air. Through the open window one hears the noises of the street.
2. I am happy to leave the city, says Mr. Brown to Mr. Picard.
3. I have a mind to go with you, answers Mr. Picard.
4. Will you be able to go with me?
5. Unfortunately, it isn't possible.
6. What a pity! Well then, will you kindly give me some final advice? Is life in France different from life in the United States?
7. Yes, Mr. Brown, the customs of the country are quite different. In general, things are done with more formality than they are here. The question of courtesy it seems to me has a profound meaning; that is, every person is worthy of respect.
8. "That's true," answers Mr. Brown.
9. I have noticed that in France business is done with more formality than it is in the United States. Business people like to chat a little with each other before taking up a business matter. They want to get to know one another.
10. I'll be very happy in France.
11. You'll have to get used to a less turbulent way of life. In general, life in France is quieter.

12. —Je l'espère. Je suis las d'être toujours bousculé.

12. I hope so (for it to be). I am tired of being forever jostled.

13. —Parlant d'autre chose, avez-vous lu les livres sur la France que je vous ai recommandés?

13. To speak of something else, did you read the books on France which I recommended to you?

14. —Oui, je les ai tous lus avec beaucoup d'intérêt.

14. Yes, I read them all with much interest.

15. —J'ai parcouru aussi les deux guides que vous m'avez prêtés: le Guide Michelin et le Guide Bleu. Il me semble que ces deux guides me rendront grand service.

15. I have also glanced through the two guides which you lent me: the Michelin Guide and the Blue Guide. It seems to me that these two guides will be helpful to me.

16. —Sans aucun doute. Quant à moi, je passerai l'été à New-York. Nos conversations m'ont donné beaucoup de plaisir. Vous allez me manquer.

16. Without any doubt. As for me, I'll spend the summer in New York. I have enjoyed our conversations very much. I shall miss you.

17. —Je penserai à vous très souvent et de temps en temps je vous écrirai.

17. I'll think of you often and from time to time I'll write you.

18. —Je serai content de recevoir vos lettres. Alors, voilà, il faut nous dire au revoir. Vous serez bien gentil de faire mes amitiés à Mme Brown et d'embrasser les enfants de ma part.

18. I'll be happy to receive your letters. Well, then we must say goodbye. Kindly give my regards to Mrs. Brown and kiss the children for me.

19. —Merci, et bonne chance!

19. Thank you, and good luck!

20. —Bon voyage, M. Brown.
Ils se serrent la main.

20. Have a safe trip, Mr. Brown.
They shake hands.

NOTE: aucun (aucune *f*), *not any, none, no one* (with emphasis) Except after **sans**, it is used with **ne. Je n'ai aucun doute.** I haven't any doubt. **Aucun de ces élèves n'est français.** None of these pupils is French.

Pronunciation and Spelling Aids

Practice aloud:

— Je suis content de quitter la ville, dit Monsieur Brown à Monsieur Picard.

(Zhuh süee kawñ-tahñ duh kee-tay la **veel**, dee muh-syeu braun a muh-syeu pee-**kar**.)

— J'ai envie de vous accompagner, répond M. Picard.

(Zhay ahñ-vee duh voo za-kawñ-pa-**nyay**, ray-pawñ muh-syeu pee-**kar**.)

— Ne pouvez-vous pas venir avec moi?

(Nuh poo-vay-voo pah vuh-neer a-vehk **mwa?**)

— Malheureusement, ce n'est pas possible.

(Ma-leu-reuz-**mahñ**, suh neh pah pu-**seebl**.)

Building Vocabulary

Words that are "false friends"

demander means to ask or ask for *not* to demand; **exiger** means to demand

rester means to stay or remain *not* to rest; **se reposer** means to rest

le crayon means the pencil *not* the crayon; **le crayon de cire** means the crayon

la fabrique means the factory *not* the fabric; **le tissu** means the fabric

la lecture means the reading selection *not* lecture; **la conférence** means the lecture

la librairie means the bookstore *not* the library; **la bibliothèque** means the library

le magasin means the store *not* the magazine; **la revue** means the magazine

actuellement means now, at present *not* actually; **réellement** means actually

large means wide *not* large; **grand** means large

les nouvelles means the news *not* novels; **le roman** means the novel

French Expressions

1. **les affaires se traitent** business is done
2. **entamer** to start, to begin; **entamer une affaire** to take up a business matter
3. **sans aucun doute** without any doubt
4. **manquer** to miss, to be lacking, to fail, to be in need of
5. **Vous allez me manquer.** I shall miss you. (*Lit.* You will be missing to me.)
6. **L'argent lui manque.** He lacks money. (*Lit.* Money is lacking to him.)
7. **Je n'y manquerai pas.** I shall not fail to do so.
8. **faire ses amitiés** to give one's regards
9. **faites-lui mes amitiés** give him, her, my regards
10. **mes amitiés à tout le monde** regards to everyone
11. **Point de nouvelles, bonnes nouvelles.** No news is good news.

Exercise No. 156—Completion of Text

1. (Through the open window) **on entend les bruits de la rue.**
2. (I have a mind) **de vous accompagner.**
3. (Will you give me) **quelques derniers conseils?**
4. **On fait les choses** (with more formality) **qu'ici.**
5. (Each person is worthy) **d'être respectée.**
6. **Ils désirent** (to get to know one another).
7. **En général la vie en France** (is more tranquil).
8. (Have you read) **les livres sur la France?**
9. (I have glanced through) **les deux guides.**
10. (I shall spend) **l'été à New-York.**
11. I shall miss you.
12. (I shall be happy) **de recevoir vos lettres.**

Grammar Notes

1. MORE IRREGULAR PAST PARTICIPLES

courir to run	**couru** run
mettre to put	**mis** put
prendre to take	**pris** taken
voir to see	**vu** seen
parcourir to scan	**parcouru** scanned
promettre to promise	**promis** promised
apprendre to learn	**appris** learned
comprendre to understand	**compris** understood

Exercise No. 157

Complete each of the following sentences with the correct past participle. Read each completed sentence aloud.

1. **J'ai déjà** (scanned *or* glanced through) **tous les guides.**
2. **Avez-vous** (understood) **tout ce que le maître a** (said)?
3. **A-t-il** (put on) **son pardessus?**
4. **Elle a** (promised) **de nous rencontrer à l'aéroport.**
5. **J'ai tout** (heard) **mais je n'ai pas tout** (understood).
6. **Avez-vous** (seen) **Mme Picard?**
7. **Les enfants ont** (run) **à l'école.**
8. **Les élèves ont** (learned) **beaucoup de locutions françaises.**
9. **Ils n'ont pas** (taken) **leurs caoutchoucs.**

10. **Nous n'avons pas** (taken) **la bouteille.**

2. AGREEMENT OF THE PAST PARTICIPLE

When a direct object *precedes* the verb, the past participle must agree with that direct object in number and gender.

Direct object after verb	Direct object before verb
(*No agreement*)	(Agreement)
Avez-vous trouvé le livre?	*Je l'ai trouvé,* (masc. sing.)
Avez-vous trouvé la lettre?	*Je l'ai trouvée,* (fem. sing.)
Avez-vous trouvé les livres?	*Je les ai trouvés,* (masc. plur.)
Avez-vous trouvé les lettres?	*Je les ai trouvées,* (fem. plur.)

The past participle does not agree with an indirect object preceding the verb. **Nous ne leur avons pas donné de cadeaux.** We did not give any gifts *to them.*

Exercise No. 158

Translate each question and answer. Read each question and answer aloud in French three times. Note the agreement of the past participle.

1. —Avez-vous recommandé ces guides (*m*)?
2. —Est-ce qu'il a écrit la réponse?
3. —Où a-t-il trouvé l'argent (*m*)?
4. —Avez-vous compris la question?
5. —A-t-elle appris le proverbe?
6. —Qui a réservé les deux places (*f*)?
7. —Quand avez-vous vu votre amie?
8. —Quand ont-ils fini l'examen (*m*)?
9. —Quand est-ce que le facteur (mail carrier) a apporté les lettres?
10. —Avez-vous entendu la sonnette (door bell)?
11. —M. Brown a-t-il parcouru tous les guides?
12. —Quelle lettre a-t-il lue[1] à M. Picard?

1. —Oui, monsieur, je les ai recommandés.
2. —Oui, monsieur, il l'a écrite.
3. —Il l'a trouvé sur le bureau.
4. —Non, monsieur, je ne l'ai pas comprise.
5. — Non, madame, elle ne l'a pas appris.
6. —Mon père les a réservées hier.
7. —Je l'ai vue hier soir.
8. —Ils l'ont fini á deux heures.
9. —Il les a apportées ce matin.
10. —Non, monsieur, je ne l'ai pas entendue.
11. — Il les a tous parcourus.
12. —Il a lu la lettre qu'il a reçue[2] de Mme Parmentier.

NOTE [1]The direct object preceding the verb, with which **lue** agrees, is **quelle lettre**. [2]**The direct object preceding the verb, with which **reçue** agrees, is the relative pronoun **qu'**, which is feminine because it refers to lettre (f).

Exercise No. 159—Questionnaire

1. Où se trouvent M. Brown et M. Picard?
2. Quel temps fait-il?
3. Qu'est-ce qu'on entend par la fenêtre?
4. Qui est content de quitter la ville?
5. Qui a envie d'accompagner M. Brown?
6. Qu'est-ce que M. Picard répond à la question, "Ne pourrez-vous pas venir avec moi"?
7. Comment fait-on les choses en France?
8. Qu'est-ce que M. Picard a remarqué en France?
9. Qui est fatigué d'être bousculé?
10. Qui a lu des livres sur la France?
11. Qui les a recommandés?
12. Quant à M. Picard, où passera-t-il l'été?
13. À qui M. Brown pensera-t-il souvent?

CHAPITRE 31 (TRENTE ET UN)

M. BROWN PART POUR LA FRANCE
MR. BROWN LEAVES FOR FRANCE

1. Il y a cinq mois que M. Brown étudie le français. Il a passé beaucoup de temps en conversation avec son professeur, M. Picard. Il a appris les règles essentielles de la grammaire et il a lu beaucoup de livres sur la France. Il a vraiment travaillé dur. Maintenant il parle bien le français et il compte se tirer d'affaires en France sans difficulté.

2. M. Brown a obtenu son billet pour le voyage, son passeport, et ses chèques de voyage. Il a tout ce qui lui faut.

3. Naturellement, M. Brown a écrit une lettre à sa représentante en France pour lui faire savoir l'heure de son arrivée. Mme Parmentier, la représentante, a promis de le rencontrer à l'aéroport.

4. C'est enfin le 31 mai, ce jour entre tous. L'avion de M. Brown part de l'aéroport Kennedy International à sept heures précises du soir. Il doit être à l'aéroport deux heures d'avance pour faire vérifier son billet et son passeport et pour faire peser ses bagages.

5. La famille ne l'accompagne pas en France parce que les enfants doivent finir l'année scolaire, et sa femme doit enseigner un cours d'été à l'université et s'occuper aussi des enfants. D'ailleurs, voyager avec quatre enfants entre cinq et douze ans est non seulement difficile, mais aussi assez coûteux.

1. Mr. Brown has been studying French for five months. He has spent a lot of time in conversation with his teacher, M. Picard. He has learned the essential rules of grammar and he has read many books on France. He really has worked very hard. Now he speaks French quite well and he expects to get along in France without difficulty.

2. Mr. Brown has obtained his ticket for the trip, his passport, and his travelers' checks. He has everything he needs.

3. Of course Mr. Brown has written a letter to his agent in France letting her know the time of his arrival. Mrs. Parmentier, the agent, has promised to meet him at the airport.

4. It is May 31 at last, the day of days. Mr. Brown's plane leaves Kennedy International Airport at 7 P.M. sharp. He must be at the airport two hours before to have his ticket and passport checked and his baggage weighed.

5. The family is not going with him to France because his children have to finish the school year and his wife has to teach a summer course at the university and also take care of the children. Besides, traveling with four children from five to twelve years of age is not only difficult but also quite expensive.

6. Naturellement la famille est dans tous ses états. Les enfants ont très peu dormi et à sept heures du matin ils sont tous levés, lavés, et habillés.

7. À trois heures de l'après-midi la famille est prête à partir pour l'aéroport. M. Brown a fait ses deux valises et il les a déjà mises dans l'auto. Ils montent tous en voiture. M. Brown se met en route et ils arrivent à l'aéroport vers cinq heures.

8. M. Brown fait vérifier son billet et son passeport, et il fait peser ses bagages. Il doit payer vingt dollars en supplément parce que le poids total dépasse les soixante-six livres permis gratis.

9. Alors M. Brown fait ses adieux à sa femme et aux enfants qui lui souhaitent "bon voyage." Il monte dans l'avion, saluant de la main son petit monde qui le regarde d'un air ému. À sept heures précises l'avion prend son vol.

10. M. Brown est en route.

6. Of course the family is extremely excited. The children have hardly slept and at seven in the morning they are all awake, washed and dressed.

7. At three in the afternoon the whole family is ready to leave for the airport. Mr. Brown has packed two valises and he has already put them in the car. They all get into the car. Mr. Brown starts off and they arrive at the airport at about five o'clock.

8. Mr. Brown has his ticket and his passport checked and he has his baggage weighed. He has to pay twenty dollars extra, because the total weight exceeds the 66 pounds allowed free.

9. Then Mr. Brown says goodbye to his wife and children, who wish him a good trip. He goes up into the plane waving to his little world, who are watching him with emotion. At 7 o'clock sharp the plane takes off.

10. Mr. Brown is on his way.

Building Vocabulary

ANTONYMS

1. **il a ouvert** he opened
   il a fermé he closed
2. **j'ai commencé** I began
   j'ai fini I finished
3. **nous avons trouvé** we found
   nous avons perdu we lost

4. **vous avez envoyé** you sent
   vous avez apporté you brought
5. **ils ont acheté** they bought
   ils ont vendu they sold
6. **elles ont donné** they gave
   elles ont reçu they received

French Expressions

1. **se tirer d'affaire, s'en tirer** to get along, to cope
2. **pour lui faire savoir** to let him know
3. **ce jour entre tous** this day of days
4. **pour faire contrôler son billet** to have his ticket checked
5. **pour faire peser ses bagages** to have his baggage weighed
6. **s'occuper de** to busy oneself with, to take care of
7. **être dans tous ses états** to be extremely excited
8. **faire les valises** to pack the suitcases
9. **monter en voiture** to get in the car
10. **se mettre en route** to set out
11. **faire ses adieux à** to say goodbye to
12. **Il est en route.** He is on his way.

Exercise No. 160—Completion of Text

1. (It is five months) **que M. Brown étudie le français.**
2. (He has learned) **les règles essentielles.**
3. (He has really worked) **beaucoup.**
4. (He has obtained) **son billet pour le voyage.**
5. (He has written) **une lettre à sa représentante.**
6. **Mme Parmentier** (has promised) **de le rencontrer.**
7. **À cinq heures** (he must be) **à l'aéroport.**
8. **La famille** (is not going with him).
9. **Les enfants** (must finish) **l'année scolaire.**
10. **M. Brown** (has packed) **les deux valises.**
11. (They all get) **en voiture.**
12. **M. Brown** (has his baggage weighed).
13. (He must pay) **vingt dollars en supplément.**

14. **M. Brown** (says goodbye to) **sa femme et ses enfants.**
15. **Il est** (on his way).

Grammar Notes

1. MORE IRREGULAR PAST PARTICIPLES

ouvrir to open	**ouvert** opened
couvrir to cover	**couvert** covered
offrir to offer	**offert** offered
savoir to know	**su** learned, [1]known
vouloir to want	**voulu** wanted
avoir to have	**eu** had
être to be	**été** been
vivre to live	**vécu** lived
plaire to please	**plu** pleased
devoir to owe	**dû** owed
falloir must[2]	**fallu** had to
paraître to appear	**paru** appeared
boire to drink	**bu** drunk
croire to believe	**cru** believed

NOTE: [1]The conversational past of **savoir**—**j'ai su**, etc.—means I have learned (found out), etc., *not* I have known, etc. [2]The verb **falloir** is used only in the impersonal third person singular (**il**), thus **il a fallu** is the only form used in the conversational past tense.

Exercise No. 161

Translate. Use the conversational past for these verbs.

Exemple: I have had (I had, I did have), **j'ai eu**

1. he has wanted
2. you opened
3. I have found out
4. Did he open?
5. we have had
6. they have been
7. I have not covered
8. Have they found out?
9. we did not open
10. she was
11. did he want?
12. I offered

2. PAST PARTICIPLES USED AS ADJECTIVES

Past participles are often used as adjectives. Like other adjectives they usually follow the noun they modify and always agree with it in number and gender.

le vase cassé	the broken vase	**le livre ouvert**	the open book
les vases cassés	the broken vases	**les livres ouverts**	the open books
la tasse cassée	the broken cup	**la porte ouverte**	the open door
les tasses cassées	the broken cups	**les portes ouvertes**	the open doors

Exercise No. 162

Complete each sentence with the correct form of the past participle in parentheses:

Example: 1. Il est assis près de la fenêtre ouverte.

1. Il est assis près de la fenêtre (ouvert)
2. Au mur il y a des affiches (f) (illustré)
3. Toutes les portes sont (fermé)
4. Le couturier Dior est bien (connu)
5. Beaucoup de ces tasses (f) sont (cassé)
6. Tous les enfants sont (levé)
7. Jean n'est pas encore (habillé)
8. Voici des revues (f) (envoyé) par M. Picard
9. Où est la chambre (réservé) pour M. Adams
10. Nous avons trouvé les billets (perdu)

Exercise No. 163—Questionnaire

1. Combien de temps y a-t-il que M. Brown étudie le français?
2. Avec qui a-t-il passé beaucoup de temps en conversation?
3. Qu'est-ce qu'il a appris?
4. Comment est-ce qu'il a travaillé?
5. Comment est-ce qu'il parle français maintenant?
6. Qu'est-ce que M. Brown a obtenu?
7. À qui M. Brown a-t-il écrit?
8. Qu'est-ce que sa représentante lui a promis?
9. À quelle heure les enfants se sont-ils levés?

10. À quelle heure est-ce que l'avion part de l'aéroport?
11. Qu'est-ce que chaque voyageur doit faire vérifier?
12. Est-ce que sa famille accompagne M. Brown en France?
13. Pourquoi est-ce que les enfants doivent rester à New-York?
14. Pourquoi est-ce que Mme Brown doit rester à New-York?

Première Partie

NOUNS

1.	l'aéroport	1.	airport
2.	le bruit	2.	noise
3.	l'arrivée	3.	arrival
4.	la copie	4.	copy
5.	la difficulté	5.	difficulty
6.	l'espoir	6.	hope
7.	la familiarité	7.	familiarity
8.	la faute	8.	mistake, fault
9.	la formalité	9.	formality
10.	l'intérêt	10.	interest
11.	la main	11.	hand
12.	le passeport	12.	passport
13.	la politesse	13.	courtesy
14.	la règle	14.	rule
15.	le séjour	15.	stay, sojourn
16.	la sortie	16.	exit, departure
17.	la valeur	17.	value
18.	l'homme, la femme d'affaires	18.	businessman, business woman

VERBS

1.	apprécier	1.	to appreciate
2.	j'apprécie	2.	I appreciate
3.	avouer	3.	to avow
4.	contrôler	4.	to control, check
5.	dépasser	5.	to exceed
6.	s'habituer à	6.	to get used to
7.	s'occuper de	7.	to be busy with, take care (charge) of
8.	elle s'occupe de	8.	she takes care of
9.	pardonner	9.	to pardon
10.	pardonnez-moi	10.	pardon me

11. prier	11. to pray, to beg
12. remarquer	12. to notice
13. traiter	13. to treat
14. courir	14. to run
15. parcourir	15. to scan, glance
16. permettre	16. to permit
17. souhaiter	17. to wish
18. surprendre	18. to surprise

ADJECTIVES

1. **différent**	1. different
2. **dernier** (dernière *f.*)	2. last
3. **digne**	3. worthy
4. **distingué**	4. distinguished
5. **nerveux** (euse f.)	5. nervous
6. **propre**	6. own
7. **sérieux** (euse *f.*)	7. serious
8. **seul**	8. alone
9. **las** (lasse *f.*)	9. tired, weary

ADVERBS

1. **d'avance**	1. in advance
2. **malheureusement**	2. unfortunately
3. **heureusement**	3. fortunately

French Expressions

1. **faire ses adieux à**	1. to say goodbye to
2. **faire ses amitiés à**	2. to give his regards to
3. **faire votre connaissance**	3. to make your acquaintance
4. **faire peser les valises**	4. to have bags weighed
5. **faire venir**	5. to send for
6. **faire savoir**	6. to let know
7. **descendre de la voiture**	7. to get out of the car
8. **monter en voiture**	8. to get into the car
9. **se mettre en route**	9. to set out
10. **se tirer d'affaire, s'en tirer**	10. to get along, to cope
11. **voulez-vous bien**	11. will you kindly
12. **à la perfection**	12. perfectly
13. **quant à moi**	13. as for me
14. **par conséquent**	14. consequently
15. **deux fois par semaine**	15. two times a week
16. **votre propre langue**	16. your own language
17. **je vous prie**	17. I beg you, please
18. **vers six heures**	18. about six o'clock

Deuxième Partie

Exercise No. 164

Translate each past participle and give the infinitive of the verb from which it is derived.

Exemple: vendu sold **vendre** to sell

1. obtenu
2. laissé
3. été
4. dit
5. fini
6. voulu
7. reçu
8. écrit
9. lu
10. appris
11. su
12. rendu
13. mis

14. obéi
15. vu
16. mangé
17. fait
18. pris
19. écouté
20. couvert
21. compris
22. ouvert
23. eu
24. permis
25. pu

Exercise No. 165

Select the group of words in Column II which best completes each sentence begun in Column I:

I	II
1. M. Brown a appris rapidement	a. qui l'attendra à l'aéroport.
2. Il parle bien le français; par conséquent	b. me rendront grand service.
3. Il a une représentante à Paris	c. deux fois par semaine chez M. Brown.
4. M. Picard n'a pas trouvé une seule faute	d. est digne d'être respectée.
5. Il y a cinq mois qu'ils se rencontrent	e. il pourra se tirer d'affaires en France.
6. Mme Brown s'occupera aussi des enfants	f. l'heure de votre arrivée?
7. Les Français croient que chaque personne	g. parce qu'il a travaillé dur.
8. Avant le départ de M. Brown	h. dans la lettre que M. Brown a écrite.
9. Les deux guides que vous m'avez prêtés	i. pendant l'absence de son mari.
10. Voulez-vous bien me faire savoir	j. son professeur lui a donné de bons conseils.

Exercise No. 166

Complete each sentence in Column I by choosing the correct expression from Column II. Be sure to use the correct verb form.

I	II
1. (Have you packed) **les valises?**	a. monter en voiture
2. (Give my regards) **à Mme Brown.**	b. descendre de la voiture
3. **Embrassez les enfants** (for me).	c. faire ses adieux
4. **Je parlerai avec vous** (in your own language).	d. me tirer d'affaire
5. (Pardon me) **si je suis fier de mes compatriotes.**	e. faire les valises
6. **Je pourrai** (to get along) **en France.**	f. pardonnez-moi
7. **J'aurai le plaisir** (of meeting you).	g. votre propre langue
8. (They get into the car) **et se mettent en route.**	h. faire votre connaissance
9. (They get out of the car) **à l'aéroport.**	i. faire mes amitiés
10. **Là M. Brown** (said goodbye) **à sa famille.**	j. de ma part

Exercise No. 167

Read each question. Translate the English answers into French. In seven of the answers there is a direct object pronoun before the verb. Be sure that the past participle agrees with the direct object pronoun in number and gender.

Exemple: 1. Oui, monsieur, je l'ai reçue.

1. **Avez-vous reçu ma lettre?**
2. **À qui est-ce que M. Brown a écrit la lettre?**
3. **M. Brown a-t-il apprécié ses services?**
4. **Qui a fait la valise?**
5. **Est-ce que les guides vous ont rendu grand service?**
6. **Qu'est-ce que la bonne a servi?**
7. **Avez-vous compris la question?**
8. **Qui n'a pas fait les leçons?**
9. **Avez-vous vu le nouveau film?**
10. **Qu'est-ce que le facteur a apporté?**

1. Yes sir, I have received it (*f*).
2. He wrote it (*f*) to Mrs. Parmentier.
3. Yes, sir, he has appreciated them (*m*).
4. Mr. Brown has packed it (*f*).
5. Yes, sir, they have given me great service.
6. She served tea with rum.
7. No, sir, I did not understand it (*f*).
8. Philippe has not done them (*f*).
9. No, madam, we have not seen it (*m*).
10. He has brought a parcel-post package (**colis postal** *m*).

Dialogue I
À l'aéroport

1. —Bonjour, Mme Parmentier. Est-ce que vous attendez quelqu'un?	1. Good day, Mrs. Parmentier. Are you expecting someone?
2. —Oui, monsieur, j'attends M. Brown de New York, le chef de la maison que je représente à Paris.	2. Yes, sir, I am waiting for Mr. Brown of New York, the head of the firm I represent in Paris.
3. —Est-ce que vous le connaissez?	3. Do you know him?
4. —Je le connais seulement par correspondance. Mais j'ai sa photo et je crois que je le reconnaîtrai. C'est un homme d'à peu près quarante ans.	4. I know him only by correspondence. But I have his photo and I think I'll recognize him. He is a man about forty years old.
5. —À quelle heure doit-il arriver?	5. At what time should he arrive?
6. —L'avion est annoncé pour sept heures.	6. The plane is scheduled to arrive at seven o'clock.
7. —Est-il en retard?	7. Is it late?
8. —Non, il est à temps. Ah! Le voilà. Il arrive. Il s'approche. Il atterrit.	8. No, it's on time. Ah! There it is. It's coming. It's approaching. It is landing.
9. —Excusez-moi, monsieur, je vais à la rencontre de M. Brown.	9. Excuse me, sir, I am going to meet Mr. Brown.

Dialogue 2
Bienvenu en France

1. —(Soyez le) Bienvenu en France, M. Brown. Comment le voyage s'est-il passé?	1. Welcome to France, Mr. Brown. How did the trip go?
2. —Merveilleusement bien! Je suis heureux d'être en France. J'ai tellement songé à ce moment.	2. Marvelously well! I am happy to be in France. I have thought about this moment so much.
3. —Et vous voilà! Je suis sûre que vous serez très content ici.	3. And here you are! I am sure that you will be very happy here.

Exercise No. 168—Lecture

Gérard n'aime pas étudier l'arithmétique

Un jour, en rentrant de l'école, Gérard dit à sa mère,—Je n'aime pas étudier l'arithmétique. C'est si difficile. Pourquoi avons-nous besoin de tant d'exercices et de tant de problèmes? Nous avons des machines à calculer, n'est-ce pas? Alors!

Mme Davis regarde son fils et dit,—Tu as tort, mon petit. On ne peut pas se passer de[1] nombres. Par exemple, on a toujours besoin de dépenser de l'argent, de faire des achats, d'estimer les distances, et puis, et puis. La mère s'arrête en voyant que Gérard ne fait pas attention à ce qu'elle dit.

A propos, continue-t-elle en souriant, le baseball ne t'intéresse pas non plus, mon petit?

Par exemple! Tu veux rire.

—Alors, si les Dodgers ont gagné quatre-vingts parties,[2] et ils en ont perdu[3] vingt, sais-tu quel pourcentage de parties ils ont gagné?

En entendant cela Gérard s'écrie,—Tu as raison, maman. Les nombres, l'arithmétique et les mathématiques sont très importants. Je crois que maintenant je vais étudier beaucoup plus.

NOTE [1]**se passer de,** *to do without* [2]**parties,** *games, matches* [3]**perdre,** *to lose.*

CHAPITRE 32 (TRENTE-DEUX)

USAGE REND MAÎTRE

PRACTICE MAKES PERFECT

FOREWORD

Mr. Brown is now in France and he writes nine letters to Mr. Picard about some of the places he visits and about his experiences and impressions.

There are many references in his letters to things he has discussed with his teacher. Much of the vocabulary in Chapters 3 to 31 is repeated in the letters.

Reread the initial texts and dialogues of the previous chapters *before* proceeding with Chapter 32 to review the vocabulary and important expressions. You will be able to do this easily and rapidly, with little or no reference to the English translation.

You should continue your pronunciation practice by reading aloud dialogues and parts of conversational texts from previous chapters as often as possible.

L'arrivée à Paris | **Arrival in Paris**

La première lettre de Paris

Paris, le 4 juin 2005
Cher ami,

    Quand l'avion est arrivé à Roissy, j'ai passé par la douane et je suis allé à la salle d'attente.
    Tout de suite une belle dame s'est approchée et elle m'a demandé:—Pardon, monsieur, êtes-vous M. Brown?
    J'ai répondu:—À votre service. Et vous êtes Mme Parmentier, n'est-ce pas? Je suis très content de faire votre connaissance. Nous nous sommes serré la main.

Paris, June 4, 2005
Dear Friend,

When the plane arrived at Roissy, I got through customs and went to the waiting room.

A beautiful lady immediately approached me and asked, "Pardon me, sir, are you Mr. Brown?"

At your service, I answered. And you are Mrs. Parmentier, are you not? I am delighted to know you. We shook hands.

—*Le plaisir est à moi, Mme Parmentier a répondu.*

Nous sommes sortis ensemble et nous avons pris un taxi pour l'Hôtel du Quai Voltaire.

Le taxi a pris le chemin de la ville en allant à toute vitesse. J'ai pensé en moi-même:—M. Picard se trompe au sujet de la vie tranquille en France.

En regardant autour de nous j'ai vu que tout, autos, camions, autobus, taxis, tout courait à vitesse vertigineuse.

À la fin j'ai crié au chauffeur:—Pas si vite, s'il vous plaît! Je ne suis pas pressé!

—*Ni moi non plus, monsieur, m'a-t-il répondu, tournant le coin à toute vitesse.*

Enfin nous sommes arrivés à l'hôtel sains et saufs. Le taxi s'est arrêté et nous sommes descendus. Mme Parmentier est entrée avec moi.

Je suis allé au bureau de réception, et j'ai dit à l'employé:—Bonjour, monsieur. Avez-vous une chambre réservée pour Brown?

—*Bienvenu à Paris, M. Brown. Certainement. Nous vous avons réservé une belle chambre au troisième étage qui donne sur le quai. C'est le numéro 35.*

—*Très bien, merci. Et quel est le prix, s'il vous plaît?*

—*Cent euro par jour, service compris.*

—*Bon. Voulez-vous bien faire monter mes bagages?*

—*Tout de suite, monsieur. Porteur! Mais vous parlez très bien le français. Y a-t-il longtemps que vous êtes en France?*

—*Je viens d'arriver, ai-je dit, assez fier de moi-même.*

—*Est-ce que vous faites un voyage d'agrément?*

—*C'est à la fois un voyage d'agrément et un voyage d'affaires.*

The pleasure is mine, answered Mrs. Parmentier. We went out together and took a taxi to the Hotel du Quai Voltaire.

The taxi took the road to the city going at full speed. I thought to myself, M. Picard is mistaken about the quiet life of France.

Looking around us I saw that everything—cars, trucks, buses, taxis—everything was rushing at a dizzying speed.

At last I shouted to the driver, "Not so fast, please! I am not in a hurry!"

Neither am I, sir! he answered me, turning the corner at full speed.

At last we arrived safe and sound at the hotel. The taxi stopped and we got out. Mrs. Parmentier went in with me.

I went to the reception desk and said to the clerk, "Good day, sir. Do you have a room reserved for Brown?"

Welcome to Paris, Mr. Brown. Certainly. We have reserved for you a fine room on the third floor, which faces the quay (wharf). It is number 35.

Very good, thank you. And what is the rate, please?

100 euros a day, including service.

Fine. Would you please have my bags taken up?

Right away, sir. Porter! But you speak French very well. Have you been in France long?

I have just arrived, I said, quite proud of myself.

Are you on a pleasure trip?

This is both (at the same time) a pleasure trip and a business trip.

J'ai bavardé un peu plus avec Mme Parmentier et ensuite nous nous sommes dit au revoir. Mme Parmentier m'a promis en partant de me téléphoner pour prendre rendez-vous.	*I chatted a little more with Mrs. Parmentier and then we said goodbye. On leaving, Mrs. Parmentier promised to telephone me to make an appointment.*
Je suis monté par l'ascenseur à ma chambre, numéro 35. Elle est très confortable. Je ne manque de rien. Je vous répète encore une fois, M. Picard, que je serai très content en France.	*I went up in the elevator to my room, number 35. It is very comfortable. I lack nothing. I repeat once more, M. Picard, that I shall be very happy in France.*
Cordialement, votre ami, *John Brown*	*Cordially, your friend,* *John Brown*

Grammar Notes of this chapter.

NOTE: Roissy is a town outside Paris where Charles de Gaulle International Airport is located.

ANTONYMS

1. **il est allé** he went
   il est venu he came
2. **il est arrivé** he arrived
   il est parti he left
3. **il est entré** he entered
   il est sorti he went out
4. **il est monté** he went up
   il est descendu he went down
5. **il s'est rappelé** he remembered
   il a oublié he forgot
6. **il a demandé** he asked
   il a répondu he answered

RELATED WORDS

1. **appeler,** to call; **s'appeler,** to be called, to be named; **se rappeler,** to recall, remember
2. **entrer,** to enter; **rentrer,** to re-enter, return home
3. **tourner,** to turn; **retourner,** to return, go back; **détourner,** to reroute
4. **venir,** to come; **revenir,** to come back; **devenir,** to become; **prevenir,** to warn
5. **voir,** to see; **revoir,** to see again

French Expressions

Présentations (pray-zahñ-tah-**syawñ**)   Introductions

1. **Permettez-moi de vous présenter Mme Parmentier, ma représentante à Paris.**
2. **Enchanté de faire votre connaissance.**

3. **Le plaisir est à moi.**
4. **Veuillez (veu-yay) me présenter à monsieur (madame)?**

1. Allow me to introduce you to Mrs. Parmentier, my agent in Paris.
2. Delighted to make your acquaintance; to know you.
3. The pleasure is mine.
4. Would you kindly introduce me to the gentleman (lady)?

Salutations—letters to friends:

1. **Mon cher Louis,** Dear Louis,
2. **Ma chère Colette,** Dear Colette,
3. **Cher ami,** Dear Friend (*m*),
4. **Chère amie,** Dear Friend (*f*),

Closings—letters to friends:

1. **Cordialement, votre ami,** Cordially, your friend,
2. **Salutations amicales de votre ami,** Warm greetings from your friend,
3. **Très affectueusement,** Very affectionately yours,
4. **Embrasse tout le monde pour moi,** Kiss everybody for me,
5. **Rappelle-moi au bon souvenir de ta famille,** Remember me to your family,

Exercise No. 169—Completion of Text

1. **Je suis allé** (to the waiting-room).
2. (Immediately) **une belle dame s'est approchée.**
3. (She asked me),—**Êtes-vous M. Brown?**
4. (I answered),—**À votre service.**
5. **Je suis content** (to make your acquaintance).
6. (The pleasure is mine), **a-t-elle répondu.**
7. (I thought to myself),—**M. Picard se trompe.**
8. (We took) **un taxi.**
9. **Tout courait** (at a dizzying speed).
10. Not so fast!
11. **J'ai crié,** —(I am not in a hurry).
12. —(Neither am I), **m'a-t-il répondu.**
13. **Avez-vous une chambre** (reserved for Brown)?
14. (What is the rate), **s'il vous plaît?**
15. (One hundred euros per day) **service compris.**

Grammar Notes

1. VERBS WITH THE AUXILIARY ÊTRE INSTEAD OF AVOIR

You have learned that the conversational past tense (present perfect) in French usually consists of the auxiliary **avoir** (*have*) plus the past participle of the verb.

In French there are sixteen verbs which take some form of the auxiliary **être** (*be*) instead of **avoir** (*have*). They are called **être**-verbs. They are translated into English the same way as **avoir**-verbs. The two most common **être**-verbs are **aller,** *to go* and **venir,** *to come.* Observe carefully the conversational past tense of **aller,** noting the auxiliary verb and the changes in the past participle.

I have gone, I went, I did go; you have gone, you went, you did go, etc.

je suis	**allé** (*m*)	(*zhuh süee za-lay*)
tu es	**allée** (*f*)	(*tu eh za-lay*)
il est	**allé** (*m*)	(*eel eh ta-lay*)
elle est	**allée** (*f*)	(*ehl eh ta-lay*)
nous sommes	**allé**	(*noo sum za-lay*)
vous êtes	**allée**	(*voo zeht za-lay*)
ils sont	**allés** (*m. plur.*)	(*eel sawñ ta-lay*)
elles sont	**allées** (*f. plur.*)	(*ehl sawñ ta-lay*)

The past participle of an **être**-verb must agree with the subject in number and gender.

je, tu, and **nous** may be masculine or feminine. If **je** or **tu** is feminine, the past participle adds the feminine singular ending **-e.** If **nous** is masculine (or masculine and feminine combined), the past participle adds **-s.** If **nous** is feminine, the past participle adds **-es. Vous,** like *you* in English, may be masculine or feminine singular, or masculine or feminine plural. The agreeing past participle therefore has four possible forms.

(masc. sing.) **allé**   (fem. sing.) **allée**   (masc. plur.) **allés**   (fem. plur.) **allées**

2. LIST OF être-VERBS

INFINITIVE

aller	to go	**entrer**	to enter, come (go) in
arriver	to arrive	**rentrer**	to return, go home
monter	to climb, mount	**venir**	to come
retourner	to return, go back	**revenir**	to return, come back
tomber	to fall	**devenir**	to become
rester	to remain, stay	**descendre**	to go (come) down
partir	to leave, depart	**naître**	to be born
sortir (de)	to go out (of)	**mourir**	to die

Conversational Past

il (elle) est allé(e)	nous sommes allés (allées)
il (elle) est arrivé(e)	nous sommes arrivés (arrivées)
il (elle) est entré(e)	nous sommes entrés (entrées)
il (elle) est rentré(e)	nous sommes rentrés (rentrées)
il (elle) est monté(e)	nous sommes montés (montées)
il (elle) est retourné(e)	nous sommes retournés (retournées)
il (elle) est tombé(e)	nous sommes tombés (tombées)
il (elle) est resté(e)	nous sommes restés (restées)
il (elle) est parti(e)	nous sommes partis (parties)
il (elle) est sorti(e) de	nous sommes sortis (sorties) de
il (elle) est venu(e)	nous sommes venus (venues)
il (elle) est revenu(e)	nous sommes revenus (revenues)
il (elle) est devenu(e)	nous sommes devenus (devenues)
il (elle) est descendu(e)	nous sommes descendus (descendues)
il (elle) est né(e)	nous sommes nés (nées)
il (elle) est mort(e)	nous sommes morts (mortes)

Note that all the **être**-verbs except **devenir**, *to become*, **mourir**, *to die* and **naître**, *to be born* are verbs of motion. They are all intransitive, that is, they do not take objects.

Exercise No. 170

Translate each short dialogue. Note the agreement of the past participle. Read each dialogue aloud three times.

1. —Philippe est-il allé à la gare pour rencontrer son père?
   —Oui. Il est sorti de la maison il y a vingt minutes.
   —Est-ce que sa soeur, Marie, est allée avec lui?
   —Oui. Sa soeur, Marie, et aussi son frère, Henri, sont allés avec lui.

2. —Madame Brown est-elle revenue de la ville?
   —Elle n'est pas encore revenue, mais elle reviendra bientôt.

—Pourquoi est-elle allée en ville?

—Elle y est allée pour faire ses achats.

3. —Pourquoi est-ce que M. Brown est revenu tard ce soir?

—Beaucoup de clients sont venus le voir l'après-midi.

—A quelle heure part-il de son bureau d'habitude?

—D'habitude il part à cinq heures précises mais aujourd'hui il n'est pas parti avant six heures moins le quart.

4. —À quelle heure est-ce que M. Brown est parti pour l'aéroport?

—Il est parti à six heures du matin.

—À quelle heure est-il monté dans l'avion?

—Il est monté dans l'avion à huit heures moins le quart.

Exercise No. 171

Supply the correct form of the participle of the verb in parentheses. Watch your endings. Read each completed sentence aloud three times.

Exemple: 1. Elle est arrivée chez elle à six heures et demie.
 1. Elle est (arriver) chez elle à six heures et demie.
 2. Nous (f) sommes (aller) à la gare en voiture.
 3. Abraham Lincoln est (naître) le 12 février 1809.
 4. Il est (mourir) le 15 avril 1865.
 5. Les enfants sont (devenir) très agités quand leur père est (monter) dans l'avion.
 6. Mme Brown est (retourner) de la ville à trois heures et quart.
 7. À quelle heure est-ce que la famille Brown est (partir) pour l'aéroport?
 8. À cinq heures précises ils sont (entrer) dans la salle d'attente.
 9. Je (m) suis (rester) trois semaines à Paris.
 10. Quand vous (m plur) êtes (partir) nous (m) sommes (arriver).

Exercise No. 172—Questionnaire

1. Qu'est-ce que M. Brown a fait quand l'avion est arrivé?
2. Qui s'est approchée dans la salle d'attente?
3. Qu'est-ce que la dame a dit?
4. Qu'est-ce que M. Brown a répondu?
5. Comment le taxi est-il allé en ville?
6. Qu'est-ce qu'il a crié à la fin?
7. Qu'est-ce que le chauffeur a répondu?
8. Qu'est-ce que M. Brown a dit à l'employé?
9. Qu'est-ce qu'il a répondu?

CHAPITRE 33 (TRENTE-TROIS)

M. BROWN REND VISITE
À LA FAMILLE PARMENTIER

MR. BROWN VISITS
THE PARMENTIER FAMILY

DEUXIÈME LETTRE DE PARIS

Cher ami,

Lundi passé, Mme Parmentier m'a appelé par téléphone pour m'inviter à prendre le thé chez elle le lendemain (the next day). Naturellement, j'ai sauté sur l'offre de visiter une famille française.

J'ai pris un taxi et à cinq heures de l'après-midi nous nous sommes arrêtés devant une maison charmante dans la rue Vaugirard. Je suis monté au troisième étage par un escalier élégant.

J'ai sonné et aussitôt j'ai entendu des pas rapides. Une petite bonne m'a ouvert la porte et elle m'a invité à entrer.

Mme Parmentier s'est approchée pour me saluer.—Bonjour, M. Brown, elle a dit, je suis contente de vous voir.

Je lui ai répondu:—Cette maison a l'air d'être du dix-huitième siècle: elle est charmante.

—Il y a beaucoup de maisons de cette époque à Paris, et plusieurs qui datent d'encore beaucoup plus loin, comme vous le savez sans doute.

Dear Friend,

Last Monday Mrs. Parmentier called me on the telephone to invite me to have tea at her house the next day. Naturally I jumped at the chance to visit a French family.

I took a taxi and at five o'clock in the afternoon we stopped in front of an attractive house in Vaugirard Street. I went up to the third floor by a graceful staircase.

I rang and immediately heard rapid footsteps. A little maid opened the door (for me) and invited me to come in.

Mrs. Parmentier approached to greet me. "Good day, Mr. Brown," she said. "I'm glad to see you."

I said to her, "This house has an eighteenth-century air: it is charming."

"There are many houses of that period in Paris and several which date from even longer ago, as you probably know."

Nous sommes entrés dans un grand salon, meublé de bon goût dans le style Louis XV (quinze). Mme Parmentier m'a présenté à son mari, et à ses deux enfants qui m'ont parus très sérieux et intelligents.

La fille, l'aînée, fait ses études dans une école privée; elle veut être médecin. Le garçon, le cadet, fait ses études au Lycée Henri IV; il veut être avocat.

Après un peu de conversation les enfants se sont retirés pour aller faire leurs devoirs.

Nous nous sommes mis à table et M. Parmentier m'a servi une tasse de thé et quelques petits gâteaux délicieux. En prenant le thé, nous avons parlé de la vie en France, des coutumes du pays, et de l'art.

M. Parmentier m'a recommandé comme curiosité de Paris le Marché aux Puces dont nous avons parlé il y a longtemps. Et Mme Parmentier m'a invité à les accompagner au Marché aux Fleurs dimanche matin.

J'ai répondu que toutes les deux excursions m'intéressaient beaucoup et j'ai accepté l'aimable invitation de madame.

Après avoir passé une heure agréable en parlant de choses et d'autres, je suis parti, charmé de mes nouveaux amis.

Je suis revenu à l'hôtel à pied, passant par les vieux quartiers de la Rive Gauche qui évoquaient d'une manière frappante l'histoire de la France.

Votre ami,
John Brown

We went into a large living room furnished with good taste in the style of Louis XV. Mrs. Parmentier introduced me to her husband and to her two children who appeared very serious and intelligent.

The girl, the elder, is studying in a private school; she wants to be a doctor. The boy, the younger one, is studying at the Henri IV lycée; he wants to be a lawyer.

After a bit of conversation, the children withdrew to do their homework.

We sat down at the table and Mr. Parmentier served me a cup of tea and some delicious little cakes. While drinking tea we talked about life in France, about the customs of the country and about art.

Mr. Parmentier recommended (to me), as a curiosity of Paris, the Flea Market, which we talked about a long time ago. And Madame Parmentier invited me to accompany them to the Flower Market on Sunday morning.

I answered that both excursions interested me very much and I accepted madame's kind invitation.

After having spent a delightful hour in talking of one thing and another, I left, charmed by my new friends.

I returned to the hotel on foot, passing through the old sections of the Left Bank which evoked in a striking manner the history of France.

Your friend,
John Brown

Building Vocabulary

SOME PROFESSIONS

1. **un docteur** doctor
2. **un médecin** medical doctor
3. **un avocat** lawyer

4. **un professeur** professor, teacher in a secondary school (**lycée**)
5. **un maître d'école** teacher (*m.*) in elementary school
6. **un ingénieur** (añ-zhay-**nyeur**) engineer
7. **un(e) écrivain** writer
8. **une femme médecin** woman doctor
9. **une avocate** woman lawyer
10. **une maîtresse** (*f.*) teacher in elementary school
11. **un acteur, un comédien** actor
12. **une actrice, une comédienne** actress

French Expressions

1. **rendre visite à** to visit (a person), to pay a visit to someone
2. **visiter** to visit (a place)
3. **Ils font leurs études.** They are studying, doing their studies
4. **Ils font leurs devoirs.** They are doing their homework
5. **Elle/il veut être docteur (avocat).** He wants to be a doctor (a lawyer).
6. **beaucoup plus loin** much longer ago, much farther away
7. **en parlant de choses et d'autres** speaking of one thing and another
8. **il y a longtemps** a long time ago

Exercise No. 173—Completion of Text

1. **Mme Parmentier** (called me) **par téléphone.**
2. **Elle m'a invité** (to have tea) **chez elle.**
3. (We stopped) **devant une maison charmante.**
4. (I went up) **au troisième étage.**
5. (I rang). **La bonne** (invited me) **à entrer.**
6. **Mme Parmentier** (approached to greet me).
7. **Elle a dit: —** (I'm glad to see you).
8. (There are many houses) **de cette époque à Paris.**
9. (We entered) **dans un grand salon.**
10. **Mme Parmentier** (introduced me) **à ses deux enfants.**
11. **L'aînée** (wants to be a) **docteur.**
12. **Ils** (retired) **pour aller faire** (their homework).
13. (We sat down) **à table.**
14. (We spoke) **de la vie en France.**
15. (I returned) **à l'hôtel à pied.**
16. **J'ai passé** (through the old sections).

Grammar Notes

1. LE PASSÉ COMPOSÉ CONVERSATIONAL PAST (PRESENT PERFECT) *OF REFLEXIVE VERBS*

Observe carefully the conversational past (present perfect) of the reflexive verb **se laver,** *to wash oneself.* Note the auxiliary verb and the changes in the past participle.

I have washed (I washed, did wash) myself

je me suis lavé (lavée)	**nous nous sommes lavés (lavées)**
tu t'es lavé (lavée)	**vous vous êtes lavé(e), (lavés lavées)**
il s'est lavé	**ils se sont lavés**
elle s'est lavée	**elles se sont lavées**

S'est-il lavé? Did he wash himself?

Est-ce qu'il s'est lavé. Did he wash himself?

Il ne s'est pas lavé. He did not wash himself.

Est-ce qui'il ne s'est pas lavé? Did he not wash himself?

The auxiliary verb **être** is used to form the conversational past of reflexive verbs.

The past participle agrees with the reflexive pronoun in number and gender when the reflexive pronoun indicates the *direct object* of the verb. The reflexive pronoun has the same gender and number as the subject.

The reflexive pronoun is sometimes the *indirect object* of the verb. In that case the past participle does *not* agree with it. Note examples:

Ils se sont fait des cadeaux.	They gave gifts *to* each other.
Ils se sont serré la main.	They shook hands. (*Lit.* They shook hands *to each other.*)
Elles s'est lavé la figure.	She washed her face. (*Lit.* She washed *to* herself the face.)

2. PRESENT AND CONVERSATIONAL PAST OF s'asseoir, *to sit down*

I sit down (I seat myself), you sit down (you seat yourself), etc.

je m'assois (ma-**swa**) or **je m'assieds** (ma-**syay**)	**nous nous asseyons** (za-say-**yawñ**)
tu t'assois (ta-**swa**) or **tu t'assieds** (ta-**syay**)	**vous vous asseyez** (za-say-**yay**)
il, elle s'assoit (sa-**swa**) or **il, elle s'assied** (sa-**syay**)	**ils, elles s'asseyent** (sa-**say**)

assieds-toi sit down, **asseyons-nous** let us sit down, **asseyez-vous** sit down

I have sat down (I sat down, I did sit down), etc.

je me suis assis (assise)	**nous nous sommes assis (assises)**
tu t'es assis (assise)	**vous vous êtes assis(e), assis(es)**
il s'est assis	**ils se sont assis**
elle s'est assise	**elles se sont assises**

3. SOME REFLEXIVE VERBS YOU HAVE MET

Infinitive	*Conversational Past*
se lever to get up	Je me suis levé(e).
se coucher to go to bed	Tu t'es couché(e).
s'habiller to dress	Il s'est habillé.
s'amuser to enjoy oneself, have a good time	Elle s'est amusée.
s'arrêter to stop	Nous nous sommes arrêtés.
s'approcher to approach	Vous vous êtes approchés.
se rencontrer to meet each other	Ils se sont rencontrés.
se connaître to know each other	Elles se sont connues.
se promener to go for a walk	Je ne me suis pas promené(e).
se tromper to be mistaken	Il ne s'est pas trompé.
se retirer to withdraw	Ne se sont-ils pas retirés?
s'asseoir to sit down	Est-ce qu'ils ne se sont pas assis?

Exercise No. 174

Translate into English the conversational past tense of the verbs listed above:

Exemple: 1. je me suis levé(e) = I got up

Exercise No. 175

Translate each question and answer. Read each question and answer aloud three times.

1. Est-ce que les enfants se sont couchés de bonne heure? Oui. Ils se sont couchés de bonne heure.
2. Est-ce que Jean s'est levé tard? Non. Il ne s'est pas levé tard.
3. Est-ce que Marie s'est habillée vite? Oui. Elle s'est habillée vite.
4. Est-ce que vous vous êtes trompé, Charles? Non. Je ne me suis pas trompé.
5. Est-ce que vous vous êtes amusée, Anne? Non. Je ne me suis pas amusée.
6. Où est-ce que vous vous êtes rencontrés, messieurs? Nous nous sommes rencontrés au bureau.
7. Où est-ce que l'autobus s'est arrêté? Il s'est arrêté au coin là-bas.
8. Est-ce que Mme Brown s'est occupée des enfants? Oui. Elle s'est occupée des enfants.
9. Est-ce que le touriste s'est senti chez lui à Paris? Comme tous les touristes, il s'est senti chez lui.

Exercise No. 176—Questionnaire

1. Qui a appelé M. Brown par téléphone?
2. À quelle heure est-ce que le taxi s'est arrêté chez Mme Parmentier?
3. Qui a ouvert la porte?
4. Qui s'est approché pour saluer M. Brown?
5. Quel air cette maison a-t-elle?
6. Où est-ce que M. Brown et Mme Parmentier sont entrés?
7. Qui sont les jeunes enfants sérieux et intelligents?
8. Où font-ils leurs études?
9. Qu'est-ce que l'aînée veut faire?
10. Pourquoi se sont-ils retirés?
11. De quoi est-ce qu'on a parlé en prenant le thé?
12. Qu'est-ce que M. Parmentier a recommandé comme curiosité?
13. Où est-ce que Mme Parmentier a invité M. Brown à les accompagner?
14. Comment est-ce que M. Brown a passé une heure agréable?
15. Est-il revenu à son hôtel à pied ou en voiture?

UNE BELLE PROMENADE
A LOVELY STROLL

TROISIÈME LETTRE

Cher ami,

Je vous écris attablé dans le café que vous m'avez fort recommandé: le Royale-Concorde. Il me reste peut-être des pieds, mais certainement pas de jambes.

Ce matin Mme Parmentier est venue me chercher à l'hôtel et nous avons commencé notre promenade en suivant les quais jusqu'au Pont Neuf.

Nous sommes restés très longtemps sur le pont, en regardant les pêcheurs qui restent des heures sans rien attraper; en regardant aussi les bateaux-mouches, et les enfants qui s'amusent à jeter des pierres dans l'eau.

Nous avons traversé le pont et continué sur la Rive Droite jusqu'à la Place de la Concorde. Je pense que cela doit être la plus belle place du monde. Les fontaines, l'obélisque, les jardins d'un côté, l'avenue des Champs-Élysées de l'autre, tout est disposé en parfaite harmonie.

Nous avons pris l'avenue des Champs-Élysées. Quelle belle avenue avec ses grands arbres, son étendue royale!

Nous nous sommes attablés dans un de ces cafés immenses pour prendre un café, mais surtout pour nous reposer. Ce qui m'a frappé tout de suite en France, c'est l'importance du café dans la vie quotidienne.

Dear Friend,

I am writing you seated at a table in the café which you have strongly recommended to me: the Royale-Concorde. I may have feet left, but certainly no legs.

This morning Mrs. Parmentier came to call for me at the hotel and we started our walk along the quays to the Pont Neuf.

We stayed on the bridge for a long time watching the fishermen, who stand for hours without catching anything, also watching the tour boats and the children amusing themselves by throwing stones in the water.

We crossed the bridge and continued on the Right Bank to the Place de la Concorde. I believe that this must be the most beautiful square in the world. The fountains, the gardens on one side, the Champs-Elysees on the other, everything is arranged in perfect harmony.

We walked up the Champs-Elysees. What a lovely avenue with its large trees, its splendid spaciousness.

We sat down at a table in one of those huge cafés to have coffee but especially to rest. What struck me at once in France is the importance of the café in daily life.

Le café est un club. On y rencontre ses amis; on y joue aux échecs; on y écrit des lettres comme je le fais maintenant.

Le café est aussi un centre de commerce. Pour les gens d'affaires c'est un deuxième bureau, même peut-être le premier.

Le café est un théâtre: les passants sont les acteurs et les actrices parfois tragiques, plus souvent comiques, mais toujours intéressants.

Ensuite nous avons continué notre route sur l'avenue des Champs-Élysées jusqu'à la Place de l'Étoile. Nous avons contemplé l'immense Arc de Triomphe qui se trouve au centre de la Place de l'Étoile.

Pour revenir au Café Royale-Concorde nous avons pris la belle avenue Marceau. À la Place de l'Alma Mme Parmentier m'a quitté. J'ai suivi les quais en admirant la Seine tout le long du chemin jusqu'à la Place de la Concorde.

Ensuite j'ai pris la rue Royale et enfin je suis tombé dans la chaise la plus proche du Café Royale-Concorde, fatigué, épuisé, et enchanté.

Votre ami, grand amoureux de Paris,
John Brown

The café is a club. There, people meet their friends; they play chess; they write letters as I am doing right now.

The café is also a business center. For business-people it is a second office, perhaps even the first.

The café is a theater: the passers-by are the actors and actresses, sometimes tragic, more often comic, but always interesting.

Then we continued on our way along the Champs-Élysées up to the Place de l'Étoile. We looked at the immense Arch of Triumph which is in the center of the Place de l'Étoile.

To return to the Café Royale-Concorde we took the beautiful avenue Marceau. At the Place de l'Alma Mrs. Parmentier left me. I followed the quays, admiring the Seine all along the way to the Place de la Concorde.

Then I took the rue Royale, and finally I fell into the nearest chair of the Café Royale-Concorde, tired, worn out, and delighted.

Your friend, in love with Paris,
John Brown

NOTE: The wide, long boulevard named **les Champs-Elysées** (**Shahñ** zay-lee-**zay**) ends at **la place Charles de Gaulle**, with **l'Arc de Triomphe** in the center. Most people still call this huge roundabout by its former name, **la Place de l'Étoile** or simply **l'Étoile,** the Star, because from the Arch, twelve avenues spread out like the points of a star.

Building Vocabulary

RELATED WORDS

1. **arrêter** to stop (someone, something); **s'arrêter** to stop (stand still); **l'arrêt** (*m*) stop (bus, train)

2. **approcher** to bring nearer; **s'approcher** to come nearer; **l'approche** (*f*) approach; **proche** near

3. **écrire** to write; **l'écrivain** writer; **l'écriture** writing, handwriting; **décrire** to describe; **la description** description

4. **la table** table; **s'attabler** to sit down at a table; **attablé** seated at a table

5. **se reposer** to rest; **le repos** rest

6. **l'amour** love; **amoureux** enamored, in love; **l'amoureux** the one in love

7. **le pays** country (not countryside); **le paysan** farmer, peasant; **le paysage** landscape

8. **tirer** to pull, to shoot; **s'en tirer** to cope, to manage; **le tiroir** (dresser-) drawer; **retirer** to pull back; **la retraite** retirement

9. **vite** quick, quickly; **la vitesse** speed

10. **curieux** curious, strange; **la curiosité** curiosity

French Expressions

1. **Elle vient me chercher.** She comes to call for (*Lit.* look for) me.
2. **d'un côté** on one side **de l'autre côté** on the other side
3. **jouer aux cartes (aux échecs, au billard)** to play cards (chess, billiards)
4. **tout le long du chemin** all along the way
5. **combien de fois?** how many times? **une fois** once; **deux fois** two times, twice; **quelquefois** sometimes; **des fois** at times; **à la fois** at once, together; **encore une fois** one more time; **plusieurs fois** several times

Exercise No. 177—Completion of Text

1. **Mme Parmentier est venue** (to look for me).
2. (We stayed) **très longtemps sur le pont.**
3. **Les pêcheurs restent des heures** (without catching anything).
4. **Les enfants s'amusent** (throwing stones).
5. (We continued) **sur le quai.**
6. **Cela doit être** (the most beautiful square) **du monde.**
7. What a beautiful avenue!
8. **Ce qui** (struck me) **c'est l'importance du café.**
9. (There people play) **aux cartes.**
10. (There one writes) **des lettres.**
11. (The passersby) **sont les acteurs et les actrices.**
12. (Then) **nous avons continué** (our way).

13. **Á la Place de l'Alma Mme Parmentier** (left me).
14. (I followed) **les quais.**
15. **Je suis tombé** (into the nearest chair).

Grammar Notes

RELATIVE PRONOUNS

a. **qui**—*who, that, which*—*is used as a subject relative pronoun.*

Connaissez-vous les acteurs *qui* **sont assis à cette table?**	Do you know the actors *who* are seated at that table?
Où est le quai *qui* **mène au Pont Neuf?**	Where is the quay *that* leads to the Pont Neuf?
J'aime bien me promener dans le parc Monceau, *qui* **se trouve pas loin de l'Étoile.**	I like to walk in Monceau Park, *which* is not far from the Étoile.

b. **que** *or* **qu'**—*whom, which, that*—*is used as a direct object relative pronoun.*

Je suis attablé dans le café *que* **vous m'avez recommandé.**	I am seated at a table in the café *that* you recommended to me.
C'est un professeur *que* **les étudiants admirent.**	He is a teacher *whom* the students admire.

c. **ce qui** (*subject*) and **ce que** *or* **ce qu'** (*object*) mean *what* (*that which*).

Savez-vous *ce qui* **est dans cette grande caisse?**	Do you know *what* (*that which*) is in that large case?
Nous avons lu tout *ce que* **vous avez écrit.**	We have read all *that* (*which*) you wrote.
Je n'ai pas entendu *ce qu'il* **a dit.**	I did not hear *what* (*that which*) he said.

d. **qui**—*whom*—*is used as the object of a preposition.*

Je ne connais pas la dame à *(avec)* **qui vous avez parlé.**	I do not know the lady to (*with*) *whom* you spoke.

e. **lequel (laquelle, lesquels, lesquelles)**—*which, whom*— *is most often used after a preposition.* It agrees with its antecedent in number and gender.

J'ai reçu votre lettre *dans laquelle* **vous décrivez "Une Belle Promenade."**	I have received your letter *in which* you describe "A Pleasant Stroll."

f. **dont** — *whose, of whom, of which* — is used as a relative pronoun instead of **de + qui** or **de +** any form of **lequel**.

Nous allons rendre visite au professeur *dont* **nous avons parlé hier.**	We are going to visit the teacher *of whom* we spoke yesterday.
Le Mont-Saint-Michel est un endroit *dont* **les omelettes sont célèbres.**	Mont-Saint-Michel is a place *whose* omelettes are famous.

g. **A relative pronoun may sometimes be omitted in English. It is never omitted in French.**

Les pêcheurs *que* **vous voyez sur le quai sont Bretons.**	The fishermen (*whom*) you see on the quay are Bretons.

Exercise No. 178

Translate each question and answer. Then read each one aloud three times.

1. Avez-vous compris tout ce que le maître a dit? Je n'ai pas tout compris.
2. Avez-vous lu les deux guides que je vous ai prêtés? Je les ai lus avec beaucoup d'intérêt.
3. Quel est le premier secret de la bonne cuisine? Tout ce qui entre dans un plat doit être de bonne qualité.
4. Est-ce qu'on peut faire du ski en montagne? Ceux qui sont jeunes et forts le font tout le temps.
5. Quel café avez-vous visité aujourd'hui? J'ai visité le Royale-Concorde dont nous avons souvent parlé.
6. Où sont les valises dans lesquelles j'ai mis mes vêtements? Elles sont dans votre chambre.

Exercise No. 179

Complete each sentence with the correct French relative pronoun:

1. Montrez-moi le chapeau (that) vous venez d'acheter.
2. Vous rappelez-vous (what) il vous a dit?
3. Les touristes (who) visitent Paris se sentent chez eux.
4. Voyons (what) se trouve dans cette caisse.
5. Voilà le guide avec (whom) nous allons visiter la cathédrale.
6. Je cherche la boîte dans (which) j'ai mis ma montre.
7. Il y a trois élèves dans ma classe (whose) les parents sont Français.
8. Tous les endroits (which) j'ai visités sont très intéressants.
9. Tout (that) se passe aux cafés est intéressant.
10. Nous ne pouvons pas trouver les élèves (whom) nous cherchons.

Exercise No. 180—Questionnaire

1. Où est-ce que M. Brown écrit sa lettre?
2. Où est-ce que Mme Parmentier est venue le chercher?
3. Où sont-ils restés très longtemps?
4. Qu'est-ce qu'ils ont vu?
5. Qu'est-ce que M. Brown pense au sujet de la Place de la Concorde?
6. Pourquoi se sont-ils attablés?
7. Qu'est-ce qui a frappé M. Brown?
8. Qu'est-ce qu'on joue dans un café?
9. Qu'est-ce que c'est un café pour les gens d'affaires?
10. Qu'est-ce qu'ils ont contemplé?
11. Où est-ce que Mme Parmentier a quitté M. Brown?
12. Qu'est-ce que M. Brown a admiré tout le long du chemin?
13. Comment M. Brown est-il tombé dans la chaise du café?

Cafés are an essential part of French life.

CHAPITRE 35 (TRENTE-CINQ)

LE MONT-SAINT-MICHEL

MONT-SAINT-MICHEL

QUATRIÈME LETTRE

Cher ami,

Devinez un peu d'où je vous écris. C'est ça! Vous avez raison. Je vous écris attablé dans un café. Vous allez croire que je ne fais que ça. C'est que le métier de touriste demande beaucoup de repos. Et où est-ce qu'on se repose mieux que dans un café?

Vous vous rappelez notre conversation au sujet de mes voyages? Eh bien, j'ai commencé mon grand cercle en partant de Paris pour la Normandie. J'ai visité le Mont-Saint-Michel et me voilà à Perros-Guirec en Bretagne. En l'honneur de ma première visite en Bretagne, je prends un calvados.

Je veux vous décrire ma visite au Mont-Saint-Michel, pendant que j'en ai la mémoire fraîche.

Pendant que le train traversait les champs et les forêts, je regardais par la fenêtre. En filant à toute vitesse je voyais les paysans qui travaillaient dans les champs. Très souvent nous avons passé par les villages.

À Pontorson, j'ai pris un taxi pour le Mont. Presque tout de suite j'ai vu ce rocher monumental isolé au milieu des sables.

Dear Friend,

Just guess from where I'm writing you. That's it! You're right. I am writing you seated at a table in a café. You're going to think that it's all I do. The thing is that the profession of tourist demands a great deal of rest. And where can on rest better than in a café?

Do you recall our conversation on the subject of my travels? Well, I started my great circle leaving Paris for Normandy. I visited Mont-Saint-Michel and here I am in Perros-Guirec in Brittany. In honor of my first visit to Brittany, I am drinking a Calvados (apple brandy).

I want to describe to you my visit to Mont-Saint-Michel while it is still fresh in my memory.

While the train was crossing the fields and forests, I was looking out the window. Going along at top speed, I saw the country people working in the fields. Very often we passed by villages.

At Pontorson, I took a taxi to the Mont. Almost at once I saw this monumental rock isolated in the middle of the sands.

Mais quand je suis arrivé au pittoresque village situé aux flancs du rocher, j'ai entendu un bruit terrifiant.

On criait, on hurlait.—Monsieur! Par ici! Les souvenirs du Mont! Les cartes postales! Monsieur! La véritable omelette de la Mère Poularde! Monsieur! Ici la vraie! Monsieur! Ici l'omelette Poularde! Les cartes! Les souvenirs! L'omelette! Ici! Ici! Monsieur! Monsieur! Monsieur!

La tête me tournait comme une toupie. J'avais envie de partir. Mais enfin je me suis dit:—En avant l'art et l'histoire. Courage!

J'ai fermé les oreilles mentalement et j'ai vite grimpé la pente rapide jusqu'à l'escalier de l'Abbaye.

La visite à l'Abbaye a duré une heure environ. Ce bâtiment gothique avec ses grandes salles, ses escaliers, ses galeries, ses cloîtres, ses jardins en terrasses est un spectacle grandiose. Je voulais rester pour contempler la sculpture mais ce n'était pas possible.

Vous savez que le visiteur d'un monument historique n'a pas de droits. On est poussé par ici, on est tiré par là et on doit suivre comme un mouton. Malgré tout j'ai reçu une impréssion imposante de cet îlot rocheux.

Maintenant je me tourne vers la Bretagne: la mer, les marins, les poissons, les chapelles et le calvados auquel les marins de la Bretagne sont dévoués. Perros-Guirec me plaît beaucoup. Je finirai peut-être par aimer le Calvados.

Très cordialement,
Votre ami,
John Brown

But when I reached the picturesque village situated on the sides of the rocky hill, I heard a terrifying din.

People were calling, yelling. "Mister! Right here! Souvenirs of the Mont! Post cards! Sir! The authentic Mother Poularde omelet! Sir! Here you get the real one! Sir! The Poularde omelet! Cards! Souvenirs! The omelet! Here! Here! Sir! Sir! Sir!"

My head was spinning like a top. I wanted to go away. But in the end I said to myself, "Onward with art and history. Courage!"

I mentally closed my ears and I quickly climbed the steep slope up to the stairs of the Abbey.

The visit to the Abbey lasted about an hour. This Gothic structure with its vast halls, its stairways, its galleries, its cloisters, its terraced gardens is a grand spectacle. I wanted to stop to contemplate the sculpture but it wasn't possible.

You know that the visitor at a historic site has no rights. You are pushed this way, pulled that way, and you have to follow like sheep. In spite of everything, I received an imposing impression of this rocky islet.

Now I turn toward Brittany: the sea, the sailors, the fish, the chapels and the Calvados to which the sailors of Brittany are devoted. I like Perros-Guirec very much. Perhaps I shall end up liking Calvados.

Cordially,
Your friend,
John Brown

Building Vocabulary

le corps (kur) body
la tête (teht) head
les cheveux (shuh-**veu**) hair
la figure (fee-**gür**) face
l'oeil (leuy) eye
les yeux (lay-**zyeu**) eyes
le nez (nay) nose
la bouche (boosh) mouth

la langue (lahñg) tongue (also, language)
la main (mañ) hand
le doigt (dwa) finger
le pied (pyay) foot
le bras (brah) arm
la jambe (zhahñb) leg
le coeur (keur) heart

French Expressions

me voici here I am
te voici here you are
le (la) voici here he (it) is
le (la) voilà there he (it) is

nous voici here we are
vous voici here you are
les voici here they are
les voilà there they are

Exercise No. 181—Completion of Text

1. (You are right).
2. (Here I am) **dans un café.**
3. (I am drinking) **un calvados.**
4. **Le train traversait** (the fields and the forests).
5. **Je regardais** (out of the window).
6. (The farmers) **travaillaient dans** (the fields).
7. (I took a taxi) **pour le Mont.**
8. (Almost at once) **j'ai vu ce rocher monumental.**
9. **On criait,—Monsieur,** (right here)!
10. **J'ai fermé** (my ears).
11. **La visite à l'abbaye** (lasted) **une heure.**
12. **Je voulais** (to stop to contemplate) **la sculpture.**
13. **On** (is pushed) **par ici, on** (is pulled) **par là.**
14. (You must follow) **comme un mouton.**

Grammar Notes

The imperfect tense—What *was happening, used to happen.*

The conversational past, as you have seen, tells what *has happened, happened,* or *did happen.*

The imperfect tense tells what *was happening* or *used to happen:* the beginning and end of actions in the imperfect tense are less precise than in the conversational past; also, the number of times an action was performed is more vague, except for the fact that the subject of the action (verb) did (would do) it on a regular or habitual basis. For convenience we can call the imperfect the *was, were, used to* tense.

Note carefully the endings of the imperfect tense of **parler, finir, vendre, prendre, avoir,** and **être.**

I was speaking, you were speaking, etc.

je parlais	nous parlions
tu parlais	vous parliez
il parlait	ils parlaient
elle parlait	elles parlaient

I was finishing, you were finishing, etc.

je finissais	nous finissions
tu finissais	vous finissiez
il finissait	ils finissaient
elle finissait	elles finissaient

I was selling, you were selling, etc.

je vendais	nous vendions
tu vendais	vous vendiez
il vendait	ils vendaient
elle vendait	elles vendaient

I was taking, you were taking, etc.

je prenais	nous prenions
tu prenais	vous preniez
il prenait	ils prenaient
elle prenait	elles prenaient

I had, you had, etc.

j'avais	nous avions
tu avais	vous aviez
il avait	ils avaient
elle avait	elles avaient

I was, you were, etc.

j'étais	nous étions
tu étais	vous étiez
il était	ils étaient
elle était	elles étaient

The imperfect tense endings of all French verbs are: Singular: **-ais** (*eh*) **-ais** (*eh*) **-ait** (*eh*); Plural: **-ions** (*yawñ*) **-iez** (*yay*) **-aient** (*eh*).

To form the imperfect tense drop the ending **-ons** from the **nous** form of the present tense and add the imperfect tense endings. This way of forming the imperfect tense applies to all verbs except **être,** whose stem is **ét-** (ayt).

Construction of the island abbey of Mont Saint Michel began in 1020.

Infinitive	Nous *form of Present*	Imperfect (*was, were, used to*)
parler	nous parlons	je parlais, tu parlais, etc.
vendre	nous vendons	je vendais, tu vendais, etc.
finir	nous finissons	je finissais, tu finissais, etc.
dormir	nous dormons	je dormais, tu dormais, etc.
prendre	nous prenons	je prenais, tu prenais, etc.
dire	nous disons	je disais, tu disais, etc.
faire	nous faisons	je faisais, tu faisais, etc.
lire	nous lisons	je lisais, tu lisais, etc.
écrire	nous écrivons	j'écrivais, tu écrivais, etc.
vouloir	nous voulons	je voulais, tu voulais, etc.
avoir	nous avons	j'avais, tu avais, etc.
être	nous sommes	j'étais, tu étais, etc.

Present and imperfect of **il y a, venir de**, and **aller**

Present	*Imperfect*
il y a there is (are)	**il y avait** there was (were)
y a-t-il? is (are) there?	**y avait-il?** was (were) there?
qu'y a-t-il? what is (are) there?	**qu'y avait-il? qu'est-ce qu'il y avait?** what was (were) there?
l **n'y a pas** there is (are) not	**il n'y avait pas** there was (were) not
Il vient de voir He has just seen.	**Il venait de voir** He had just seen.
Je vais arriver I am going to arrive.	**J'allais arriver** I was going to arrive.

Exercise No. 182

Translate the following brief exchanges. Practice them aloud:

1. —Qu'est-ce que M. Brown faisait quand vous êtes entré dans le salon?

    —Il lisait à haute voix (aloud) une lettre qu'il venait de recevoir de sa représentante à Paris.

    —M. Picard que faisait-il?

    —Il l'écoutait.

2. —Que faisiez-vous pendant que le train traversait les champs et les forêts?

    —Je regardais par la fenêtre.

    —Qu'est-ce que vous voyiez?

—Je voyais les paysans qui travaillaient dans les champs.

3. —Y avait-il beaucoup de vendeurs au Mont-Saint-Michel?

—Il y en avait une armée.

—Qu'est-ce qu'ils vendaient?

—Ils vendaient les souvenirs du Mont.

4. —Jouez-vous souvent au tennis?

—Autrefois (formerly) je jouais presque tous les jours mais cette année j'ai joué une fois seulement.

Exercise No. 183

Each of these sentences indicates an action that was happening for an unspecified amount of time (*imperfect tense*) and another action that interrupted it at a definite time (*conversational past tense*). Complete with the correct French verbs. Practice aloud. Translate the completed sentences into English:

1. **Les vendeurs** (were calling and yelling) **quand je suis arrivé au marché.**
2. **Pendant que** (I was listening to) **la radio, on m'a telephoné.**
3. **Quand** (we were doing) **nos devoirs, ils sont entrés dans notre chambre.**
4. **Elle est tombée quand elle** (was getting out) **de l'auto.**
5. **Quand le taxi** (was going) **à toute vitesse, j'ai crié:—Pas si vite!**
6. **Nous lui avons rendu visite quand** (he was) **malade.**
7. (There were) **beaucoup de personnes à l'aéroport quand notre avion est arrivé.**
8. **Pendant que** (we were waiting for) **l'autobus, il a commencé à pleuvoir.**
9. **Nous les avons rencontrés quand** (we were coming) **du cinéma.**
10. **M. Brown est revenu pendant que les enfants** (were sleeping).

NOTE: in all of the above, the clause taking the imperfect tense provides a kind of background action or condition that was happening when a more precise, one-time action interrupted or took place, which would thus be expressed by the passé composé (conversational past).

Exercise No. 184—Questionnaire

1. D'où est-ce que M. Brown écrit?
2. Qu'est-ce que le métier de touriste demande?
3. Où est le café?
4. Qu'est-ce que M. Brown prend en l'honneur de sa première visite en Bretagne?
5. Qu'est-ce que M. Brown faisait pendant que le train traversait les champs et les forêts?
6. Qu'est-ce qu'il voyait?
7. Qu'est-ce qu'il pouvait voir dans les villages?
8. Qu'a-t-il entendu quand il est arrivé?
9. Pourquoi avait-il d'abord envie de partir?
10. Pourquoi est-ce que M. Brown voulait rester?
11. Quelle impression M. Brown a-t-il reçue?
12. Où se tourne-t-il maintenant?

CHAPITRE 36 (TRENTE-SIX)

LE GRAND GUIGNOL

PUPPET SHOW

CINQUIÈME LETTRE

Cher ami,

Je suis revenu à Paris de mon voyage en Bretagne de plus en plus amoureux de la France.

Ce matin je suis allé au Louvre pour le visiter à fond.

Si la tête me tournait comme une toupie au Mont-Saint-Michel à cause du bruit, elle me tournait dix fois plus vite en sortant du silence du Louvre. Je me suis dit:—Imbécile! Pourquoi n'es-tu pas sorti il y a deux heures? Crois-tu que le Louvre va s'envoler?

Enfin, après un bon déjeuner arrosé d'un bon vin, j'étais délassé et avide de nouvelles aventures.

Je me suis tourné vers le Jardin des Tuileries attiré par le soleil et les fleurs. Je marchais tranquillement quand tout à coup j'ai entendu des éclats de rires. Je me suis approché, tout curieux.

J'ai vu un joli petit théâtre, la scène encadrée d'un rideau de velours bleu ciel. Les bancs qui formaient la petite salle étaient comblés d'enfants. Ils riaient à la folie.

Dear Friend,

I returned from my trip to Brittany more and more in love with France.

This morning I went to the Louvre to visit it thoroughly.

If my head was spinning like a top at Mont-Saint-Michel because of the noise, it was spinning ten times faster when I left the silence of the Louvre. I said to myself, Fool! Why didn't you leave two hours ago? Do you think the Louvre is going to fly away?

Well, after a good lunch washed down with a good wine, I was refreshed and eager for new adventures.

I turned toward the Tuileries Gardens attracted by the sun and the flowers. I was strolling quietly along when all of a sudden I heard bursts of laughter. I drew near, very curious.

I saw a pretty little theatre, the stage framed by a sky-blue velvet curtain. The benches which formed the tiny auditorium were crowded with children. They were laughing wildly.

Sur la scène il n'y avait que Guignol. Il ne bougeait pas. Il ne disait rien. Mais ce n'était pas nécessaire. Il n'avait qu'à apparaître, et les enfants éclataient de rire.

J'ai pris une place à coté d'une toute petite fille qui m'a saisi par la main en criant:—Papa! Très flatté, j'ai répondu:—Bonjour, ma chérie.

Sa maman, toute rose, lui a dit:—Regarde, Cri-Cri, voilà Gringalet, le fils de Guignol. Et à moi:—Christine pense que tous les messieurs s'appellent papa.

　—Mais j'en suis ravi, madame, ai-je dit, en souriant.

Un fou rire nous a fait regarder la scène. Le petit Gringalet était en train de donner de grands coups de tête dans le ventre de Guignol. Les enfants n'étaient pas du tout fâchés. Au contraire, ils en étaient ravis.

J'ai dit au revoir à Cri-Cri et à sa mère, et l'enfant m'a répondu gentiment:—Au revoir, papa.

Je dois vous dire qu'à ce moment là, ma femme et mes enfants me manquaient beaucoup.

Salutations amicales de votre ami,
John Brown

On the stage there was only Guignol. He was not moving. He was not saying anything. But it wasn't necessary. He had only to appear and the children would burst out laughing.

I took a seat next to a very little girl who seized my hand and called out: Daddy! Very flattered, I answered, Hello, my dear.

Her mother said to her, blushing, Look, Cri-Cri, there is Gringalet, Guignol's son. And to me, Christine thinks that all men are called daddy.

But I'm delighted, Madame, I said, smiling.

A wild shout of laughter made us look at the stage. Little Gringalet was butting Guignol in the stomach with his head. The children were not at all annoyed. On the contrary, they were delighted.

I said goodbye to Cri-Cri and her mother and the child answered nicely, Goodbye, daddy.

I must tell you that at that moment I missed my wife and my children very much.

Greetings from your friend,
John Brown

NOTE: Guignol (gheen-**yul**) Chief character in French puppet shows. His son is called **Gringalet** (grañ-ga-**lay**).

Building Vocabulary

ANTONYMS

1. **le bruit** noise, **le silence** silence
2. **fatigué** tired, **délassé** refreshed
3. **apparaître** to appear, **disparaître** to disappear
4. **rire** to laugh, **pleurer** to weep
5. **fâché** annoyed, angry, **ravi** delighted
6. **nouveau (nouvel) nouvelle** (*f*) new, **vieux (vieil) vieille** (*f*) old
7. **mener** to lead, **suivre** to follow
8. **monter en voiture** to get into the car, **descendre de la voiture** to get out of the car

NOTE: nouvel and **vieil** are forms used before masculine nouns beginning with a vowel or mute **h: un nouvel article; un vieil homme**

French Expressions

1. **de plus en plus** more and more
2. **à fond** thoroughly
3. **tout à coup** suddenly
4. **à la folie** wildly, uproariously
5. **il n'y avait que Guignol** there was only Guignol
6. **éclater de rire** to burst out laughing

Exercise No. 185—Completion of Text

1. (I returned) **de mon voyage.**
2. **J'étais** (more and more) **amoureux de la France.**
3. **Ce matin** (I went) **au Louvre.**
4. (My head) **me tournait comme une toupie.**
5. (I said to myself), — **Imbécile.**
6. **Pourquoi n'es-tu pas sorti** (two hours ago)?
7. (I was) **délassé.**
8. (I was walking) **tranquillement.**
9. (I approached) **tout curieux.**
10. **Les bancs** (were) **comblés d'enfants.**
11. (They were laughing) **à la folie.**
12. **Guignol** (was not moving).
13. He was saying nothing.
14. **Les enfants** (were not at all) **fâchés.**

Grammar Notes

1. PRESENT, IMPERFECT, CONVERSATIONAL PAST OF rire, *to laugh;* **vivre,** *to live*

Present

I laugh, you laugh, etc.

je ris (ree)	nous rions
tu ris (ree)	vous riez
il rit (ree)	ils rient (ree)
elle rit (ree)	elles rient (ree)

Imperative: ris rions riez

I live, you live, etc.

je vis	nous vivons
tu vis	vous vivez
il vit	ils vivent
elle vit	elles vivent

Imperative: vis vivons vivez

Imperfect

I was laughing, you were laughing, etc.

je riais	nous riions	je vivais	nous vivions
tu riais	vous riiez	tu vivais	vous viviez
il riait	ils riaient	il vivait	ils vivaient
elle riait	elles riaient	elle vivait	elles vivaient

I was living, you were living, etc.

Conversational Past

I laughed, you laughed, etc.

j'ai ri, etc.   **nous avons ri**, etc.

I lived, you lived, etc.

j'ai vécu, etc.   **nous avons vécu**, etc.

Like **rire**: **sourire**, *to smile*; like **vivre**: **survivre**, *to survive*; **revivre**, *to revive*

NOTE: In pronouncing the imperfect forms for **nous** and **vous** in the verb **rire**, do not pronounce the double **ii** as two separate vowels; rather, slightly elongate the sound.

2. **THE IMPERFECT IS OFTEN USED WITH vouloir, pouvoir, savoir, devoir** and **avoir**. The conversational past is used less often with these verbs.

Il nous devait cinq dollars.   He owed us five dollars.

Je ne pouvais pas lui écrire.   I was not able to write him.

3. **THE PAST INFINITIVE**

The *past infinitive* is formed by the auxiliary **avoir** or **être** plus the *past participle* of the verb.

Present Infinitive	*Past Infinitive*
parler **to speak**	avoir parlé **to have spoken**
finir **to finish**	avoir fini **to have finished**
aller **to go**	être allé **to have gone**
sortir **to go out**	être sorti **to have gone out**

You have learned that prepositions (except **en**) take the present infinitive in French instead of the present participle as in English.

sans apprendre without learning   **en admirant** (while) admiring

avant de partir before leaving   **en sortant** (on) leaving

Prepositions may also take past infinitives

après avoir appris after having learned; **après être allé** after going (*Lit.* after having gone)

NOTE: **après** always takes a past infinitive.

Exercise No. 186

Complete the following sentences in French with the imperfect tense of all of the verbs in parentheses:

Exemple: 1. Les enfants riaient à la folie.

1. **Les enfants** (were laughing) **à la folie.**
2. **Mme Parmentier** (was living) **à Paris.**
3. **Les paysannes** (were washing) **le linge.**
4. (Were they) **fâchés?**
5. **Jean** (was coming) **du cinéma.**
6. **Nous** (were paying a visit to) **M. Duval.**
7. **M. Brown** (was he thinking) **à** (*about*) **sa famille?**
8. **Marie** (was getting out) **de la voiture.**
9. **Je** (was coming back) **de l'hôtel à pied.**
10. **Nous** (were going up) **au troisième étage.**
11. **Toute la ville** (was smiling).
12. (I was) **content de vous voir.**
13. **Un bel** (*handsome*) **homme** (was approaching).
14. **Ils** (were beginning) **à parler français.**
15. **Elle** (was eating) **des gâteaux délicieux.**
16. **Ils** (used to meet) **tous les jeudis.**
17. **Nous** (did not have) **d'argent.**
18. **Elles** (did not want) **aller.**
19. (Were you able) **lui rendre visite?**
20. **Personne ne** (knew) **combien il** (owed).

NOTE [1]Verbs ending in **-cer** have a soft **c** (like s) and verbs ending in **-ger** have a soft **g** (*zh*) before **e** or **i.** To keep the **c** and **g** soft before endings beginning with **a** or **o,** the **c** must add a cedilla; and the **g** must be followed by a silent **e.** Thus:

commencer

Present: nous commençons

Imperfect: je commençais, il commençait

manger

Present: nous mangeons

Imperfect: je mangeais, ils mangeaient

but

Imperfect: nous commencions

Future: nous commencerons

Imperfect: nous mangions

Future: nous mangerons

Exercise No. 187—Questionnaire

1. **Pourquoi M. Brown est-il allé au Louvre?**
2. **Qu'est-ce que M. Brown s'est dit?**
3. **Où s'est-il tourné?**
4. **Qu'est-ce qu'il a entendu tout à coup?**
5. **Qu'est-ce qu'il a vu quand il s'est approché?**
6. **Qui ne bougeait pas?**
7. **Qu'est-ce que les enfants faisaient chaque fois que Guignol apparaissait?**
8. **Où est-ce que M. Brown a pris une place?**
9. **Qu'est-ce que la petite fille a crié?**
10. **Qu'est-ce que le petit Gringalet était en train de faire?**
11. **Est-ce que les enfants étaient fâchés?**
12. **Qu'est-ce que Cri-Cri a répondu quand M. Brown lui a dit au revoir?**

Première Partie

NOUNS

1. l'arbre	1. tree
2. l'avocat	2. lawyer
3. l'ascenseur	3. elevator
4. le banc	4. bench
5. le camion	5. truck
6. le champ	6. field
7. le chemin	7. road
8. le docteur	8. doctor
9. la douane	9. customs
10. l'écrivain	10. writer
11. l'escalier	11. staircase
12. la figure	12. face
13. la fontaine	13. fountain
14. la forêt	14. forest
15. les gens	15. people
16. la jambe	16. leg
17. le lycée	17. high school
18. la mémoire	18. memory
19. la manière	19. manner
20. le paysan	20. peasant
21. le pas	21. step
22. la pierre	22. stone
23. le repos	23. rest
24. la rivière	24. stream, river
25. le village	25. village
26. la vitesse	26. speed
27. le ventre	27. stomach

VERBS

1. s'approcher (de)	1. to approach
2. s'arrêter	2. to stop
3. boire	3. to drink
4. crier	4. to cry out, to shout
5. décrire	5. to describe
6. disparaître	6. to disappear
7. descendre	7. to descend
8. durer	8. to last
9. essayer	9. to try
10. jeter	10. to throw
11. marcher	11. to walk
12. monter	12. to go up, mount
13. oublier	13. to forget
14. pousser	14. to push
15. se rappeler	15. to recall
16. se retirer	16. to retire
17. retourner	17. to go back
18. rentrer dans	18. to reenter
19. rire	19. to laugh
20. sauter	20. to leap, to jump
21. se tromper	21. to be mistaken

ADJECTIVES

1. amoureux (amoureuse *f*)	1. amorous, in love
2. chéri	2. dear, beloved
3. délassé	3. refreshed
4. fâché	4. angry, vexed
5. fatigué	5. tired
6. flatté	6. flattered
7. fier (fière *f*)	7. proud
8. frais (fraîche *f*)	8. fresh
9. frappant	9. striking
10. gracieux (gracieuse *f*)	10. graceful
11. meublé	11. furnished
12. neuf (neuve *f*)	12. (brand-)new
13. nouveau (nouvelle *f*)	13. new, another
14. plusieurs	14. several
15. proche	15. near
16. sain	16. healthy
17. sauf	17. safe

ADVERBS

1. aussitôt que	1. as soon as
2. enfin	2. finally
3. ensuite	3. then, next
4. longtemps	4. long, a long while
5. cordialement	5. cordially
6. tellement	6. so, in such manner

PREPOSITIONS

1. parmi	1. among
2. au bord de	2. on the edge of
3. au milieu de	3. in the middle of

French Expressions

1. d'accord	1. agreed, okay
2. en avant	2. forward, onward
3. à la fois	3. together, at the same time
4. de plus en plus	4. more and more
5. tout à coup	5. suddenly
6. faire leurs études	6. to study
7. faire leurs devoirs	7. to do their homework
8. rendre visite à	8. to pay a visit to
9. jouer aux cartes	9. to play cards
10. le plaisir est à moi	10. the pleasure is mine
11. le café me plaît	11. I like the café
12. je ne manque de rien	12. I lack nothing

Deuxième Partie

Exercise No. 188

Translate each sentence. Then read it aloud three times.

1. M. Brown est parti pour Paris.
2. Sa femme est restée à la maison.
3. Mme Picard est sortie il y a une heure.
4. Elle n'est pas encore rentrée.
5. Nous sommes montés en ascenseur.
6. Ils sont descendus à pied.

7. Pourquoi êtes-vous revenue si tard, Marie?

8. Je suis allée au marché pour faire mes achats.

9. Son grand-père est mort ce matin.

10. Ma grand-mère est née le cinq juin 1927.

Exercise No. 189

Fill in the correct form of the past participle of each verb in parentheses; watch for agreement between subject or preceding direct object and verb:

Exemple: 1. Une belle dame s'est approchée.

1. Une belle dame s'est (approcher).

2. Ils se sont (rencontrer) à la gare.

3. J'ai (prendre) un taxi pour l'hôtel.

4. Nous sommes (sortir) ensemble.

5. Le taxi s'est (arrêter) devant le théâtre.

6. Elle est (arriver) saine et sauve.

7. M. Brown est (descendre) de la voiture.

8. On lui a (réserver) un belle chambre.

9. Ma soeur est (naître) le 5 janvier.

10. Il a (mettre) son pardessus.

11. Qu'est-ce que vous avez (dire)?

12. Je n'ai pas (faire) les valises.

13. Ont-ils (demander) des renseignements?

14. Les fenêtres sont (ouvrir). Qui les a (ouvrir)?

Exercise No. 190

Complete each sentence by selecting from the parentheses the tense of the verb that fits best. Translate each sentence.

1. Demain nous ___ visite à la famille Brown. (rendrons, rendions, avons rendu)

2. Hier soir les enfants ___ au ciné. (iront, allaient, sont allés)

3. Les élèves n'écoutaient pas pendant que le professeur ___ . (parlera, parlait, a parlé)

4. Où ___ l'hiver dernier? (passerez-vous, passiez-vous, avez-vous passé)

5. Je ne les ___ jusqu'à demain. (verrai pas, voyais pas, ai pas vu)

6. Nous faisions nos devoirs pendant qu'ils ___ aux cartes. (joueront, jouaient, ont joué)

7. Elles sont restées à la maison parce qu'il ___ à verse. (pleuvra, pleuvait, a plu)

8. ___ un voyage en Europe l'été prochain? (ferez-vous, faisiez-vous, avez-vous fait)

9. Il nous ___ cinq dollars hier. (prêtera, prêtait, a prêté)

10. À quelle heure est-ce que ___ hier matin? (vous vous lèverez, vous vous leviez, vous vous êtes levé)

Exercise No. 191

Complete each sentence in French. Then read it aloud three times.

1. (It was pouring) **quand M. Picard a frappé à la porte.**
2. (I was very happy) **lorsque** (*when*) **j'ai reçu sa lettre.**
3. **Ils prenaient du thé au rhum** (when Mr. Brown received) **un télégramme.**
4. **Nous dînions** (when my agent telephoned me).
5. **Autrefois** (we used to go) **souvent au théâtre.**
6. (I did not know)[1] **ce qu'ils disaient.**
7. (We were not able)[1] **trouver le stylo.**
8. (Did they want)[1] **voyager partout?**
9. (She did not have[1] time) **d'aller au ciné.**
10. (She was to) **nous rendre visite hier.**

NOTE [1]Use the imperfect.

Dialogue
Au poste d'essence

M. Brown entre au poste d'essence pour faire le plein d'essence.	Mr. Brown goes to the gas station to fill up the tank.
Tout de suite un jeune homme s'approche pour le servir.	Immediately a young man approaches to serve him.
—Bonjour, monsieur, lui dit le jeune homme.	Good day, sir, the young man greets him.
—Bonjour, jeune homme, répond M. Brown. Voulez-vous bien faire le plein?	Good day, young man, answers Mr. Brown. Will you fill it up, please?
—Tourisme ou super?	Regular or Super?
—Tourisme, s'il vous plaît. Voulez-vous bien vérifier l'huile, l'eau, et les pneus?	Regular, please. Will you please check the oil, water, and the tires?
—Avec plaisir, monsieur, répond l'employé.	With pleasure, sir, the employee replies.
Le jeune homme fait le plein, vérifie l'huile, l'eau et les pneus.	The young man fills the tank, checks the oil, the water and the tires.
—Tout est bien, dit-il à notre touriste.	Everything is all right, he says to our tourist.
—Merci beaucoup. Combien est-ce que je vous dois?	Many thanks. How much do I owe you?
—Ça fait 33 euro, 40 cent.	It comes to 33 euros, 40 cents.
M. Brown lui donne deux billets de vingt euro, et le jeune homme lui rend la monnaie, six euro, 60 cent.	Mr. Brown gives him two 20-euro bills and the young man gives him the change, six euros and 60 cents.
M. Brown fait le compte et il voit que tout est en ordre.	Mr. Brown figures out the amount and sees that all is in order.
—Très bien, dit-il à l'employé.	Very good, he says to the employee.
Merci beaucoup et au revoir.	Thank you very much and goodbye.
Le jeune homme répond:—Au revoir et bon voyage.	The young man answers, Goodbye and happy trip.

Exercise No. 192—Lecture 1

Une excursion à Versailles

Un jour M. Brown a invité les enfants de Mme Parmentier à l'accompagner en excursion à Versailles. Ce n'est pas très loin de Paris et ils sont arrivés sans aucune difficulté. En route pour le palais M. Brown a eu une idée originale.

—Mangeons sur l'herbe dans le grand parc au bord du lac. On m'a dit que c'est permis.

—Merveilleux! Allons-y.

Ils sont entrés dans une épicerie pour acheter du jambon, un fromage de camembert et une bouteille de vin rouge. Dans une boulangerie à côté ils ont acheté deux baguettes et trois éclairs.

— Moi, j'ai un appétit de loup, a dit l'aînée en sortant de la boulangerie.

— Allons manger tout de suite, a dit M. Brown. Mais que faire pour les ustensiles?

— Voyons ce qu'il y a dans nos poches, a dit le garçon. Il a trouvé un canif.[1]

— Voilà! Et nous allons boire dans la bouteille.[2]

Ils sont entrés au palais par la grande grille, mais au lieu de faire la visite ils sont sortis pour traverser le jardin immense.

Le jardin avec ses statues, fontaines et bosquets[3] a fait une forte impression sur M. Brown. Les deux enfants étaient d'accord.—Je vous assure que le jardin est le bijou de Versailles, a dit le cadet. Mais le palais nous ennuie à mourir.

M. Brown a répondu en riant,—Nous ne sommes pas forcés d'y aller.

Arrivés au lac ils se sont assis sur l'herbe pour manger. Ils ont causé d'une chose et d'une autre en mangeant, et M. Brown était frappé encore une fois par leur intelligence. Les enfants ont mangé comme deux loups et ils se sont amusés énormément.

Tous les trois ils se souviendront[4] longtemps de cette excursion à Versailles.

NOTE   [1]penknife [2]from the bottle. [3]groves of trees. [4]will remember; **se souvenir de,** *to remember.*

Exercise No. 193—Lecture 2

L'Avenue de l'Opéra

Nous nous promenons sur l'avenue de l'Opéra. C'est une belle avenue large qui mène du Palais Royal à l'Opéra.

Il y a beaucoup de monde sur l'avenue. Tous les touristes s'y rencontrent. Les trottoirs sont bordés de boutiques de luxe où on peut acheter toutes sortes de belles choses, si on a de l'argent: des bijoux, de la lingerie fine, des gants, de la céramique, des blouses, des articles de cuir, et aussi des livres, car nous sommes en France où on aime lire. Il y a même une petite boutique et une librairie dans l'Opéra.

Il y a aussi un café-restaurant bien connu sur la Place de l'Opéra: le Café de la Paix. Allons-y prendre un demi,[1] voulez-vous? Avec plaisir.

NOTE [1]a beer.

CHAPITRE 37 (TRENTE-SEPT)

LA GRANDE RUE DU VILLAGE
MAIN STREET

FOREWORD

As a means of testing your understanding, a series of English questions, to be answered in French, are given in Chapters 37–40 under the heading Test of Reading Comprehension, instead of the usual French Questionnaire. You can check your responses in the Answers Section at the back of the book.

Cher ami,

J'ai remarqué que malgré la différence qui existe entre les villages français, ils ont tous une grande rue qui mène à une place entourée d'arbres.

Derrière les arbres, les boutiques du village sont bien rangées, en ordre. La teinturerie est souvent peinte en violet. La vitrine de la boulangerie-pâtisserie à côté est remplie de gâteaux délicieux. Le boucher au coin a pendu ses gigots élégants à l'air libre. Quelques mouches s'y promènent tranquillement, mais personne n'y prête attention.

Dans la vitrine de l'épicerie on voit un tas de boîtes de sardines, et quand on y passe on sent le parfum fort de café. La blanchisseuse joue l'artiste. Elle arrange sa vitrine avec des papiers bleus, roses et violets pour faire un tableau d'une blouse blanche. La laiterie est toujours comblée.

Sur la place, à peu près au milieu du village, il y a la mairie d'un côté et l'église de l'autre. Au fond de la place se trouve l'école. Quelquefois on entend des rires, des chansons, mais en général le silence domine.

L'aspect de la rue change à toute heure. Pour ne rien manquer du spectacle je me lève de bonne heure et je sors. La matinée est grise. Toutes les fenêtres et tous les volets sont fermés. On dort. J'entends un coq. Puis un autre. Les chiens réveillés commencent à se saluer. Tout le monde se réveille. On ouvre les volets, on ouvre les fenêtres.

Voilà un garçon, le premier, qu'on envoie chercher le pain. Il se précipite dans la rue, court à vitesse vertigineuse, et s'arrête soudain au coin pour examiner quelque chose qui attire son attention. Ensuite il reprend sa route au pas militaire. En voilà un autre. Et encore un. Ce que les Français man-

gent comme pain! Notre héros, le premier, revient avec un pain presque aussi long que lui, qu'il fait tourner comme une canne.

Il n'est que sept heures et demie. Je dois tout de même vous quitter, car j'ai rendez-vous avec les jeunes Parmentier pour faire une excursion à Chartres.

Je vous laisse en vous serrant la main, jusqu'à ma prochaine lettre dans laquelle je vous écrirai nos aventures de cet après-midi.

Votre ami,

John Brown

BUILDING VOCABULARY

la canne cane

la chanson song

le coq (kuk) rooster

l'église church

le gigot (zhee-goh) leg of lamb

la mairie townhall

la mouche fly

le tableau picture, painting

le volet shutter

la vitrine shop window

dominer to reign *fig.* dominate

pendre to hang

se précipiter to hurl oneself, rush

reprendre to take again

se réveiller to wake up

comblé crowded

entouré surrounded

peint painted

rangé arranged

réveillé awakened

sage well-behaved

soudain suddenly

à l'air libre in the open air

au milieu de in the middle of

pour ne rien manquer in order to miss nothing

Boutiques et marchands shops and shopkeepers

Note the fairly regular pattern in the naming of the boutique or establishment where the various trades are performed.

la blanchisseuse laundress

la blanchisserie laundry

le boucher butcher

la boucherie butcher shop

le boulanger baker

la boulangerie bakery

le bureau de tabac tobacco shop

le(la) coiffeur (-euse) hairdresser

la confiserie candy shop

le (la) confiseur, confiseuse confectioner, candy-maker

le cordonnier shoemaker

la cordonnerie shoe repair shop, cobbler's

la couturière dressmaker

la droguerie drugstore

l'épicier grocer

l'épicerie grocery

la laiterie dairy

la papeterie stationery shop

la pâtisserie pastry shop, pastry

la pharmacie pharmacy, drugstore

le (la) pharmacien(ne) pharmacist

le tailleur tailor

la teinturerie dry-cleaner's

Exercise No. 194—Test of Reading Comprehension

Answer these questions fully in French:

1. What has Mr. Brown noticed?
2. Where does the street often lead to?
3. What is behind the trees?
4. What shop is often painted violet?
5. Where can one see delicious cakes? A pile of cans of sardines? A white blouse that looks like a painting?
6. Where are the flies walking tranquilly about?
7. What three buildings are on the square?
8. Why does Mr. Brown get up early?
9. What does he hear first?
10. Who rushes into the street?
11. Why does he suddenly stop?
12. With what does our hero return?
13. Why must Mr. Brown stop writing?
14. What will he describe in his next letter?

Exercise No. 195—Completion of Text

1. **La rue mène** (to a square surrounded by trees).
2. **Les boutiques du village sont** (well arranged).
3. **La teinturerie** (is painted) **en violet.**
4. **La vitrine de la pâtisserie** (is filled with delicious cakes).
5. **Le boucher** (has hung his legs of lamb) **à l'air libre.**
6. **Quelques mouches** (are walking on them) **tranquillement.**
7. (In the middle of the village) **il y a la mairie.**
8. **Des fois on entend** (laughter and songs).
9. (In order not to miss anything of the spectacle) **je me lève de bonne heure.**
10. People are sleeping.
11. **Les chiens réveillés commencent** (to greet each other).

12. **Tout le monde** (wakes up).
13. (What the French eat) or (how the French eat) **comme pain!**
14. **Notre héros** (returns with a loaf of bread).
15. (I must nevertheless) **vous quitter.**

Grammar Notes

ORDER OF SINGLE OBJECT PRONOUNS

You have learned:

Direct Object				**Indirect Object**			
me me		**nous** us		**me** (to) me		**nous** (to) us	
te you (fam.)		**vous** you		**te** (to) you		**vous** (to) you	
le him, it (m)		**les** them		**lui** (to) him		**leur** (to) them	
la her, it (f)				(to) her			

Reflexives (Direct and Indirect Objects)

me myself	**nous** ourselves
te yourself	**vous** yourself, yourselves
se himself, herself	**se** themselves
itself, oneself	

1. The partitive pronoun (**en**—*some, any, none, not any, of it, of them*) is often omitted in English, but *en* is never omitted in French.

Avez-vous du beurre?	Have you any butter?
J'*en* ai une livre.	I have a pound (of it).
A-t-elle acheté des oeufs?	Has she bought some eggs?
Elle *en* a acheté une douzaine	She has bought a dozen (of them).

2. The use of **y** to a place already mentioned.

Combien de temps restera-t-il à Paris?	How long will he stay in Paris?
Il *y* restera trois semaines.	He will stay there three weeks.

3. Object pronouns precede the verb except in the affirmative imperative.

Avez-vous acheté *les* peintures?	Have you bought the paintings?
Je ne *les* ai pas achetées.	I have not bought them.
Ne *les* achetez pas.	Do not buy them.
Achetez-*les*.	Buy them.

4. Sometimes a verb has two object pronouns (listed below). Their placement is explained below.

me	le	lui	y	en
nous	la	leur		
te	les			
vous				

a. If there are pronoun objects of different persons (more than one in the same sentence), both precede the verb with **me, te, nous, vous** (first and second persons) coming before **le, la, l', les** (third person). This order is different in English.

M'enverrez-vous les billets?   Will you send me the tickets?

Nous *vous les* enverrons demain.   We shall send *them to you* tomorrow.

b. If there are two pronoun objects of the third person, the direct object (**le, la, l',** or **les**) precedes the indirect object (**lui** or **leur**).

Avez-vous prêté votre crayon à Jean?   Did you lend your pencil to John?

Oui. Je *le lui* ai prêté.   Yes. I lent *it to him*.

c. When **y** or **en** is used with another object pronoun, it follows that object pronoun, and is placed with the verb that it *goes with* (in meaning):

A-t-elle mis les tasses sur le buffet?   Has she put the cups on the buffet?

Elle *les y* a mises.   She has put *them there*.

Il n'a pas eu l'occasion de *m'en* informer.   He did not have a chance to inform *me of it*.

d. If **y** and **en** both appear, **y** precedes **en**.

This combination is rarely seen except with il y a (there is, are).

Combien de chaises y a-t-il dans le salon?   How many chairs are there in the parlor?

Il *y en* a six.   There are six (*of them*).

e. In the affirmative imperative the order of two object pronouns is exactly as in English.

Donnez-les-moi. Envoyez-m'en.   Give *them to me*. Send *me some* (*of it*).

NOTE: moi is used for **me, toi** for **te,** in the affirmative imperative, except before **en** when the contraction **m'en** and **t'en** is used.

Exercise No. 196

Practice the following sentences aloud. They will help give you a feel for the double object pronoun. Of course, in ordinary conversation a simple *yes* or *no* answer would serve, or an answer with only one pronoun object. Thus in Question No. 1 the answer might also be:

Oui. *or* **Oui, nous l'avons envoyée. Non.** *or* **Non, nous ne l'avons pas envoyée.**

Translate the questions and answers into English after completing the exercise.

1. **Est-ce que vous avez envoyé la poterie à M. Brown?**
   Oui, nous la lui avons envoyée.
2. **Est-ce que beaucoup de monde se rencontre sur l'avenue de l'Opéra?**
   Tous les touristes s'y rencontrent.
3. **Envoyez-moi les journaux français, s'il vous plaît.**
   Nous vous les enverrons demain.
4. **Est-ce que le garçon vous a donné l'addition?**
   Il ne me l'a pas encore donnée.
5. **Avez-vous demandé les billets à l'employé?**
   Je ne les lui ai pas encore demandés parce qu'il est très occupé.
6. **Combien d'assiettes y a-t-il dans cette caisse?**
   Il y en a vingt-cinq douzaines.
7. **Lui avez-vous rendu l'argent que vous lui avez emprunté?** (borrowed)
   Je le lui rendrai ce soir.
8. **La bonne a-t-elle mis sur le bureau la porcelaine que M. Brown vient de recevoir?**
   Elle l'y a mise.
9. **Me prêterez-vous votre parapluie?**
   Je vous le prêterai; mais rendez-le-moi demain, s'il vous plaît.
   Merci beaucoup. Je vous le rendrai demain.
10. **Montrez-moi, s'il vous plaît, la nouvelle robe que vous avez achetée. Je ne peux pas vous la montrer parce qu'elle n'est pas encore arrivée du magasin.**

CHAPITRE 38 (TRENTE-HUIT)

UNE EXCURSION À CHARTRES
A TRIP TO CHARTRES

Cher ami,

Mes jeunes amis sont venus me chercher de bonne heure car j'ai voulu revenir à temps pour aller à l'opéra le soir. Cette fois-ci ils avaient préparé (they had prepared) un bon déjeuner qu'on avait l'intention de prendre en route sur l'herbe, comme à Versailles. Mais cette fois-ci ils avaient apporté (they had brought) un beau panier rempli d'une nappe, de serviettes, de couteaux, de fourchettes, et aussi d'un poulet.

La voiture que j'avais louée (I had rented) nous attendait en bas. Nous y sommes montés tout en parlant et en riant, et nous voilà en route.

Je conduisais à mon aise, quand tout à coup j'ai entendu un son que j'ai reconnu tout de suite.

—Qu'est-ce que c'est? ont demandé les enfants.

J'ai stoppé et nous sommes descendus.—Nous avons crevé un pneu, j'ai répondu.

J'ai voulu changer le pneu et les enfants voulaient m'aider. Très heureux ils ont commencé à chercher le cric. Mais, malheur! il n'y avait pas de cric dans l'outillage. Que faire?

De temps en temps une auto passait à toute vitesse. Malgré nos signaux désespérés personne ne s'est arrêté. Il était presque midi et le soleil donnait à plomb sur nos têtes. Nous nous sommes assis sous un arbre près de la route pour attendre notre destin.

Bientôt un grand camion s'est approché rapidement et il s'est arrêté court avec un grand bruit de freins devant nous. Le camionneur est descendu.

—Vous êtes à plat? Voulez-vous un coup de main? Ce grand gaillard avait une voix très douce. Il souriait.

—Nous n'avons pas de cric, lui ai-je dit.

—Mais c'est un désastre, m'a-t-il répondu, en cherchant le sien (his).

—En tout cas nous avons un pneu de rechange.

—C'est toujours ça! Tout le monde s'est mis à la besogne. En cinq secondes tout était prêt.

Je n'osais pas lui offrir un pourboire. Il avait tant de dignité naturelle. Mais les deux enfants ont eu une idée astucieuse.—Voulez-vous bien déjeuner avec nous? Nous avons un poulet énorme.

—Très volontiers, a répondu le camionneur. À condition que j'ajoute mon jambon et ma bouteille de vin.

Nous nous sommes assis sous l'arbre et nous avons déjeuné de bon appétit.

—Le jambon est délicieux, avons-nous dit avec enthousiasme.

Il a souri.—Ma femme ne me néglige pas.

Le déjeuner fini, nous avons tous fait la sieste. Ensuite nous avons fait nos adieux. Le gros camion est parti vers Paris et nous avons repris la route pour Chartres.

Et voilà qu'encore une fois je n'ai pas le temps de vous décrire mes impressions, car ce soir je vais à l'opéra et je dois m'habiller.

Bien cordialement à vous,

John Brown

Building Vocabulary

le camion truck

le camionneur truckdriver

le désastre disaster

le coup de main a helping hand

le destin fate

le gaillard jovial fellow

le malheur misfortune

le panier basket

le nappe tablecloth

la serviette napkin

le son sound

ajouter to add, join

couper to cut

louer to rent

négliger to neglect

oser to dare

court short

désespéré desperate

gros (grosse *f*) big, fat

sous under

en bas below, downstairs

l'automobile (la voiture) the car

le cric (kree) jack

le poste d'essence gas station

les freins brakes

le pneu tire

le pneu de rechange spare tire

l'outillage tool kit

le volant steering wheel

stationner to park

changer l'huile to change the oil

conduire to drive, to conduct

être à plat to have a flat

crever un pneu to burst (puncture) a tire

faire le plein d'essence to fill up the tank

stopper to stop, come to a halt

vérifier to check

French Expressions

1. **Qu'est-ce qui est arrivé?** What happened?
2. **crever un pneu** to get a flat (tire)
3. **le soleil donnait à plomb** the sun was shining directly
4. **être à plat** to have a flat
5. **un coup de main** a helping hand
6. **c'est toujours ça** it's always like that
7. **se mettre à la besogne** to set to work
8. **et voilà qu'encore une fois** and so it is that once more

Exercise No. 197—Test of Reading Comprehension

1. Why did Mr. Brown's young friends call for him early?
2. What had they prepared?
3. Where was the car that Mr. Brown had rented?
4. What did he hear all of a sudden?
5. What had happened?
6. What did the young children want to do?
7. Why could they not change the tire?
8. What did the truckdriver who came along soon offer to do?
9. Why didn't Mr. Brown dare to offer him a tip?
10. What clever idea did the children have?
11. What did they eat and drink for lunch?
12. What did the children say about the truckdriver's ham?
13. What did the truckdriver say about his wife?
14. What did they do after lunch?
15. Why, once again, doesn't Mr. Brown have time to describe his impressions of Chartres?

Exercise No. 198—Completion of Text

1. **Mes amis sont venus** (to get me).
2. (They had prepared) **un bon déjeuner.**
3. a tablecloth, some napkins, some knives, some forks
4. (And there we were) **en route.**
5. (All of a sudden) **j'ai entendu un son.**
6. We have blown a tire.

7. (There was no jack) **dans l'outillage.**
8. (Nobody) **s'est arrêté.**
9. (We sat down) **sous un arbre.**
10. (Soon a large truck) **s'est approché rapidement.**
11. **Voulez-vous** (a helping hand)?
12. (At any rate) **nous avons un pneu de rechange.**
13. **Tout le monde** (set to work).
14. **Je n'osais pas** (to offer him a tip).
15. **Voulez-vous bien** (to have lunch with us)?

Grammar Notes

1. **THE PAST PERFECT (PLUPERFECT) TENSE.** What *had happened.* MODEL VERBS, **parler, finir, vendre.**

j'avais parlé (fini, vendu)	I had spoken (finished, sold)
tu avais parlé (fini, vendu)	you had spoken (finished, sold)
il avait parlé (fini, vendu)	he had spoken (finished, sold)
elle avait parlé (fini, vendu)	she had spoken (finished, sold)
nous avions parlé (fini, vendu)	we had spoken (finished, sold)
vous aviez parlé (fini, vendu)	you had spoken (finished, sold)
ils avaient parlé (fini, vendu)	they had spoken (finished, sold)
elles avaient parlé (fini, vendu)	they had spoken (finished, sold)
avait-il parlé (fini, vendu)?	had he spoken (finished, sold)?
il n'avait pas parlé (fini, vendu)	he had not spoken (finished, sold)
n'avait-il pas parlé (fini, vendu)?	had he not spoken (finished, sold)?

The past perfect tense is usually formed by the auxiliary verb **j'avais,** etc. (*I had,* etc.) plus the past participle of the verb. See below for **être** verbs.

Exercise No. 199

Change these sentences from the conversational past to the past perfect. Then, translate the changed sentence into English:

Exemple: 1. Il avait appris les règles essentielles. He had learned the essential rules.

1. **Il a appris les règles essentielles.**
2. **Nous avons vraiment travaillé dur.**
3. **Ils n'ont pas encore obtenu leurs billets.**
4. **A-t-il écrit une lettre à son ami?**

5. Qui a promis de le rencontrer à l'aéroport?
6. J'ai oublié mon parapluie.
7. Est-ce qu'ils ont réservé une chambre pour M. Brown?
8. Avez-vous lu beaucoup de guides?
9. Ses jeunes amis ont préparé un bon déjeuner.
10. A-t-il loué une voiture?

2. THE PAST PERFECT OF être-VERBS, MODEL VERB aller

I had gone, you had gone, etc.

j'étais allé (allée)	nous étions allés (allées)
tu étais allé (allée)	vous étiez allée(s), allée(s)
il était allé	ils étaient allés
elle était allée	elles étaient allées

être-verbs in the past perfect take the auxiliary **j'étais, etc.,** instead of **j'avais, etc. J'étais, etc.,** is the imperfect of **être,** *to be*. As an auxiliary verb it is translated *I had*, etc., not *I was*, etc.

Reflexive verbs also take the auxiliary **j'étais, etc.,** in the past **perfect.**

Conversational Past **Une belle dame s'est approchée.** *A beautiful lady approached.*

Past Perfect **Une belle dame s'était approchée.** *A beautiful lady had approached.*

Exercise No. 200

Change these sentences from the conversational past to the past perfect. Then, translate the changed sentence into English:

Exemple: 1. Mes jeunes amis étaient venus me chercher.

My young friends had come to get me.

1. Mes jeunes amis sont venus me chercher.
2. Un grand camion s'est approché rapidement.
3. Nous nous sommes assis sous un grand arbre.
4. Je suis allé à la salle d'attente.
5. Nous ne sommes pas sortis ensemble.
6. Ils sont arrivés sains et saufs.
7. Le taxi s'est arrêté devant l'hôtel.
8. Êtes-vous allé au bureau de douane?
9. Nous nous sommes dit au revoir.
10. Elles ne sont pas restées à Paris deux semaines.

3. THE POSSESSIVE PRONOUNS **le mien**, *mine*, **le tien**, *yours*, etc.

*In French as in English there are possessive adjectives and possessive pronouns. The possessive adjectives (**mon, ton, son,** etc.) are very important and useful words. You have learned and used them a great deal. The possessive pronouns are used rather infrequently. Study the following examples:*

Possessive Adjectives	Possessive Pronouns
Son père (his or her father) **est jeune.**	**Le mien** (mine) **est agé.**
Sa soeur (his or her sister) **est docteur.**	**La mienne** (mine) **est avocate.**
Ses livres (his or her books) **sont neufs.**	**Les miens** (mine) **sont vieux.**
Ses plumes (his or her pens) **sont bonnes.**	**Les miennes** (mine) **sont mauvaises.**

The possessive pronoun agrees in number and gender with the noun for which it stands or substitutes. Here is the complete table of possessive pronouns:

Singular

Masculine	Feminine	
le mien	**la mienne**	*mine*
le tien	**la tienne**	*yours*
le sien	**la sienne**	*his, hers*
le nôtre (nohtr)	**la nôtre**	*ours*
le vôtre (vohtr)	**la vôtre**	*yours*
le leur	**la leur**	*theirs*

Plural

Masculine	*Feminine*
les miens	**les miennes**
les tiens	**les tiennes**
les siens	**les siennes**
les nôtres	**les nôtres**
les vôtres	**les vôtres**
les leurs	**les leurs**

After the verb **être, à** + an independent pronoun is generally used rather than the possessive pronoun:

Cette montre est à moi, à toi, à lui, à elle.   This watch is mine, yours, his, hers.

Ces places sont à nous, à vous, à eux, à elles.   These seats are ours, yours, theirs (*m*) theirs (*f*).

Exercise No. 201

Read aloud in French these sentences and related questions; then, translate them into English.

1. **Nous avons de bons professeurs. Comment trouvez-vous les vôtres?**
2. **Allons au bureau de poste dans votre voiture. La nôtre a crevé un pneu.**
3. **Prêtez-moi votre plume, s'il vous plaît. La mienne n'écrit pas.**
4. **J'ai oublié mon parapluie. Voulez-vous bien me prêter le vôtre?**
5. **Vous n'avez pas de cric. Voulez-vous emprunter (borrow) le mien?**
6. **La bicyclette de Paul coûte plus cher que la mienne, mais la mienne est meilleure que la sienne.**
7. **Louise et moi nous avons acheté des billets de théâtre hier. J'ai les miens, mais elle a malheureusement perdu les siens.**
8. **Voici nos chapeaux. Celui-ci est à moi. Celui-là est à vous.**

The cathedral of Chartres is one of the finest examples of Gothic architecture.

CHAPITRE 39 (TRENTE-NEUF)

M. BROWN ACHÈTE UN BILLET DE LOTERIE

MR. BROWN BUYS A LOTTERY TICKET

Cher ami,

Je ne suis pas joueur, M. Picard. C'est à dire que jusqu'à la semaine dernière je n'avais jamais été joueur.

Ce qui est arrivé? Je vais vous raconter tout.

Comme vous le savez bien il y a des postes de vente de billets de loterie partout à Paris.

Quand je suis arrivé à Paris j'ai remarqué tout de suite qu'on s'occupait beaucoup de la Loterie Nationale. Je voyais des affiches illustrées dans le métro, dans les autobus, dans les rues, enfin un peu partout. Quand (Whenever) je voyais une de ces affiches je commençais à rêver:—Si je gagnais le premier prix, le gros lot, j'aurais (would have) assez d'argent pour voyager partout en Europe l'année prochaine. Ma femme m'accompagnerait (would accompany me) et les enfants iraient (would go) à l'école quelque part en France pour apprendre le français. Ma femme pourrait (would be able) faire la connaissance des Parmentier et nous pourrions (could) peut-être faire un voyage ensemble tous les quatre.

Je pourrais (would be able) acheter beaucoup de belles choses. J'achèterais (would buy) des objets d'art, non pas pour les vendre, mais pour les garder chez moi. Je serais (would be) l'homme le plus heureux du monde.

C'est ainsi que je rêvais.

Mercredi passé je descendais la rue de Rivoli. Au coin de la rue Cambon j'ai vu un de ces petits postes de vente de billets de loterie. La jeune fille qui était de service m'a vu regarder l'annonce "Loterie Nationale." Elle m'a dit:

—Monsieur, achetez ce billet. C'est le bon. Il vous portera bonheur.

—Comment savez-vous que celui-là est le bon?

—Parce qu'il a trois zéros. Regardez.

J'ai regardé et en effet le numéro finissait en trois zéros. Je me suis dit,—Celui-là, il sort de l'ordinaire.

Allons-y!

Et voilà comment je suis devenu joueur!

Le lendemain, je me suis levé de bonne heure, j'ai sonné tout de suite pour demander mon café, mes croissants et mon journal. Ils sont arrivés tous à la fois, mais à ce moment je ne m'intéressais qu'au journal. Je l'ai ouvert vite, le coeur battant. Mais où est-ce qu'on les a cachés, ces numéros? Ah, les voilà! Qu'est-ce que je vois? Le numéro qui a gagné le gros lot finit en trois zéros: 26,000. Je ne respire plus. Je cherche mon billet, en faisant des voyages dans la lune. Enfin je le trouve. Je peux à peine le tenir. Voilá les trois zéros. Voilà le deux. Mais, malheur! C'est un cinq, pas un six. Tant pis! Et j'ai pris mon petit déjeuner, en riant de moi-même. J'ai décidé que les émotions d'un joueur ne sont pas pour moi. J'aime la vie tranquille comme je vous l'ai dit à New-York.

Très cordialement, votre ami,

John Brown

Building Vocabulaire

l'affiche (*f*) poster

l'annonce (*f*) advertisement

le bonheur happiness

le coeur heart

French Expressions

1. **être de service** to be on duty
2. **il sort de l'ordinaire** it is something out of the ordinary
3. **allons-y** let's go, let's take it
4. **tant pis** so much the worse
5. **à peine** scarcely, hardly
6. **quelque part** somewhere

Exercise No. 202—Test of Reading Comprehension

1. What kind of man had Mr. Brown never been?
2. What had he noticed right away when he came to France?
3. When he saw one of the illustrated posters what did he dream of doing?
4. If he won the first prize, for what would he have sufficient money?
5. What would his wife do?
6. What would the children do?
7. From whom did Mr. Brown buy a lottery ticket?
8. What did he ring for the next morning?
9. What was the only thing that interested him at the moment?
10. What happened when he saw that the winning number had three zeros?
11. What was he doing mentally while he looked for his ticket?
12. What number did Mr. Brown have?
13. What number won the prize?
14. What did Mr. Brown decide?
15. What sort of life does he like?

Exercise No. 203—Completion of Text

1. (I had never been) **joueur.**
2. **Il y a** (lottery ticket stalls) **partout à Paris.**
3. **J'ai remarqué tout de suite** (that people were very much taken up with) **la Loterie Nationale.**
4. (I saw illustrated posters) **dans le métro.**
5. (If I won the first prize) **j'aurais assez d'argent pour voyager partout en Europe.**
6. (I would be able to buy) **beaucoup de belles choses.**
7. **Je serais** (the happiest man in the world).
8. (And that is how) **je suis devenu joueur.**
9. **Je me suis levé** (early).
10. **A ce moment** (I was interested only in the newspaper).
11. (I look for) **mon billet.**
12. **Je peux** (scarcely hold it).
13. **Mais malheur!** (It's a five, not a six).
14. **J'ai pris mon petit déjeuner** (laughing at myself).

Grammar Notes

1. THE PRESENT CONDITIONAL, WHAT *would happen.* MODEL VERBS **parler, finir, vendre**

The present conditional may be called the *would* tense. Its use in French is much the same as in English.

je parlerais (finirais, vendrais)	I would speak (finish, sell)
tu parlerais (finirais, vendrais)	you would speak (finish, sell)
il parlerait (finirait, vendrait)	he would speak (finish, sell)
elle parlerait (finirait, vendrait)	she would speak (finish, sell)
nous parlerions (finirions, vendrions)	we would speak (finish, sell)
vous parleriez (finiriez, vendriez)	you would speak (finish, sell)
ils parleraient (finiraient, vendraient)	they (*m*) would speak (finish, sell)
elles parleraient (finiraient, vendraient)	they (*f*) would speak (finish, sell)

The personal endings of the present conditional of all verbs are **-ais, -ais, -ait; -ions, -iez, -aient.** They are exactly like the endings of the imperfect tense.
To form the present conditional, add the conditional endings to the *infinitive* as a base. If the *infinitive* ends in **-re,** as in **vendre,** drop the final **e** before adding the conditional endings.

Thus the base for the present conditional is the same as the base for the future.

Compare:

Infinitive	Future	Present Conditional
to	*I shall, you will, etc.*	*I would, you would, etc.*
parler	je parlerai, tu parleras, etc.	je parlerais, tu parlerais, etc.
finir	je finirai, tu finiras, etc.	je finirais, tu finirais, etc.
vendre	je vendrai, tu vendras, etc.,	je vendrais, tu vendrais, etc.

2. THE IRREGULAR PRESENT CONDITIONAL

Those verbs that have an irregular base for the future have the same irregular base for the conditional. Review and compare:

Infinitive		Future		Pres. Cond.	
to		shall, will		would	
avoir	pouvoir	j'aurai	je pourrai	j'aurais	je pourrais
être	devoir	je serai	je devrai	je serais	je devrais
aller	recevoir	j'irai	je recevrai	j'irais	je recevrais
envoyer	vouloir	j'enverrai	je voudrai	j'enverrais	je voudrais
venir	valoir	je viendrai	je vaudrai	je viendrais	je vaudrais
tenir	voir	je tiendrai	je verrai	je tiendrais	je verrais
courir	savoir	je courrai	je saurai	je courrais	je saurais
faire	falloir	je ferai	il faudra	je ferais	il faudrait

Exercise No. 204

Change these sentences from the future to the present conditional. Read both French sentences aloud. Translate each sentence in the present conditional into English.

Exemple: 1. Je voyagerais partout en Europe.

I would travel everywhere in Europe.

1. Je voyagerai partout en Europe.
2. Il visitera la France et l'Italie.
3. Nous apprendrons le français.
4. Ma famille ne m'accompagnera pas.
5. Elle pourra acheter beaucoup de belles choses.

6. Aura-t-il assez d'argent?
7. Ils achèteront des objets d'art.
8. Serez-vous content de rester ici?
9. Elle ne vous connaîtra pas.
10. Ils ne feront pas leurs devoirs.
11. Je vous enverrai les revues.
12. Ils ne viendront pas la semaine prochaine.

NOTE: Sometimes in English, we use the word « would » with a verb to indicate an act that was a regular occurrence, that happened habitually. In such cases, continue to use the imperfect tense.

When I was 12 years old, I would go to the movies on Saturdays.

Quand j'avais douze ans, j'allais au cinéma le samedi.

If I were you, I wouldn't go to the movies this weekend.

Si j'etais toi, je n'irais pas au cinéma ce weekend.

M. BROWN S'EN VA
MR. BROWN GOES AWAY

Cher ami,

Quand je suis parti de New York j'étais assez bien renseigné sur la France. J'avais lu quelques livres sur son histoire et sur les coutumes du pays. Je savais parler français passablement.

Maintenant que je suis sur le point de partir de France il me semble que je parle avec beaucoup plus de facilité. J'ai visité beaucoup de ces endroits dont nous avons parlé dans nos conversations. Dans mes lettres je ne pouvais décrire que très peu de tout ce que j'ai vu et appris. Le reste, je dois le laisser pour notre prochaine rencontre.

J'aime tant de choses en France: Paris, les monuments historiques, le paysage, la peinture, et la cuisine. Mais j'aime surtout les Français. J'aime leur sentiment marqué de la dignité de l'homme, leur sens vif du comique, leur politesse et leur passion pour la discussion.

La vie en France est vraiment plus tranquille qu'à New York, malgré mes premières impressions dans le taxi qui me conduisait à vitesse vertigineuse de l'aéroport à l'hôtel.

Comme vous savez c'était un voyage d'agrément aussi bien qu'un voyage d'affaires. Heureusement j'ai bientôt terminé mes affaires et je pouvais me dévouer complètement aux distractions.

Je n'avais pas le temps d'aller ni au Maroc ni en Corse. Dommage! Mais j'ai préféré passer mon temps à mieux connaître la France. Il y a tant à voir, à faire et à apprendre. Tout m'a enchanté.

J'aurai beaucoup à vous dire au sujet des personnes que j'ai rencontrées, des endroits que j'ai visités, et de tout ce que j'ai appris des coutumes, de la vie, de la langue, et des arts de la France.

Certainement je reviendrai en France. Je voudrais revenir l'année prochaine. Mais cette fois-ci toute la famille m'accompagnerait. Je suis sûr que je pourrais faire le guide sans difficulté. Je n'ai pas gagné le gros lot de la loterie, mais tout de même, je reviendrai.

Celle-ci est la dernière lettre que je vous écris avant de partir pour New-York le premier août. Je me donnerai le plaisir de vous téléphoner dès mon arrivée pour vous inviter à dîner en famille.

Sans doute nous passerons des heures en parlant de la France et de notre Paris bien aimé.

À bientôt,

Votre ami,
John Brown

BUILDING VOCABULARY

le comique comic(al)	**le sens** sense
la facilité facility	**s'en aller** to go away
la marque mark, symbol	**conduire** to drive
le reste remainder, rest	**renseigné** informed
la rencontre meeting	**dès** as early as, from

French Expressions

1. **je m'en vais** I go away
2. **tu t'en vas** you go away
   il, elle s'en va he, she goes away
   nous nous en allons we go away
   vous vous en allez you go away
   ils, elles s'en vont they go away
3. **être sur le point de partir** to be about to leave
4. **tant à voir** so much to see
5. **faire le guide** to act as guide
6. **dès mon arrivée** immediately on my arrival
7. **combien de choses** how many things
8. **beaucoup de choses** many things
9. **tant de choses** so many things

Exercise No. 205—Test of Reading Comprehension

1. Before leaving for France, how had Mr. Brown obtained knowledge of that country?
2. How much was he able to describe in his letters?
3. What does he like best in France?
4. What does he like about the French people?
5. How does he compare life in France with life in the United States?
6. When had he gotten a different impression?
7. Who would accompany him on his next trip to France?
8. What is he sure of?
9. When is he leaving for New York?
10. What will he be glad to do immediately upon his arrival home?
11. What does he think he and Mr. Picard will do when they are together again?

Grammar Notes

1. THE PAST CONDITIONAL. *What would have happened.*

I would have spoken	*I would have gone*
you would have spoken, etc.	*you would have gone, etc.*
j'aurais parlé	je serais allé(e)
tu aurais parlé	tu serais allé(e)
il aurait parlé	il serait allé
elle aurait parlé	elle serait allée
nous aurions parlé	nous serions allés, allées
vous auriez parlé	vous seriez allé(s), allée(s)
ils auraient parlé	ils seraient allés
elle auraient parlé	elles seraient allées

The past conditional is formed by the auxiliary **j'aurais, etc.**, plus the past participle, for all **avoir**-verbs (=verbs which take the present tense of **avoir** as auxiliary verb in the **passé composé** construction); and by the auxiliary **je serais, etc.**, plus the past participle, for all **être**-verbs (including reflexive verbs).

2. CONDITIONAL SENTENCES, si (*if*)-CLAUSES

A conditional sentence is one that includes a **si** (*if*)-clause. Compare the tenses of the verbs used in the following French conditional sentences with those used in the corresponding English sentences:

1. **Si je le vois, je lui parlerai.**
2. **S'il gagne le prix, il ira en Europe.**
3. **Si je le voyais, je lui parlerais.**
4. **S'il gagnait le prix, il irait en Europe.**
5. **Si je l'avais vu, je lui aurais parlé.**

6. **S'il avait gagné le prix, il serait allé en Europe.**

1. If I see him, I shall speak to him.
2. If he wins the prize, he will go to Europe.
3. If I saw him, I would speak to him.
4. If he won the prize, he would go to Europe.
5. If I had seen him, I would have spoken to him.
6. If he had won the prize, he would have gone to Europe.

The tenses of conditional sentences in French are often the same as the tenses in the corresponding English conditional sentences. Note, however, these differences:

As in English, French uses the present tense to imply future action in the **si**-clause. It *never* uses a future tense in the **si**-clause. See sentences 1 and 2.

French uses the imperfect tense in the **si**-clause where English can use either the past or *should* or *were to*. See sentences 3 and 4.

3. SI (*WHETHER*)

When **si** means *whether*, it is followed by the same tenses as in English.

Je ne sais pas s'il fera un voyage en Europe l'été prochain.	**I don't know whether he will take a trip to Europe next summer.**

1. Si j'ai le temps, je vous accompagnerai jusqu'à la gare.
2. Si vous la voyez, faites-lui mes amitiés.
3. Si vous revenez à Paris, j'espère avoir le plaisir de vous revoir.
4. Si nous pouvons vous aider, nous le ferons.
5. Si les affaires ne retiennent M. Brown à Paris, il visitera la Côte d'Azur.
6. Si nous vivions en France, les enfants iraient à l'école pour apprendre le français.
7. Si vous parliez plus lentement, je vous comprendrais mieux.
8. Seriez-vous surpris si je vous disais que j'étudie le français?
9. Si j'allais à Paris, je rendrais visite à la famille de Mme Parmentier.
10. Si j'avais assez d'argent, je ferais un voyage autour du monde.
11. Ils auraient réussi à l'examen s'ils avaient travaillé dur.
12. Si elle avait cherché un peu plus longtemps, elle l'aurait trouvé.
13. Nous serions allés au cinéma si nous avions fini nos devoirs plus tôt.
14. Si M. Brown n'avait pas lu les guides, il n'aurait pas su se tirer d'affaire en France.

1. If I have time, I shall accompany you as far as the station.
2. If you see her, give her my regards.
3. If you return to Paris, I hope to meet you again.
4. If we are able to help you, we shall do so.
5. If business does not detain Mr. Brown in Paris, he will visit the Riviera.
6. If we were living in France, the children would go to school to learn French.
7. If you spoke more slowly, I would understand you better.
8. Would you be surprised if I told (were to tell) you that I am studying French?
9. If I went to Paris, I would pay a visit to the family of Mrs. Parmentier.
10. If I had enough money, I would take a trip around the world.
11. They would have passed (succeeded in) the examination if they had worked hard.
12. If she had looked a little longer, she would have found it.
13. We would have gone to the movies if we had finished our homework sooner.
14. If Mr. Brown had not read the guidebooks, he would not have known how to get along in France.

Première Partie

NOUNS

1. l'annonce		1. advertisement	
2. le bijou		2. jewel	
3. le bonheur		3. happiness	
4. la boutique		4. shop	
5. le coq		5. rooster	
6. l'essence (*f*)		6. gasoline	
7. l'église (*f*)		7. church	
8. l'herbe (*f*)		8. grass	
9. l'huile (*f*)		9. oil	
10. le jambon		10. ham	
11. la lune		11. moon	
12. demain, le lendemain		12. tomorrow, the next day	
13. le métro		13. subway	
14. la nappe		14. tablecloth	
15. le panier		15. basket	
16. le reste		16. remainder	
17. le sentiment		17. feeling	
18. la serviette		18. napkin	
19. le son		19. sound	
20. le trottoir		20. sidewalk	
21. la vitrine		21. shop window	

VERBS

1. ajouter		1. to add	
2. battre		2. to beat	
3. cacher		3. to hide	
4. conduire		4. to drive	
5. couper		5. to cut	

6. ennuyer	6. to bore, annoy
7. il nous ennuie	7. he bores us
8. gagner	8. to earn, win
9. louer	9. to rent
10. négliger	10. to neglect
11. oser	11. to dare
12. reprendre	12. to take again
13. respirer	13. to breathe
14. réveiller	14. to awake
15. rire de	15. to laugh at
16. rêver	16. to dream
17. se souvenir (de)	17. to remember
18. Je me souviens.	18. I remember.

ADJECTIVES

1. ne-aucun aucune $(f)^1$	1. no, no one, none
2. délicieux délicieuse (f)	2. delicious
3. gros grosse (f)	3. big, large, stout
4. sage	4. well-behaved
5. entouré	5. surrounded
6. renseigné	6. informed

NOTE: [1]**Aucun** may be used as a pronoun or as an adjective. Thus:

Aucun de ses amis n'était à la station.	None of his friends was at the station.
Il n'a eu aucune intention de l'acheter.	He had no intention of buying it.

ADVERBS

1. soudain	1. suddenly
2. tant	2. so much, so many
3. vraiment	3. truly

French Expressions

1. être de service	1. to be on duty
2. être à plat	2. to have a flat
3. faire le compte	3. to add up the bill
4. faire le plein d'essence	4. to fill up the tank
5. faire le guide	5. to act as guide
6. se mettre à la besogne	6. to set to work
7. il sort de l'ordinaire	7. it's out of the ordinary
8. tant pis	8. too bad
9. c'est toujours ça	9. that's all to the good

Deuxième Partie

Exercise No. 206

Translate the following sentences accurately. All the tenses you have learned are illustrated here.

1. Elles sont allées au marché pour faire des achats.
2. Les Français ont fait une forte impression sur M. Brown.
3. Il est allé à la gare pour demander des renseignements.
4. Je pourrai me tirer d'affaire en France parce que je parle bien le français.
5. Après-demain nous rendrons visite à M. Duval.
6. Le jeune homme avait déjà fait le plein d'essence et vérifié l'huile.
7. L'été prochain M. Brown pourra faire le guide pour toute la famille.
8. Si M. Brown avait eu plus de temps, il aurait fait un voyage au Maroc.
9. À l'Hôtel du Quai Voltaire nous n'avons manqué de rien.
10. Après avoir terminé ses affaires, M. Brown s'est dévoué complètement aux distractions.
11. Je vais écrire une lettre à ma représentante pour lui faire savoir la date de mon arrivée.
12. Après avoir fait nos adieux, nous sommes montés dans l'avion.
13. Je pensais aux conseils de mon professeur pendant que le taxi filait à toute vitesse par les rues de Paris.
14. Autrefois M. Brown faisait traduire sa correspondance française, mais à l'avenir (in the future) il la traduira lui-même.
15. Les enfants s'amusaient à jeter des pierres dans l'eau.
16. Si vous trouvez les caoutchoucs que j'ai laissés chez vous, rendez-les-moi, s'il vous plaît.
17. Je n'oublierai pas de vous les rendre.
18. Je n'avais jamais vu un spectacle pareil.
19. Lorsque M. Brown voyageait en Europe, Mme Brown s'occupait des enfants.
20. Je n'ai jamais été en France mais je compte y aller l'été prochain.

Exercise No. 207

Complete the following sentences in French.

1. **M. Brown** (is a businessman from New York).
2. **Il a fait** (a trip to Paris in order to visit his agent).
3. **Il voulait** (to get acquainted with her).
4. **Avant de partir pour la France** (he had learned to speak French well).
5. (He had also read many books) **sur la France.**
6. **Il a écrit** (many letters to his friend and teacher).
7. **Il a décrit** (many of the interesting places of which they had spoken in their conversations).
8. **Malgré ses premières impressions** (he had found life in France more tranquil than in the United States).
9. **Il pensait au taxi** (which had taken him to his hotel).
10. (The dizzying speed of the taxi) **ne lui avait pas fait plaisir.**
11. **Heureusement** (he soon finished his business matters).
12. **Il aime surtout les Français,** (their politeness and their marked feeling for the dignity of man).
13. **Tout de même** (he did not have time to go to Morocco or Corsica).
14. **Il y avait** (so much to see, so much to do, so much to learn).
15. **Il avait beaucoup appris** (about the customs, the life, the language and the arts of France).
16. **L'année prochaine** (he will return to France).
17. **Toute la famille** (would accompany him).
18. (He has not won the first prize in the lottery) **mais il aura** (enough money).
19. **Celle-ci est la dernière lettre** (which Mr. Brown will write before leaving France).
20. **Sans aucune doute** (he will invite Mr. Picard to dinner with his family) **quand il sera de retour à New-York.**

Exercise No. 208—Lecture

Nice, la capitale de la Côte d'Azur

Il y a vraiment deux villes dans Nice: la ville italienne et la ville française, la vieille ville et la ville moderne. On peut se promener dans les vieux quartiers où on n'entend rien que l'italien, car ce n'est qu'en 1860 que Nice est devenue française. Dans ce quartier, on vend des macaronis, des raviolis, des olives et des saucisses. L'air est parfumé d'ail et de sauce tomate. On crie, on chante, on marchande. C'est un quartier tout à fait italien.

Mais à deux pas, en traversant la Place Masséna, on se trouve dans la ville française. On monte le boulevard Victor Hugo sous une allée de superbes arbres et on admire les boutiques magnifiques. On voit des voitures longues comme des trains. C'est la ville de luxe.

Nice est aussi un centre sportif. Il y a un club de tennis magnifique; il y a l'hippodrome de Cagnes, tout près; les célèbres sports d'hiver à Beuil, dans les montagnes; le yachting et les bains de mer. Il est vrai que la plage est pierreuse (rocky), mais ça ne fait rien; on y va tout de même pour adorer le soleil.

La ville où l'on est né, où l'on va à l'école, où l'on gagne son pain, cette ville-là existe aussi. Cette ville a son commerce: le tourisme, les fleurs, les parfums, les olives, la pêche. Elle a sa vie culturelle: la musique, qu'elle prend très au sérieux, l'opéra, le théâtre, les conférences, les librairies. Comme dans les autres villes de la France il y a le goût de la science, et le gout de l'art.

Mais après tout, la vraie gloire de Nice est sa situation. Elle se lève de la mer bleue aux collines ornées de villas fleuries jusqu'aux pieds des montagnes couvertes de neige. Le ciel est d'un bleu intense comme la mer. L'air est doux, embaumé.

Tout y est pour rendre le monde heureux.

ENGLISH-FRENCH DICTIONARY

There are a few conventions used in this text's dictionary, which are important to highlight: 1. Gender of nouns is given by including le or la in the French translation. Only when the noun is listed in the plural form les, or requires l' due to its first letter being a vowel or mute h, will the abbreviations m and f appear to indicate masculine or feminine.   2. In the English-French part of the dictionary, a verb is given in the infinitive form in French, although the word to does not appear before the English verb that precedes it. By contrast, in the French-English section, French verbs will be translated by to + verb in the English following.   3. French adjectives whose feminine forms are created by merely adding a silent e, or whose masculine forms already end in silent e, will appear just in the masculine form. However, if there are other patterns in spelling the feminine endings, both masculine and feminine forms should appear. The same omission and inclusion just described also occur if the plural form of the adjective is created by adding s or if the masculine form of the adjective ends in s. There are a number of nouns that have special endings for the feminine and the plural: these will follow the same rule as the adjectives.

Please be aware that these pages constitute even less than a "starter dictionary." The meaning(s) of words are chosen most often by how they were used in the dialogues or supplemental stories. There are many good bilingual dictionaries to be found in large and small bookstores, retail and used. However, I (ed.) would discourage pocket dictionaries; your selection should be long enough to give an example for each major meaning of a word. In general, these dictionaries will cost no more than $15; however, if you plan to continue French study and usage, purchase a dictionary that has been published or revised no earlier than 2000, since there are so many new terms regularly entering both languages.

A

a (an) un, une
able capable
able (to be) *v* pouvoir
aboard: all aboard! en voiture!
about de; sur; autour de *(around)*; **What's it about?** De quoi s'agit-il?
above au dessus de; en haut
absolutely absolument
accept *v* accepter
accident l'accident *m*
accompany *v* accompagner
accomplish *v* accomplir
according to selon
accurate juste, exact
accustomed: to get accustomed to s'habituer à
acquaintance la connaissance; **to make the acquaintance of** faire la connaissance de

acquainted with (to be) connaître
across en travers, à travers
active actif, active
actor l'acteur *m*, l'actrice *f*; le comédien, la comédienne
actually réellement
add *v* ajouter, additionner
address l'adresse *f*
address *v* adresser
admire *v* admirer
admission l'entrée *f*
admit *v* admettre
adore *v* adorer
adorned orné
advance *v* avancer
advantage l'avantage *m*
advertise *v* annoncer
advertisement l'annonce *f*

advice le conseil

advise *v* conseiller

affair l'affaire *f*

afraid (to be) avoir peur

after ensuite, après

afternoon l'après-midi *m*, **in the afternoon** (p.m.) de l'après-midi

afterward après

again encore

against contre

age l'âge *m*

agent l'agent *m*, le représentant

ago il y a; **ten years ago** il y a dix ans

agree to *v* consentir à; être d'accord

agreeable agréable

agreed entendu, d'accord

aid *v* aider

air l'air *m*; **in the open air** en plein air

airmail par avion

airplane l'avion *m*

airport l'aéroport *m*

alike pareil, pareille; semblable

all tout, toute, tous, toutes; **not at all** pas du tout; **all right** parfait, entendu

allow *v* permettre

allowed permis

almost presque

alone seul

along le long de

already déjà

also aussi

although bien que; quoique

always toujours

ambassador l'ambassadeur *m*

ambitious ambitieux, ambitieuse

American américain; l'Américain (the American)

among parmi

amount la somme

amuse *v* amuser

and et; **and so on** ainsi de suite

angry fâché **to get angry** se fâcher

animal l'animal *m*

announce *v* annoncer

annoy *v* ennuyer

another un autre, une autre; **one more** encore un (une)

answer la réponse

answer *v* répondre

any quelque; de *(partitive)*; **anybody, anyone** quelqu'un

anything quelque chose

apartment l'appartement *m*

appear *v* apparaître; paraître *(to seem)*

appetite l'appétit *m*

apple la pomme

appointment le rendez-vous

appreciate *v* apprécier

approach *v* s'approcher de

April avril *m*

arise *v* se lever

arm le bras

around autour de

arrange *v* arranger

arrival l'arrivée *f*

arrive *v* arriver

art l'art *m*

article l'article *m*

artist l'artiste *m/f*

artistic artistique

as . . . as aussi . . . que; **as well as** aussi bien que; **as little as** aussi peu que; **as much as** autant que; **as long as** tant que; **as if** comme si

ashtray le cendrier

ask (for) *v* demander

ask (questions) *v* poser des questions

asleep endormi

assist *v* aider à

assortment l'assortiment *m*

assure *v* assurer

astonish *v* étonner

astute astucieux, astucieuse

at à; **at first** d'abord; **at last** enfin; **at once** tout de suite; **at home** chez moi, chez soi, etc.

attention l'attention *f*; **pay attention to** *v* faire attention à

August août *m*

aunt la tante

author l'auteur *m*

automobile l'automobile *f*, l'auto *f*; la voiture

autumn l'automne *m*

avenue l'avenue *f*

awake éveillé

awaken *v* réveiller

away absent; **to go away** s'en aller

B

baby le bébé, l'enfant *m/f*

back le dos *(body);* **to be back** être de retour; **in back of** derrière

backwards en arrière

bad mauvais

badly mal

baggage les bagages (m)

baker le boulanger

bakery la boulangerie

ball la balle, le ballon

banana la banane

bank la banque, la rive *(river)*

bar la buvette *(drinking)*

barber le barbier

bargain *v* marchander

basket le panier

bath le bain; **bathroom** la salle de bain

bathe *v* se baigner

be *v* être; **be hungry** avoir faim; **be right** avoir raison; **be wrong** avoir tort; **be sleepy** avoir sommeil; **be thirsty** avoir soif; **be in the act of** être en train de

beautiful beau, bel, belle

because parce que

become *v* devenir

bed le lit

bedroom la chambre à coucher

beef le boeuf; **beefsteak** le bifteck

beer la bière

before avant *(time)* devant *(place)*

begin *v* commencer; se mettre à

beginning le commencement

behind derrière

believe *v* croire

bell la cloche; **housebell** la sonnette

below en bas

belt la ceinture

bench le banc

besides d'ailleurs

best le meilleur *adj;* le mieux *adv*

better meilleur *adj;* mieux *adv;* **so much the better** tant mieux

between entre

bicycle la bicyclette, le vélo

big grand

bill la note *(at hotels);* le compte, l'addition *(at restaurants);* **bill of fare** le menu

birthday l'anniversaire *m*

bit (a) un peu

black noir

blanket la couverture

blouse la blouse

blow le coup

blue bleu

boat le bateau

body le corps

book le livre

bookstore la librairie

born (to be) *v* naître; **born** né(e)

borrow *v* emprunter

both les deux

bottle la bouteille

bottom le bas; le fond

box la boîte

boy le garçon

bracelet le bracelet

brake *n* le frein; *v* freiner

brandy le cognac, l'eau de vie *f*

brave courageux, courageuse

bread le pain

break *v* casser; rompre

breakfast le petit déjeuner; **to have breakfast** prendre le petit déjeuner

breathe *v* respirer

brief bref, brève

bright clair

bring *v* apporter; **bring back** rapporter

broad large

broken cassé

brother le frère

brown brun

brush *n* la brosse; *v* brosser

build construire; bâtir

building l'immeuble *m,* le bâtiment

burn *v* brûler

bus l'autobus *m*

business l'affaire *f;* **in business** dans les affaires; **to do business in** faire le commerce de

businessman, -woman l'homme, la femme d'affaires

busy occupé
but mais
butcher le boucher
butcher shop la boucherie
butter le beurre
buy *v* acheter
buyer l'acheteur *m*
by par

C

cab le taxi
cake le gâteau
calendar le calendrier
call *v* appeler; **to be called** s'appeler
calm calme
camera l'appareil photographique *m*
can la boîte de conserve
can (to be able) *v* pouvoir
candy store la confiserie
capital city la capitale
car la voiture *(auto)*; le wagon *(railroad)*; le tram *(streetcar)*; **by car** en voiture
card la carte; **postcard** la carte postale
care le soin; **take care of** s'occuper de, soigner
carry *v* porter; **carry away** emporter
case le cas; la caisse *(box)*; **in any case** en tout cas
cashier le caissier
castle le château, les châteaux
cat le chat
catch *v* attraper; **catch cold** attraper un rhume
cause la cause; la raison
cease *v* cesser
ceiling le plafond
celebrate *v* célébrer, fêter
center le centre
ceramics la céramique
certain certain; sûr
certificate le certificat
chair la chaise
chance la chance; **Good luck!** Bonne chance!
change *v* changer; **change money** changer de l'argent; **change (coins)** la monnaie
charm *v* enchanter; charmer
charming charmant; ravissant
chat *v* causer
cheap bon marché

cheaper meilleur marché
check le chèque
check *v* vérifier; contrôler
cheerful gai
cheese le fromage
chicken le poulet
child l'enfant *m/f*
chocolate le chocolat
choose *v* choisir
Christmas la Noël
church l'église *f*
cigar le cigare
circle le cercle
city la ville; **to the city (downtown)** en ville
city hall l'hôtel de ville *m*
class la classe; la sorte
clean propre
clear clair
clerk l'employé de bureau *m*
clever habile, adroit
climate le climat
clock l'horloge *f*
close *v* fermer
closed fermé
cloth l'étoffe *f*; le drap
clothe *v* habiller
clothes les vêtements *m*; les habits *m*
club le cercle; le club
coast la côte
coat le manteau; **overcoat** le pardessus; **raincoat** l'imperméable *m*
coffee le café
cold froid; **It (weather) is cold.** Il fait froid; **I am cold.** J'ai froid; **I have a cold.** Je suis enrhumé.
color la couleur; **What is the color of . . . ?** De quelle couleur est . . . ?
comb *n* le peigne; *v* peigner
come *v* venir; **come back** revenir; **come in** entrer
comfortable confortable, commode
commerce le commerce
common courant; ordinaire
companion le copain, la copine
compare *v* comparer
complete complet, complète
compliment le compliment
computer l'ordinateur *m*

concern la maison *(business);* **That does not concern (*v*) me.** Cela ne me regarde pas.

concert le concert

conduct *v* conduire

conductor le receveur *(on train, bus, etc.)*

confess *v* avouer

confidentially entre nous

congratulate *v* féliciter

congratulation la félicitation

consent *v* consentir

consequently par conséquent

considerable considérable

consist of *v* consister en, à

contain *v* contenir

content (to be) être content; être satisfait

continue *v* continuer

contrary le contraire; **on the contrary** au contraire

contribute *v* contribuer

conversation la conversation

cook *n* le cuisinier; *v* cuire; faire la cuisine

cookbook le livre de recettes

cool frais, fraiche; **It (weather) is cool.** Il fait frais.

corner le coin

correct correct; exact; **That's right.** C'est correct.

correspondence la correspondance

cost *n* le prix; **cost** *v* coûter

costume le costume

cotton le coton

count *v* compter

country la campagne *(opposite of city);* le pays *(nation)*

course le cours; le plat *(of meal);* **Of course!** Bien entendu! Mais oui!

cousin le cousin, la cousine

cover *n* la couverture; *v* couvrir

covered couvert

cream la crème

cross *v* traverser

crowd la foule

cry *v* crier, s'écrier *(shout);* pleurer *(weep)*

cup la tasse

curiosity la curiosité

custom l'usage *m;* la coutume

customary habituel, habituelle

customer le client

customhouse, customs la douane

customs official le douanier

cut *v* couper

D

daily quotidien, quotidienne

dairy la laiterie

dance *n* la danse, le bal; *v* danser

dangerous dangereux, dangereuse

darling (my) mon chéri; ma chérie

date la date

daughter la fille

day le jour, la journée; **day after tomorrow** après-demain; **day before yesterday** avant-hier

dead mort

dear cher, chère

death la mort

December décembre *m*

decide *v* décider

declare *v* déclarer

deed le fait; l'action *f*

delay *v* tarder

delicious délicieux, délicieuse

delighted ravi, enchanté

delightful ravissant

deliver *v* livrer

demand *v* exiger

dentist le dentiste

department le département

department store le grand magasin

departure le départ

descend *v* descendre

describe *v* décrire

description la description

design le dessin

desire le désir; l'envie *f;* **to have a desire to (a mind to)** avoir envie de

desk le bureau

dessert le dessert

detain *v* retenir

develop *v* développer

devoted dévoué

dictionary le dictionnaire

die *v* mourir

difference la différence

different différent

difficult difficile

difficulty la difficulté
dine *v* dîner
dining room la salle à manger
dinner le dîner
direction la direction
dirty sale
disagreeable désagréable
disappear *v* disparaître
discontented with mécontent de
discover *v* découvrir
discuss *v* discuter
dish le plat; l'assiette *f* (plate)
distance la distance
distribute *v* distribuer
district le quartier
divide *v* diviser
do *v* faire
doctor le médecin, le docteur
dog le chien
door la porte
doubt le doute
downstairs en bas
downtown le centre, en ville
dozen la douzaine
drama le drame
dream *v* rêver; **dream of** *v* songer à
dress *n* la robe; *v* habiller; s'habiller
dress designer le couturier
dressmaker le couturier
dressmaking la couture
drink *n* la boisson; **drink** *v* boire
drive *v* conduire (a *car*)
driver le chauffeur
drop *v* laisser tomber (Lit. *let fall*)
drugstore la pharmacie
dry sec, sèche
duck le canard
during pendant; durant
duty le devoir
dwell *v* demeurer
dye *v* teindre

E

each chaque *adj*; chacun, chacune *pron*
ear l'oreille *f*
early de bonne heure; tôt

earn *v* gagner
earth la terre
easily facilement
east l'est *m*
Easter Pâques *f pl*; **Happy Easter** Joyeuses Pâques
easy facile
eat *v* manger
edge le bord; **at the edge of** au bord de
effect l'effet *m*
effort l'effort *m*
egg l'oeuf *m*
either l'un ou l'autre; **either . . . or** ou . . . ou
electric(al) électrique
elegant élégant
elevator l'ascenseur *m*
else: someone else quelqu'un d'autre
embassy l'ambassade *f*
embroidered brodé
employee l'employé *m*; l'employée *f*
empty vide
end la fin
end *v* terminer
England l'Angleterre
English anglais; l'anglais *(language)*; l'Anglais *(Englishman)*
enjoy *v* jouir de; **enjoy oneself** s'amuser
enough assez
enter *v* entrer (dans)
entirely tout à fait
envelope l'enveloppe *f*
equal égal
erase *v* effacer
especially surtout
essential essentiel, essentielle
estimate *v* estimer
etc. et cetera
European européenne; l'Européen *(the European)*
even même; **even though** quand même
evening le soir; **Good evening!** Bonsoir; **yesterday evening** hier soir, **tomorrow evening** demain soir; **this evening** ce soir
ever jamais; toujours
every chaque; **every day** tous les jours
everybody tout le monde
everyone chacun, chacune
everything tout

everywhere partout

exact précis, exact

examine *v* examiner

exceed *v* dépasser

excellent excellent

except sauf, excepté

excite *v* exciter; agiter

exclaim *v* s'écrier

excursion l'excursion *f*

excuse *v* excuser; **Excuse me!** Excusez-moi! Pardon-nez-moi!

exit la sortie

expect *v* espérer; attendre

explain *v* expliquer

express l'express *(train)*

exquisite exquis

extra en plus, supplémentaire

eye l'oeil *m*; les yeux *pl*

eyeglasses les lunettes *f pl*

F

face la figure; le visage

fact le fait; **in fact** en effet

factory l'usine *f*; la fabrique

fail *v* manquer; **Do not fail to write me.** Ne manquez pas de m'écrire; **without fail** sans faute

fall *n* la chute; *v* tomber

false faux, fausse

family la famille

famous célèbre

far loin; **as far as** jusqu'à

fare le prix de la place; le prix du voyage

farther plus loin

farthest le plus éloigné

fashion la mode

fashionable à la mode

fast *adj* vite, rapide; *adv* vite, rapidement

fasten *v* attacher

fat gros, grosse; gras, grasse

father le père

fault la faute

favor *n* le service; **do a favor** rendre un service

fear *n* la peur; *v* avoir peur; craindre

feather la plume

February février *m*

feel *v* sentir; **He feels at home.** Il se sent chez lui. **How do you feel?** (health) Comment vous portez-vous?

feeling le sentiment

fetch *v* apporter; aller chercher

few peu; **few people** peu de gens

field le champ

figure *v* calculer

fill *v* remplir; **fill the tank with gas** faire le plein d'essence.

film le film

finally enfin; finalement

find *v* trouver

fine *adj* fin; *n* l'amende *(money)*

finger le doigt

finish *v* finir; terminer

fire le feu, l'incendie

firm *adj* ferme; *n* la maison *(business)*

first le premier, la première; **at first** d'abord

fish le poisson

fit convenable *(suitable)*

fit *v* aller à; **This dress fits me well.** Cette robe me va bien.

flat plat; **I have a flat tire.** Je suis à plat.

flatter *v* flatter; **You flatter me.** Vous êtes trop aimable.

flavor le goût; la saveur

flight le vol

floor le plancher; l'étage *m (story)*

flour la farine

flower la fleur

fly *v* voler

follow *v* suivre

following suivant

fond of (to be) aimer; être friand de *(foods)*

food la nourriture; les vivres *m pl*, les victuailles *f pl*

foot le pied; **on foot** à pied

for pour; **for me** pour moi; car *(since, because)*

force *n* la force; *v* forcer

foreigner l'étranger, l'etrangère

forest la forêt

forget *v* oublier

forgive *v* pardonner

fork la fourchette

form la forme

form *v* former

formality la formalité
former (the) celui-là, celle-là, ceux-là, celles-là
formerly autrefois
fortunate heureux, heureuse
fortunately heureusement
forward en avant
found trouvé
fountain la fontaine, le jet d'eau
fountain pen le stylo
fragrant parfumé
frame *n* le cadre; *v* encadrer
franc le franc
free libre, gratis, gratuit
French français; le français *(language)*; le Français (Frenchman)
frequently souvent, fréquemment
fresh frais, fraîche
Friday vendredi
friend l'ami, l'amie
friendly aimable
frighten *v* effrayer
from de
front le devant; **in front of** devant
fruit le fruit
full plein
fun l'amusement *m;* **have fun** s'amuser
funny drôle
fur la fourrure
furious furieux, furieuse
furnish *v* meubler *(a room)*
furnished meublé
furniture les meubles
further plus loin
future l'avenir *m;* **in the future** à l'avenir

G

gaiety la gaîeté
gain *v* gagner
gamble *v* jouer
gambler le joueur
game le jeu: la partie
garage le garage
garden le jardin
gasoline l'essence *f;* **gasoline station** le poste d'essence
gate la porte
gay gai

gem la pierre précieuse
general général; **in general** en général; **general delivery** poste restante
generous généreux, généreuse
gentle doux, douce
gentleman le monsieur; **gentlemen** les messieurs; **ladies and gentlemen** mesdames et messieurs
genuine authentique
geography la géographie
German allemand; l'allemand *(language);* l'Allemand *(the German)*
Germany l'Allemagne *f*
get *v* obtenir; recevoir; **to get acquainted with** *v* se familiariser avec
get into *v* monter (en voiture)
get up *v* se lever
gift le cadeau
girl la fille
give *v* donner
give back *v* rendre
glad content, heureux
gladly volontiers
glass le verre; **fine glass** le cristal
glitter *v* briller
glove le gant
go *v* aller
go away *v* s'en aller
go back *v* retourner
go down *v* descendre
go home *v* rentrer
go in *v* entrer
go out *v* sortir
go to bed *v* se coucher
go to sleep *v* s'endormir
go up *v* monter
God Dieu *m*
gold l'or *m*
good *adj* bon, bonne; *adv* bien; **Good morning!** Bonjour! **Good afternoon!** Bonjour! **Good evening!** Bonsoir! **Good night!** Bonne nuit! Bonsoir!
goodbye au revoir; adieu; **bid goodbye to** faire ses adieux à
goodness la bonté
goods la marchandise
grand magnifique
granddaughter la petite-fille

grandfather le grand-père
grandmother la grand-mère
grandson le petit-fils
grant *v* accorder
grape le raisin
grasp *v* saisir
grateful reconnaissant
gray gris
great grand
green vert
greet *v* saluer
greeting la salutation
grocer l'épicier *m*
grocery store l'épicerie *f*
ground la terre
group le groupe
guard le garde *v* garder
guess *v* deviner
guide *n* le guide; *v* guider

H

hair les cheveux
hairdo la coiffure
hairdresser le coiffeur, la coiffeuse
half *adj* demi; *n* la moitié
ham le jambon
hand la main; **shake hands** se serrer la main
handbag le sac à main
handkerchief le mouchoir
handsome beau, bel, belle
happen *v* arriver; se passer; **What is happening?** Qu'est-ce qui se passe?
happy heureux, heureuse
hard difficile *(difficult)*; dur *(not soft)*
hat le chapeau
have *v* avoir; **have to** *(must)* *v* devoir; **have something done** *v* faire
he il
head la tête
headache mal à la tête; **I have a headache.** J'ai mal à la tête.
health la santé; **Here's to your health!** À votre santé!
hear *v* entendre
heart le coeur
heaven le ciel; **Good Heavens!** Mon Dieu!
heavy lourd
help *v* aider

her la; lui; son, sa, ses
here ici; **here is (are)** voici
herself se; elle-même
high haut
him le; lui
himself se; lui-même
hire *v* louer
his son, sa, ses; à lui; le sien, la sienne, les siens, les siennes
history l'histoire *f*
hold *v* tenir
holiday le jour de fête; **vacation holidays** les vacances *m*
home la maison; **at home** à la maison; chez moi, chez lui, etc.
hope *v* espérer
horse le cheval, les chevaux
horseback *v* à cheval
hospital l'hôpital *m*, la clinique
hot chaud; **It (weather) is hot.** Il fait chaud. **I am hot.** J'ai chaud.
hotel l'hôtel *m*
hour l'heure *f*
house la maison
how comment; combien; **How are you?** Comment allez-vous? **How much does that cost?** Combien cela coûte-t-il? **How much money?** Combien d'argent? **How many books?** Combien de livres? **How often?** Combien de fois? **How pretty!** Que c'est joli!
however cependant; pourtant
hundred cent
hunger la faim
hungry (to be) avoir faim
hurry *v* se dépêcher, se hâter; **I am in a hurry.** Je suis pressé.
hurt *v* faire mal à
husband le mari

I

I je; moi
ice cream la glace
if si; **if not** sinon
ill malade
illustration l'illustration *f*
imagine *v* s'imaginer
immediately tout de suite; immédiatement

imperfect défectueux, défectueuse
import *v* importer
important important
importer l'importateur *m*
impossible impossible
in dans; en
inch le pouce
included compris
incorrect inexact
increase *v* augmenter
incredible incroyable
indeed en effet; vraiment; **Yes, indeed!** Mais oui!
indicate *v* indiquer
indispensable indispensable
industrious diligent
industry l'industrie *f*
infant le petit enfant; le bébé
influence l'influence *f*
inform *v* informer; faire savoir
information les renseignements *f pl;* **He asks for information.** Il demande des renseignements.
inhabit *v* habiter
ink l'encre *f*
inn l'auberge *f*
inquire *v* prendre des renseignements
inside dedans
insist *v* insister
instantly à l'instant
instead of au lieu de
instruct *v* enseigner
instrument l'instrument *m*
intelligent intelligent
intend *v* avoir l'intention de; compter (faire quelque chose)
interest l'intérêt *m;* **to be interested in** s'intéresser à
interesting intéressant
into dans; en
introduce *v* présenter
invitation l'invitation *f*
invite *v* inviter
irritate *v* irriter; agacer
it il, elle, ce; **It's late.** Il est tard. **It's five o'clock.** Il est cinq heures. **It's true.** C'est vrai.
Italian italien; l'italien *(language);* l'Italien, l'Italienne *(the Italian)*
Italy l'Italie *f*

its son, sa, ses
itself se; lui-même; elle-même

J

jacket la veste; le veston
January janvier *m*
jewel le bijou, les bijoux
joke la plaisanterie
joke *v* plaisanter
journey le voyage
joyous joyeux
judge le juge
juice le jus; **orange juice** le jus d'orange
July juillet *m*
jump *v* sauter
June juin *m*
just juste; **I have just eaten.** Je viens de manger.

K

keep *v* garder
key la clef
kill *v* tuer
kind *adj* gentil, aimable; *n* la sorte
kindly: Will you kindly . . . ? Voulez-vous bien . . . ?
kindness la bonté
kiss *n* le baiser; *v* embrasser
kitchen la cuisine
knife le couteau
knock *v* frapper
know *v* savoir *(to have knowledge of, to know how);* connaître *(to be acquainted with)*

L

lack *v* manquer; **I lack nothing.** Je ne manque de rien.
lady la dame; **ladies and gentlemen** mesdames et messieurs
lamb l'agneau *m;* **leg of lamb** le gigot
lamp la lampe
land *v* atterrir *(airplane);* débarquer *(ship)*
landscape le paysage
language la langue; le langage
large grand; gros, grosse
last le dernier, la dernière; **last night** hier soir
late tard; en retard
laugh *v* rire; **They laugh at him.** Ils se rient de lui.

laundry la blanchisserie
lay v poser
lazy paresseux, paresseuse
lead v conduire
leap v sauter
learn v apprendre
least le moins; **at least** au moins
leather le cuir
leave v partir; quitter
left gauche; **to the left** à gauche
leg la jambe
lemon le citron
lemonade la limonade
lend v prêter
length la longueur
less moins; **less than five** moins de cinq
lesson la leçon
let v permettre *(permit)*
letter la lettre
library la bibliothèque
lie v mentir *(tell a lie)*
lie down v se coucher
life la vie
lift v lever
light la lumière
like *adv* comme; *adj* pareil, pareille; *v* aimer; vouloir;
  I would like je voudrais
likewise également; aussi
linen le lin; le linge
liner le paquebot
lip la lèvre
list *n* la liste
listen v écouter
little petit; peu de; **little money** peu d'argent
live v vivre; habiter, demeurer *(dwell)*
lively gai; vif, vive
living room le salon
long long, longue; **He left a long time ago.** Il est
  parti il y a longtemps.
look v regarder; chercher *(look for)*; **Look out!** Attention!
lose v perdre
lost perdu
lot beaucoup; **a lot of people** beaucoup de monde
loud haut, fort; **in a loud voice, aloud** à haute voix
love *n* l'amour *f*; *v* aimer; **in love** amoureux, amoureuse

lovely charmant
low bas, basse *f*
luck la chance
lucky heureux, heureuse
luggage les bagages *m*
lunch le déjeuner; **I have lunch.** Je prends le déjeuner.

M

madam madame
magazine la revue
magnificent magnifique
maid la bonne
mail le courrier
majority la majorité, la plupart
make v faire
man l'homme *m*
manner la manière
manufacture v fabriquer
many beaucoup; **many others** beaucoup d'autres
map la carte
March mars *m*
market le marché
marvelous merveilleux, merveilleuse
match *n* l'allumette *f*
matter l'affaire; la chose; **in the matter of** au sujet de,
  quant à; **It does not matter.** N'importe.
mattress le matelas
May mai *m*
may pouvoir *(be able)*
me me; moi
meal le repas
mean v vouloir dire
meanwhile (in the) en attendant
measure la mesure
measure v mesurer
meat la viande
mechanic le mécanicien
medicine le médicament
meet v rencontrer
meeting la rencontre; le rendez-vous; la réunion
  (many people)
memory la mémoire; le souvenir
mend v raccommoder, réparer
merchandise la marchandise
merchant le marchand, le commerçant

message le message
metal le métal
middle le milieu; **in the middle of** au milieu de
midnight minuit *m*
mild doux, douce
milk le lait
million le million
mind l'esprit *m*; **I have a mind to** j'ai envie de
mine à moi; le mien, la mienne, les miens, les miennes
minute la minute; **Wait a minute!** Attendez un instant!
mirror le miroir
miscellaneous divers
misfortune le malheur
Miss mademoiselle
miss *v* manquer; **I shall miss you.** Vous me manquerez.
mistake la faute
mistaken (to be) *v* se tromper
Mister monsieur
mode la mode
model le modèle
modern moderne
moment le moment; **Just a moment!** Un instant!
Monday lundi
money l'argent; la monnaie *(coins)*
money order le mandat-poste
month le mois
moon la lune
more plus; **more than** plus que, plus de *(before a number)*; **not any more** ne . . . plus
morning le matin; la matinée; **in the morning (a.m.)** du matin
most le (la) plus; **most of the people** la plupart des gens; **for the most part** pour la plupart
mother la mère; la maman
motor *n* le moteur; *v* aller en auto
mountain la montagne
mouth la bouche
move *v* bouger; déménager *(to new home)*
movies le ciné; le cinéma
much beaucoup; **much more** beaucoup plus
museum le musée
music la musique
musician le musicien
must *v* devoir; falloir; **I must (ought to) do it.** Je dois le faire. **I must (have to) go.** Il me faut aller.

my mon, ma, mes
myself me; moi-même

N

name le nom; **What is your name?** Comment vous appelez-vous?
namely c'est-à-dire
napkin la serviette
narrow étroit
nation la nation
naturally naturellement
nature la nature
near près de; proche
nearly presque; à peu près
neat propre
necessary nécessaire; **It is necessary** il faut
neck le cou
necklace le collier
necktie la cravate
need *v* avoir besoin de
neglect *v* négliger
neighbor le voisin
neither non plus; **neither . . . nor** ne . . . ni . . . ni
never ne . . . jamais
nevertheless tout de même
new nouveau, nouvel, nouvelle; neuf, neuve
news les nouvelles; **What's the news?** Quelles sont les nouvelles? **What's new?** Quoi de neuf? **news program or newsreel** les actualités *f pl*
nice gentil, gentille
night la nuit; le soir
no non; **No parking!** Défense de stationner! **No Smoking!** Défense de fumer!
nobody personne; ne . . . personne
noise le bruit
none ne . . . aucun
noon le midi
nor, neither . . . nor ne . . . ni . . . ni
north le nord
nose le nez
not ne . . . pas; ne . . . point
notebook le cahier
nothing ne . . . rien
notice *v* remarquer
notify *v* avertir
November novembre *m*
now maintenant; **now and then** de temps en temps

nowhere nulle part
number le nombre; le numéro

O

obey *v* obéir
object l'objet *m*
oblige *v* obliger
observe *v* observer
obtain *v* obtenir
occupation le métier; l'occupation *f*
October octobre *m*
of de; **of it, of them** en; **I have some** *(of it, of them).* J'en ai.
offer *v* offrir
office le bureau
officer l'officier *m*
often souvent; **quite often** assez souvent
oil l'huile *f*
old ancien, ancienne; vieux, vieil, vieille; **How old are you?** Quel âge avez-vous?
once une fois; **at once** tout de suite; **all at once** tout à coup; **once more** encore une fois
one un, une; on *(people, you)* **How does one say?** Comment dit-on?
only seul; seulement; ne . . . que
open *adj* ouvert; *v* ouvrir
opera l'opéra *m*
opposite en face de, vis-à-vis
or ou; **either . . . or** ou . . . ou
order *n* l'ordre *m*, la commande; **in order to** afin de; *v* commander
ordinary ordinaire, banal
other autre
otherwise sinon
our notre, nos
out dehors
outside dehors; hors de
over dessus; au dessus de
overcoat le pardessus
owe *v* devoir
own *adj* propre; *v* posséder

P

pack *v* emballer; **He packs his bags.** Il fait ses valises.
pain *n* mal; *v* faire mal à
painting la peinture
pair la paire

pale pâle
pancake la crêpe
pants le pantalon
paper le papier
parcel le paquet
parcel post le colis postal
pardon *v* pardonner
park le parc
park *v* stationner *(a car)*
part la partie
pass *v* passer
passenger le voyageur, le passager
passport le passeport
past passé; **the past week** la semaine passée
pastry shop la pâtisserie
pause *n* la pause; *v* faire une pause
pay *v* payer
pea le petit pois
pear la poire
pearl la perle
pedestrian le piéton
pen la plume
pencil le crayon
people le peuple: les gens; on
perceive *v* apercevoir
percent pourcent
perfect parfait; **Perfect!** Parfait! Très bien!
performance la représentation; la séance
perfume le parfum
perhaps peut-être
permit *v* permettre
permitted permis
person la personne
pharmacy la pharmacie
photograph *n* la photo; **take a photograph** prendre or faire une photo
physician le médecin
pick up *v* ramasser
picture *n* le tableau. l'image *f*
piece le morceau; la pièce
pillow l'oreiller *m*
pin l'épingle *f*
pitcher *(milk)* le pot au lait
pity la pitié **What a pity!** Quel dommage!
place l'endroit *m*; le lieu; **to take place** avoir lieu; **in place of** au lieu de
plane *(air)* l'avion *m*

plate l'assiette *f*

play *n* la pièce de théâtre; *v* jouer

pleasant agréable

please *v* plaire; *(If you)* **please.** S'il vous plaît. **That pleases me.** Cela me plaît.

pleasure le plaisir

pocket la poche

point le point; **on the point of departure** sur le point de partir

police la police

policeman l'agent de police *m*

politely poliment

poor pauvre

porter le porteur

portrait le portrait

possess *v* posséder

possible possible

poster l'affiche *f*

postman le facteur

post office la poste; le bureau de poste

potato la pomme de terre

pottery la poterie

pound la livre

powder la poudre

practice *v* pratiquer

praise *v* louer

pray *v* prier

precede *v* précéder

precious précieux, précieuse

prefer *v* préférer; aimer mieux

prepare *v* préparer

present *n* le cadeau; *adv* présent; **at present** actuellement; **to be present at** assister à; *v* offrir, présenter

press *v* presser; **press clothes** repasser des vêtements

pretty joli

price le prix

prize le prix

probably probablement; sans doute

produce *v* produire

profession la profession

professor le professeur

profit le profit

program le programme

prohibit *v* défendre

promise *v* promettre

pronounce *v* prononcer

propose *v* proposer

protect *v* protéger

provided that pourvu que

publish *v* éditer, publier

publisher l'éditeur *m*

pull *v* tirer

punish *v* punir

pupil l'élève *m/f*

purchase *n* l'achat *m*; l'emplette *f*; *v* acheter

purchaser l'acheteur, acheteuse

purse le porte-monnaie

push *v* pousser

put *v* mettre; poser; **to put on** mettre

Q

quality la qualité

quantity la quantité

quarter le quart; le quartier *(neighborhood)*

question *n* la question; *v* poser des questions

quick rapide

quickly rapidement; vite

quiet *adj* tranquille; calme **Keep quiet!** Restez tranquille! *v* calmer

quit *v* quitter

quite tout à fait; **quite often** assez souvent

quote *v* citer

R

radio la radio

railroad le chemin de fer

rain la pluie

rain *v* pleuvoir; **It is raining.** Il pleut.

raincoat l'imperméable *m*

raise *v* lever; élever

rapid rapide

rapidly rapidement

rate le tarif

rather plûtot; **rather than** plûtot que; **I would rather** j'aimerais mieux

razor le rasoir

reach *v* arriver

read *v* lire

ready prêt

realize *v* comprendre; se rendre compte de

really vraiment; en vérité

rear le fond; **in the rear** au fond

reason la raison

recall *v* se rappeler *(remember)*

receipt la quittance

receive recevoir

recognize *v* reconnaître

recommend *v* recommander

recommendation la recommendation

record le disque *(phonograph)*; *v* enregistrer

recover *v* se remettre *(health)*

red rouge

reference la référence; **in reference to** à propos de

reflect *v* réfléchir

refreshment le rafraîchissement

refund *v* rembourser

refuse *v* refuser

regards: give my regards to faites mes amitiés à

regret *v* regretter

relate *v* raconter

relative le parent

rely upon *v* compter sur

remainder le reste

remarkable remarquable

remember *v* se rappeler; se souvenir de

remembrance le souvenir

remove *v* enlever

rent *v* louer

repair *v* réparer

repeat *v* répéter

reply *n* la réponse; *v* répondre

represent *v* représenter

representative le représentant

request *v* demander

require *v* exiger, demander, réclamer

resemble *v* ressembler à

reserve *v* retenir; réserver

residence la résidence; la maison

respect *n* le respect; *v* respecter

responsible responsable

rest le reste *(remainder)*; le repos *(repose)*; *v* se reposer

rested délassé

restless agité

result le résultat

retail en détail

retain *v* retenir

retire *v* se retirer; prendre sa retraite

return *n* le retour; *v* revenir *(come back)*; rendre *(give back)*; retourner (go *back)*

review la révision

rice le riz

rich riche

ride *v* se promener; **in a car, on a bicycle, on horse-back** en voiture, à bicyclette, à cheval

right droit; **to the right** à droite

right juste, exact; **That's right.** C'est exact (juste); **You are right.** Vous avez raison.

ring *n* l'anneau *m*, la bague, l'alliance *f* *(wedding ring)*; *v* sonner

river le fleuve, la rivière

road le chemin; la route

room la chambre

rough rude

round rond

route la route

row le rang

rubbers les caoutchoucs

ruler la règle *(measuring)*

rum le rhum

run *v* courir

S

sad triste

sadly tristement

safe sauf; **safe and sound** sain et sauf

sailor le marin

salad la salade

sale la vente

salesperson le vendeur

salt le sel

same même; **all the same** tout de même

sample l'échantillon *m*

satisfactory satisfaisant

satisfy *v* contenter; satisfaire

Saturday le samedi

sauce la sauce

saucer la soucoupe

sausage la saucisse, le saucisson

say *v* dire

scarcely à peine

scarf l'écharpe *f*, le foulard, le fichu

scene la scène

schedule l'horaire *m*

school l'école *f;* **to school** à l'école

scissors les ciseaux *m*

sea la mer; **at sea** en mer

seaport le port de mer

seashore la plage

season la saison

seat la place

seated assis

second le (la) deuxième

see *v* voir

seek *v* chercher

seem *v* sembler; paraître

seize *v* saisir

seldom rarement

sell *v* vendre

send *v* envoyer

sense le sens; **common sense** le bon sens

sentiment le sentiment

separate *v* séparer

September septembre *m*

serious sérieux, sérieuse

servant la bonne; le (la) domestique

serve *v* servir

set *v* mettre, placer; **set out** se mettre en route

several plusieurs

sew *v* coudre; **sewing** la couture

shake *v* secouer; **shake hands** se serrer la main

shape la forme

shave *v* se raser

shawl le châle

shine *v* briller

ship *v* expédier

shipment l'envoi *m*

shirt la chemise

shoe la chaussure, le soulier

shoemaker le cordonnier

shop la boutique

shop window la vitrine

shopping (to go) faire des achats, des courses

short court

shoulder l'épaule *f*

shout *v* crier

show *v* montrer

shut *adj* fermé; *v* fermer

sick malade

sickness la maladie

side le côté; **at the side of** à côté de

sidewalk le trottoir

signify *v* signifier

silence le silence

silk la soie; **a silk dress** une robe de soie

silken, silky soyeux, soyeuse

silver l'argent

similar semblable

simple simple

since depuis *(time);* puisque *(because)*

sincerely sincèrement; **Yours sincerely** Votre tout devoué

sing *v* chanter

singer le chanteur, la chanteuse

single seul; célibataire *(unmarried)*

sir monsieur

sister la soeur

sit *v* être assis; **sit down** s'asseoir; **Sit down.** Asseyez-vous.

size la taille; la grandeur

skin la peau

skirt la jupe

sky le ciel

sleep le sommeil

sleep *v* dormir; **fall asleep** s'endormir; **I am sleepy.** J'ai sommeil.

slowly lentement

small petit

smell *n* l'odeur *f;* *v* sentir

smile *n* le sourire; *v* sourire

smoke *n* la fumée; *v* fumer **No smoking!** Défense de fumer!

snapshot la photo

snow *n* la neige; *v* neiger

so (thus) ainsi; **and so forth** ainsi de suite

soap le savon

sock la chaussette

soft doux, douce *f*

software le logiciel

soldier le soldat

solid solide

some quelque, quelques; des

somebody quelqu'un

someone quelqu'un

something quelque chose

sometimes parfois

somewhere quelque part

son le fils

song la chanson

soon bientôt; **sooner** plus tôt; **as soon as possible** aussitôt que possible

sorry (to be) regretter

sort la sorte

sound le son

soup la soupe; le potage

south le sud; le Midi

southern du sud

Spain l'Espagne *f*

Spanish espagnol; l'espagnol *(language)*; l'Espagnol *(Spaniard)*

speak *v* parler

special delivery exprès

spectator le spectateur

speed la vitesse; **at full speed** à toute vitesse

spend *v* dépenser; passer *(time)*

spinach les épinards *m pl*

spirit l'esprit *m*

spit *v* cracher

splendid splendide

spoil *v* gâter

spoon la cuiller; la cuillère

sport le sport

spring le printemps; **in spring** au printemps

stairs l'escalier *m*

stamp le timbre *(postage)*

stand *v* être debout **Stand up!** Levez-vous!

starch l'amidon *m*; **No starch** Sans amidon

start *v* commencer

station la gare *(railroad)*

stay *n* le séjour *(visit)*; *v* rester

steak le bifteck

steamer le paquebot

steel l'acier *m*

stenographer le sténographe

step le pas

stick le bâton

still *adj* calme, tranquille; *adv* encore; toujours; **It is still raining.** Il pleut toujours.

stocking le bas; le collant *(pantyhose)*

stop *v* s'arrêter, cesser; **The taxi stops.** Le taxi s'arrête.

store le magasin; la boutique

story l'histoire *f*; l'étage *m* *(of house or building)*

straight droit

strange curieux, curieuse

stranger l'étranger, l'étrangère

strawberry la fraise

street la rue

strike *v* battre; frapper

stroll *v* faire une promenade (un tour)

strong fort

student l'étudiant *m*, l'étudiante *f*

studious diligent

study l'étude *f*; *v* étudier

stupid stupide

style le style; **in style** à la mode

subject le sujet; **change the subject** parler d'autre chose

suburbs la banlieue

succeed *v* réussir

success le succès; la réussite

such tel, telle, tels, telles; **such a man** un tel homme

suddenly tout à coup

suffer *v* souffrir

sufficient suffisant, **That's sufficient.** Cela suffit.

sugar le sucre

suggest *v* proposer

suit le costume; le complet; l'ensemble *m*

suitable convenable

sum la somme

summary le résumé

summer l'été *m*, **in summer** en été

sun le soleil

Sunday dimanche

supermarket le supermarché, le magasin à grande surface

supper le souper

suppose *v* supposer

sure sûr

surname nom de famille *m*

surprise *v* surprendre

surprised surpris

surroundings les environs *m*

sweater le chandail, le pullover

sweet doux, douce

swift rapide

swim *v* nager

sympathetic sympathique

T

table la table; **to set the table** mettre la table

tablecloth la nappe

tailor le tailleur

take *v* prendre; **take away** emporter

talk *v* parler; causer

tall grand

tank le réservoir; **fill the tank with gas** faire le plein d'essence

taste *n* le goût; *v* goûter

tax l'impôt *m*

taxi le taxi

tea le thé

telegram le télégramme

telegraph *v* télégraphier

telephone *n* le téléphone; *v* téléphoner, appeler: donner un coup de fil

television la télévision

tell *v* dire; raconter

temperature la température

text le texte

than que

thank *v* remercier

thanks merci; les remerciements

that ce, cet, cette; celui, celle; cela; qui, que

the le, la, les

theater le théâtre

their leur, leurs

theirs le leur, la leur, les leurs; à eux, à elles

them les, leur; eux, elles

then alors; puis; ensuite

there là; y; voilà; **There he is!** Le voilà! **There is (are)** il y a; **over there** là-bas

therefore donc

these ces; ceux, celles

they ils, elles

thick épais, épaisse

thing la chose; l'objet

think *v* penser; croire; **I think so.** Je crois que oui.

thirst la soif; **I'm thirsty.** J'ai soif.

this ce, cet, cette; **this one** celui-ci, celle-ci; ceci

thoroughly à fond

those ces; ceux, celles

though quoique

thought la pensée; l'idée *f*

thousand mille; mil *(dates)*

throat la gorge; **have a sore throat** avoir mal à la gorge

throw *v* jeter

thumb le pouce

Thursday jeudi

thus ainsi

ticket le billet; **one way ticket** le billet simple, le billet d'aller; **round-trip ticket** le billet d'aller-retour

ticket-window le guichet

time le temps; l'heure *f (hour)*; **from time to time** de temps en temps; **What time is it?** Quelle heure est-il? **to have a good time** s'amuser; **one time** une fois; la fois **How many times?** Combien de fois? **At times** parfois; **sometimes** quelquefois

timetable l'horaire *f*

tip *n* le pourboire *(gratuity)*: *v* donner un pourboire

tire le pneu *(car)*; **spare tire** le pneu de rechange

tired fatigué

tiresome ennuyeux, ennuyeuse

to à, en, vers, pour

tobacco le tabac

today aujourd'hui

together ensemble

tomato la tomate

tomorrow demain; **till tomorrow** à demain

tone le ton

tongue la langue

tonight ce soir

too aussi *(also)*; trop *(too much)*

tooth la dent

toothache mal aux dents

toothbrush la brosse à dents

toothpaste la (pâte) dentifrice

total *n* le total; le montant

touch *v* toucher

tour le tour; le voyage

tourist le (la) touriste

toward vers; envers

towel la serviette; **bath towel** la serviette de bain; **dishtowel** le torchon

town la ville

toy le jouet

traffic la circulation

train *n* le train

tranquil tranquille

translate *v* traduire

travel *v* voyager

traveler le voyageur

tray le plateau

treat *v* traiter

tree l'arbre *m*

tremendous énorme

trip le voyage; **to take a trip** faire un voyage

trouble *n* la difficulté; *v* déranger; inquiéter; **Don't trouble yourself!** Ne vous dérangez pas!

trousers le pantalon

true vrai

truly vraiment; **Yours truly,** Agréez, Monsieur, l'assurance de ma considération distinguée.

trunk la malle

truth la vérité

truthful sincère

try *v* essayer; tâcher

turn *v* tourner; **Turn left!** Prenez la première à gauche!

twice deux fois

U

ultimately à la fin

umbrella le parapluie

unbelievable incroyable

uncle l'oncle *m*

uncover *v* découvrir

under sous; au-dessous de

undergo *v* subir

understand *v* comprendre

undertake *v* l'entreprendre

undertaking l'entreprise *f*

undress (to) se déshabiller

unequal inégal

unexpected inattendu

unfair injuste

unfamiliar peu connu

unfortunately malheureusement

unheard of inouï

unite *v* unir

united uni

United States les États-Unis *m pl*

university l'université *f*

unknown inconnu

unless à moins que

unoccupied inoccupé; libre

unpack *v* déballer

unpleasant désagréable

unsatisfied mécontent

until jusqu'à; **until now** jusqu'à présent

up to jusqu'à

upon sur

upstairs en haut

us nous

use *v* se servir de

useful utile

useless inutile

usher *n* l'ouvreur *m*

usual ordinaire; **usually** d'ordinaire

utensil l'ustensile *m*

V

vacation les vacances

vain: in vain en vain

valise la valise

valley la vallée

valuable de valeur

varied varié

variety la variété

various divers

vase le vase

veal le veau; **veal stew** la blanquette de veau

vegetable le légume

verify *v* vérifier

very très

vicinity les environs

view *n* la vue; *v* voir

village le village

vinegar le vinaigre

visit *n* la visite; *v* visiter; rendre visite à

visitor le visiteur, la visiteuse

visa le visa

voice la voix; **in a loud voice** à haute voix; **in a low voice** à demi-voix

voyage le voyage

W

wages le salaire

wait *v* attendre; **wait for** attendre

waiter le garçon

wake *v* réveiller; se réveiller

walk *n* la promenade; *v* aller à pied; **go for a walk** se promener

wallet le portefeuille

wardrobe la garde-robe; l'armoire *f*

warm chaud; **It (weather) is warm.** Il fait chaud. **I am warm.** J'ai chaud.

wash *v* laver; **I wash (myself).** Je me lave.

washroom le cabinet de toilette

watch la montre

water l'eau *f*

way la manière; **by the way** à propos

we nous

weak faible

wear *v* porter

weather le temps **What's the weather?** Quel temps fait-il? **The weather is nice (bad).** Il fait beau (mauvais).

week la semaine; **twice a week** deux fois par semaine

weep *v* pleurer

weigh *v* peser

welcome bienvenu; **Welcome!** Soyez le bienvenu (la bienvenue)! **You're welcome (Don't mention it).** Il n'y a pas de quoi.

well bien; **Well!** Eh bien!

west l'ouest *m*

what *adj* quel, quelle, quels, quelles

what? *subject of verb* qu'est-ce qui?

what? *object of verb* que? qu'est-ce que?

what? *object of preposition* quoi?

when quand; lorsque

where où

whether si

which *adj* quel, quelle, quels, quelles

which *relative pronoun* qui, que

which *(that which)* ce qui. ce que

which one lequel, laquelle

which ones lesquels, lesquelles

while pendant que

white blanc *m* blanche *f*

who? *interrogative pronoun* qui? qui est-ce qui? *relative pronoun* qui

whom? *interrogative pronoun* qui? qui est-ce que? *relative pronoun* que

width la largeur

wife la femme

willingly volontiers

win *v* gagner

wind le vent; **It's windy.** Il fait du vent.

window la fenêtre

wine le vin

winter l'hiver *m*

wipe *v* essuyer

wise sage

wish *v* désirer; vouloir

with avec

withdraw se retirer

without sans; **do without** se passer de

woman la femme

wonder la merveille

wonderful merveilleux; merveilleuse **wonderfully** à merveille

wood(s) le bois

wool la laine; **a woolen shirt** une chemise de laine

word le mot

work *n* le travail; l'oeuvre *f*; *v* travailler

worker l'ouvrier, l'ouvrière

work of art l'objet d'art *m*

world le monde

worry *v* s'inquiéter; **Don't worry!** Ne vous inquiétez pas!

worst le pire

worth la valeur

worthy digne

wrap *v* emballer

write écrire

writer l'écrivain

written écrit

wrong faux, fausse

wrong (to be) avoir tort; **He is wrong.** Il a tort.

Y

year l'an *m*, l'année *f*

yellow jaune

yes oui; si; **Yes, indeed!** Mais oui!

yesterday hier; **day before yesterday** avant-hier

yet encore; **not yet** pas encore

you vous; tu, te, toi

young jeune

your votre, vos; ton, ta, tes

yours à vous, à toi

yourself vous-même, toi-même

Z

zero le zéro

zoo le jardin zoologique

DICTIONNAIRE FRANÇAIS-ANGLAIS

There are a few conventions used in this dictionary that are important to highlight:

1. Gender of nouns is given by including **le** or **la** in the French translation. When the noun is listed only in the plural form **les**, or requires **l'** due to its first letter being a vowel or mute **h**, will the abbreviations *m* and *f* appear to indicate masculine or feminine.

2. French adjectives whose feminine forms are created by merely adding a silent **e**, or whose masculine forms already end in silent **e**, will appear just in the masculine form. However, if there are other patterns in spelling the feminine endings, both masculine and feminine forms should appear. The same omission and inclusion just described also occur if the plural form of the adjective is created by adding **s** or if the masculine form of the adjective ends in **s**. There are a number of nouns which have special endings for the feminine and the plural: these will follow the same rule as the adjectives.

A

à to, at, on, in, until

abord: d'abord at first

accord *m* harmony; **d'accord** agreed, granted

achat *m* purchase; **aller faire des achats** to go shopping

acheter to buy

actualités *f pl* newsreel

actuellement now, at present

addition *f* bill

affaire *f* business, affair; **M. Brown est dans les affaires.** Mr. Brown is in business.

affiche *f* poster

âge *m* age; **Quel âge avez-vous?** How old are you?

agent *m* agent; **l'agent de police** policeman

aider to help

ail *m* garlic

ailleurs elsewhere; **d'ailleurs** besides

aimer to like, love; **aimer mieux** to prefer

aîné *m*, **l'aînée** *f* oldest or older son or daughter

ainsi thus, so; **ainsi de suite** and so forth

air *m* air, look, expression; **à l'air libre** in the open air

ajouter to add, join

aller to go; **s'en aller** to go away; **Comment allez-vous?** How are you? **Ça va bien.** I am well. **Cette robe me va bien.** This dress fits me.

allumette *f* match

alors well, then, in that case, and so

amateur *m* lover (*of things*), fancier

ambassade *f* embassy

ami m, **amie** *f* friend

amour *m* love

amoureux *m*, **amoureuse** *f* lover

s'amuser to enjoy oneself, have fun; **amusons-nous** let's have some fun

an *m* year

ancien *m*, **ancienne** *f* old, ancient; former

anglais English; **l'anglais** English (*language*); **l'Anglais** (*Englishman*)

Angleterre *f* England; **en Angleterre** in England

anneau *m* ring

année *f* year; **l'année scolaire** school year

anniversaire *f* birthday, anniversary

annoncer to announce; advertise

apercevoir to perceive, observe

appartement *m* apartment

apparaître to appear

appeler to call; **s'appeler** to be called (named); **Comment vous appelez-vous?** What is your name? **Je m'appelle** My name is

appétit *m* appetite

apporter to bring

apprécier to appreciate

apprendre to learn, teach

s'approcher de to approach, get near, go up to; **Je me suis approché de la voiture.** I approached the car.

après after, afterward; **après-demain** the day after tomorrow

après-midi *m* afternoon; **de l'après-midi** in the afternoon, p.m.

arbre *m* tree

argent *m* money, silver

arrêt *m* stop, halt

s'arrêter to stop; **L'autobus s'arrête là-bas.** The bus stops over there.

arrière behind, backwards

arrivée *f* arrival

arriver (à) to arrive (at), reach, happen. **Qu'est-ce qui est arrivé?** What has happened?

art *m* art

ascenseur *m* elevator

aspect *m* appearance, look

s'asseoir to sit down; **Asseyez-vous.** Sit down.

assiette *f* dish, plate

assez enough; **c'est assez** that's enough; **assez souvent** quite often

assis *m*, **assise** *f* seated

assortiment *m* assortment

astucieux *m*, **astucieuse** *f* astute, wily

s'attabler to sit down at table; **attablé** seated at table

attendant waiting; **en attendant** in the meantime

attendre to wait (for); await

atterrir to land; **L'avion atterrit.** The plane is landing.

attraper to catch; **attraper un rhume** to catch cold

auberge *f* inn

aucun *m*, **aucune** *f* none, no one, not any

au dessous de below, under

au dessus de above, over

aujourd'hui today

aussi also, as; **moi aussi** I/me too; **aussi bien que** as well as

aussitôt soon, immediately; **aussitôt que possible** as soon as possible.

autant que as much (many) as; **Je travaille autant que jamais.** I am working as much as ever.

autour de around

autre other, another, different; **quelque chose d'autre** something else

autrefois formerly

avance *f* advance; **d'avance** beforehand, in advance; **en avance** ahead of; early

avancer to advance, progress

avant before; **avant-hier** day before yesterday

avec with

avide eager

avion *m* airplane; **en avion** by airplane

avocat *m* lawyer

avoir to have; **avoir peur de** to be afraid of; **avoir raison (tort)** to be right (wrong); **avoir envie de** to have a mind to; **avoir besoin de** to have need of; **avoir l'intention de** to intend to; **avoir mal de tête (mal aux dents, mal à la gorge)** to have a headache (toothache, sore throat); **Quel âge avez-vous? J'ai dix ans.** How old are you? I am ten years old.

avouer to confess

annonce *f* advertisement, announcement

B

bagages *m pl* baggage

baguette *f* wand; long loaf of bread

bain bath *m*; **la salle de bain** bathroom

banc *m* bench

banlieue *f* suburbs

barbe *f* beard

bas *m* stocking; **le bas collant** nylons, pantyhose

bas *m*, **basse** *f* low; **en bas** downstairs; **tout bas** in a low voice; **là-bas** over there

bateau *m* boat

bâtiment *m* building

bâtir to build

battre to beat

bavard talkative

beau *m*, **bel** *m* (before a vowel or sometimes h), **belle** *f* beautiful

beaucoup (de) much, very much, many; **beaucoup d'autres** many others; **beaucoup plus** much more; **merci beaucoup** many thanks

besogne *f* work, job; **se mettre à la besogne** to set to work

besoin *m* need; **avoir besoin de** to need Nous en avons besoin tout de suite. We need it (have need of it) at once.

beurre *m* butter

bibliothèque *f* library; bookcase

bien well, fine, very; **bien sûr** surely; **assez bien** quite well; **bien des fois** many times

bientôt soon; **à bientôt** see you soon

bienvenu welcome; **soyez le bienvenu** (be) welcome!

bijou *m s*, **les bijoux** *m pl* jewel(s)

billet *m* bill, ticket, note; **le billet d'aller-retour** round-trip ticket; **le billet d'aller (le billet simple)** one-way ticket

blanc *m*, **blanche** *f* white

blanchisserie *f* laundry

bleu *m* **bleue** *f* blue (color)

blouse *f* smock

boeuf *m* beef; **le boeuf bourguignon** beef stew Burgundy-style

boire to drink

bois *m* wood

boisson *f* beverage, drink

boîte *f* box; **la boîte aux lettres** letter box

bon *m*, **bonne** *f* good; **bon marché** cheap; **c'est bon** that's fine

bonheur *m* happiness

bonne *f* the maid

bord *m* edge; **au bord de la mer** at the seaside

bouche *f* mouth

boucher *m* butcher

boucherie *f* butcher shop

bouger to move, budge

boulangerie *f* bakery

bousculé pushed around, jostled

bout *m* bit, tip, end; **faire un bout de toilette** wash up a bit

bouteille *f* bottle

boutique *f* shop

bras *m* arm

briller to shine

brise *f* breeze

bruit *m* noise

brun brown

bureau *m* office; **le bureau de poste** post office

buvette *f* bar

C

ça (cela) that, it

cacher to conceal, hide

cadeau *m* gift

cadet *m*, **la cadette** *f* the younger, youngest one (*in a family*)

cahier *m* notebook; **le cahier de musique** music book

caisse *f* case, box; cash register

calculer to figure

calvados *m* brandy of Brittany

camarade *m/f* comrade, friend

camion *m* truck

camionneur *m* truck-driver

campagne *f* the country, countryside; **à la campagne** in the country

canif *m* penknife

caoutchoucs *m pl* rubbers

car for, because, since

carte *f* menu, map, card; **la carte postale** postcard

cas *m* case; **en tout cas** in any case

casser to break

cause *f* cause, case; **à cause de** because of

causer to chat, to talk

ce, cet, cette this or that

ceci this

ceinture *f* belt

cela (ça) that

célèbre famous

célébrer to celebrate

celui *m*, **celle** *f* this one *or* that one

cendrier *m* ashtray

une centaine about a hundred, a hundred or so

centimètre (cm) *m* centimeter (2.5 cms equal 1 inch)

cependant however

certain certain, sure

ces these *or* those

cesser to cease, stop

cesse *f* stoppage; **sans cesse** continually

ceux *m pl*, **celles** *f pl* these *or* those

chacun *m*, **chacune** *f* each, each one

chaise *f* chair

chaleur *f* heat

chambre *f* room; **la chambre à coucher** bedroom

champ *m* field

changer to change, revise; **changer de l'argent** to change money; **changer de place** to change one's seat

chanson *f* song

chanter to sing

chanteur *m*, **chanteuse** *f* singer

chapeau *m* hat

chaque each, every

château *m* **les châteaux** *m pl* chateau, castle

chaud hot, warm; **le chaud** heat, warmth; **il fait chaud** it (weather) is warm (hot); **j'ai chaud** I am (feel) warm, hot

chaussette *f* sock

chaussure *f* shoe, **une paire de chaussures** a pair of shoes

chemin *m* road; **le chemin de fer** railroad

chemise *f* shirt

cher *m*, **chère** *f* dear; expensive **plus cher** dearer

chercher to look for, to seek

chéri *m*, **chérie** *f* dear one, darling; **mon chéri, ma chérie** my dear, my darling

cheval *m s*, **chevaux** *m pl* horse

cheveux *m pl* hair

chez at the house (home) of; **chez moi** at my house; **chez les Brown** at the Browns' house

chien *m* dog

choisir to choose

chose *f* thing; **quelque chose** something

ciel *m* sky, heaven

cinéma *m* cinema, movies; movie house

citer to cite, to mention; to quote

clair clear, bright

classe *f* class; **en classe** in school

clef *f* key

coeur *m* heart; **par coeur** by heart

coin *m* corner

colis postal *m* **colis postaux** *m pl* parcel post package(s)

colline *f* hill

combien (de) how much, how many; **Combien cela coûte-it?** How much does this cost?

comique comic

comme like, as, for, how; **comme ci, comme ça** so-so; **Comme il est tard!** How late it is!

commencer to begin

comment how **Comment ça va?** How are you?

commission *f* allowance, errand

commode convenient, comfortable

compagnie *f* company

complet complete; **le complet** suit of clothes

comprendre to understand

compris understood, included

compte *m* the bill; **faire le compte** to add up the bill

compter to count; to intend, to count on

conduire to drive, to conduct, lead

conférence *f* lecture

connaissance *f* knowledge, acquaintance; **faire la connaissance de** to make the acquaintance of, to meet

connaître to know, to be acquainted with

connu known

conseil *m* advice

conséquent following; **par conséquent** consequently

construire to construct, to build

content happy

continuer to continue, keep on

contre against; **par contre** on the other hand

contrôler to control, to check

coq *m* rooster

corps *m* body; group of people acting together

corriger to correct

costume *m* costume; **le costume tailleur** suit (woman's)

côté *m* side; **à côté de** at the side of, next to

se coucher to lie down, go to bed

couleur *f* color; **De quelle couleur est . . . ?** What is the color of . . . ?

coup *m* blow, stroke; **tout à coup** all of a sudden; **un coup de main** a helping hand; **donner un coup de pied** to kick

couper to cut

courant common, current: **au courant** well-informed

courir to run

courrier *m* mail

cours *m* course

court short

couteau *m* knife

coûter to cost

coutume *f* custom, habit

couture *f* dress designing; dressmaking; sewing

couturier *m* dress designer, dressmaker

couvert covered; **le couvert** place setting (*at table*)

couverture *f* cover

couvrir to cover

cravate *f* necktie

crayon *m* pencil

crème *f* cream

crêpe *f* pancake

crever to break, to puncture; **crever un pneu** to have a blowout

crier to cry out

croire to believe, to think; **je crois que oui (non)** I think so (not)

croix *f* cross

cuisine *f* kitchen, cooking

cuisinier *m* cook;

cuisinière *f* cook; stove

cuiller *f* spoon

curieux *m*, **curieuse** *f* curious

D

dame *f* lady

dans in, into

date *f* date

de of, from, by, with

debout standing; **il est (il reste) debout** he is standing

débrouillard resourceful

découvrir to discover, uncover

décrire to describe

défense *f* prohibition, defense; **Défense de fumer!** No smoking. **Défense de stationner!** No parking.

dehors outside, outdoors

déjà already

déjeuner *m* lunch; **petit déjeuner** breakfast

délassé refreshed; rested

demain tomorrow; **à demain** until tomorrow; **demain matin** tomorrow morning

demander to ask, ask for; **se demander** to wonder

déménager to move

demeurer to reside, to live

demi half; **le demi** glass of draft beer

dent *f* tooth; **mal aux dents** toothache

départ *m* departure

dépasser to exceed **Le poids des bagages dépasse cent livres.** The weight of the baggage exceeds 100 lbs.

se dépêcher to hurry

depuis since, for (*duration*)

dernier *m* **dernière** *f* last, final

derrière behind

dès since, from, as early as; **dès mon arrivée** immediately upon my arrival

descendre to descend, go down

désespérer to despair, to be without hope

désirer to desire, want, wish

dessert *m* dessert

dessin *m* design, drawing

dessous under, underneath; **au-dessous de** under

dessus over, above **au-dessus de** on, upon

dette *f* debt

devant in front of, before

devenir to become

deviner to guess

devoir *m* duty; **les devoirs** homework; **faire ses devoirs** to do his (her) homework

devoir to owe; to be obliged to; to have to; to be supposed to

difficile difficult

difficulté *f* difficulty

digne worthy

dîner to dine; **le dîner** dinner

diplôme *m* diploma

dire to say, tell; **c'est-à-dire** that is to say; **dites-moi** tell me

distingué distinguished

distraction *f* recreation

divers various, several

doigt *m* finger

domestique *m/f* servant

dominer to reign, to dominate

dommage *m* injury; **Quel dommage!** What a pity!

donc therefore

donner to give

dont of which, of whom, whose

dormir to sleep

douane *f* customs, customhouse

doute *m* doubt; **sans doute** of course, probably

douzaine *f* dozen

doux *m*, **douce** *f* gentle, sweet, mild

drap *m* cloth, sheet

droit *m* law; right; **droit** *adj* right, straight; **à droite** to the right; **tout droit** straight ahead; **la main droite** the right hand

durant during

E

eau *f* water; **l'eau de vie** brandy

échantillon *m* sample

écharpe *f* long scarf

éclat *m* brightness, glitter; **de tout son éclat** in all its brilliance

éclater to burst out, to resound

école *f* school

écouter to listen to; **Nous écoutons le professeur.** We listen to the teacher.

écran *m* screen

s'écrier to cry out

écrire to write

écrivain *m* writer

effet *m* effect; **en effet** in fact

égaler to equal

égayer to cheer up

église *f* church

élève *m/f* pupil, student

elle she, it; her; **elle-même** herself; **elles** they

embouchure *f* mouth (of river)

embrasser to kiss

employé *m* employee, clerk

employer to employ

emporter to carry away, to take away

emprunter to borrow

en in, into, while, on to; of it, of them

encadré framed

enchanté delighted; charmed

encore still, yet, again; **encore une fois** once more; **encore un (une)** one more, another; **pas encore** not yet

encre *f* ink

endroit *m* place

enfant *m/f* child

enfin finally

ennuyer to bore, annoy; **s'ennuyer** to be bored

ennuyeux *m*, **ennuyeuse** *f* boring

ensemble together, whole

enseigner to teach

ensuite then, next

entendre to hear, understand; **entendu** agreed, all right; **bien entendu** of course

entouré surrounded

entre between; **entre nous** confidentially

entrecôte *m* small steak

entrée *f* entrance; first course (dish) of a meal

entreprendre to undertake

entrer (dans) to enter, come in

envie *f* wish, desire, longing; **J'ai envie de dormir.** I feel like sleeping

environ about, nearly, approximately

environs *m pl* vicinity, neighborhood; suburbs

s'envoler to fly away

envoyer to send

épicier *m* grocer

épicerie *f* grocery store

épuisé worn out

equivaloir to equal

escalier *m* staircase

Espagne *f* Spain

espagnol Spanish; **l'espagnol** *(language)* **l'Espagnol** *(Spaniard)*

espérer to hope, hope for, expect

essayer to try, to try on

essence *f* gasoline; **faire le plein d'essence** to fill the tank with gasoline

est *m* east

estomac *m* stomach; **mal à l'estomac** stomach ache

et and

étage *m* story or floor (of house)

étalage *m* display

état *m* state; **coup d'état** political takeover; **dans tous ses états** terribly excited

été *m* summer; **en été** in summer

étoffe *f* cloth

étoile *f* star (of heavens)

étonner to astonish

être to be; **être en train de** to be in the act of

étrennes *f pl* New Year's presents

étude *f* study; **ils font leurs études** they are carrying on their studies

étudiant *m* student

étudier to study

évoquer to evoke

excepté except

excuser to excuse; **Excusez-moi.** Excuse me.

exemple *m* example; **par exemple** for example

exiger to demand

expliquer to explain

exprimer to express

extra extra; **c'est de l'extra** it's especially good

F

fabrique *f* factory
facile easy
fâché annoyed, angry
facilité *f* facility
facteur *m*, **factrice** *f* mail carrier
faim *f* hunger; **avoir faim** to be hungry
faire to make, to do

Il fait ses adieux à son ami. He is saying goodbye to his friend.

Faites mes amitiés à Mme Picard. Give my regards to Mrs. Picard.

Il fait beau (mauvais). The weather is nice (bad).

Il fait le compte. He adds up the bill.

Je veux faire sa connaissance. I want to meet him.

Ils font leurs devoirs. They are doing their homework.

Elle fait ses achats. She is shopping.

Ils font des progrès. They are making progress.

Il fait peser ses valises. He is having his bags weighed.

Il fait le plein d'essence. He is filling up the tank with gasoline.

Cela nous fait plaisir. That pleases us.

Ça ne fait rien. That doesn't matter.

Nous allons faire un voyage. We are going to take a trip.

fait *m* act, deed, fact; **tout à fait** entirely, quite
fait done (*past participle of* **faire**)
falloir to be necessary; **il faut** it is necessary; **il faudra** it will be necessary
famille *f* family; **en famille** together with the family
fatigué tired
faut: il faut it is necessary
faute *f* mistake
faux *m*, **fausse** *f* false
féliciter to congratulate
femme *f* woman; wife
fenêtre *f* window
fermer to close
fermier *m* farmer
fête *f* holiday, festival
feu *m* fire, light; **les feux d'artifice** fireworks
fichu *m* scarf
fier *m*, **fière** *f* proud
figure *f* face

fil *m* thread
filer to spin; **en filant à toute vitesse** running at full speed
fille *f* girl; daughter; **la jeune fille** girl
film *m* film; **le film policier** detective film; **le film de reportage** documentary film
fils *m* son
fin *f* end; **à la fin de** at the end of
finir to finish
flatté flattered
fleur *f* flower; **Marché aux Fleurs** Flower Market
fleuve *m* river
fois *f* time; **deux fois** two times; **combien de fois** how many times; **encore une fois** one more time; **quelque-fois** sometimes
folie *f* madness; **à la folie** madly
fond *m* bottom; **au fond** basically; in the rear; **à fond** thoroughly
force *f* strength
forcer to force
forêt *f* forest
foulard *m* square scarf
fourchette *f* fork
fort strong, strongly
fournir to furnish
fourrure *f* fur
frais *m* coolness, freshness; **frais** *m*, **fraîche** *f* cool; fresh; **il fait frais** it is cool
fraise *f* strawberry
français French; **le français** French (*language*); **le Français** (*Frenchman*); **la Française** (*Frenchwoman*)
frapper to knock, strike
freins *m pl* brakes
frère *m* brother
friand de fond of
friandise *f* treat
froid cold; **le froid** the cold, coldness; **il fait froid** it (the weather) is cold; **j'ai froid** I am cold
fumer to smoke; **Défense de fumer!** No smoking!

G

gagner to gain, win, earn
gai gay
le garçon boy, waiter; **le garçon à tout faire** office boy

garder to guard, to keep; **il garde sa chambre** he keeps to his room

gare f railroad station

gâteau m cake

gauche left; awkward; **la main gauche** the left hand

gens m pl people, persons, folk

gentil m, **gentille** f nice, kind

gigot m leg of lamb

gilet m cardigan sweater, vest

glace f ice cream

goût m taste, flavor

grâce f grace; **grâce à vous** thanks to you

grand big, large, great, tall

grand'mère f grandmother

grand-père m grandfather

gras m, **grasse** f fat

gratte-ciel m skyscraper

gris gray

gros m, **grosse** f big, large, stout, thick: **en gros** wholesale; all together

guichet m ticket window

Guignol m Punch and Judy, puppet show

H

s'habiller to dress oneself, to get dressed

habiter to live in, to inhabit

habitude f habit, custom; **d'habitude** usually

s'habituer à to get accustomed to; to get used to

hache f ax

haie f edge

haut high, loud; **à haute voix** in a loud voice

hauteur f height

herbe f grass

héros m hero

heure f hour; **de bonne heure** early; **Quelle heure est-il?** What time is it?

heureux m, **heureuse** f happy

hibou m owl

hier yesterday; **hier soir** last night; **hier matin** yesterday morning

hiver m winter; **en hiver** in winter

homme m man; **l'homme d'affaires** businessman

hors d'oeuvre m appetizers

huile f oil, cooking oil

I

ici here

idée f idea; **Quelle bonne idée!** What a fine idea!

imperméable m raincoat

importer to matter; **n'importe (pas)** it doesn't matter

ingénieur m engineer

intéresser to interest; **s'intéresser à** to be interested in

intérêt m interest

isolé isolated

itinéraire m itinerary, route

J

jamais ever; **ne . . . jamais** never; **Mieux vaut tard que jamais.** Better late than never.

jambe f leg

jambon m ham

jardin m garden

jaune yellow

jeter to throw

jeu m game

jeune young; **la jeune fille** girl

joie f joy

joli pretty

jouer to play; **jouer à** to play (a game or sport); **jouer de** to play (an instrument)

joueur m gambler, player

jouir de to enjoy

jour m day; **tous les jours** every day; **le jour de l'an** New Year's Day; **de jour en jour** from day to day

journal m newspaper

journée f the day; **toute la journée** all day

jupe f skirt

jus m juice; **le jus d'orange** orange juice

jusque up to, until, as far as; **jusqu'à présent** up to now; **jusqu'ici** as far as here

K

kilogramme (kg) m kilogram (*2.2 pounds*)

kilomètre (km) m kilometer (*5/8 of a mile*)

L

la f the

la f her, it

là there; **là-bas** over there

laine *f* wool; **un fichu de laine** a woolen scarf

laisser to let, to leave

lait *m* milk

langue *f* language; tongue

large wide

largeur *f* width

lavabo *m* washroom, sink

laver to wash; **se laver** to wash oneself

le *m* the

le *m* him, it

leçon *f* lesson

légume *m* vegetable

lendemain the next day

lent slow

lequel *m*, **laquelle** *f*, **lesquels** *m pl*, **lesquelles** *f pl* who, whom, which; which one? which ones?

les *pl* the

les them

lettre *f* letter; **les belles-lettres** literature

leur, leurs *possessive adjective*

leur *indirect object pronoun* (to) them

lever to raise, to lift; **se lever** to get up, to stand up; to rise; **levez-vous** stand up

libre free; **à l'air libre** in the open air

lieu *m* place; **au lieu de** instead of; **avoir lieu** to take place

librairie *f* bookstore

lin *m* linen (cloth)

linge *m* linen (bed linen, clothing)

lire to read

lit *m* bed; **au lit** in bed

livre *m* book

livre *f* pound

loi *f* law

loin far; **loin d'ici** far from here

long *m*, **longue** *f* long; **le long du chemin** along the way

la longueur length

longtemps a long time; **plus longtemps** longer

lorsque when; **lorsqu' il est arrivé** when he arrived

louer to rent

loup *m* wolf

lourd heavy

lui *indirect object pronoun* (to) him, (to) her

lui *independent pronoun* him

lumière *f* the light

lune *f* moon

luxe *m* luxury; **les articles de luxe** luxury articles

lycée *m* French secondary school

M

ma *f* my

madame madam, Mrs.

mademoiselle young lady, Miss

magasin *m* store; **le magasin à grande surface** supermarket; **les grands magasins** department stores

main *f* hand: **la main gauche** left hand; **la main droite** right hand; **à la main gauche (droite)** on the left (right); **ils se donnent (serrent) la main** they shake hands

maintenant now

mais but; **mais oui** of course, yes indeed

maison *f* house, home; **à la maison** at home

maître *m* master, teacher

maîtresse *f* teacher, mistress

mal badly; **le mal** pain; **j'ai mal à la tête, (mal aux dents, à l'estomac)** I have a headache (toothache, stomachache); **ça fait mal aux yeux** it hurts the eyes

malade sick; **malade** *m/f* sick person

malgré in spite of

malheur *m* misfortune

malheureux *m*, **malheureuse** *f* unhappy, unfortunate

malheureusement unfortunately

manger to eat

manière *f* manner

manquer to lack, to need; **je ne manque de rien** I lack nothing; **manquer** to fail, to miss; **Ne manquez pas de faire vos devoirs.** Don't fail to do your homework. **Vous me manquerez.** I shall miss you.

manteau *m* coat, cloak

marchand *m* merchant, storekeeper; **marchand de vin** wine merchant

marchander to bargain

marchandise *f* merchandise

marché *m* the market; **faire son marché** to do one's marketing

marcher to walk, to march

mari *m* husband

marier to marry; **se marier** to get married

marin *m* sailor, seaman

matin *m* morning; **du matin** in the morning, a.m.

matinal early-rising

matinée *f* morning

médecin *m* medical doctor, physician

meilleur better; **le meilleur** best; **meilleur marché** cheaper

même same, even, self; **la même chose** the same thing; **tout de même** all the same; **moi-même** myself; **même les plus riches** even the wealthiest

mener to lead

mer *f* sea; **en mer** at sea

merci thanks; **merci beaucoup** many thanks

mère *f* mother

merveille *f* marvel; **à merveille** wonderfully

merveilleux *m*, **merveilleuse** *f* wonderful

mes my

métier *m* trade, business; **C'est mon métier.** That's my trade.

mètre *m* meter (about 39 inches)

mettre to put, to put on; **se mettre à table** to sit down at the table; **se mettre en route** to set out; **se mettre à** + *infinitive* to begin to; **Il se met à écrire.** He is beginning to write.

meubler to furnish

meubles *m pl* furniture

midi *m* noon; **le Midi** south of France

mieux *adv* better; **tant mieux** so much the better; **Ça va mieux.** I feel better. **Mieux vaut tard que jamais.** Better late than never.

milieu *m* middle; **au milieu de** in the middle of

miroir *m* mirror

mode *f* fashion; **à la mode** in style

moi me, to me, I

mois *m* month

moins less, minus; **moins de cinq** fewer than five

mon, ma, mes *possessive adjective* my

monde *m* world; **tout le monde** everybody

monnaie *f* coin, money, change; **en monnaie** in change

monsieur *m* gentleman, sir, Mr.; **les messieurs** gentlemen

montagne *f* mountain

montant *m* total

monter to go up, to ascend, to carry up; **monter en voiture** to get into the car

montre *f* watch

montrer to show

morceau *m* piece, morsel

mort dead; **la mort** death

mot *m* word

mouchoir *m* handkerchief

mourir to die; **ennuyer à mourir** to bore to death

moyens *m pl* means

mur *m* wall; **au mur** on the wall

N

naître to be born; **né** born

nager to swim

nappe *f* tablecloth

nation *f* nation

ne; ne . . . pas not; **ne . . . jamais** never; **ne . . . rien** nothing; **ne . . . plus** no longer; **ne . . . ni . . . ni** neither nor; **ne . . . que** only; **je n'ai qu'un professeur** I have only one teacher

nécessaire necessary

neige *f* snow

neiger to snow

neuf (neuve *f***)** *new*

nez *m* nose

ni . . . ni neither . . . nor; **ni moi non plus** neither do I

Noël *f* Christmas

noir black

nom *m* name

nombre *m* number

non no; **non plus** neither

nord *m* north

note *f* bill; grade (school); **la note d'hôtel** hotel bill

notre, nos our possessive adjective

nouveau *m*, **nouvel** *m* (before vowel or h), **nouvelle** *f* new

nouvelles *f* pl news; **Point de nouvelles bonnes nouvelles.** No news is good news. **Quelles sont les nouvelles?** What is the news?

nuit *f* night

O

obéir to obey

objet d'art *m* art object

obtenir to obtain

occasion *f* opportunity, occasion, chance

s'occuper de to busy oneself with, to take care of; **Mme Davis s'occupe des enfants.** Mrs. Davis takes care of the children.

oeuf *m* egg

oeil *m* eye; **les yeux** eyes

oeuvre *f* work; **le chef d'oeuvre** masterpiece

offrir to offer

on one, people, you, we, they; **on dit** one says; people (they, you, we) say; it is said

oncle *m* uncle

or *m* gold; **la montre d'or** the gold watch

ordinateur *m* computer

oreille *f* ear

original original; creative

oser to dare

ou or

où where

oublier to forget

outillage *m* tool kit

ouvert open

ouvreur *m*, **ouvreuse** *f* usher

ouvrier *m*, **l'ouvrière** *f* worker

ouvrir to open

P

pain *m* bread, loaf of bread; **les petits pains** rolls

pâle pale

panier *m* the basket

pantalon *m* trousers

paquebot *m* steamship, liner

Pâque *f* Passover

Pâques *f pl* Easter; **Joyeuse Pâques!** Happy Easter!

par by, through; **par ici** this way; **par-ci par-là** here and there

parapluie *m* umbrella

paraître to seem, to appear

parce que because

parcourir to glance through

pardessus *m* overcoat

pardonner to pardon; **pardonnez-moi** pardon me

pareil (pareille *f*) like, equal, similar, such

parfait perfect

parfois at times

parler to speak; **parlant d'autre chose** speaking of something else, to change the subject

parmi among

part *f* share, part; **de ma part** for my part; **quelque part** somewhere; **nulle part** nowhere

partie *f* the part (first, second, etc.); the game

partir (de) to leave; **partir en voyage** to leave on a trip

partout everywhere

pas, ne . . . pas not; **pas du tout** not at all; **pas encore** not yet

pas *m* step; **un faux pas** slip, social error

passeport *m* passport

passer to spend, to pass; **se passer de** to do without; **Qu'est-ce qui se passe?** What is happening?

passionnant fascinating

pauvre poor

payer to pay; **payer ses repas** to pay for one's meals

pays *m* country

paysage *m* landscape, scenery

paysan *m* peasant, farmer

pêche *f* peach; fishing

pêcheur *m* fisherman

peinture *f* painting

pendant during; **pendant que** while

penser (à) to think (of); **je pense que oui** I think so; **Il pense à son ami.** He is thinking of his friend.

perdre to lose

père *m* father; **tel père tel fils** like father like son

permettre to permit

personne person, nobody

peser to weigh; **faire**

peser to have weighed

petit small, little; **petit à petit** little by little

peu little, few; **un peu plus** a little while longer; **peu de choses** few things; **beaucoup de choses** many things

peur *f* fear; **avoir peur** to be afraid

peut-être perhaps

phrase *f* sentence

pièce *f* room; piece; play (theater)

pied *m* foot; **à pied** on foot

pierre *f* stone

pierreux *m*, **pierreuse** *f* rocky

pire *adj* worse

pis *adv* worse

place *f* place; seat; square

plaire to please; **il plaît** it pleases; **s'il vous plaît** please (if it pleases you)

plaisir *m* pleasure; **le plaisir est à moi** the pleasure is mine

plat *m* dish, plate, course

plat flat; **être à plat** to have a flat (tire)

plateau *m* tray

plein full; **faire le plein (d'essence)** to fill the tank

pleurer to weep

pleuvoir to rain; **Il pleut à verse.** It's pouring.

plomb *m* lead; **soleil de plomb** sun beating down

pluie *f* rain

plupart (de) *f* most (of), the majority; **la plupart des places** most of the places; **pour la plupart** for the most part

plus more; **plus de cinq** more than five; **non plus** either; **en plus** in addition; **plus tôt** sooner; **de plus en plus** more and more; **plus ou moins** more or less

plusieurs several

plutôt rather

pneu *m* tire; **pneu de rechange** spare tire

poche *f* pocket

poids *m* weight

point *m* point; **Il est sur le point de partir** He is about to leave. **ne . . . point** not at all; **Il ne parle point.** He doesn't speak at all.

petits pois *m pl* peas

poison *m* poison

poisson *m* fish

politique political

pomme *f* apple; **la pomme cuite** baked apple

pomme de terre *f* potato

pont *m* bridge

port de mer *m* seaport

porte *f* door

porte-parapluie *m* umbrella stand

porter to bear; to carry; to wear; **se porter** to feel (health); **Comment vous portez-vous?** How do you feel?

porteur porter

poser to pose; to put; **poser des questions** to ask questions

poste *f* post office; **le mandat-poste** money order; **poste-restante** general delivery

poste *m* post, station; **le poste d'essence** gasoline station

pot au lait *m* milk pitcher

poterie *f* pottery

poularde *f* fatted chicken

poulet *m* chicken

pour for, to, in order to, for the sake of

pourboire *m* tip, gratuity

pourcentage *m* percentage

pourquoi why

pourtant however

pouvoir to be able, can, may

précise precise, sharp; **à cinq heures précises** at five o'clock sharp

préférer to prefer

premier *m*, **première** *f* first

prendre to take; **prendre des renseignements** to get information; **prendre le petit déjeuner** to have breakfast

près (de) near, close to; **à peu près** pretty near, more or less

presque almost, nearly

prêt ready

prêter to lend

prier to pray; to beg

prix *m* price, prize; **à prix fixe** at a fixed price

problème *m* problem

prochain next

proche near

produire to produce

produit *m* product

profond profound, deep

programme *m* program

progrès *m* progress; **faire des progrès** to make progress

projet *m* project

promenade *f* walk, stroll, ride; **faire une promenade** to take a walk; **une promenade à bicyclette** a bicycle ride

se promener to go for a walk; **se promener en voiture** to go for a drive

promettre to promise

propagande *f* propaganda

propos: à propos by the way; **à propos du film** with reference to the film

propre own; clean, neat; **leur propre langue** their own language

puce *f* flea; **le Marché aux Puces** the Flea Market

puis then

puisque since
punir to punish

Q

qualité *f* quality
quand when
quant à as for, as to; **quant à moi** as for me
quantité *f* quantity
quartier *m* quarter; neighborhood
que, qu'est-ce que *interrogative pronoun object* what? **Que voulez-vous? Qu'est que vous voulez?** What do you want?
que *relative pronoun object* whom, that, which; **Voilà les clefs que vous cherchiez.** There are the keys (that) you were looking for.
que *conjunction* that; than; **Je sais qu'il a raison.** I know that he is right. **Il est plus grand que moi.** He is taller than I.
quel *m*, **quelle** *f adj* what, which; **Quelle cravate avez-vous choisie?** Which necktie have you chosen? *interrogative pronoun* what? which? **Quel est le prix?** What's the price?
quelconque any, whatsoever; **un dessert quelconque** some sort of dessert
quelque some, any; **quelque chose d'autre** something else; **quelques films** some films; **quelque part** somewhere; **quelque peu** somewhat; **quelquefois** sometimes
quelqu'un *m*, **'une** *f* someone, somebody; **quelques-uns** *n*, **-unes** *f* some, several
qu'est-ce qui *interrogative pronoun subject* what? **Qu'est-ce qui est arrivé?** What has happened?
qui *interrogative pronoun subject or object* who? whom? **Qui est-ce?** Who is it? **Qui cherchez-vous?** Whom are you looking for? **De qui parlez-vous?** Of whom are you speaking?
qui *relative pronoun subject* who; **Connaissez-vous l'homme qui demeure ici?** Do you know the man who lives here?
question *f* question; **poser des questions** to ask questions
une quinzaine two weeks; **dans une quinzaine** in two weeks (*fifteen days*)
quitter to leave; **Il quitte la chambre.** He leaves the room.

quoi *pronoun used with prepositions* what **À quoi pensez-vous?** What are you thinking of? **Il n'y a pas de quoi.** Don't mention it. You're welcome.
quoique although
quotidien *m*, **quotidienne** *f* daily; everyday

R

raconter to tell (a story)
radio *f* radio
raison *f* reason; **il a raison** he is right
ramasser to pick up
rang *m* row
se rappeler to recall, to remember; **Je ne me rappelle pas son adresse.** I don't recall his address.
rapporter to bring back
rapprocher to bring nearer
rasoir *m* razor; **le rasoir de sûreté** safety razor; **le rasoir électrique** electric razor
rayon *m* shelf
recevoir to receive
réchauffer to warm up, to warm up again
recommencer to begin again
recommander to recommend
refuser to refuse
regarder to look at; to concern **dans tout ce qui regarde les en-têtes** in everything that concerns the headings
règle *f* rule
regretter to regret, to be sorry; **Je le regrette beaucoup.** I'm very sorry.
remarquer to notice
remercier to thank
remplir to fill; **rempli de** filled with
remporter to carry back
rencontre *f* meeting; **Je vais à la rencontre de Mme D.** I am going to meet Mrs. D.
se rencontrer to meet each other
rendre to give back; to render; **rendre visite à** to pay a visit to (somebody); **rendre service à** to do a service to, to aid; **se rendre compte de** to realize
renseignement *m* information; **prendre des renseignements** to ask for information, to make inquiries
rentrer to come home
renvoyer to send back

répéter to repeat
répondre to answer, to reply
réponse *f* answer
repas *m* meal
repos *m* rest, repose
se reposer to rest
réserver to reserve
respirer to breathe
ressembler to resemble, to be alike; **ils se ressemblent** they resemble each other
reste *m* remainder, rest
rester to remain; **rester (être) debout** to stand
retard *m* delay; **en retard** late; **Nous sommes en retard.** We are late.
retenir to hold back, to retain; to reserve; **retenir une place** to reserve a seat
se retirer to withdraw
retour *m* return; **M. Black est de retour.** Mr. Black is back.
retourner to return, to go back
réussir to succeed
réveiller to awaken; **se réveiller** to wake up
revenir to come back, to return
rêver to dream
revoir to see again; **au revoir** goodbye
la revue magazine
le rhum rum
le rhume cold; **Je suis enrhumé.** I have a cold.
riche rich
rideau *m* curtain
rien *m* nothing; **ne . . . rien** nothing; **rien de plus facile** nothing easier; **de rien** or **il n'y a pas de quoi** you're welcome
rire to laugh; **se rire de** to laugh at
rive *f* bank (of river)
rivière *f* stream, river, branch of a river
robe *f* dress
rôle *m* role, part
roman *m* novel
rond round, plump
roue *f* wheel
rouge red
rue *f* street

S

sage good, well behaved; wise
sain healthy

saison *f* season
saisir to seize, to grasp
sale dirty; nasty
salle *f* room; **salle de classe** classroom; **salle à manger** dining room; **salle d'attente** waiting room; **salle de bain** bathroom
salon *m* living room, parlor
saluer to greet
sans without
santé *f* healthy; **À votre santé!** Here's to you! Your health!
satisfait satisfied
saucisse *f* sausage
sauf except; **sauf** *m*, **sauve** *f* safe; **sain et sauf** safe and sound
sauter to jump; to hop
savoir to know; **savoir-faire** tact, know-how; **savoir-vivre** good manners
savon *m* soap
séance *f* performance
séjour *m* sojourn
selon according to
semaine *f* week; **deux fois par semaine** twice a week
sembler to seem, to appear
sens *m* sense, opinion, direction; **le bon sens** common sense; **sens unique** one-way (street)
sentiment *m* feeling, sentiment
sentir to feel; to perceive; to smell; **Il se sent chez lui.** He feels at home.
serviette *f* napkin; **serviette de bain** bath towel
servir to serve
seul alone
seulement only; **non seulement . . . mais aussi** not only . . . but also
si if; whether; **sinon** otherwise
siècle *m* century
soeur *f* sister
soie *f* silk; **une robe de soie** a silk dress
soirie *f* silk fabric
soif *f* thirst; **il a soif** he is thirsty
soigner to take care of
soir *m* evening; **ce soir** this evening, tonight
soleil *m* sun
somme *f* sum
sommeil *m* sleep; **j'ai sommeil** I am sleepy
son *m* sound
son, sa, ses *possessive adj* his, her, its

songer (à) to dream (of)

sonner to sound, to ring

sorte *f* sort, kind

sortie *f* departure, exit

sortir to go out, to leave; **il sort de l'ordinaire** it's out of the ordinary

soucoupe *f* saucer

soudain suddenly

souffrir to suffer

souhaiter to wish for, to desire

soulier *m* shoe, pump

souper *m* supper

sourire to smile

sous under

se souvenir de to remember; **Nous ne nous souvenons pas de tous les circumstances.** We do not remember all the circumstances.

souvent often; **assez souvent** quite often; **plus souvent** more often

stationner to park; **Défense de stationner!** No parking allowed!

sténo *m* stenographer

style *m* style

stylo *m* fountain pen

sucre *m* sugar

sucrier *m* sugar bowl

sud *m* south

suffire to be sufficient; **cela suffit** that's enough

suite *f* sequence, result, continuation; **tout de suite** immediately; **et ainsi de suite** and so forth

suivre to follow

sujet *m* subject; **au sujet de** about, in the matter of

supplément *m* supplement, extra; **en supplément** in addition, extra

sur on, upon, over, above, about

sûr sure; **bien sûr** surely

surprendre to surprise

surtout above all, especially

sympathique nice, pleasant

T

tabac *m* tobacco

tâcher to try

tant so much, so many; **tant mieux!** good! so much the better! **tant pis!** so much the worse! **tant d'exercises** so many exercises

tantôt soon

tard late

tarte *f* tart, pie

tasse *f* cup

tel *m*, **telle** *f*, **tels** *m pl*, **telles** *f pl* such, like; **Tel père tel fils.** Like father, like son. **un tel homme** such a man

téléphoner to telephone

temps *m* time; weather; **de temps en temps** from time to time; **Quel temps fait-il?** How is the weather? **à temps** in time

tenir to hold, to keep;

tenir table ouverte to keep open house

terminer to finish

tête *f* head; **mal de tête** *or* **mal à la tête** headache

tiens! well!

timbre *m* stamp; **le timbre-poste** postage stamp

tirer to draw, to pull; **se tirer d'affaire** to get along

tissu *m* texture, fabric

toit *m* roof

tomber to fall

ton *f* tone

ton, ta, tes *possessive adj* your

tort *m* wrong; **Vous avez tort.** You are wrong.

tôt soon, early; **plus tôt** sooner, earlier; **le plus tôt possible** as soon as possible

toucher to touch

toujours always, still; **Comme toujours.** As ever. **Il pleut toujours.** It is still raining.

tourner to turn

tout *m* (**toute** *f*, **tous** *m pl*, **toutes** *f pl*) all, whole, every; **tout le monde** everybody; **en tout cas** in any case; **pas du tout** not at all; **tout à fait** quite, entirely; **tout à coup** all of a sudden

traduire to translate

trajet *m* flight, trip

travail *m* work

travailler to work

très very

tremper to soak

triste sad

se tromper to be mistaken

trop too, too much, too many; **trop tard** too late; **trop de livres** too many books; **trop d'argent** too much money

trottoir *m* sidewalk

trouver to find; **se trouver** to be (somewhere); **Où se trouve mon chapeau?** Where is my hat?

U

unité *f* unit; unity

unir to unite; **uni** united; **les États-Unis** *m pl* the United States

usage *m* custom, usage; **L'usage rend maître.** Practice makes perfect.

usine *f* factory

ustensile *m* utensil

utile useful

V

valeur *f* value

valoir to be worth; **Cela ne vaut rien.** That isn't worth anything.

varier to vary, to change

veau *m* veal; **la blanquette de veau** veal stew

vedette *f* star (theater or film)

velours *m* velvet

vendeur *m* **vendeuse** *f* seller, salesman, saleswoman

vendre to sell

venir to come; **venir de** to have just; **La caisse vient d'arriver.** The case has just arrived.

vent *m* wind; **Il fait du vent.** It is windy.

vente *f* sale; **en vente** on sale

ventre *m* stomach

vérité *f* truth

verre *m* glass (for drinking)

vers about, toward

verser to pour; to spend (money)

vert green

vêtements *m pl* clothes

(il) veut dire it means **Que veut dire ce mot?** What does this word mean?

viande *f* meat

vide empty

vie *f* life; **l'eau de vie** *f* brandy

vieux *m*, **vieil** *m* (before a vowel or h), **vieille** *f* old; **le vieux portrait** the old portrait; **le vieil arbre** the old tree; **les vieux quartiers** the old sections

vif *m*, **vive** *f* alive, living, lively

ville *f* city, town; **en ville** to the city, downtown; **Mme Morelle va en ville pour faire ses achats.** Mrs. Morelle goes downtown to shop.

vin *m* wine

visage *m* face

visite *f* visit; **Nous allons lui rendre visite.** We are going to pay him a visit.

visiter to visit (places); **Nous visiterons tous les musées.** We shall visit all the museums.

vite rapidly, quickly, fast

vitesse *f* speed; **à toute vitesse** at full speed

vitrine *f* shop window

vivre to live

voici here is, here are; **le voici** here he is; **me voici** here I am; **les voice** here they are

voie *f* way, thoroughfare; **voie publique** public thoroughfare

voilà there is, are (*pointing*); there now! behold! that's that! **la voilà** there she is

voir to see

voiture *f* car, carriage; **en voiture** by car; **En voiture!** All aboard!

voix *f* voice; **à haute voix** in a loud voice

vol *m* flight; **L'avion prend son vol.** The airplane takes off.

volontiers gladly, with pleasure

votre, vos *possessive adj* your

vouloir to want, wish; **Voulez-vous bien me dire . . . ?** Will you kindly tell me . . . ? **Je voudrais l'acheter.** I should like to buy it.

voyage *m* voyage, trip; **Bon voyage!** Pleasant journey! **M. Brown est en voyage.** Mr. Brown is on a trip, **le voyage de commerce** the business trip; **le voyage d'agrément** pleasure trip

voyager to travel

voyageur *m*, **voyageuse** *f* traveler, passenger

vrai true; **C'est vrai.** It's true.

vraiment really, truly; **Vraiment!** Really!

vue *f* sight, view; **Je le connais de vue.** I know him by sight.

W

wagon-lit *m* sleeping car (train); **le wagon-restaurant** dining-car

Y

y there

Z

zéro *m* zero

ANSWER KEY

Exercise No. 1

1. Qui
2. homme d'affaires
3. ville
4. Il y a
5. père
6. mère
7. fils; et
8. s'appellent; et
9. cinq pièces
10. cuisine; salle de bain
11. bureau; rue
12. Il est
13. vingtième
14. toute la journée

Exercise No. 2

1. La
2. une
3. Le; la
4. Le
5. La
6. une
7. un
8. La
9. La; une
10. L'; le
11. L'; la
12. une; un

Exercise No. 3

1. les chambres
2. les harpes
3. des pièces
4. les fils
5. les hommes
6. des salons
7. les Américains
8. des étages
9. les bureaux
10. des personnes
11. les oncles
12. des enfants
13. les héros
14. les rues
15. des avenues

Exercise No. 4

1. M. Brown est un homme d'affaires américain.
2. Il habite à New-York.
3. Il y a six personnes dans la famille.
4. Il demeure dans une maison particulière.
5. Il y a cinq pièces dans la maison.
6. M. Brown est le père.
7. Mme Brown est la mère.
8. Le bureau se trouve/est dans la rue Whitehall.
9. M. Brown prend le train.
10. Il travaille au bureau.

Exercise No. 6

1. Qui
2. importateur
3. objets d'art
4. Au printemps
5. Il désire
6. parler
7. aussi
8. Mais
9. C'est pourquoi
10. le professeur
11. un ami de M. Brown
12. (un) rendez-vous

13. Ils parlent
14. rapidement
15. très intelligent
16. un bon professeur

Exercise No. 7

1. est
2. Est-il
3. Il ne parle pas
4. Parle-t-il
5. Il apprend
6. Il désire
7. Il n'étudie pas
8. Il sait
9. Ont-ils
10. Il compte
11. faire
12. parler

Exercise No. 8

1. (d)
2. (f)
3. (g)
4. (b)
5. (c)
6. (e)
7. (a)
8. (j)
9. (h)
10. (i)

Exercise No. 9

1. le français
2. le Français
3. merci
4. aussi
5. peut-être
6. le bureau
7. presque
8. toujours
9. très bien
10. rapidement
11. un peu
12. là

13. de
14. ici
15. grand
16. mais
17. où
18. bon
19. mauvais
20. avec
21. des articles
22. des endroits
23. C'est pourquoi
24. Comment allez-vous?

Exercise No. 11

1. est assis
2. beaucoup de choses
3. Il faut savoir
4. qu'est-ce que c'est que ça?
5. joue; chante
6. au-dessus du piano
7. entre
8. des lettres
9. C'est assez
10. À jeudi

Exercise No. 12

1. du
2. au
3. des
4. du
5. à l'
6. à la
7. aux
8. au
9. a l'
10. des

Exercise No. 13

1. Au-dessus
2. près de la
3. Sur le
4. au-dessus du bureau
5. entre les
6. autour de la

7. derrière la
8. devant le
9. dans la
10. avec; dans le

Exercise No. 14

1. M. Brown est assis dans le salon.
2. M. Picard est assis près de lui.
3. Il y a beaucoup de choses autour de nous.
4. Oui, elle chante bien.
5. Madame Brown joue bien du piano.
6. Il est sur le piano.
7. Il est au mur au-dessus du piano.
8. La bibliothèque est près d'une fenêtre.
9. Le miroir est entre les fenêtres.
10. Le bureau est près de la porte.
11. Une chaise est devant le bureau.
12. Il y a des livres sur la petite table.

Revision 1, Chapitres 1–5

Exercise No. 15

1. (g)
2. (e)
3. (i)
4. (h)
5. (j)
6. (k)
7. (l)
8. (a)
9. (d)
10. (c)
11. (b)
12. (f)

Exercise No. 16

1. toute la journée
2. s'il vous plaît
3. Peut-être
4. Bonsoir
5. en ville
6. C'est pourquoi
7. Comment allez-vous?
8. Où

9. Qu'est-ce que c'est que ça?
10. Qui
11. Qu'est-ce qui
12. Quand

Exercise No. 17

1. (d)
2. (f)
3. (i)
4. (k)
5. (h)
6. (g)
7. (c)
8. (a)
9. (j)
10. (b)
11. (e)

Exercise No. 18

1. devant la maison
2. autour de la table
3. près de la porte
4. derrière le bureau
5. sur le piano
6. Les livres du garçon
7. La mère de la fille
8. Le maître des enfants
9. au mur
10. À qui

Exercise No. 19

1. Qui est M. Brown?
2. C'est un homme d'affaires américain.
3. Où habite(demeure)-t-il?
4. Il demeure dans les environs de New-York.
5. Pourquoi apprend-il le français?
6. Il désire faire un voyage en France.
7. Qui est son professeur?
8. Son professeur est M. Picard.
9. Pourquoi apprend-il rapidement?
10. Il apprend rapidement parce qu'il est intelligent.
11. Combien d'enfants y a-t-il dans la famille Brown (or dans la famille de M. Brown)?

12. Il y a quatre enfants.

13. Combien de pièces y a-t-il dans la maison des M. Brown?

14. Il y a cinq pièces, une salle de bain, et une cuisine.

Exercise No. 20

Mr. Brown Is Learning French

Mr. Brown is an American businessman who imports art objects from France. That is why he wants to take a trip to France in the spring. He wants to talk with his agent. He also wants to visit some interesting places in France. But he does not know how to speak French.

Mr. Brown has a good teacher. He is a Frenchman who lives in New York and who is named Mr. Picard. Every Tuesday and Thursday the teacher takes the train to go to the home of his student. There the two gentlemen talk in French. Mr. Brown is very intelligent and he learns rapidly. During the first lesson, for example, he learns greetings and farewells by heart. He already knows how to say, "Good day," "How are you?" "See you soon," and "Until tomorrow." He already knows how to say in French the names of many things that are in his living room, and he knows how to answer the questions, "What is that?" and "Where is . . . ?" M. Picard is very satisfied with his student's progress and he says, "Very good. That's enough for today. So long."

Exercise No. 21

1. sont importants
2. quelques verbes
3. Pourquoi
4. Parce que
5. avec elle
6. d'autres pays
7. en bateau ou en avion
8. Combien
9. très rapidement

10. Ça suffit (or c'est assez) pour aujourd'hui

Exercise No. 22

1. J' etudie
2. ils ne parlent pas
3. nous comptons
4. elles désirent
5. Je travaille
6. Habitez-vous
7. Il écoute
8. Il ne coûte pas
9. Nous travaillous
10. Vous étudiez
11. Elles bavardeut
12. Elle ne visite pas
13. Vous commencez
14. Importe-t-il
15. Qui parle?
16. Les enfants jouent

Exercise No. 23

1. Henri me joue pas bien du piano.
2. Paul n'étudie pas . . .
3. Nous ne parlons pas . . .
4. Ils n'écoutent pas . . .
5. Mes enfants, ne jouez pas . . .
6. Elle ne désire pas . . .
7. Qui n'étudie pas . . .?
8. Nous ne travaillons pas . . .
9. Elle ne compte pas . . .
10. Vous ne travaillez pas . . .

Exercise No. 25

1. Les messieurs sont assis dans le salon chez M. Brown.
2. M. Picard commence à parler.
3. M. Brown écoute avec attention.
4. M. Picard pose les questions.
5. M. Brown répond aux questions.
6. Oui, monsieur, les verbes sont importants.
7. Oui, il importe des objets d'art.
8. Il désire faire un voyage en France.
9. Il compte visiter la France, le Maroc, et peut-être la Corse.

10. Il va voyager en avion.
11. M. Brown apprend rapidement.

Exercise No. 26

1. ouvre
2. Entrez, monsieur.
3. Passez au salon, s'il vous plaît.
4. Ma fille
5. Avez-vous
6. J'ai
7. Nous sommes
8. l'aîné
9. dix ans
10. la plus jeune *or* la cadette
11. Ils bavardent.
12. accepte

Exercise No. 27

1. avez-vous
2. J'ai
3. a-t-elle
4. Elle a
5. Avez-vous
6. Nous n'avons pas
7. as-tu
8. Je n'ai pas
9. ont-elles
10. Elles n'ont pas
11. a
12. a
13. avez-vous
14. J'ai

Exercise No. 28

1. va-t-il
2. Il va
3. Allez-vous
4. nous allons
5. vont-ils
6. va
7. Vas-tu
8. va
9. Allez-vous
10. Nous n'allons pas
11. allez-vous
12. Nous allons
13. Comment allez-vous? or Comment ça va?
14. Ça va bien

Exercise No. 29

1. est
2. est
3. est
4. est
5. est-il
6. n'est pas
7. Êtes-vous
8. je suis
9. sont
10. Ils sont
11. sont-ils
12. Ils sont
13. Êtes-vous
14. nous ne sommes pas

Exercise No. 30

1. M. Picard sonne à la porte.
2. La bonne ouvre la porte.
3. M. Brown attend M. Picard dans le salon.
4. Anne est malade.
5. Oui, elle est enrhumée.
6. Il a quatre enfants.
7. Il y a six personnes dans sa famille.
8. Ils s'appellent Charles, Thomas, Elizabeth, et Anne.
9. Charles a dix ans.
10. Oui, ils vont à l'école, excepté Anne.
11. Il invite M. Picard à visiter son bureau.
12. Oui, il accepte l'invitation.

Exercise No. 31

1. grandes
2. On peut
3. journaux
4. est assis
5. de vous voir
6. J'aime bien
7. Je vois

8. De quelle couleur
9. bleu
10. Mon Dieu!
11. Pas loin d'ici
12. Tant mieux! Allons-y!

Exercise No. 32
1. assise
2. petits
3. intelligente
4. jolies
5. confortable
6. haute
7. gris
8. intelligents
9. bon
10. jolies
11. grands
12. vieux
13. belle
14. rouge; bleu
15. noires
16. vieux

Exercise No. 33
1. belle
2. bonne
3. intelligentes
4. bonnes
5. blanches
6. longue
7. Tout, beau
8. Quel
9. quelle
10. Quels
11. toute
12. tous

Exercise No. 34
1. Le bureau de M. Brown est très confortable.
2. Les fenêtres du bureau sont grandes.
3. Il y a des posters aux murs.
4. Il y a des journaux français sur la table.
5. Le ciel sur l'affiche/le poster est bleu.

6. Le soleil est jaune.
7. Comment allez-vous, M. Brown?
8. Très bien, merci.
9. J'ai faim.
10. Moi aussi.

Exercise No. 35
1. Il est au vingtième étage d'un gratte-ciel.
2. Il n'est pas grand.
3. Oui, il est confortable.
4. Il y a des posters aux murs.
5. Il y a beaucoup de papiers sur le bureau de M. Brown.
6. Près de la porte il y a un petit bureau.
7. Entre les fenêtres il y a une longue table.
8. Le soleil est jaune.
9. Les cheminées sont noires.
10. La colline est verte.
11. Oui, madame, le ciel est bleu.
12. Le château est blanc.
13. Le toit est rouge.
14. Oui, il a faim.

Exercise No. 36
1. Ses parents
2. Son ami
3. Voici
4. n'est-ce pas
5. J'apprends
6. n'est pas difficile
7. Je l'étudie
8. Le français me plaît
9. à merveille
10. Je comprends
11. Vous êtes
12. Pas du tout; la vérité

Exercise No. 37
1. Are you learning French? Yes, I am learning French.—Is Charles learning French? No, he is not learning French.
2. Are you writing a letter? I am not writing a letter.—What are you writing? I am writing the French lesson.

3. What are you reading? I am reading a French newspaper.—What is Anne reading? She is reading a French magazine.

4. Do you understand your teacher when he speaks fast? No, Madam, but we understand the teacher when he speaks slowly.

5. What does Mr. Brown sell? He sells art objects.—Does he sell wholesale or retail? He only sells wholesale.

6. Who is Mr. Brown waiting for? He is waiting for M. Picard.—Where is he waiting for him? He is waiting for him in the living room.

Exercise No. 38

1. Nous vendons
2. Nous apprenons
3. Je comprends
4. Les parents lisent
5. Rendez-vous
6. Je prends
7. Elles ne prennent pas
8. Nous répondons
9. lit
10. Vous ne comprennez pas
11. Écrivons
12. élirent
13. vendent-ils
14. Lisez
15. Elle inscrit
16. Entendez-vous

Exercise No. 39

1. M. Dupont habite New York.
2. Oui. Il parle bien français.
3. Non, monsieur, ses parents ne sont pas américains. Ils sont canadiens.
4. Il sait que M. Brown apprend le français.
5. Il entre un jour dans le bureau de M. Brown.
6. Il salue M. Brown en français.
7. M. Brown apprend à parler, à lire, et à écrire le français.
8. Il étudie diligemment.
9. M. Picard est son professeur de français.
10. C'est un bon professeur.

11. Il comprend bien quand M. Picard parle français.
12. Il apprend les mots et les expressions de la vie quotidienne.
13. M. Brown va faire un voyage en France.
14. Il espère partir au printemps.

Exercise No. 40

1. (c)
2. (e)
3. (a)
4. (g)
5. (i)
6. (b)
7. (j)
8. (d)
9. (h)
10. (f)

Exercise No. 41

1. Je parle français.
2. Ils demeurent aux États-Unis.
3. Nous avons faim.
4. La revue est blanche et noire.
5. Les maisons sont rouges.
6. J'ai quinze ans.
7. Les professeurs posent des questions.
8. Nous répondons aux questions.
9. Il attend son ami.
10. J'écris des lettres.

Exercise No. 42

1. travaillons
2. apprennent
3. ne savez pas
4. écris
5. lisent
6. ne comprends pas
7. étudie
8. prenez
9. attendent
10. ne répondez pas
11. lisez
12. n'attendez pas

Exercise No. 43

1. j'ai faim; je n'ai pas faim.
2. je suis enrhumé; je ne suis pas . . .
3. j'étudie la leçon; je n'étudie pas . . .
4. j'attends le professeur; je n'attends pas . . .
5. je compte voyager; je ne compte pas . . .
6. j'apprends à écrire le français; je n'apprends pas . . .
7. je lis la revue; je ne lis pas . . .
8. j'écris la lettre; je n'écris pas . . .
9. je comprends les questions; je ne comprends pas . . .
10. j'accepte l'invitation; je n'accepte pas . . .
11. je commence à lire; je ne commence pas . . .
12. je réponds à la question; je ne réponds pas . . .

Exercise No. 44

1. Qui
2. Qui
3. Qui est-ce que
4. qui
5. qui
6. Qu'est-ce que
7. Qu'
8. Qui
9. Qu'est-ce qui
10. Que
11. Qu'est-ce que
12. Qu'est-ce qui

Exercise No. 45

Mr. Brown already knows the names of all the objects in his house. Now he is beginning to study the verbs because he wants to learn to read, write, and speak in French. He also wants to learn the numbers in French. Since he wants to visit his agent in Paris, who does not speak English, he wants to learn to speak French as soon as possible. Therefore he needs much practice with people who speak French well. Luckily he has two French friends who are in business near his office in Whitehall Street.

One day Mr. Brown goes to visit these French gentlemen. The two gentlemen listen with attention while Mr. Brown talks with them in French. After ten minutes of conversation, the gentlemen ask their friend many questions, and they are happy with his progress.

Exercise No. 46

Thursday, April twenty-second, at nine o'clock in the evening, M. Picard arrives at the house of his student, Mr. Brown. The oldest son, a ten-year-old boy, opens the door, and greets the teacher politely. They go into the living room where Mr. Brown is usually waiting for his teacher.

But this evening he is not there. Mrs. Brown is not there either. M. Picard is very much surprised, and he asks the boy, "Where is your dad?" The son answers sadly, "My dad is sick. He is in bed because he has a bad cold."

The teacher is a bit annoyed but he only says, "What a pity! Well, next week we shall study for two hours. Until next Tuesday, then. Goodbye, little one." The boy answers "Goodbye, sir."

Exercise No. 47

1. Ils prennent
2. ces tasses
3. fleurs bleues
4. célèbre
5. Chaque région
6. très jolie
7. aussi jolie
8. Vous connaissez
9. C'est vrai
10. beaucoup de
11. Comme vous dites
12. C'est un plat simple
13. encore une tasse
14. Tout

Exercise No. 49

1. Nous disons
2. Je vois

3. Il ne dit pas
4. Il dit
5. Dit-il?
6. Que dites-vous?
7. Que voyez-vous?
8. Ils voient
9. Vois-tu?
10. Je ne vois pas
11. Ils disent
12. Que disent-ils?
13. Elle ne voit pas
14. Voyons
15. Dites-moi

Exercise No. 50

1. cette
2. ces
3. ce
4. ces
5. cette
6. cet
7. ces
8. cette
9. ces
10. cet
11. ces
12. cet

Exercise No. 52

1. Ils sont assis dans la salle à manger.
2. Ils prennent du café avec des gâteaux.
3. M. Brown dit,—Comment trouvez-vous ces tasses et ces soucoupes?
4. La tasse blanche est de Limoges.
5. La porcelaine de Limoges est célèbre.
6. Il est de Vallauris.
7. Elle est célèbre pour sa poterie.
8. Elle est en Provence.
9. Elle est très jolie.
10. M. Brown connaît bien son métier.
11. Il a des échantillons de poterie ordinaire.
12. Elle est simple.
13. Il offre encore une tasse de café.
14. Il dit,—Merci bien. Tout est délicieux.

Exercise No. 53

1. Vous savez
2. aussi importante que
3. à quoi
4. Je crois que oui; voulez dire
5. Vous avez raison; sont indispensables
6. Nous avons besoin
7. Sans l'argent; grand'chose
8. En attendant; vous avancez rapidement
9. C'est
10. A jeudi prochain

Exercise No. 54

1. Je veux
2. Je peux (puis)
3. Voulez-vous
4. Pouvez-vous
5. Nous voulons
6. Nous ne pouvons pas
7. Ils ne veulent pas
8. Pouvez-vous
9. Veut-il
10. Peut-elle

Exercise No. 55

a) trente
b) dix
c) cinquante
d) quarante-neuf
e) seize
f) trente-huit
g) dix-sept
h) quinze
i) soixante-deux
j) soixante-huit
k) vingt-quatre
l) treize

Exercise No. 56

a) deux et six font huit
b) dix et sept font dix-sept
c) sept fois huit font cinquante-six
d) neuf fois sept font soixante-trois
e) dix-neuf moins huit égalent onze

f) dix-huit moins six égalent douze

g) soixante divisé par dix égalent six

h) soixante-neuf divisé par trois égalent vingt-trois

Exercise No. 57

1. Il y a sept jours dans une semaine.
2. Il y a douze mois dans une année.
3. Il y a vingt-quatre heures dans une journée.
4. Il y a soixante minutes dans une heure.
5. Il y a soixante secondes dans une minute.
6. Il y a trente jours dans le mois de septembre.
7. Il y a trente-six étudiants dans la classe.
8. J'ai dix-sept ans.
9. Il a dix-neuf ans.
10. Il y a trois automobiles dans le garage.

Exercise No. 58

1. Il sait déjà que les noms des choses et des personnes sont importants.
2. Les nombres sont aussi importants que les noms et les verbes.
3. Nous avons besoin de nombres pour le commerce.
4. Il pense tout de suite au commerce.
5. Nous avons besoin de nombres pour téléphoner.
6. M. Brown veut comprendre et employer les nombres correctement.
7. Il avance rapidement.
8. dix, vingt, trente, quarante, cinquante, soixante

Exercise No. 59

1. Combien de fois; en voyage
2. On; pour acheter des billets
3. dans les grands magasins
4. Connaissez-vous
5. Je le connais
6. vaut
7. à peu près
8. Vous voulez acheter
9. Vous donnez
10. Il me rend

Exercise No. 60

1. What are you doing? I am writing a letter.
2. What is Jean doing? He is playing piano.
3. What is Marie doing? She is studying the French lesson.
4. What are the girls doing? They are shopping.
5. What are you doing, child? I am playing ball.
6. What is Mr. Martin doing? He is having the baggage weighed.
7. Do you believe this story? I do not believe it.
8. Does your friend believe it? He doesn't believe it either.

Exercise No. 61

a) quatre cents
b) mille
c) sept cent cinquante-trois
d) mille neuf cent soixante-quatorze
e) quatre-vingt-quinze
f) soixante-dix-sept
g) quatre-vingt-six
h) soixante et onze
i) six cent soixante-dix
j) quatorze mille cinq cent quatre-vingt-six

Exercise No. 63

1. Il le connaît parce qu'il est importateur d'articles francais.
2. Le premier janvier, deux mille.
3. Le franc existait en France avant l'euro.
4. Douze pays européens ont adopté l'euro.
5. L'euro vaut plus.
6. Les questions de M. Picard sont faciles.
7. Usage rend maître.

Exercise No. 64

1. Savez-vous
2. Nous connaissons
3. Nous ne savons pas
4. Il sait (comment)
5. Je sais
6. Ils ne connaissent pas
7. Je connais
8. Savez-vous (comment)

9. Connaissent-ils

10. savoir

Exercise No. 65

1. Nos
2. ma
3. notre
4. Leurs
5. ses
6. vos
7. votre
8. Son
9. Sa
10. Leurs
11. notre
12. son
13. ton; mon
14. son
15. leur

Exercise No. 66

10 dix

20 vingt

30 trente

40 quarante

50 cinquante

100 cent

22 vingt-deux

44 quarante-quatre

66 soixante-six

88 quatre-vingt-huit

110 cent dix

220 deux cent vingt

16 seize

32 trente-deux

48 quarante-huit

64 soixante-quatre

80 quatre-vingts

160 cent soixante

Exercise No. 67

1. Nous dînons au restaurant.
2. L'addition pour tout le monde monte à 170 (cent soixante-dix) euros.
3. Nous laissons 27 (vingt-sept) euros.

4. Je porte une valise très lourde à la gare.
5. Elle pèse 30 (trente) kilos ou 66 (soixante-six) livres.
6. En France on compte les distances en kilomètres.
7. M. Brown sait changer les kilomètres en milles.
8. M. Brown achète trois paires de chaussures.
9. Le sujet de la prochaine conversation est les heures de la journée.
10. M. Brown dit, "Mieux vaut tard que jamais."

Exercise No. 68

1. À quelle heure
2. La première séance; quatre heures et demie de l'après-midi
3. d'autres questions
4. la gare
5. demande des renseignement
6. un billet d'aller et retour
7. est-ce que le train part
8. Arrive-t-il
9. de bonne heure
10. Les voici
11. Merci bien or Merci beaucoup, monsieur
12. À votre service

Exercise No. 69

1. part
2. partez-vous
3. Nous dormons
4. ne dort pas
5. sert
6. Sentez-vous
7. Je ne sens pas
8. sortent-ils
9. Je sors
10. Ne dormez pas

Exercise No. 70

1. Sept heures et demi du sois
2. dix heures et quart du soir
3. six heures et demie du matin
4. midi
5. quatre heures et demie de l'après-midi

6. sept heures moins vingt du soir
7. à neuf heures du soir
8. quatre heures dix de l'après-midi
9. huit heures moins le quart du matin
10. neuf heures moins vingt du matin

Exercise No. 71

1. Tout le monde veut savoir quelle heure il est.
2. M. Brown joue le rôle du voyageur.
3. M. Picard joue le rôle de l'employé du guichet.
4. Il désire un billet de première classe.
5. Un billet d'aller et retour coûte 22 (vingt-deux) euros.
6. M. Picard joue le rôle de l'employé au cinéma.
7. M. Brown demande des renseignements.
8. Il y a trois séances à ce ciné.
9. Il achète deux billets pour la troisième séance.
10. Il paie 12 (douze) euros pour ces deux billets.

Exercise No. 72

1. (f)
2. (h)
3. (a)
4. (j)
5. (b)
6. (i)
7. (c)
8. (d)
9. (e)
10. (g)

Exercise No. 73

1. demander des renseignements
2. Nous avons besoin d'
3. connaît son métier
4. changer de l'argent
5. pens-tu
6. Aimez-vous
7. j'ai faim
8. voulez-vous dire
9. Nous payons nos repas
10. Vous avez raison
11. Tu as tort
12. avez-vous besoin

Exercise No. 74

1. (c)
2. (h)
3. (a)
4. (d)
5. (g)
6. (k)
7. (b)
8. (e)
9. (l)
10. (f)
11. (i)
12. (j)

Exercise No. 75

1. je pense à mon ami . . .
2. je veux faire . . .
3. je peux acheter . . .
4. je porte . . .
5. je pars . . .
6. je compte . . .
7. je dis . . .
8. je connais . . .
9. je donne . . .
10. je sais . . .

Exercise No. 76

1. nous ne posons pas...
2. nous ne calculons pas . . .
3. nous ne trouvons pas . . .
4. nous ne lisons pas . . .
5. nous n'écrivons pas . . .
6. nous ne dînons pas . . .
7. nous ne connaissons pas . . .
8. nous n'achetons pas . . .
9. nous n'avons pas . . .
10. nous ne savons pas . . .

Exercise No. 77

The Brown Family Drops in on Mom

It is the first time that the Brown family is visiting Mrs. Brown at her office. Today Mr. Brown has the day off; he takes advantage of this occasion to take a walk with the children and pay a visit to his wife at the university. Mr. Brown and his four children enter quite a stately building and go up in the elevator to the fifteenth floor where Mrs. Brown's office is located. Anne, the youngest, who is only five years old, is very curious. She asks her father many questions about the students circulating in the halls.

When they arrive at the office, the mother gets up and says, "What a pleasant surprise! How glad I am to see you!" The children admire all the objects they see in the office: the computer, the bookcases (*rayons de livres*, shelves of books), and on the walls the diplomas and certificates, a beautiful world map and especially the posters. Everybody is very happy.

Charles, the oldest, looks out of the large window and sees the blue sky and the sun which is shining. Below, he and his sister Anne look at the automobiles which are going down the street. From the fifteenth floor they seem very small.

The visit over, the whole family enters a little restaurant that is not far from the university, for Mrs. Brown must be back in one hour for another class. They all eat heartily, especially the children, because they are very hungry.

Exercise No. 78
1. J'aime beaucoup voir
2. ne m'intéressent pas
3. Ils adorent
4. toutes les vedettes de l'écran
5. Ils les connaissent
6. près de chez vous
7. à pied
8. Nous préférons
9. Donc; de bonne heure

Exercise No. 79
1. Je viens
2. Ils ne viennent pas
3. vient
4. viennent
5. Venez
6. Venez-vous
7. Nous revenons
8. revient-il
9. Elle ne vient pas
10. venez-vous
11. devenir
12. Je veux devenir

Exercise No. 80
1. les
2. la
3. l'
4. les
5. le
6. la
7. le
8. vous
9. nous
10. nous
11. y
12. y
13. vous
14. m'
15. t'

Exercise No. 81
1. M. Brown sait demander des renseignements.
2. Ils préfèrent le théâtre.
3. Ils préfèrent le ciné.
4. Oui, monsieur, ils les connaissent bien.
5. Il est près de la maison de M. Brown.
6. Ils préfèrent les places du quatorzième ou du quinzième rang.
7. De là il est possible de bien voir et entendre.
8. Ils arrivent de bonne heure.

Exercise No. 82
1. Vous savez (comment)
2. un événement important
3. Commençons
4. Comme (Que)
5. une date triste

6. une date victorieuse
7. Finissons
8. aussi bien que
9. D'ailleurs
10. Il m'apprend
11. C'est vous
12. Pas du tout

Exercise No. 83
1. finissez-vous
2. Nous finissons
3. choisissez-vous
4. Je choisis
5. punit
6. il n'obéit pas
7. bâtissent
8. Remplissez
9. Ils ne finissent pas
10. remplit
11. Choisissons

Exercise No. 84
1. première
2. troisième
3. quatorzième
4. cinquième
5. douzième
6. premier
7. dernière
8. neuvième
9. derniers

Exercise No. 85
1. le dix-huit avril mil sept cent (*or* dix-sept cent) soixante-quinze
2. le douze octobre mil quatre cent (*or* quatorze cent) quatre-vingt douze
3. le vingt-deux février mil huit cent (*or* dix-huit cent) neuf
4. le premier mai mil neuf cent (*or* dix-neuf cent) cinquante-six

Exercise No. 86
1. Il apprend vite parce qui'il aime les questionnaires en français.

2. M. Picard va citer quelques dates de l'histoire de France.
3. M. Brown va citer un événement important pour chacune.
4. Il cite la prise de la Bastille.
5. Il cite la bataille de Waterloo.
6. C'est une date triste.
7. Il cite la victoire des Alliés à la fin de la première guerre mondiale.
8. C'est une date glorieuse pour les Parisiens.

Exercise No. 87
1. Voyons; la géographie de France.
2. que je vous pose
3. recevoir un prix
4. est situé
5. de café, coton, et sucre
6. le fleuve le plus long
7. beaucoup plus long que
8. plus petit que
9. la plus haute montagne
10. plus haut que
11. que vous avez raison
12. est terminé

Exercise No. 88
1. Je mets
2. Qui soumet
3. Pourquoi mettez-vous?
4. Que mets-tu? *or* Qu'est-ce que tu mets?
5. Nous ne soumettons pas
6. Ils ne mettent pas
7. Je n'admets pas
8. Permet-il?
9. Pourquoi permettez-vous?
10. Remettez le
11. Ne permet-il pas?
12. Permettez-moi

Exercise No. 89
1. Are French films better than American films?
2. Some are better, some are worse. In France and in the United States one can see the best

and also the worst films. In general, I like the French films better.

3. Robert sings badly. Richard sings worse than Robert. But Bernard sings worst of all.

4. Herbert writes well. But you write better than he. Renée writes best of all.

5. Where do they make the best porcelain? They make it in Limoges.

6. Better late than never.

Exercise No. 90

1. aussi, que
2. plus aimable que
3. la meilleure plume
4. si bonne que
5. plus grande que
6. le plus diligent
7. la plus jeune
8. plus intéressant que
9. le plus long
10. la plus grande ville
11. plus long que
12. mal
13. les meilleurs films
14. la pire (la plus mauvaise)
15. plus de

Exercise No. 91

1. La question est: Sur quel grand fleuve est-ce que la ville de Paris est située?

2. Il est situé à l'embouchure de la Seine.

3. C'est un grand marché de café, de coton et de sucre.

4. Le Mississippi est plus long et plus large que la Loire.

5. Le Mount McKinley est plus haut que le Mont Blanc.

6. a. M. Dupont est le plus jeune des trois.
   b. M. Arnaud est le plus âgé des trois.
   c. Mme Millet est plus âgée que M. Dupont.
   d. M. Dupont est le plus riche.
   e. M. Arnaud est le moins riche.

f. Mme Millet n'est pas si riche que M. Dupont, or Elle est moins riche que M. Dupont.

Exercise No. 92

1. une journée typique
2. à six heures et demie
3. matinal
4. de bonne heure
5. Que mangez-vous
6. du café, des petits pains et des oeufs
7. Parfois
8. au bureau
9. mon courrier; les réponses
10. Que faites-vous
11. me voir
12. finissez-vous
13. Je quitte
14. Nous nous mettons

Exercise No. 93

1. se
2. se
3. se, s'
4. vous
5. vous
6. se
7. se
8. nous
9. vous
10. s'
11. m'
12. toi
13. vous
14. me
15. se

Exercise No. 94

1. What is your name? My name is Albert.
2. At what time do you get up? I get up at 7 A.M.
3. At what time do you go to bed? I go to bed at 11 P.M.
4. Do you dress quickly? I dress very quickly.
5. How are you? I'm feeling well, thank you.

6. How is your father? He is not well. He has a cold.

7. At what time does Mr. Brown sit down to table? He sits down to table at 7 P.M.

8. Are the boys having a good time playing baseball? Yes, they are having a very good time.

Exercise No. 95

1. Il se lève à six heures et demie.
2. Il se lave et il s'habille.
3. Il s'habille dans une demi-heure plus ou moins.
4. A sept heures à peu près il se met à table dans la salle à manger.
5. Elle se lève de bonne heure.
6. Ils déjeunent ensemble.
7. Il prend du jus d'orange, du café, des petits pains, et des oeufs.
8. Parfois il mange des crêpes au lieu des oeufs.
9. Il est prêt à partir à sept heures et demie.
10. Il arrive à son bureau à neuf heures.
11. Il prend son déjeuner à une heure.
12. Il mange un sandwich, un café et un dessert quelconque.
13. Des clients viennent le voir dans l'aprèsmidi.
14. Il finit sa journée à cinq heures.

Exercise No. 96

1. bien renseigné
2. tout de même
3. Nous restons
4. votre marché
5. des fruits, des légumes, du lait, du beurre, du fromage et du café
6. des bas et des casseroles
7. stationner
8. à son aise
9. de bons camarades
10. J'ai envie de déménager

Exercise No. 97

1. du, du

2. du; du; des
3. de
4. des
5. des
6. d'
7. de la; de la; des
8. de
9. de l'
10. de

Exercise No. 98

1. Oui, nous en vendons beaucoup.
2. Oui, elle en achète.
3. Non, je n'en ai pas (un).
4. Prenez-en
5. N'en mangez pas.
6. Il en a trente.
7. Merci. Je n'en veux pas.
8. Oui, ils en ont assez.

Exercise No. 99

1. M. Picard est toujours curieux.
2. Il sait déjà que M. Brown rentre assez tard.
3. La famille Brown ne termine pas son dîner bien avant huit heures et demie.
4. Parce que les enfants ne veulent pas se coucher.
5. Ils les font au supermarché.
6. On achète des fruits, des légumes, du lait, du café, des conserves, toutes sortes de viande, et ainsi de suite (and so on).
7. On n'y trouve pas de pardessus.
8. Plusieurs des grands magasins ont des succursales.
9. Ils aiment leurs maîtres d'école.
10. M. Picard a envie de déménager à la banlieue.

Exercise No. 100

1. (i)
2. (e)
3. (f)
4. (h)
5. (g)
6. (a)

7. (c)
8. (j)
9. (b)
10. (d)

Exercise No. 101

1. le fleuve le plus long
2. plus grande que
3. plus fatigué que
4. si grand que
5. plus haut que
6. la plus haute montagne
7. le premier jour
8. le 30 janvier 1988 (mil neuf cent quatre-vingt-huit)
9. de la famille
10. mon meilleur ami

Exercise No. 102

1. Do you take coffee or chocolate for your breakfast? I take neither one nor the other. I drink a glass of water.
2. Do you want cream and sugar in your coffee? I want some cream but I do not want any sugar.
3. What do they eat for breakfast in France? They eat very little; generally rolls and coffee.
4. What do they eat for breakfast in the United States? Usually they begin with orange juice. Then they eat any cereal, a piece of toast or eggs. Americans are also very fond of pancakes with syrup. Of course there is also coffee, tea, or milk to drink.

Exercise No. 103

1. Oui, je les invite.
2. Non, je ne le préfère pas.
3. Oui, ils les connaissent bien.
4. Oui, nous vous attendons.
5. Non, je me lève tard.
6. Nous nous couchons à onze heures.
7. Oui, ils s'habillent très vite.
8. Je m'appelle Albert Martin.
9. Nous les finissons à quatre heures de l'après-midi.

10. Oui, ils le finissent maintenant.

Exercise No. 104

1. fatiguée; pareille
2. Ils se mettent à table
3. Ils sont (or restent) debout
4. sont assis
5. De temps en temps; au lieu de
6. attraper un rhume
7. la plupart de
8. à l'heure
9. Nous sommes, les bienvenus
10. de bonne heure; tard

Exercise No. 105

A Visit to the Liner *Queen Elizabeth 2*

It is Saturday. Mr. Brown gets up at eight o'clock and looks out of the window. The sky is blue. The sun is shining. He says to his wife. "Today let's visit the liner *Queen Elizabeth 2*, which arrived this morning. I have some goods on board. We'll have a good opportunity to visit the ship."

"Fine," says Mrs. Brown.

At nine o'clock, they leave in the car and in about an hour they arrive at the pier. At the entrance they see a group of boys who are eating ice cream and who are talking in French.

Mr. Brown greets the boys and he talks a bit with the nearest one. Here is the conversation:

"Good morning, young man. Are you French?"

"No sir, I'm American."

"But you speak French very well."

"Well these boys who work on the liner are my friends and they are teaching me how to speak correctly. They are my teachers. Besides, I study French in high school and every day I read a few pages of French. By the way, are you French?"

"No, young man, I am American like you and like you I am studying French. But I have only one teacher."

"I see. But you speak very well."

"Thank you. Goodbye and good luck."

"Goodbye, sir."

Mr. Brown goes back to his wife who is waiting for him smiling, and they continue on their way for the visit to the ocean liner.

"Il est sympathique, ce garçon," Mr. Brown says to his wife. Then he translates the sentence ("He's a likable boy.") to see his wife's reaction.

Exercise No. 106

1. Quel mauvais temps!
2. Entrez, entrez; trempé
3. votre imperméable
4. Mettez
5. ça va mieux
6. attraper un rhume
7. on ne doit pas sortir
8. Venez
9. leur apporte
10. Prenez
11. Permettez-moi
12. il pleut toujours

Exercise No. 107

1. lui
2. nous
3. lui
4. leur
5. leur
6. Lui
7. m'
8. lui
9. lui
10. nous
11. nous
12. moi
13. leur
14. lui
15. lui

Exercise No. 108

1. Il pleut à verse.
2. La bonne ouvre la porte.
3. Il le met dans le porte-parapluies.
4. Il les laisse à l'entrée.
5. Ils entrent dans la salle à manger.
6. Ils prennent du thé au rhum.
7. Elle met sur la table des tasses, des soucoupes, une théière pleine de thé, un sucrier, des cuillers à thé et une bouteille de rhum.
8. Après elle sort de la salle à manger.

Exercise No. 109

1. en prenant
2. à pleuvoir
3. il fait chaud
4. il fait très froid
5. il pleut souvent
6. Je préfère (or J'aime mieux)
7. préférez-vous (or aimez-vous mieux)
8. parlons plutôt
9. de chaleur et de froid
10. doit
11. il fait beau

Exercise No. 111

1. ne, rien
2. n'—pas encore
3. ne—jamais
4. n'—pas—non plus
5. ne—rien; ne—rien
6. Ne—pas
7. n'—plus
8. ne—pas non plus
9. n'—rien
10. n'—qu'
11. Rien
12. Pas encore
13. ne—jamais
14. n'—ni—ni

Exercise No. 112

1. Ils parlent du climat.
2. Le climat de la France est quelque peu différent de celui des États-Unis.
3. Il fait chaud. Des fois il fait très chaud.
4. Il préfère l'automne.
5. Il préfère le printemps.
6. Il y a une différence assez marquée entre les saisons en France.
7. Il pleut beaucoup, il fait du vent, le ciel est gris.
8. Le ciel est bleu clair et l'air est doux, embaumé.

Exercise No. 113

1. nous allons continuer
2. très désagréable
3. qui ont les moyens
4. Est-ce qu'il n'y a pas d'hiver
5. Il ne fait jamais froid
6. Il fait mettre
7. nager le matin
8. On peut voir
9. doit être
10. Si vous avez le temps

Exercise No. 114

1. Which pottery do you prefer, that of Vallauris or that of Biot? I prefer that of Biot.
2. Which hat do you like better? This one or that one? I prefer that one.
3. Which climate is milder, that of France or that of Canada? That of France is milder.
4. How do you like these dresses? I like this one. I find the colors of that one too bright (Lit. brilliant).
5. Which seats do you prefer, those in the first rows or those in the rear? We prefer those in the first rows.
6. What kind of handkerchiefs are you going to buy? I am going to buy those which are cheapest.

Exercise No. 115

1. celles
2. ceux
3. celui-là
4. celles-là
5. celles-là
6. ceux-là
7. celui-ci; celui-là
8. celle-ci; celle-là
9. celui
10. cela

Exercise No. 116

1. Ils quittent Paris en hiver parce que l'hiver est désagréable.
2. Ils vont en Suisse ou à la Côte d'Azur.
3. L'hiver est doux. Le soleil brille presque tous les jours.
4. En été il fail plus chaud, mais il y a toujours une jolie brise de mer.
5. Sur la Côte d'Azur on peut nager le matin et faire du ski l'après-midi
6. On peut voir les montagnes couvertes de neige.
7. Il fait frais pendant la nuit.
8. Il fait très froid dans les montagnes.
9. Les montagnes sont à une distance d'à peu près quatre-vingts kilomètres de la plage.
10. M. Brown va essayer de faire ce petit voyage au mois de juin.

Exercise No. 117

1. la bonne cuisine française
2. un des plus grands plaisirs
3. à déjeuner
4. Cela arrive
5. nous fait cadeau
6. Ramenez
7. Je vais vous dire
8. Tout ce qui; de bonne qualité
9. Il faut avoir
10. du beurre, du beurre, et encore du beurre

Exercise No. 118

1. avec moi
2. pour toi

3. chez moi

4. chez nous

5. chez elle

6. sans eux

7. près d'elle

8. autour de nous

9. à nous

10. à elles

Exercise No. 119

1. Lui; Elle

2. Moi

3. moi; nous; eux

4. toi

5. moi

6. lui

7. elle et moi

8. Moi

9. à vous

10. à lui

Exercise No. 120

1. La bonne cuisine française est un des plus grands plaisirs du touriste en France.

2. Oui. Il connaît un peu la cuisine française.

3. Elle nous fait cadeau de beaucoup d'expressions d'usage courant.

4. Il doit faire une liste de ses plats préférés.

5. Vraiment, non. La cuisine française n'est pas compliquée.

6. Le troisième secret est: du beurre, du beurre et encore du beurre.

7. Oui. Il va tout de suite les raconter à sa femme.

8. M. Brown est un mari modèle.

9. M. Brown a un appétit de loup.

10. M. Picard va casser la croûte avec lui.

Exercise No. 121

1. (c)

2. (f)

3. (a)

4. (e)

5. (g)

6. (i)

7. (k)

8. (b)

9. (d)

10. (l)

11. (h)

12. (j)

Exercise No. 122

1. j'ai froid

2. j'ai chaud

3. il fait chaud

4. il pleut beaucoup

5. il fait frais

6. il fait froid

7. un imperméable

8. je porte un pardessus

9. tombe

10. toutes les saisons

Exercise No. 123

1. (d)

2. (f)

3. (a)

4. (g)

5. (i)

6. (h)

7. (e)

8. (b)

9. (j)

10. (c)

Exercise No. 124

1. lui

2. lui

3. l'

4. le

5. la; se

6. moi; vous

7. les

8. la

9. m'

10. leur

Exercise No. 125

1. Je ne connais personne.
2. Nous ne mangeons jamais de viande.
3. Je n'ai qu'un professeur.
4. Elle ne veut plus ce chapeau-là.
5. Jeanne ne va pas encore à l'école.
6. Je ne suis pas fatiguée non plus.
7. Nous n'avons plus de temps.
8. Pourquoi ne dites-vous rien?
9. Nous n'avons ni temps ni argent.

Exercise No. 126

An Unusual Program at the Movies

This evening Mr. and Mrs. Brown are going to the movies. They don't like the majority of Hollywood films, especially the Westerns in which the cowboys fire shots at everybody and are constantly galloping. Detective stories don't interest them either.

But this evening there is an unusual program in a theater very near their home. The picture is called "A Trip to France." This is a documentary film on the country which Mr. Brown is going to visit in a few months. There are scenes portraying the history of France, others which show its countryside, its rivers, its mountains, its large cities, etc. That is to say that it is a most interesting film for tourists.

The Browns arrive at the theatre at 8:30. Almost all the seats are taken, so they have to sit in the third row. Mr. Brown does not like this because the movements on the screen hurt his eyes. Fortunately they are able to change their seats after a quarter of an hour, and they take seats in the thirteenth row.

The Browns enjoy this picture very much. They find it fascinating.

On leaving the theatre Mr. Brown says to his wife, "You know Alice, I believe that I will get along well in France. I understood almost everything they said."

Exercise No. 127

1. quelques
2. prêt
3. très à mon aise
4. Ils se ressemblent
5. partout
6. comme vous dites
7. quelques-unes de ces
8. Les pêcheurs et les marins
9. Les fermiers
10. Les ouvriers des mines
11. Nous n'avons pas besoin
12. ne ressemblent pas
13. discuter

Exercise No. 128

1. étudions, étudiant
2. venons, venant
3. lisons, lisant
4. achetons, achetant
5. voulons, voulant
6. disons, disant
7. choisissons, choisissant
8. finissons, finissant
9. bâtissons, bâtissant
10. connaissons, connaissant
11. apprenons, apprenant
12. appelons, appelant
13. comptons, comptant
14. dormons, dormant
15. mettons, mettant
16. faisons, faisant
17. avons, ayant
18. sommes, étant

Exercise No. 129

1. quelqu'un
2. quelques
3. Quelques-uns
4. Quelques-unes
5. quelques-unes
6. quelques

7. quelques

8. quelques

9. quelques-unes

10. quelqu'un

Exercise No. 130

1. Il va poser quelques questions à M. Picard sur les Français.

2. Il demande si les Français se ressemblent plus ou moins.

3. Oui. Il est vrai qu'il y a de très grandes différences entre tous les Français.

4. Il y a des différences entre les Français à cause de la géographie et aussi à cause de leurs métiers.

5. Les pêcheurs de la Bretagne sont très dévots et très dévoués au Calvados.

6. Les gens du Midi sont bavards et blagueurs.

7. Non. Ils ne ressemblent pas trop aux montagnards de l'Auvergne.

8. Oui. Les Français aiment beaucoup discuter.

9. Ils sont fiers de leur tradition de démocratie, de philosophie, de belles-lettres et de science.

10. Ils aiment tous la bonne cuisine et le bon vin.

Exercise No. 131

1. vient de recevoir

2. est en train d'admirer

3. non seulement . . . mais aussi

4. que vous n'aimez pas

5. n'est-ce pas?

6. les beaux-arts

7. la peinture, la sculpture et l'architecture

8. Je compte sur le plaisir

9. tout à fait exceptionnel

10. Je vous admire

Exercise No. 132

1. Elle achète

2. Préférez-vous

3. je préfère

4. Répétons

5. J'espère

6. vous levez-vous

7. Je me lève

8. célèbre

9. s'appelle

10. jettent

11. appelle

12. Je répète

Exercise No. 133

1. Il vient de recevoir une grande caisse de marchandise.

2. M. Picard est en train de la regarder et de l'admirer.

3. Il y a des échantillons de riches étoffes de soie.

4. La belle étoffe de laine est de la maison Dior.

5. M. Picard croit que M. Brown n'aime pas la mode.

6. M. Brown est amateur des arts.

7. Il va voir l'art des grands maîtres.

8. Il espère visiter aussi les musées de l'art moderne.

9. M. Brown s'intéresse à l'art, à l'histoire et aux belles-lettres.

10. Ils vont former une société d'estime mutuelle.

Exercise No. 134

1. la grande fête nationale

2. On célèbre

3. Tout le monde

4. toute la journée; toute la nuit

5. les Guignols

6. célébrée

7. en dormant

8. Le jour de l'An

9. les étrennes

10. table ouverte

11. doit être

12. Tout le monde quitte Paris

13. par-ci ou par là

Exercise No. 135

1. Il tient

2. Nous obtenons

3. Je ne retiens pas

4. tient table ouverte

5. Nous commençons à travailler

6. changeons-nous

7. prononcez-vous
8. Nous le prononçons
9. Nous ne mangons pas
10. nous nageons
11. Nous corrigeons
12. Recommençons

Exercise No. 136
1. on
2. personne ne
3. On
4. rien
5. personne
6. rien
7. Rien
8. Personne
9. personne
10. Personne ne

Exercise No. 137
1. Ils vont parler des jours de fête en France.
2. On célèbre le quatorze juillet dans les rues.
3. On danse dans les rues.
4. On vend des crêpes, des gauffres, des glaces et toutes sortes de friandises.
5. Il y a les petits chevaux de bois et les Guignols pour les enfants.
6. Il faut dire la Noël.
7. On dort parce qu'on a réveillonné toute la nuit.
8. Les enfants reçoivent leurs cadeaux le jour de l'An.
9. On les appelle les étrennes.
10. La ville est morte.

Exercise No. 138
1. Je voyagerai
2. Je visiterai
3. faudra
4. Je ferai
5. J'irai
6. Je passerai
7. Je prendrai
8. Je reviendrai
9. mieux que moi

10. sera
11. qui arrive à tout le monde
12. chez soi

Exercise No. 139
1. Where will you go next summer? I shall go to France. When will you leave N.Y.? I shall leave May 31.
2. How much time will you spend in France? I shall spend three months there. Will you travel by plane or by boat? I shall travel by plane.
3. Will you take a trip to Morocco? I shall take a trip to Morocco. Will Mr. Picard be able to go with you? Unfortunately, he will not be able to go with me.
4. Will you see your agent in Paris? Yes indeed. She will be waiting for me at the airport. How long will you stay in Paris? I shall stay there two weeks.
5. Will you visit the Riviera? Of course I shall visit it. When will you return to the U.S.? I shall return September 1.

Exercise No. 140
1. Il visitera
2. Je voyagerai
3. Nous irons
4. Ils n'écriront pas
5. Il faudra
6. Verrez-vous?
7. Ils ne partiront pas
8. Nous vendrons
9. Ne finira-t-il pas?
10. Elle n'apprendra pas
11. Il sera
12. Viendrez-vous?
13. J'aurai
14. Tu n'écouteras pas
15. Nous étudierons
16. Je ne ferai pas
17. Pourrez-vous?
18. Irez-vous?

Exercise No. 141

1. Il voyagera en avion.
2. Il verra la Vénus de Milo, la Mona Lisa et la salle de céramique grecque.
3. Il passera par le jardin des Tuileries.
4. Il prendra un taxi à la Place de l'Étoile.
5. Il visitera la Tour Eiffel.
6. Il se promènera en taxi au Bois de Boulogne.
7. M. Brown connaît le Paris des guides.
8. On se sent chez soi à Paris.
9. Le soir du quatorze juillet on voit jouer les grandes fontaines à Versailles.
10. Il se trempera dans la mer et dans le soleil à la Côte d'Azur.
11. Il reviendra à Paris par la route des Alpes.

Exercise No. 142

1. (e)
2. (g)
3. (l)
4. (n)
5. (b)
6. (c)
7. (i)
8. (o)
9. (m)
10. (j)
11. (h)
12. (k)
13. (d)
14. (a)
15. (f)

Exercise No. 143

1. la ceinture de cuir leather belt
2. la robe de soie silk dress
3. la montre d'or gold watch
4. la salle de bain bathroom
5. la chemise de laine woolen shirt
6. le bureau de poste post office
7. le voyage d'affaires business trip
8. le cahier de musique music book
9. le tissu de coton cotton cloth
10. le bracelet d'argent silver bracelet
11. l'objet d'art art object
12. le chapeau de paille straw hat

Exercise No. 144

1. J'achèterai une cravate.
2. Elle coûtera vingt euros.
3. J'irai en France.
4. Je reviendrai aux États-Unis le 31 décembre.
5. Je me coucherai à minuit.
6. Je me lèverai à six heures du matin.
7. Je ne lui dirai rien.
8. Personne n'ira avec moi.
9. Je travaillerai toute la journée.
10. Nous nous rencontrerons à l'entrée du théâtre.

Exercise No. 145

1. Ils n'ont pas peur l'exprimer leurs idées.
2. Nous n'avons pas besoin de continuer.
3. Elle a l'intention de porter son manteau neuf.
4. Avez-vous envie de m'accompagner?
5. Il fera son possible pour vous aider.
6. Allez-vous faire des achats au Marché aux Puces?
7. M. Brown est en train d'ouvrir la caisse.
8. Avez-vous peur de dire la vérité?
9. Allez-vous vous promener en voiture au Bois de Boulogne?
10. Vous savez que M. Brown ne s'intéresse pas à la mode.

Exercise No. 146

1. mon chapeau
2. ton manteau
3. sa chemise de laine
4. sa robe de soie
5. notre ceinture de cuir
6. vos gants rouges
7. leur imperméable
8. leur fichu
9. Cette robe
10. Cette cravate
11. Ces gants
12. Cette jupe

Exercise No. 147

Mrs. Brown's Birthday

It is March 22, Mrs. Brown's birthday. She is thirty-five years old today. To celebrate this festive day the Brown family is going to dine in an elegant restaurant on Madison Avenue in New York.

When they enter the restaurant they see a beautiful basket full of white roses on the table reserved for the Browns. Naturally Mrs. Brown is very much surprised. She thanks and kisses her dear husband warmly.

At the end of a delicious dinner Anne, the youngest, says in a low voice to the other children, "Now!" And each of the four children takes a pretty little box from under the table. These are presents for their mother.

Anne gives her a silk handkerchief; Elizabeth, a linen blouse; Thomas, a pair of gloves; and Charles, a woolen scarf.

The following week, Mr. Brown figures out the bill for that day, which follows:

Dinner $160

Tip 24

Flowers 40

Gifts . . . . _126_

Total $350

"What a coincidence," says Mr. Brown. "Three hundred fifty dollars, ten times thirty-five years."

Exercise No. 148

1. à la main
2. vient d'arriver
3. qui suit
4. Je partirai
5. J'ai l'intention
6. très occupé
7. Par conséquent
8. Depuis quelque temps; deux fois par semaine
9. une seule faute
10. Voulez-vous bien

Exercise No. 149

1. Je leur enverrai
2. recevra
3. Ils sauront
4. Il ne voudra pas
5. courront
6. ne vaudront pas
7. Ils nous devront
8. Ils tiendront
9. Traduirez-vous
10. Nous ne suivrons pas
11. Je ferai
12. Nous pourrons

Exercise No. 150

1. Combien de temps
2. pendant les mois
3. Depuis quand
4. depuis dix ans
5. depuis deux ans
6. depuis trois heures
7. Combien de temps
8. Il y a trois jours
9. Depuis quand demeurez-vous
10. Nous y demeurons

Exercise No. 151

1. Ils sont assis dans le salon chez M. Brown.
2. Il tient deux lettres à la main.
3. Il va lire sa lettre à Mme Parmentier.
4. Il partira de New-York le 31 mai.
5. Il passera deux mois en France; *or* Il y passera deux mois.
6. Il restera à Paris trois semaines.
7. Il espère voyager au Maroc en avion, et peut-être en Corse.
8. Mme Parmentier est très occupée.

9. Il veut faire la connaissance de Mme Parmentier.
10. Il écrit d'avance dans l'espoir de pouvoir arranger un rendez-vous.
11. Il y a cinq mois que M. Brown prend des leçons de français.

Exercise No. 152
1. Il est en train de lire
2. J'ai reçu
3. pendant les mois
4. Je compte sur le plaisir
5. que je parlerai en français
6. vous féliciter
7. Vous avez connu
8. si je suis fier
9. Vous verrez
10. Je pourrai

Exercise No. 153
1. Did Mr. Picard ask Mr. Brown some difficult questions? Yes, he asked him some difficult questions. Did Mr. Brown answer well? Yes, he answered all the questions well.
2. When did Mr. Brown write the letter to his agent? He wrote the letter two weeks ago today. To whom did he read a copy of the letter? He read the copy to Mr. Picard.
3. Did Mr. Picard find many mistakes in the letter? He did not find a single mistake. What book helped Mr. Brown a great deal? The book, "Commercial Correspondence" helped him a great deal.
4. Did Mr. Brown appreciate the services of Mrs. Parmentier? Yes, he always appreciated her loyal services. What did Mr. Picard say when Mr. Brown finished reading the letter? He said, "It is a nice letter."

Exercise No. 154
1. reçu
2. décidé
3. apprécié
4. contribué

5. vendu
6. écrit
7. lu
8. rendu
9. fait
10. entendu; dit
11. fini
12. servi

Exercise No. 155
1. M. Brown a écrit une lettre à sa représentante.
2. Il a lu la copie de cette lettre à son professeur.
3. Il n'a pas trouvé une seule faute.
4. Mme Parmentier sera à Paris pendant les mois de juin et juillet.
5. Elle va rencontrer M. Brown (*or* Elle va le rencontrer) à l'aéroport Charles de Gaulle.
6. Il va parler en français avec elle.
7. Il l'a connue comme représentante de toute confiance.
8. M. Brown est certain qu'il sera content parmi les Français.
9. Les deux messieurs auront leur dernier rendez-vous mardi prochain.
10. Ils se rencontreront au bureau de M. Brown.
11. M. Picard lui donnera quelques derniers conseils.

Exercise No. 156
1. Par la fenêtre ouverte
2. J'ai envie
3. Voulez-vous bien me donner
4. avec plus de formalité
5. Chaque personne est digne
6. se connaître l'un l'autre
7. est plus tranquille
8. Avez-vous lu
9. J'ai parcouru
10. Je passerai
11. Vous allez me manquer *or* Vous me manquerez
12. Je serai content

Exercise No. 157

1. parcouru
2. compris; dit
3. mis
4. promis
5. entendu; compris
6. vu
7. couru
8. appris
9. pris
10. pris

Exercise No. 158

1. Have you recommended these guides? Yes, I have recommended them.
2. Did he write the answer? Yes, he wrote it.
3. Where did he find the money? He found it on the desk.
4. Did you understand the question? No, I did not understand it.
5. Has she learned the proverb? No, she hasn't learned it.
6. Who reserved the two seats? My father reserved them yesterday.
7. When did you see your friend? I saw her yesterday evening.
8. When did they finish the examination? They finished it at two o'clock.
9. When did the postman bring the letters? He brought them this morning.
10. Did you hear the bell? No, I did not hear it.
11. Has Mr. Brown scanned all the guidebooks? He has scanned them all.
12. What letter did he read to Mr. Picard? He read the letter which he received from Mrs. Parmentier.

Exercise No. 159

1. Ils se trouvent dans le bureau de M. Brown.
2. Il fait chaud.
3. On entend les bruits de la rue.
4. M. Brown est content de quitter la ville.
5. M. Picard a envie d'accompagner M. Brown. (*or* de l'accompagner.)
6. Il répond,—Malheureusement, ce n'est pas possible.
7. On fait les choses avec plus de formalité en France.
8. Il a remarqué que les affaires se traitent en France avec plus de formalité qu'ici.
9. M. Brown est fatiqué d'être bousculé.
10. M. Brown a lu des livres sur la France.
11. M. Picard les a recommandés.
12. M. Picard passera l'été à New-York.
13. M. Brown pensera souvent à M. Picard.

Exercise No. 160

1. Il y a cinq mois
2. Il a appris
3. Il a vraiment travaillé
4. Il a obtenu
5. Il a écrit
6. a promis
7. il doit être
8. ne l'accompagne pas
9. doivent finir
10. a fait
11. Ils montent tous
12. a fait peser ses bagages
13. Il doit payer
14. fait ses adieux à
15. en route

Exercise No. 161

1. il a voulu
2. vous avez ouvert
3. j'ai su
4. A-t-il ouvert?
5. nous avons eu
6. ils ont été
7. je n'ai pas couvert
8. Ont-ils su?
9. nous n'avons pas ouvert
10. elle a été
11. A-t-il voulu?
12. j'ai offert

Exercise No. 162

1. ouverte
2. illustrées
3. fermées
4. connu
5. cassées
6. levés
7. habillé
8. envoyées
9. reservée
10. perdus

Exercise No. 163

1. Il y a cinq ans qu'il étudie le français.
2. Il a passé beaucoup de temps en conversation avec son professeur M. Picard.
3. Il a appris les règles essentielles de la grammaire.
4. Il a vraiment travaillé beaucoup.
5. Il parle bien le français maintenant.
6. M. Brown a obtenu son billet, son passeport et ses chèques de voyage.
7. Il a écrit à sa représentante.
8. Sa représentante lui a promis de le recontrer à l'aéroport.
9. Ils se sont levés à sept heures du matin.
10. Il part à sept heures précises.
11. Chaque voyageur doit faire vérifier son billet et son passeport.
12. Sa famille n'accompagne pas M. Brown (or ne l'accompagne pas) en France.
13. Ils doivent finir l'année scolaire.
14. Elle doit rester à New-York pour s'occuper aussi des enfants.

Exercise No. 164

1. obtained **obtenir**
2. left **laisser**
3. been **être**
4. said **dire**
5. finished **finir**
6. wanted **vouloir**
7. received **recevoir**
8. written **écrire**
9. read **lire**
10. learned **apprendre**
11. known **savoir**
12. given back **rendre**
13. put **mettre**
14. obeyed **obéir**
15. seen **voir**
16. eaten **manger**
17. done, made **faire**
18. taken **prendre**
19. listened **écouter**
20. covered **couvrir**
21. understood **comprendre**
22. opened **ouvrir**
23. had **avoir**
24. permitted **permettre**
25. been able **pouvoir**

Exercise No. 165

1. (g)
2. (e)
3. (a)
4. (h)
5. (c)
6. (i)
7. (d)
8. (j)
9. (b)
10. (f)

Exercise No. 166

1. Avez-vous fait
2. Faites mes amitiés
3. de ma part
4. dans votre propre langue
5. Pardonnez-moi
6. me tirer d'affaires
7. de faire votre connaissance
8. Ils montent en voiture
9. Ils descendent de la voiture
10. a fait ses adieux

Exercise No. 167

1. Oui, monsieur, je l'ai reçue.
2. Il l'a écrite à Mme Parmentier.

3. Oui, monsieur, il les a appreciés.
4. M. Brown l'a faite.
5. Oui, monsieur, ils m'ont rendu grand service.
6. Elle a servi du thé au rhum.
7. Non, monsieur, je ne l'ai pas comprise.
8. Philippe ne les a pas faites.
9. Non, madame, nous ne l'avons pas vu.
10. Il a apporté un colis postal.

Exercise No. 168

Gerard Does Not Like To Study Arithmetic

One day upon returning home from school Gerard says to his mother, "I don't like to study arithmetic. It's so difficult. Why do we need so many exercises and so many problems? We have calculators, don't we? Well, then!"

Mrs. Davis looks at her son and says. "You are wrong, my dear (*Lit.* my little one). We cannot do without numbers. For example, one always needs to spend money, go shopping, estimate distances and . . . and . . ." The mother stops speaking on seeing that Gerard is not paying attention to what she says.

"By the way, dear," she continues, smiling, "baseball doesn't interest you either?"

"What an idea! You're joking."

"Well then if the Dodgers have won eighty games and they have lost twenty do you know what percentage of games they have won?"

On hearing this, Gerard exclaims, "You're right, mother. Numbers, arithmetic and mathematics are very important. I think that now I'm going to study much more."

Exercise No. 169
1. à la salle d'attente
2. Tout de suite
3. Elle m'a demandé
4. J'ai répondu
5. de faire votre connaissance
6. Le plaisir est à moi
7. J'ai pensé en moi-même
8. Nous avons pris un taxi
9. à vitesse vertigineuse
10. Pas si vite!
11. Je ne suis pas pressé
12. Ni moi non plus
13. reservée pour Brown
14. Quel est le prix
15. cent euros francs par jour

Exercise No. 170

1. Did Philippe go to the station to meet his father? Yes, he left the house 20 minutes ago. Did his sister Marie go with him? His sister Marie and also his brother Henri went with him.
2. Has Mrs. Brown returned from the city? She has not returned yet but she will return soon. Why did she go to the city? She went there to do her shopping.
3. Why did Mr. Brown return so late this evening? Many clients came to see him in the afternoon. At what time does he usually leave his office? Usually he leaves at five o'clock sharp, but today he did not leave until a quarter to six.
4. At what time did Mr. Brown leave for the airport? He left at six o'clock in the morning. At what time did he get on the plane? He got on the plane at a quarter to eight.

Exercise No. 171
1. arrivée
2. allées
3. né
4. mort
5. devenus; monté
6. retournée
7. partie
8. entrés
9. resté
10. partis; arrivés

Exercise No. 172

1. Il a passé par la douane et il est allé à la salle d'attente.
2. Une belle dame s'est approchée.
3. Elle a dit,—Pardon monsieur, êtes-vous M. Brown?
4. Il a répondu,—À votre service.
5. Le taxi est allé en ville à toute vitesse.
6. À la fin il a crié,—Je ne suis pas pressé!
7. Le chauffeur a répondu,—Ni moi non plus.
8. Il a dit,—Bonjour, monsieur. Avez-vous une chambre réservée pour M. Brown?
9. Il a répondu,—Bienvenu à Paris, Monsieur Brown.

Exercise No. 173

1. m'a appelé
2. prendre le thé
3. Nous nous sommes arretés
4. Je suis monté
5. J'ai sonné; m'a invité
6. s'est approchée pour me saluer
7. Je suis contente de vous voir
8. Il y a beaucoup de maisons
9. Nous sommes entrés
10. m'a presenté
11. veut être
12. se sont retirés; leurs devoirs
13. Nous nous sommes mis
14. Nous avons parlé (causé)
15. Je suis revenu
16. par les vieux quartiers

Exercise No. 174

1. I got up
2. You went to bed. (You lay down.)
3. He got dressed.
4. She enjoyed herself.
5. We stopped.
6. You approached.
7. They met each other.
8. They knew each other.
9. I did not take a walk.
10. He was not mistaken.

11. Did they not withdraw?
12. Did they not sit down?

Exercise No. 175

1. Did the children go to bed early? They went to bed early.
2. Did Jean get up late? No, he did not get up late.
3. Did Marie dress quickly? Yes, she dressed quickly.
4. Were you mistaken, Charles? No, I was not mistaken.
5. Did you have a good time, Anne? No, I did not have a good time.
6. Where did you meet, gentlemen? We met at the office.
7. Where did the bus stop? It stopped at the corner over there.
8. Did Mrs. Brown take care of the children? She took care of the children.
9. Did the tourist feel at home in Paris? Like all tourists, he felt at home.

Exercise No. 176

1. Mme Parmentier a appelé M. Brown par téléphone.
2. Il s'est arrêté à cinq heures.
3. Une petite bonne a ouvert la porte.
4. Mme Parmentier s'est approchée pour le saluer.
5. Elle a l'air d'être du dix-huitième siècle.
6. M. Brown et Mme Parmentier sont entrés dans un grand salon.
7. Ce sont les enfants de Mme Parmentier.
8. Ils font leurs études au Lycée Henri IV et dans une institution privée.
9. L'ainé veut être docteur.
10. Ils se sont retirés pour aller faire leurs devoirs.
11. On a parlé de la vie en France.
12. M. Parmentier a recommandé le Marché aux Puces.
13. Mme Parmentier l'a invité à les accompagner au Marché aux Fleurs.

14. Il a passé une heure agréable en parlant d'une chose et d'une autre.

15. Il est revenu à pied.

Exercise No. 177

1. me chercher
2. Nous sommes restés
3. sans rien attraper
4. à jeter des pierres
5. Nous avons continué
6. la plus belle place
7. Quelle belle avenue!
8. m'a frappé
9. On y joue
10. On y écrit
11. Les passants
12. Ensuite; notre route
13. m'a quitté
14. J'ai suivi
15. dans la chaise la plus proche

Exercise No. 178

1. Did you understand all that the teacher said? I did not understand all (of it).
2. Did you read the two guides that I lent you? I read them with much interest.
3. What is the first secret of good cooking? All that enters into a dish must be of good quality.
4. Can one ski in the mountains? Those who are young and strong do it all the time.
5. What café did you visit today? I visited the Royale-Concorde of which we have often spoken.
6. Where are the valises in which I have put my clothes? They are in your room.

Exercise No. 179

1. que
2. ce qu'
3. qui
4. ce qui
5. qui
6. laquelle
7. dont

8. que
9. ce qui
10. que

Exercise No. 180

1. Il écrit sa lettre (or Il l'écrit) attablé dans le café Royale-Concorde.
2. Elle est venue le chercher à l'hôtel.
3. Ils sont restés très longtemps sur le Pont Neuf.
4. Ils ont vu des pêcheurs, des bateaux-mouches, et des enfants.
5. Il pense que cela doit être la plus belle place du monde.
6. Ils se sont attablés pour prendre un café, mais surtout pour se reposer.
7. L'importance du café dans la vie quotidienne l'a frappé.
8. Dans un café on joue aux échecs.
9. Le café est un deuxième bureau pour les gens d'affaires.
10. Ils ont contemplé l'immense Arc de Triomphe.
11. Elle a quitté M. Brown à la Place de l'Alma.
12. Il a admiré la Seine.
13. Il est tombé fatigué, épuisé, et enchanté dans la chaise du café.

Exercise No. 181

1. Vous avez raison
2. Me voici
3. Je prends (Je bois)
4. les champs et les forêts
5. par la fenêtre
6. Les fermiers; les champs
7. J'ai pris un taxi
8. Presque tout de suite
9. Par ici
10. les oreilles
11. a duré
12. m'arrêter pour contempler
13. est poussé; est tiré
14. On doit suivre

Exercise No. 182

1. What was Mr. Brown doing when you entered the living room? He was reading aloud a letter which he had just received from his agent. What was Mr. Picard doing? He was listening to him.
2. What were you doing while the train was crossing the fields and the forests? I was looking out of the window. What did you see? I saw the peasants who were working in the fields.
3. Were there many vendors at Mont Saint Michel? There was an army of them. What were they selling? They were selling souvenirs of the Mont.
4. Do you often play tennis? Formerly I played (used to play) almost every day, but this year I have played only once.

Exercise No. 183

1. (criaient et hurlaient) The vendors were calling and yelling when I arrived at the market.
2. (j'écoutais) While I was listening to the radio somebody telephoned me.
3. (nous faisions) When we were doing our homework, they entered our room.
4. (descendait) She fell when she was getting out of the car.
5. (allait) When the taxi was going at full speed, I cried, "Not so fast."
6. (il était) We visited him when he was ill.
7. (Il y avait) There were many people at the airport when our plane arrived.
8. (nous attendions) While we were waiting for the bus, it began to rain.
9. (nous venions) We met them when we were coming from the movies.
10. (dormaient) Mr. Brown returned while the children were sleeping.

Exercise No. 184

1. Il écrit attablé dans un café.
2. Le métier de touriste demande beaucoup de repos.
3. Le café est dans la ville de Perros-Guirec.
4. Il prend un Calvados.
5. Il regardait par la fenêtre.
6. Il voyait les paysans qui travaillaient dans les champs.
7. Il pouvait voir les femmes qui lavaient le linge.
8. Il a entendu un bruit terrifiant.
9. La tête lui tournait comme une toupie.
10. Il voulait rester pour contempler la sculpture.
11. Il a reçu une impression imposante.
12. Il se tourne vers la Bretagne.

Exercise No. 185

1. Je suis revenu
2. de plus en plus
3. je suis allé
4. Ma
5. Je me suis dit
6. il y a deux heures
7. J'étais
8. Je marchais
9. Je me suis approché
10. étaient
11. Ils riaient
12. ne bougeait pas
13. Il ne disait rien
14. n'étaient pas du tout
15. J'ai dit

Exercise No. 186

1. riaient
2. vivait
3. lavaient
4. étaient-ils
5. venait
6. rendions visite à
7. pensait-il
8. descendait
9. revenais
10. montions
11. souriait
12. j'étais
13. s'approchait

14. commençaient
15. mangeait
16. se rencontraient
17. n'avions pas
18. ne voulaient pas
19. Pouviez-vous
20. savait; devait

Exercise No. 187

1. M. Brown est allé au Louvre pour le visiter à fond.
2. Il s'est dit,—Imbécile.
3. Il s'est tourné vers le Jardin des Tuileries.
4. Il a entendu des rires immodérés.
5. Il a vu un petit, joli théâtre.
6. Guignol ne bougeait pas.
7. Les enfants éclataient de rire.
8. Il a pris une place à côté d'une toute petite fille.
9. Elle a crié,—Papa.
10. Le petit Gringalet était en train de donner de grands coups de tête dans le ventre de Guignol.
11. Non, monsieur, les enfants n'étaient pas fâchés.
12. L'enfant a répondu gentiment.—Au revoir, papa.

Exercise No. 188

1. Mr. Brown has left for Paris.
2. His wife remained at home.
3. Mrs. Picard went out one hour ago.
4. She hasn't returned yet.
5. We went up in the elevator.
6. They went down on foot.
7. Why did you return so late, Marie?
8. I went to the market to do my shopping.
9. His grandfather died this morning.
10. My grandmother was born June 5, 1927.

Exercise No. 189

1. approchée
2. rencontrés
3. pris

4. sortis
5. arrêté
6. arrivée
7. descendu
8. reservé
9. née
10. mis
11. dit
12. fait
13. demandé
14. ouvertes; ouvertes

Exercise No. 190

1. **(rendrons)** Tomorrow we shall pay a visit to the Brown family.
2. **(sont allés)** Yesterday evening the children went to the movies.
3. **(parlait)** The pupils were not listening while the teacher was talking.
4. **(avez-vous passé)** Where did you spend last winter?
5. **(verrai)** I shall not see them until tomorrow.
6. **(jouaient)** We were doing our homework while they were playing cards.
7. **(pleuvait)** They remained at home, because it was pouring.
8. **(Ferez-vous)** Will you take a trip to Europe next summer?
9. **(a prêté)** He lent us five dollars yesterday.
10. **(vous vous êtes levé)** At what time did you get up this morning?

Exercise No. 191

1. Il pleuvait à verse
2. J'étais très content
3. quand M. Brown a reçu
4. quand ma représentante m'a téléphoné
5. nous allions
6. Je ne savais pas
7. Nous ne pouvions pas
8. Voulaient-ils voyager *or* Est-ce qu'ils voulaient voyager
9. Elle n'avait pas le temps
10. Elle devait

Exercise No. 192

An Excursion to Versailles

One day Mr. Brown invited Mrs. Parmentier's children to accompany him on an excursion to Versailles.

It is not very far from Paris and they arrived without any difficulty. On the way to the palace, Mr. Brown had a novel idea.

"Let's lunch on the grass in the big park at the edge of the lake. I'm told that it's allowed."

"Wonderful! Let's go."

They entered a grocery to buy some ham, a Camembert cheese and a bottle of red wine. In a bakery next door they bought two loaves of French bread and three eclairs.

"I'm as hungry as a wolf," said the older one as they left the bakery.

"Let's eat right away," said Mr. Brown. "But what to do about utensils?"

"Let's see what there is in our pockets," said the younger one. The boy found a penknife.

"Here! And we'll drink out of the bottle."

They entered the palace through the great iron gate but instead of taking the tour they went out, crossing the immense garden. The garden with its statues, fountains and groves of trees made a strong impression on Mr. Brown. The two children were in agreement. The younger one said: "I assure you that the garden is the jewel of Versailles. But the palace bores us to death."

Mr. Brown answered laughing, "We're not obliged to go there."

When they arrived at the lake they sat down on the grass to eat. They talked of one thing and another while eating and Mr. Brown was struck once more by their intelligence. The children ate like two wolves and they had a wonderful time. All three of them will remember this excursion to Versailles for a long time.

Exercise No. 193

Avenue de l'Opéra

We are strolling along the Avenue de l'Opéra. It is a fine wide avenue, which leads from the Palais Royal to the Opera.

There are many people on the avenue. All the tourists meet there. The sidewalks are lined with luxury shops where one can buy all sorts of beautiful things, if one has money: jewels, fine lingerie, gloves, china, blouses, leather goods and also books, for we are in France where people like to read. There is even a small shop and a bookstore inside the Opera House.

There is also a well-known café-restaurant on the Place de l'Opéra: the Café de la Paix. Let's go have a beer, shall we? With pleasure.

Exercise No. 194

1. M. Brown a remarqué que malgré la différence qui existe entre les villages français, ils ont tous une grande rue.
2. La rue mène souvent à une place entourée d'arbres.
3. Derrière les arbres, les boutiques du village sont bien rangées.
4. La teinturerie est souvent peinte en violet.
5. On peut voir de délicieux gâteaux dans la vitrine de la pâtisserie. Dans la vitrine de l'épicerie. Dans la vitrine de la blanchisseuse.
6. Les mouches se promènent tranquillement sur les gigots pendus devant la boucherie.
7. La mairie, l'église et l'école sont toutes sur la place.
8. M. Brown se lève de bonne heure pour ne rien manquer du spectacle de la rue.
9. D'abord il entend un coq chanter.
10. Un petit garçon se précipite dans la rue.

11. Il s'arrête soudain pour examiner quelque chose qui attire son attention.
12. Notre héros revient avec un pain presque aussi long que lui.
13. Il est sept heures et demie et M. Brown a rendez-vous avec les jeunes Parmentier pour faire une excursion à Chartres.
14. Il décrira les aventures de cet après-midi.

Exercise No. 195

1. à une place entourée d'arbres
2. bien rangées
3. est peinte
4. est remplie de gâteaux délicieux
5. a pendu ses gigots
6. s'y promènent
7. Au milieu du village
8. des rires et des chansons
9. Pour ne rien manquer du spectacle
10. On dort
11. à se saluer
12. se réveille
13. Ce que les Français mangent
14. revient avec un pain
15. Je dois tout de même

Exercise No. 196

1. Did you send the pottery to Mr. Brown? We sent it to him.
2. Do many people meet each other on the Avenue de l'Opéra? All tourists meet one another there.
3. Please send me the French newspapers. We shall send them to you tomorrow.
4. Has the waiter given you the bill? He hasn't given it to me yet.
5. Did you ask the employee for the tickets? I haven't asked him for them yet because he is very busy.
6. How many dishes are there in this case? There are 25 dozen (of them).
7. Did you return the money (to him), which you borrowed from him? I shall return it to him this evening.
8. Has the maid put on the desk the porcelain which Mr. Brown has just received? Yes, she has put it there.
9. Will you lend me your umbrella? I'll lend it to you; but please return it to me tomorrow. Many thanks. I'll return it to you tomorrow.
10. Please show me the new dress you have bought. I cannot show it to you, because it has not yet arrived from the store.

Exercise No. 197

1. M. Brown a voulu revenir à temps pour aller à l'opéra.
2. Ils avaient préparé un bon déjeuner.
3. La voiture attendait en bas.
4. Il a entendu un son qu'il a reconnu tout de suite.
5. Ils avaient crevé un pneu.
6. Les jeunes enfants voulaient aider à changer le pneu.
7. Il n'y avait pas de cric dans l'outillage de la voiture.
8. Le camionneur leur a offert un coup de main.
9. Le camionneur avait tant de dignité naturelle.
10. Les enfants l'ont invité à déjeuner avec eux.
11. Ils ont mangé leur poulet et le jambon du camionneur, et ont bu la bouteille de vin.
12. Ils ont dit, "Ce jambon est délicieux."
13. Il a dit, "Ma femme ne me néglige pas."
14. Ils ont fait la sieste, ensuite ils ont fait leurs adieux.
15. M. Brown doit s'habiller pour aller à l'opéra.

Exercise No. 198

1. me chercher
2. Ils avaient préparé
3. une nappe, des serviettes, des couteaux, des fourchettes
4. Et nous voilà
5. Tout à coup
6. Nous avons crevé un pneu
7. Il n'y avait pas de cric

8. Personne ne
9. Nous nous sommes assis
10. Bientôt un grand camion
11. un coup de main
12. En tout cas
13. s'est mis à la besogne
14. lui offrir un pourboire
15. déjeuner avec nous

Exercise No. 199

1. **Il avait appris les règles essentielles** . . . He had learned the essential rules.
2. **Nous avions vraiment travaillé** . . . We had really worked hard.
3. **Ils n'avaient pas encore obtenu** . . . They had not yet obtained their tickets.
4. **Avait-il écrit** . . . **?** Had he written a letter to his friend?
5. **Qui avait promis** . . . **?** Who had promised to meet him at the airport?
6. **J'avais oublié** . . . I had forgotten my umbrella.
7. **Avaient-ils reservé** . . . **?** Had they reserved a room for Mr. Brown?
8. **Aviez-vous lu** . . . **?** Had you read many guidebooks?
9. **Ses jeunes amis avaient préparé** . . . His young friends had prepared a good lunch.
10. **Avait-il loué** . . . **?** Had he rented a car?

Exercise No. 200

1. **Mes jeunes amis étaient venus me chercher** . . .
2. **Un grand camion s'était approché** . . . A large truck had approached rapidly.
3. **Nous nous étions assis** . . . We had sat down under a large tree.
4. **J'étais allé** . . . I had gone to the waiting room.
5. **Nous n'étions pas sortis** . . . We had not gone out together.
6. **Ils étaient arrivés** . . . They had arrived safe and sound.

7. **Le taxi s'était arrêté** . . . The taxi had stopped in front of the hotel.
8. **Étiez-vous allé** . . . **?** Had you gone to the customs office?
9. **Nous nous étions dit** . . . We had said good-bye to each other.
10. **Elles n'étaient pas restées** . . . They had not stayed in Paris two weeks.

Exercise No. 201

1. We have good teachers. How do you find yours?
2. Let's go to the post office in your car. Ours has a flat tire.
3. Please lend me your pen. Mine does not write.
4. I have forgotten my umbrella. Will you lend me yours?
5. You have no jack. Do you want to borrow mine?
6. Paul's bicycle costs more than mine, but mine is better than his.
7. Louise and I bought theatre tickets yesterday. I have mine, but unfortunately she has lost hers.
8. Here are our hats. This one is mine and that one is yours.

Exercise No. 202

1. Il n'avait jamais été joueur.
2. Il avait remarqué que l'on s'occupait beaucoup de la Loterie Nationale.
3. Il a rêvé gagner le gros lot.
4. Il aurait assez d'argent pour voyager partout en Europe.
5. Sa femme l'accompagnerait.
6. Les enfants iraient à l'école quelque part en France.
7. M. Brown a acheté un billet de loterie d'une jeune fille dans un poste de vente de billets de loterie.
8. Le lendemain il a sonné pour demander du café, des croissants et le journal.
9. Il ne s'intéressait qu'au journal.

10. Il ne respirait plus et commençait à chercher son billet.
11. Il faisait des voyages dans la lune.
12. M. Brown avait le numéro 25.000.
13. Le numéro qui a gagné le gros lot était 26.000.
14. M. Brown a décidé que les émotions du joueur n'étaient pas pour lui.
15. Il aime la vie tranquille.

Exercise No. 203

1. Je n'avais jamais été
2. des postes de vente de billets de loterie
3. qu'on s'occupait beaucoup de
4. Je voyais des affiches illustrées
5. Si je gagnais le premier prix
6. Je pourrais acheter
7. l'homme le plus heureux du monde
8. Et voilà comment
9. de bonne heure
10. Je ne m'intéressais qu'au journal
11. Je cherche
12. à peine le tenir
13. C'est un cinq, pas un six
14. en riant de moi-même

Exercise No. 204

1. **Je voyagerai partout en Europe** . . . I would travel everywhere in Europe.
2. **Il visiterait** . . . He would visit France and Italy.
3. **Nous apprendrions** . . . We would learn French.
4. **Ma famille ne m'accompagnerait pas.** My family would not accompany me.
5. **Elle pourrait acheter** . . . She would be able to buy many beautiful things.
6. **Aurait-il . . . ?** Would he have enough money?
7. **Ils achèteraient** . . . They would buy some art objects.
8. **Seriez-vous . . . ?** Would you be glad to remain here?

9. **Elle ne vous connaîtrait pas** . . . She would not know you.
10. **Ils ne feraient pas** . . . They would not do their homework.
11. **Je vous enverrais** . . . I would send you the magazines.
12. **Ils ne viendraient pas** . . . They would not come next week.

Exercise No. 205

1. M. Brown avait lu quelques livres sur l'histoire de France et sur ses coutumes.
2. Il ne pouvait décrire que très peu de ce qu'il avait vu et appris.
3. Il aime surtout les Français.
4. Il aime leur politesse, leur sentiment de la dignité de l'homme, et leur sens vif du comique.
5. Il pense que la vie est plus tranquille en France.
6. Il avait eu une impression différente dans le taxi quand il venait d'arriver.
7. Toute la famille l'accompagnerait.
8. Il est sûr qu'il pourrait faire le guide sans difficulté.
9. Il part le premier août.
10. Il se donnera le plaisir de téléphoner à M. Picard dès son arrivée.
11. Il pense qu'ils passeront des heures à parler de la France et de son Paris bien aimé.

Exercise No. 206

1. They went to the market to shop.
2. The French people made a strong impression on Mr. Brown.
3. He went to the railroad station to ask for information.
4. I shall be able to get along in France because I speak French well.
5. After tomorrow we shall visit Mr. Duval.
6. The young man had already filled the tank and checked the oil.
7. Next summer Mr. Brown will be able to act as guide for his whole family.

8. If Mr. Brown had had more time, he would have taken a trip to Morocco.

9. At the Hotel Quai Voltaire, we lacked nothing.

10. After having finished his business matters, Mr. Brown devoted himself completely to recreation.

11. I'm going to write a letter to my agent to let her know the date of my arrival.

12. After saying goodbye, we got into the plane.

13. I was thinking of my teacher's advice while the taxi was racing at full speed through the streets of Paris.

14. Formerly Mr. Brown had his French correspondence translated, but in the future he will translate it himself.

15. The children were amusing themselves by throwing stones into the water.

16. If you find the rubbers which I left at your home, return them to me please.

17. I shall not forget to return them to you.

18. I had never seen such a sight.

19. When Mr. Brown was traveling in Europe, Mrs. Brown was taking care of the children.

20. I have never been in France, but I intend to go there next summer.

Exercise No. 207

1. est un homme d'affaires de New-York.

2. un voyage à Paris pour rendre visite à sa représentante.

3. faire sa connaissance.

4. il avait appris à bien parler français.

5. Il avait aussi lu beaucoup de livres sur la France.

6. beaucoup de lettres à son ami et professeur.

7. beaucoup des endroits intéressants dont ils avaient parlé dans leurs conversations.

8. il avait trouvé la vie en France plus tranquille qu'aux Etats-Unis.

9. qui l'avait conduit à son hôtel.

10. La vitesse vertigineuse du taxi.

11. il a bientôt terminé ses affaires.

12. leur politesse et leur sentiment marqué de la dignité de l'homme.

13. il n'a pas eu le temps d'aller ni au Maroc ni en Corse.

14. tant à voir, à faire et à apprendre.

15. des coutumes, de la vie, de la langue et des arts de la France.

16. il reviendra en France.

17. l'accompagnerait.

18. Il n'a pas gagné le gros lot de la loterie mais il aura assez d'argent.

19. que M. Brown écrira avant de quitter la France.

20. il invitera M. Picard à dîner en famille.

Exercise No. 208

Nice, Capital of the Riviera

There are really two cities in Nice: the Italian city and the French city; the old city and the new city. One can walk in the old districts where one hears nothing but Italian, for Nice became French only in 1860. In this district they sell macaroni, ravioli, olives, and sausage. The air is perfumed with garlic and tomato sauce. People shout, sing, bargain. This part of the city is entirely Italian.

But close by, crossing the Place Massena, you are in the French city. You walk up Boulevard Victor Hugo under a row of splendid trees and you admire the magnificent shops. You see cars as long as trains. It is a city of luxury.

Nice is also a sports center. There is a magnificent tennis club; there is the race track at Cagnes, nearby; the famous winter sports at Beuil in the mountains; yachting and sea bathing. It is true that the beach is rocky (stony) but that does not matter. You go there anyway to worship the sun.

The city where people are born, where they go to school, where they earn a living, this city exists too. This city has its commerce: tourism, flowers, perfume, olives, fishing. It has its cultural life: music, which it takes very seriously, opera, theater, lectures and bookstores. As in other cities of France, there is an interest in science and an interest in art.

But after all the real glory of Nice is its location. It rises from the blue sea to the hills adorned with flower-covered villas up to the foothills of the mountains covered with snow. The sky is intensely blue like the sea. The air is mild and balmy.

Everything is there to make people happy.

SUMMARY OF VERB CONJUGATIONS

Regular Verbs

In the verb conjugations below, note that subject pronouns **elle** and **on,** although not listed, use the same form of the verb as **il,** that is, third person singular; **elles,** third person plural, uses the same form of the verb as **ils.**

Infinitive Present Participle Past Participle	Present Tense	Future Pres. Conditional	Imperfect Convers. Past
parler to speak **parlant parlé**	je parle nous parlons	je parlerai je parlerais	je parlais j'ai parlé
finir to finish **finissant fini**	je finis nous finissons	je finirai je finirais	je finissais j'ai fini
vendre to sell **vendant vendu**	je vends nous vendons	je vendrai je vendrais	je vendais j'ai vendu

Auxiliary Verbs

Infinitive Present Participle Past Participle	Present Tense	Future Pres. Conditional	Imperfect Convers. Past
avoir to have **ayant eu**	j'ai nous avons	j'aurai j'aurais	j'avais j'ai eu
être to be **étant été**	je suis nous sommes	je serai je serais	j'étais j'ai été

Common Irregular Verbs

Infinitive Present Participle Past Participle	Present Tense	Future Pres. Conditional	Imperfect Convers. Past
aller to go **allant allé**	je vais nous allons	j'irai j'irais	j'allais je suis allé
s'asseoir to sit down **s'asseyant être assis**	je m'assieds (assois) nous nous asseyons	je m'assoirai je m'assoirais	je m'asseyais je me suis assis
battre to beat **battant battu**	je bats nous battons	je battrai je battrais	je battais j'ai battu
boire to drink **buvant bu**	je bois nous buvons	je boirai je boirais	je buvais j'ai bu
conduire to conduct **conduisant conduit**	je conduis nous conduisons	je conduirai je conduirais	je conduisais j'ai conduit
connaître to know **connaissant connu**	je connais nous connaissons	je connaîtrai je connaîtrais	je connaissais j'ai connu
courir to run **courant couru**	je cours nous courons	je courrai je courrais	je courais j'ai couru
couvrir to cover **couvrant couvert**	je couvre nous couvrons	je couvrirai je couvrirais	je couvrais j'ai couvert
croire to believe **croyant cru**	je crois nous croyons	je croirai je croirais	je croyais j'ai cru
devoir to owe, must **devant dû**	je dois nous devons	je devrai je devrais	je devais j'ai dû
dire to say **disant dit**	je dis nous disons	je dirai je dirais	je disais j'ai dit
dormir to sleep **dormant dormi**	je dors nous dormons	je dormirai je dormirais	je dormais j'ai dormi
écrire to write **écrivant écrit**	j'écris nous écrivons	j'écrirai j'écrirais	j'écrivais j'ai écrit
envoyer to send **envoyant envoyé**	j'envoie nous envoyons	j'enverrai j'eenverrais	j'envoyais j'ai envoyé
faire to do, make **faisant fait**	je fais nous faisons	je ferai je ferais	je faisais j'ai fait
falloir to be necessary **—fallu**		il faudra il faudrait	il fallait il a fallu

lire to read	je lis	je lirai	je lisais
lisant lu	nous lisons	je lirais	j'ai lu
mentir to lie	je mens	je mentirai	je mentais
mentant menti	nous mentons	je mentirais	j'ai menti
mettre to put	je mets	je mettrai	je mettais
mettant mis	nous mettons	je mettrais	j'ai mis
mourir to die	je meurs	je mourrai	je mourais
mourant mort	nous mourons	je mourrais	je suis mort
naître to be born	je nais	je naîtrai	je naissais
naissant né	nous naissons	je naîtrais	je suis né
offrir to offer	j'offre	j'offrirai	j'offrais
offrant offert	nous offrons	j'offrirais	j'ai offert
ouvrir to open	j'ouvre	j'ouvrirai	j'ouvrais
ouvrant ouvert	nous ouvrons	j'ouvrirais	j'ai ouvert
paraître to appear	je parais	je paraîtrai	je paraissais
paraissant paru	nous paraissons	je paraîtrais	j'ai paru
partir to set out, leave	je pars	je partirai	je partais
partant parti	nous partons	je partirais	je suis parti
plaire to please	je plais	je plairai	je plaisais
plaisant plu	nous plaisons	je plairait	j'ai plu
pleuvoir to rain		il pleuvra	il pleuvais
pleuvant plu		il pleuvrait	il a plu
pouvoir to be able	je peux (puis)	je pourrai	je pouvais
pouvant pu	nous pouvons	je pourrais	j'ai pu
prendre to take	je prends	je prendrai	je prenais
prenant pris	nous prenons	je prendrais	j'ai pris
recevoir to receive	je reçois	je recevrai	je recevais
recevant reçu	nous recevons	je recevrais	j'ai reçu
rire to laugh	je ris	je rirai	je riais
riant ri	nous rions	je rirais	j'ai ri
savoir to know	je sais	je saurai	je savais
sachant su	nous savons	je saurais	j'ai su